THE COURSE IN BUDDHIST REASONING AND DEBATE

The Course in
Buddhist Reasoning and Debate

*An Asian Approach to Analytical Thinking Drawn
from Indian and Tibetan Sources*

Daniel Perdue

SNOW LION
BOSTON & LONDON
2014

Snow Lion
An imprint of Shambhala Publications, Inc.
Horticultural Hall
300 Massachusetts Avenue
Boston, Massachusetts 02115
www.shambhala.com

9 8 7 6 5 4 3 2 1

First Edition
Printed in the United States of America

⊛ This edition is printed on acid-free paper that meets the
American National Standards Institute z39.48 Standard.
♻ Shambhala makes every effort to print on recycled paper.
For more information please visit www.shambhala.com.

Distributed in the United States by Penguin Random House LLC
and in Canada by Random House of Canada Ltd

Designed by Gopa & Ted2, Inc.

Library of Congress Cataloging-in-Publication Data

Perdue, Daniel.
The course in Buddhist reasoning and debate: An Asian approach to
analytical thinking drawn from Indian and Tibetan sources /
Daniel Perdue.—First edition.
pages cm
ISBN 978-1-55939-421-5 (hardcover: alk. paper)
1. Buddhist logic. 2. Debates and debating—Religious aspects—
Buddhism. I. Title.
BC25.P463P466 2013
160.88'2943—dc23
2013013348

Contents

Conclusion

Preface

THIS BOOK IS called a "course" because it is a set of explanations and exercises that have the goal of helping you the reader, who would then become the student, to develop new understanding and gain new skills in reasoning, or at least add new techniques to the skills you already have. This course is every inch the reflection of courses I have taught in several Buddhist centers and colleges over several decades. It is as if I had perfected my course guidelines and written up my lectures. Now, to the greatest extent possible, everyone who is interested can take the course.

Although this course can prove useful for Tibetan language students, the main intent is to help people gain the basic reasoning and debate skills that are practiced in Buddhist debate. Thus, in this book there is very little explanation of Tibetan language concerns, justifications for translation terms, and so on. Those interested in these topics can refer to my *Debate in Tibetan Buddhism* (1992) and many other books and articles on Tibetan philosophical debate. Often in this text I suggest further reading in some of those sources, and several of them are listed in the bibliography.

Even though I often refer you to other works, I do not necessarily assume that you will go forth and get them. I have written this as a stand-alone book, so that what you need to complete the course and gain the skills is provided here. I suggest further reading in other works especially for those who are interested in going further in the study of Buddhist philosophy, but this book alone is adequate for the purpose of conveying the basic essentials for this style of reasoning. Since this book is a stand-alone resource, there is some duplication of material that has been covered in my own and others' writings. However, none of those other sources focuses completely on conveying the style of reasoning.

The procedures and strategies of Buddhist reasoning and debate are explained here mainly in terms of the traditional topics of Buddhist philosophy, but it remains true that explaining those topics is still not the main intent of this book. By no means are the techniques of this style of reasoning limited to topics of Buddhist philosophy, and it is my hope that these techniques can be communicated far beyond the Buddhist community. I am confident that every aspect of this style of reasoning and rational discourse could be rewritten in terms of reasoning about mathematics, biology, law, and other areas of human interest. What is communicated here is just another tool.

The spirit of this broad applicability of reasoning is reflected in the custom of calling the final degree in most academic areas a PhD or doctor of philosophy. Even if a person gets a PhD in chemistry or dance and never once took a course in philosophy, the degree is a doctor of philosophy. The reason for this is that the essential accomplishment the person must have completed is some measure of skill in rationality, which is the heart of "the love of wisdom" that is philosophy.

BACKGROUND

More than two decades ago, I wrote my big book on debate, *Debate in Tibetan Buddhism.*[1] At the time, I thought I was writing a book that would prepare people for debate; however, it seems it does not really work that way. At least, that is not the typical experience. That book worked best to prepare students to read Tibetan literature on reasoning and philosophy. I wrote in the chapter on the procedure in debate in *Debate in Tibetan Buddhism,* "The purpose for this chapter is to supply a detailed annotation to the textual form of the debates, not so much to prepare one for actual debate as to prepare one to absorb the debates translated in this work."[2] Although I thought that work would also train people in the debating skills, it seems it worked only for those who immersed themselves in the environment of Buddhist reasoning and debate—the monasteries, nunneries, and Buddhist centers where debate is practiced. So, this present book is my new attempt to communicate the basics of Buddhist reasoning and debate for the many people who want to learn, and I bring to this new effort decades of experience in teaching Buddhist reasoning and debate in college classrooms and Buddhist centers.

This book is also intended to be a handy guide that encourages. It seems that something of a difficulty arose from the size of *Debate in Tibetan Buddhism,* at nearly one thousand pages. I was told by Sidney Piburn, who was then vice president and editor-in-chief at Snow Lion Publications, that soon after that book was published in 1992, he and Jeffrey Cox, the president of Snow Lion, were in Dharamsala in Himachal Pradesh, northern India, visiting with the Dalai Lama. They gave a copy of my book to the Dalai Lama, who laughed and made that gesture of weighing a heavy thing, and said, "Too big! People will be discouraged." So in an effort to counter the weight of that book and help people to once again be encouraged, I have written this new book.

Debate in Tibetan Buddhism was more theoretical in approach. I was recording what I had learned from many great Tibetan teachers within the context of graduate Tibetan language courses at the University of Virginia, in my own study, and in my fieldwork in the Tibetan monasteries reestablished in India. That text is in line with the Buddhist commentarial tradition. In the religious and philosophical literature of South Asia—Jain, Hindu, and Buddhist alike—there is a drift in the commentaries from shorter and pithier to more expansive and more detailed. Early on, a topic such as an explanation of valid cognition (Sanskrit: *pramāṇa,* Tibetan: *tshad ma*) would be presented in a very pithy way, with a mere reference to topics in a form that is brief and easily memorized. During that time, in a world in which the vast majority of people were illiterate, such a text was understood to be for a rarefied group of monastic scholars. Also, those scholars were trained to understand the contents only with tremendous support of oral explanations from other scholars who had studied the topics in the past. Consider that the Hindu Vedas were not written down for centuries after they appeared on the Indian subcontinent. Showing the priority given to the spoken word, even today the Vedas are an authentic canon only in their verbal form, not the written. Over the centuries, in all the early South Asian traditions, more and more of the oral explanations were written down, so the books grew longer and longer. When the Tibetans composed the Collected Topics literature on valid cognition, the sort of text that is translated in part in *Debate in Tibetan Buddhism,* they must have thought they were doing a great service to students in gathering so much information from so many sources and putting it all in one place. No doubt that is true. Their efforts made it easier to get on with the study.

Several hundred years after the Tibetans created the Collected Topics genre of literature for studying topics of Buddhist reasoning and debate, I wrote an even longer version covering part of the material, recording even more of the oral commentary, so that a reader would have less need to meet with teachers who could explain the content. This is why I say that my big book on debate is in line with the Buddhist commentarial tradition. It is not at all pithy, and records even more explanations from the oral tradition than anything that came before. I had gotten the commentary from expert teachers, I wrote it down, and there it is.

However, it has not done everything I hoped it would do. That book alone does not work to communicate to people how to debate in the Buddhist style. The main problem is that you cannot learn to debate from *reading* alone. You have to *verbalize* it. *Debate in Tibetan Buddhism* is a great record of the oral commentary, and for nearly twenty years it has served as the essential guide for the topics, but the book itself is too far removed from the oral tradition. Think about it. Everyone who ever learned to debate in this long tradition—dating back to a time long before the Buddha himself—did so in *speaking* with others, usually teachers and fellow students. All along, from the earliest, pithiest texts to the most expansive, it was assumed that the tradition of oral commentary was there in the background, giving support.

This reliance on the oral tradition indicates a very important emphasis in South Asian religions: you only know what you know, not what you can access. As Kensur Yeshi Thupten, a great scholar and debater, once told me, in the monastery they have a saying when a monk is having trouble coming up with the answer and says that he knows exactly where it is in the text. The others say that such a monk has his "learning in a box," referring to a box where he has his books stored. Of course, this is mocking, for the fact that you know where the information is in a book does not necessarily imply that you know the information. In fact, when people say that, they roll their eyes as if trying to read the text, and saying that usually means that they don't *know* the information. So, you only know what you know. This comment has great import for our time in which we seem to feel that if the knowledge is out there and we have access to it, then that is good enough.

PREPARATION

I first began to study logic and reasoning as a philosophy major at the University of Virginia in the late 1960s. It was because of an introductory logic course with Professor David Yalden-Thomson that I became a philosophy major. I later added on a second major in religious studies and made the effort to take courses in all the world religions. Of these, Buddhism most piqued my interest and seemed to answer most of my questions.

Thus, in 1973, I began graduate work in religious studies, intending to study Zen Buddhism. That was the first year for Professor Jeffrey Hopkins at the University of Virginia, and he convinced me to at least try Tibetan studies, a program that he was just starting at UVa. As he told me then, if I focused on Japanese Buddhism, since there was no professor of Japanese Buddhism on the faculty at that time, I would spend two or three years "reading dog stories in Japanese." However, if I started studying Tibetan, we would begin immediately with Buddhist texts. I went along with his advice, and I am so glad I did. It was a most fortuitous turn of events. The Tibetan approach suited me quite well. Though in time I have come to have a sense of the heart of Japanese Buddhism, I don't think I could have reached that understanding without first approaching Buddhism through the Tibetan style.

Over the next several years Professor Hopkins established a thoroughgoing program in Tibetan studies at the University of Virginia and brought in many great Tibetan scholars who were able to train us in logic and debate to the point where we all gained basic competence. Since logic and reasoning is not the endgame but a tool taught to beginners for the sake of their progress on the spiritual path, these visiting Tibetan scholars such as Lati Rinpoche, Denma Lochö Rinpoche, and Kensur Yeshi Thupten always referenced the place of basic reasoning in relation to the whole of Buddhist practice and philosophy.

Subsequently, during my graduate years I decided to focus on Buddhist reasoning and debate as practiced by the Tibetans. In 1983 I completed my dissertation, "Practice and Theory of Philosophical Debate in Tibetan Buddhist Education," and earned my PhD. I revised that dissertation and spent months adding an index so readers would be able to find what they wanted somewhere in the more than nine hundred pages. It was published as *Debate in Tibetan Buddhism* by Snow Lion Publications in 1992. My tremendous appreciation for this style of reasoning and debate has only grown over the years. I am amazed at its effectiveness and its broad applicability.

Since graduating, I have taught topics of Buddhist reasoning and debate in Tibetan language courses and in courses wholly in English at Buddhist centers and at several colleges and universities for more than three decades. Over the years I would occasionally receive messages from people from around the world who were studying alone or in groups and who wondered whether or not I had any additional materials. At first I was surprised when I would receive those messages. It seemed to me that I had been very generous in putting everything in one place. In time I have come to understand something of what they were asking for. I have sat in classrooms with good students who had read the appropriate parts of *Debate in Tibetan Buddhism* but were still unable to proceed in debate. So, over the years, I have developed many techniques for communicating this basic information to the people in the room, and I have wondered many times about how to expand the class. This book is part of that effort.

ACKNOWLEDGMENTS

I had the opportunity to write up these materials because Virginia Commonwealth University, in Richmond, Virginia, gave me a semester of research leave during the spring 2011 semester. These materials had been in waiting for years, for it is very difficult to find the time and energy to write while teaching so many students in so many courses every semester. So I thank the university, especially those who made the decision to support me. I would also like to thank Michael Wakoff, an editor at Shambhala Publications, who made a sincere effort to make this a better manuscript. Because of his extensive background in philosophy, he was also able to make several important comments in regard to logic. I am grateful, too, to my longtime friend Sue Carrington who helped me immensely in reviewing the initial page proofs. I would like to extend my gratitude to four former students who helped in various ways to improve this book. Christopher Runyon contributed many examples of comparisons involving variables, which are incorporated into exercise 26.3 in chapter 26, "Efforts and Practices." Sean Burns contributed several helpful comments in regard to the Buddhist truth table narrative in chapter 23, "Procedures in Debate." Both Runyon and Burns are especially well positioned to comment on the meeting of Buddhist and Greek-based logic and epistemology, as both were accomplished students of Western logic and philosophy and, in addition, both finished at the top of their classes when they took the course on Buddhist reasoning and debate. Subsequently, they both served very capably as teaching assistants for future classes. Kyle Gigliotti created the "Defender's Answers Decision Tree" and has graciously allowed me to use it in chapter 23, "Procedures in Debate." Finally, I wish to express my heartfelt gratitude to Jeremy Williams who used his great skills to create all of the illustrations in this book and has pitched in to help whenever I asked, from months before we sent this manuscript to Snow Lion Publications in 2011 up until 2014 when Shambhala Publications will publish it. I look forward to working with Jeremy in the future.

THE PRESENT COURSE

The Course in Buddhist Reasoning and Debate is the result of my years in the classroom, teaching this material to hundreds of students. I call it a "course" because I have taught it as a course so many times and because it is an effective program of study that meets several goals and objectives. In the traditional Buddhist setting, in my own experience, and in the experience of many American students, this course—this program of study—gives the students new skills and a new approach to the flood of information coming our way. I have pared down the material to just what is required to get you going, and then you can go on wherever you want, whether in Buddhist studies or any other area of human investigation. What is here is by no means all of Buddhist reasoning and debate. What is here is a start. There are oceans left over. In that regard, it is like *Debate in Tibetan Buddhism*, for the title of that work is greater than the contents. Still, in both cases, it's enough to get you going. The goal is to convey the basics and to help you develop the skills. This book is intended to make these analytical tools available to everyone. Many students have found it valuable, and I include some of their comments here.

This course in Buddhist reasoning and debate will continue to serve in the traditional role of introducing students to the vast literature on Buddhist thought. In addition to that, it will be helpful as an introduction to what is usually called "critical thinking," in conjunction with, or as a companion to, traditional critical thinking instruction. Since this is a style of reasoning that is suitable as a door of entry for students interested in Buddhist and Hindu philosophical thought, it will naturally assist any students of philosophy in organizing their thoughts. When I first entered philosophy in the late 1960s, there was a tremendous bias against Eastern thought. I remember one day in class, when Professor David Yalden-Thomson was wondering why one good student had dropped out of our philosophy of mind course, another student reported that that student had dropped the course because he had become a religious studies major and needed to concentrate his efforts over there. Professor Yalden-Thomson said, "It's a shame that anyone would abandon rationality for superstition." We still see the same sort of bias today, and in regard to Asian approaches in medicine, there is an even stronger bias. But, slowly, slowly over the years, I have seen a change in the philosophers' attitudes toward Eastern thought, and I think that in time we will see much of the same in the doctors' attitudes. The proof is in the pudding.

For any philosophers who might be interested, I prefer the term "analytical thinking" rather than the usual "critical thinking" because I mean to affirm the capacity of reasoning and debate not only to discover faulty reasoning but also to test and confirm good reasoning. Clearly this is the intent of every undertaking in "critical thinking," but the word "critical" seems to convey too much of a sense of finding fault. It is not the same as "critique" as used in art, for a "critique" can occasionally be nothing but praise. I think that "critical" could probably be understood in the same way, but that is not the way we usually hear it.

APPLICATION OF THE COURSE

Although the procedures and examples in this book are expressed in Buddhist philosophical terms—and that thought is certainly useful and interesting—what I most want to convey here are the underlying procedures and rational tools. As one student wrote, "The subject itself, while at first glance is seemingly very dependent upon Tibetan Buddhist conventions to no practical purpose, teaches the fundamentals of logic and can easily be applied in everyday thought." In line with this sentiment, I think it would be quite possible to re-create every argument and example in this book with arguments and examples from other fields, especially those with clear definitions—mathematics, biology, medicine, and perhaps law.

What's more, this stuff is great fun for kids! In the traditional setting, in the monasteries of Tibet and in India before them, this basic training in reasoning and debate was a topic of study for the young monks (and now nuns as well) in the range of nine to twelve years of age. There is a phenomenon that occurs when we are around that age that we become more rational, not so childlike any more. We have all been exposed to the cold, intellectual brutality of twelve-year-olds. They love the challenge. They love the clarity and precision. They love the control. As one student wrote, "This course enables students to move through discussions in a logical manner. Debate is better than video games." It was a proud moment for me. It may be that kids learn by video games, but no game is so fast and fantastic as the mind.

Thus, I say that this book would make a fine support for home schooling. Again, do not be put off by the Buddhist terminology. You don't have to believe this stuff, compelling though it may be. You just have to understand how the debaters use the terminology. Anyway, it's awfully challenging to find a product that is not impermanent. So how could an assertion such as "All products are impermanent" be an offense to anyone? Parents teaching their children at home will find it interesting to create their own examples, comparisons, and arguments.

I have provided exercises in the book. After all, it is a course. In addition, you should make up your own exercises and examples. Since, in all likelihood, no instructor is there with you, you will have to do the exercises on your own or with your debate partners. It will definitely help you to work through this material with a partner. We are always smarter as a group than we are individually. This is true for everyone. I have generally not supplied answers to the exercises, but all the information needed to do the exercises is in the material covered in the book, and you can discover the answers by using your wits. That is part of the process.

I think, if you look in the right place, you will find lectures, sample debates, and materials. One day I searched online for Buddhist debate and came up with a lot of videos. There were just a couple in English, and those were by former students of mine. All the rest that I found were of Tibetan monks and nuns debating in the monastic setting in Tibet and India. Among the comments posted for these videos, there was one saying, "I sure wish I could understand what they are saying." Well, I wish you could too. Rather than trying to translate everything they are saying, what we need to do is to bring the material and the procedures over into English, so that you can understand. After all, almost no Tibetan, accomplished in debate or not, would understand simple debates in Sanskrit, though their tradition of debate was adopted from Indian Sanskrit debates.

It should be clear that I am very enthusiastic about this style of reasoning. Buddhist debate has worked for me, and I have seen it work for hundreds of others who have never stopped thanking me, as I have never stopped thanking my teachers. This book and the supporting materials I hope to create are my attempt to bring this valuable material to the many around the world who are interested to learn it. If I did not know it to be so valuable, I would not have spent my life on it.

Technical Notes

On the Sanskrit

THE SANSKRIT TERMS are almost always given in full transliteration, complete with diacritics, even when in the text. The exceptions are when the Sanskrit is cited in a quote from another source. The transliteration scheme for Sanskrit is aimed at easy pronunciation, using *śh, ṣh,* and *ch* rather than the standard *ś, ṣ,* and *c;* also, *chh* is used rather than *ch.* The intent of this style is to avoid excluding nonspecialists or newcomers and to provide a basis for learning.

Even words originally in Sanskrit that have become English loan words, like "nirvana," are given with the diacritics and in italics, as *nirvāṇa.* The justification for this style is that there is not that much we need to learn to pronounce the words correctly, and we should be fully ready to do it. Remember that for the vast majority of human history, the vast majority of humans could not read or write, but now it is different. Ours is a time of high literacy rates in a global community where communicating from one side of the world to the other takes only seconds. Therefore, we do not have to obscure the sounds or avoid complexity in the way we represent sounds. People can do it.

Although I cannot fairly claim to be a great Sanskritist, I am clear about this: if you mispronounce the terms, no matter how advanced your learning, people think you don't know what you are talking about. Just learn these four things, and you will have already gone a long way toward the goal. First, when a vowel is shown with a line over the top, as *ā, ī,* or *ū,* it is a long vowel, a double-beat sound. Second, when a letter is shown with a dot under it, as *ṛ, ḍ, ṭ, ṇ,* or *ṣ,* the letter is a retroflex sound, meaning that you bend the tip of the tongue back so that it points toward the top of your head. That gives the letters a more resonant sound. For instance, the normal *d* sound is a dental, made by bringing the tip of the tongue near the back of the front teeth, but for the retroflex *ḍ,* the tongue is bent back. Practice this, and you will quickly hear the difference. Third, the letters *ñ* and *ṃ* have diacritical markings, but they just represent how the letters are written in Sanskrit, nothing about the pronunciation. All of these letters are sometimes capital letters, but there is no difference in the way they sound. Fourth, the inflection of multisyllabic Sanskrit words usually falls on the first or second syllable rather than the next to last syllable as is typical in English.

On the Tibetan

The system for transliterating Tibetan is that formulated by Turrell Wylie ("A Standard System of Tibetan Transliteration," *Harvard Journal of Asian Studies* 22 [1959]: 261–67). Tibetan words represented with English letters in the text—names of persons, places, and so on—are given in "loose phonetics" for the sake of easy pronunciation.

On the Footnotes and Endnotes

The footnotes give information needed for understanding the text narrative. The endnotes provide references for the citations, so readers may refer to them if they wish to follow up in the cited text.

On the Use of Mathematical-Style Notation

I have sometimes used mathematical-style notation in order to make clear what is modifying what. For instance, it can be confusing to refer to "non-impermanent phenomena," for that might seem to refer to phenomena that are not impermanent; thus, including only permanent phenomena. However, in Tibetan, that term is meant to refer not only to permanent phenomena but also to non-existents, which are also not *impermanent* phenomena. Thus, I put such terms in mathematical-style notation, for example, "non-(impermanent phenomenon)," to clear away any ambiguity about how the terms are supposed to be read.

Preliminaries for Buddhist Reasoning and Debate

1. Introduction

THE FIRST LINES of the *Tao-te Ching** are:

> The Tao that can be told of is not the eternal Tao;
> The name that can be named is not the eternal name.[1]

This indicates that the full understanding of the Dao cannot be communicated by words. Buddhist debate is not like that. It is always all about the words. What you said—that is what we are talking about. However, just as the profound meaning of the Dao cannot be carried by words alone, so Buddhist debate cannot be communicated by reading and writing alone.

This chapter introduces you to what you need to know in order to master the content of this book. The first essential is that, in order to gain competence in the Buddhist style of debate, you need to *verbalize* what you are analyzing. Thinking about it is not enough. To verbalize the analysis, you need a partner or two, another mind and voice to respond to. In many physical activities from folding the laundry to pole-vaulting to dancing, we speak of "muscle memory." Of course the muscles don't remember anything, so this phenomenon must be a function of consciousness, but we have all had the experience that, when you do something over and over again, it becomes second nature. You don't need to think about it so much anymore. It seems that this phenomenon is all the more so with the activity of using the tongue when speaking. One bit of advice sleep experts give to patients who struggle with falling asleep is to settle into a comfortable position and then don't move, especially don't move the mouth and tongue. This must be because the movement of the mouth and tongue alert the brain and cause

---

*You may prefer *Dao De Jing* and the *Dao* rather than the old Wade-Giles transliterations.

us to stay awake. Of course, for the reptilian brain in us, this activity must first be connected to eating, but for those of us who are fortunate enough to be able to speak, moving the tongue when speaking alerts the brain to be active in a more sophisticated way. At least, that is what we hope for. Practicing debate out loud, especially if you can do it with someone else so there is the mystery of another mind, gives you a facility of tongue that is most helpful. And, because of the close connections between speech and intellectual activity, the process of verbalizing your analysis causes you to develop new connections. Of course, it gives you a facility of mind too. One student who completed this course wrote, "I've left this class with a much more facile mind and tongue. Great tool for logic in real life situations." Practice in debate can also help give you more confidence. You know that what you are saying is right, and so you deliver your lines with a greater stability and confidence, with less of that flutter in your breast and voice that can betray you.

REQUIREMENTS FOR RATIONAL DISCOURSE

Three things are essential for a sensible and productive debate to be possible: competence in rational procedure, composure, and memory. If any of these are missing, the debate will not proceed well. The main goal of this book is especially to assist in the development of rational procedure, but with practice, composure and memory also come along. "Composure" means coolness under fire. Many verbal encounters are won simply by browbeating the opponent, by overpowering or shaming the other person. We are able to maintain our composure by having a rightness of position, in the style of Gandhi's or Dr. Martin Luther King, Jr.'s nonviolent campaigns of "holding the truth" (Skt. *satyagraha*). By practicing debate and knowing when we are in the right, our confidence grows. Thus, knowing the rightness of your position and your statements is one fruit of training. We are able to hold our own ground in the face of someone who disputes us because we have trained for these situations, and we know what we are doing. I have heard that there is a saying in the military: "The more you sweat in training, the less you bleed on the battlefield." In the same way, the more you develop your skills in analytical thinking and debate, the less you will be browbeaten by bullies who don't know what they are talking about. Memory and presence of mind develop with practice, so that you will be able to remain in the discussion. It is amazing how many disputes you can win simply by staying on topic.

What You Need to Succeed in Buddhist Reasoning and Debate

When I teach this course, I ask two students from former classes to debate a topic of their own choice in front of the assembled new students. For the students, this is like spying on another camp to see what they are doing. The new students cannot understand fully what they are hearing, but they get a sense of it from observing what the more advanced students are doing. So, believe it or not, the way to read this book is to first *peruse* chapter 25, "Bringing It All Together: Debating a Comparison of Phenomena," then *peruse* chapter 23, "Procedures in Debate," and then come back to the beginning, starting with this introduction, and read the book closely. Just peruse those later chapters, just *glance* at them to the point of wondering. Don't beat your head against the wall trying to understand every detail. That would be counterproductive. Just begin to lay down the grooves. The early glance is like looking at pictures of a place you are soon going to visit. Then, later, when you build up to chapters 23 and 25 in order, you will be proud of your success in understanding every detail. You can develop these skills in eight to sixteen weeks, especially if you work with a partner and verbalize the exercises and speak them out loud.

This approach seems to be relatively easier for philosophy majors, mathematics majors, science majors, economics majors, musicians, and actors. With philosophy, math, science, and economics majors, they have some training in reasoning already, so this is just another approach. Also, all but the actors are used to working with symbolic languages in their respective disciplines, which matures the brain since you are always moving things around mentally. In return, the philosophy, math, science, and economics majors report that Buddhist reasoning and debate gave them a new tool that better enables them to work in their disciplines. I think the actors do well with it because they are good at memorizing lines, and then naturally, after speaking the lines a few times, the new connections have developed.

There is some memorization here. I recommend that you learn several terms, definitions, divisions, paradigms, and so on. I think memorization has gotten a bad name in modern American education. I have never regretted having immediate access to anything I learned by heart. Again, nothing is so fast and fantastic as the mind. It seems to me that if you build up a body of facts to which you always have immediate access, then in time you develop the ability to see the patterns. This is what we call learning. But, without the basic information in your ready-access memory, you have little to draw on. Just having access to the information in books and online is not good enough. That is having your learning in a box. The computer is not your mind. Your mind is your mind.

So, what do you need to do in order to gain basic competence in Buddhist debate?

1. Find a debate partner or two. You don't have to be in the same room in our sci-fi era, but you do need to speak with a partner rather than just write out your lines in the debate.
2. Read over the material in this book part by part in order. To the extent that you wish, follow up with further reading in *Debate in Tibetan Buddhism, Mind in Tibetan Buddhism, Tibetan Logic,* and any of the many other works I suggest, though it may be best initially to stick with just what is here.[2] Then, if you can, listen to the online lecture that corresponds. (I plan to produce videos of my lectures on Buddhist reasoning and debate and place them online.) Then read over the same material one more time. Thus: read, listen, read.
3. Practice with your partner, following the examples in this book and anywhere else you can find them. This should include making up your own examples and questions. This book and the supporting material you can search for are intended to be like a programmed text for learning basic Buddhist reasoning.

I cannot be there with all who would care to learn. It might be nice, but I'm afraid I can't. Even so, you can do it—you and your partner.

I really do think you need a debate partner or two. I don't know the mysteries of the mind well enough, but there is clearly something in the energy between two people talking that is lacking in one's own internal review. Studying Buddhist debate on your own is sort of like when you continue reading your biology text or driving on the interstate even though you are tired or distracted and then suddenly you realize that you are not present in the activity. You had zoned out. In trying to discover Buddhist reasoning on your own, there is a lack of vividness for almost everyone working individually. However, in conversation with another intelligent person, you are drawn out to be more present and alert. Perhaps it is the demand to be present in your conversation that makes phone conversations so dangerous while driving. So, if you want to gain this skill, do the exercises, follow the lead of the people you will find in your search, and practice speaking the debate exercises with your partner.

A Change as a Result of Practicing Buddhist Reasoning and Debate

Do not be discouraged if you do not get it immediately. This stuff is not difficult. Honestly. I'm not just putting a shine on it. There is challenging material down the road, or at least it still seems so to me, but this is the most basic material. It may seem obscure at first, but really it is easy. Really. As one former student said, "It clicked at some point and now I'm wondering, 'This is it?'"

Sometimes people hear the debates and become intrigued. For instance, I had one good student who reported that, one day in a coffee shop near one of the colleges where I taught this topic, she overheard two students practicing debate. Of course, she did not know what they were doing, but she said she was intrigued because, even though they were clearly speaking English, she could not understand what they were saying. So she joined the class and did quite well. Once you get going, it is a vibrant exchange. It can become like second nature. Anyway, if you work to develop a good rational procedure, why wouldn't you want to keep it handy at all times?

It was only after several years of teaching this material that it began to seem to me that learning these basic procedures actually changes our brains. We wear in new connections. This happens all the time, I think. Maybe it always happens with learning. I don't know. I am not a brain scientist. However, I have talked with some brain scientists about this. As I understand it, it has something to do with neuroplasticity, a quality of the brain that is comparable to the flexibility of the joints. And, like the flexibility of the joints, neuroplasticity lessens as we age, so it becomes harder to make new connections.

I have an example in this regard. It is from the time when our graduate Tibetan language class at the University of Virginia was learning early debate topics under Lati Rinpoche. We had gotten to the challenging topic of substantial and isolate phenomena, which is covered in chapter 14 in *Debate in Tibetan Buddhism*. There was a student in that class who was about ten or twelve years older than the rest of us. On about the second day, when Lati Rinpoche was explaining substantial and isolate phenomena, all of us younger ones were able to give answers, but this older student said in despair, "I just don't know where you are coming from on this! How are you able to come up with those answers?" Now I see this as a story of slightly reduced neuroplasticity. By the next time we met, this good student had it down cold by following up with the books. The person's age required that it just took a little longer to make the new connections.

Another story on this is from the courses I have taught on this topic. There has grown up a sort of legend of a benchmark in the process that the students speak of as a "click." It is like everything falls into place. That which was not going the right way now starts going the right way. And then it's easy. No kidding. You get it. I can remember having this experience myself. In several comments, students speak of experiencing this "click" when they finally got it:

> It is a little difficult at first, but after the first test it will click. Like a flash of lightning! Debate is so helpful because you can actually use it in life.

> I was lost for the first part of the semester, and about half way through, it all clicked, and I got it.

> Challenging [course] but I felt great when I "got it." I think the class really helped with my fear of public speaking. After having to do this, a normal prepared presentation isn't nearly as scary.

> My work ethic has increased dramatically because of the demands of this class. Very difficult, but very rewarding after the proverbial "click."

> Buddhist Debate. It is a difficult class, yet so simple.... All of the information we were going over seemed so foreign to me. However, I feel that working actively to understand what we were learning, I gained an understanding that could not have been taught in the classroom. It's a little like when you hear a saying your whole life and one day you just really understand it.

How Buddhist Reasoning and Debate Can Help You

As we all know, rationality does not apply just to topics of theology and philosophy. Rather, it applies everywhere. Thus, I offer this course as a great introduction to one approach to rational inquiry. Though the information is expressed in terms of Buddhist philosophy, do not think that these techniques apply only to Buddhist topics. If you learn the techniques, you can use them for any topic. It is a way of organizing information, whatever kind of information. It is not limited to Buddhist topics. The Buddhist debaters have done a great job of stressing the reasoning forms to find their limits, and the system is designed to take a person into topics of Buddhist philosophy. However, I have found—and so too have hundreds of students found—that the techniques apply broadly, not just to Buddhist topics. It is another tool in your toolkit. Here are some comments from students who took this course that illustrate this:

> I gained a little self-confidence in this class.

> I will take my skills from this class and use them *every* day throughout my life.

> The price for education is very high, but one cannot put a price on the amount of knowledge I have acquired because of this class. This class helps me to acquire knowledge in all facets of life.

> This course was unlike any I had taken . . . and was certainly the most philosophically stimulating and most rewarding course. It has improved my reasoning skills [and] short-term memory and boosted my confidence, making me less afraid to speak in front of people. My mind has been restructured to think in a way previously unfamiliar to me, and I am always grateful to learn about another culture's thought systems.

> Although I was familiar with the use of consequences in argument, this course really helped me become more disciplined in my approach.

> The lessons I've learned in this course alone are able to be applied to *every* aspect of my life. I've become a better listener, and I've also learned how to be a more successful arguer, if there is such a thing. All in all, this class has made me more open to different ideas and ultimately more flexible.

> The rewards of the critical thinking and logic skills that I developed in this class go far beyond the realm of Buddhist Reason and Debate. I am more concise in my speech and much more confident about the thoughts I assert—because I know they are well thought out.

This class has been the most influential of my entire academic career. In learning the skills of debate, I have sharpened my critical thinking skills. The material covered is applicable to most everyday encounters, which contributes to better understanding and a greater awareness.

I found myself being able to apply the knowledge that I learned in class. For example, I never understood the fact that there are so many overgeneralizations until I really applied the material learned in class. I think and feel that this class would be helpful for law students because it teaches you how to understand the logic of things.

This class really improved my critical analysis skills and has helped my communication in school, work, friendship, even with my boyfriend! It was so much fun learning this new method of logic and comparison and feeling connected to the great Tibetan debaters.

This course was challenging but rewarding. It was like learning a new language or a math formula. The information in this class is very different from Western styles of debate and philosophy; I liked the challenge though. The class was enjoyable; it helped me to work on my memory skills, study skills, knowledge of Eastern philosophy, my public speaking skills, and my confidence. It is a demanding course but well worth the effort!

I provide these comments to support my claim that learning this style of Buddhist reasoning and debate will be supportive to analytical thought in any area of your life. It is a way of organizing the information, which assists in your own thought, your own speech, your own writing, and your assessment of the speech and writing of others.

One day in conversation, Professor James Cargile, who teaches philosophy at the University of Virginia and was one of the readers of my dissertation, came up with a good analogy for the differing approaches in Western and Buddhist styles of reasoning. Though he was well accomplished in Western logic, reading my dissertation was his first meeting with an Asian approach to critical thinking. One thing that was important to Professor Cargile was to establish that what is rational in one system must also be rational in the other and indeed must be rational everywhere. We agreed on this for sure. In our meetings, I emphasized to Professor Cargile that Buddhists think that one's reasoning abilities have to be internal, not mechanized, because a person can be liberated only by internal understanding. He compared this style of reasoning, which must be internalized in some way, to learning to grapple up the side of a mountain on your own, whereas the Western approach is like building a *ferrocarril.* (It seems that *ferrocarril* is a Spanish word for "railroad," but in our conversation that day, he gestured and explained that he meant one of those short railways that run up the side of a steep mountain.) His point was that on a ferrocarril, anyone can reach the top of the mountain. Similarly, by application of logical principles, one can find the result whether or not you have become a rational person internally. However, if you have to grapple up the side of a mountain on your own—that is, to understand the result by your own wits—then the means for that has to be within oneself.

Final Comment: This course will have a value corresponding closely to the measure of what you put into it. Although verbalizing the analysis with a partner is essential for gaining competence in debate and just thinking about it will not get you there, it is also essential to think about it. For almost every debater I have ever met—Tibetan, American, and otherwise—this approach ignites a fire of passion that spreads throughout all of their intellectual life. The key is to constantly apply what you are learning. Keep it close like a new, favorite toy. Check to see how it can apply to information coming your way or if it applies at all. Just keep pushing, and you will find the value.

HAIKU

Unique debate class
Man, kids talked all the time
Like I did today.

2. The Human Situation

───────────

HAVING BEEN BORN as we have, we now face death. Nothing more is required to assure us that we shall die but that we have been born. Once a plant has sprouted, it is definite that in time that plant will die. Every structure we build will come down in time. Having met as we have assures us that we shall part. When you move into a new home, you can confidently put a sign on the refrigerator that says, "The day when you no longer live here is surely coming." If a mountain system rises up, though it may last for millions of years, in time it will wear away and be gone. Geologists estimate that the Appalachian mountain system that runs from northern Georgia up to Maine may be the oldest mountain system in the world, perhaps as old as 600 million years. The northern tip of this mountain system is found in the north of Scotland and another part of it is now in Morocco in the west of Africa. You can imagine how long ago they were formed and how long it took the geological plates to drift so far apart, moving at approximately the rate that your fingernails grow. The geologists believe that formerly some of the mountains in this system were as much as ten miles high, more than four miles taller than Mt. Everest, and now, millions of years after they arose, none is more than a mile high! If in time even these great mountains wear away, what need is there to wonder about this frail body?

The Tibetan Book of the Dead* literature puts forth an assertion that we shall survive after the end of this life. These texts explain the process of dying, what life is like in the period between—after the end of this life and before the beginning of the next—and how we take rebirth. Thus, they say there are no dead persons, there are only dying persons—and we are all dying persons. From the point of conception, we begin the process of death.

───────────

*Rather than being a single text, the Tibetan Book of the Dead is a genre of literature with several different versions; thus, it is not italicized here.

Moment by moment, with every breath, we draw closer to death. When you finish reading this paragraph, you are closer to death than when you began it. When you walk out of this room, you are closer to death than when you entered it. Although these things are clearly accurate, they are difficult to bear in mind, and the implications of these truths humble us. Moreover, they imply that our time is precious and fleeting, and we must do what we wish to do now, while there is still time.

Clearly, the thought of the Tibetan Book of the Dead is that this life within us cannot be stamped out. There is no choice but to live, and ultimately, if you want peace and happiness, there is no choice but to try to figure out life. Especially from the point of view of a system that asserts a round of rebirth, every day and every life is like the movie *Groundhog Day* in which the world-weary character played by Bill Murray lives and relives February 2nd over and over again until he manages to do what has to be done.

For whatever reason, we all want life, and we act to preserve our lives. Some say it is because of a fear of the unknown that lies beyond this life. Some say it is because of attachment to this life: we have what we have, and we want to keep it. Some find a biological explanation for why we seek to preserve our lives. Everything about us is laid out for the preservation of our lives. But we want to live only if we can live with some measure of peace, free of suffering. No one wants to live in constant and horrible misery. Thus, we hope to live, but, beyond that, we hope to live free of suffering.

Still, as I say, having been born as we have, we now face death. And, on top of that, before we die, we will face difficulties. So, it is not a question of whether or not we will die. Nor is it a question of whether or not we will suffer. Thus, given the reality of suffering and death, is there anything we can do? The first impulse is to flee. We wonder whether or not it might be possible to avoid death and suffering. Naturally, we wonder whether or not there is any way to get out of this fix. The constant vulnerability to death and suffering frustrates our wish to live in peace. Even if everything is fine in this moment, it is difficult to be at peace. At this point, we cannot stop death, and we cannot prevent difficulties from coming our way. So what do we have? What can we control? It is a matter of how we respond. Everyone knows the quote attributed to Albert Einstein that insanity is doing the same thing over and over again and expecting a different result. Our responses to life events are often quite consistent. We do the same things over and over again, and we usually get the same results. Thus, our propensities just keep piling up, and often we only gain more difficulties. But, if every day is like *Groundhog Day,* then every day is a chance to get smart, to get it right. As hard as it may be, when difficulties arise, we have a choice of whether to respond with anger or with patience. Even if you don't believe in a round of rebirth and that an action of anger can give you a long, miserable life in hell, the intelligent will consider whether or not anger will benefit them in this difficult situation. In the film *The Godfather,* Michael Corleone said, "Don't hate your enemies—it clouds your judgment."

Against the backdrop of inescapable death and certain suffering, we all want happiness and don't want suffering. It is a constant longing that drives us morning, noon, and night, and sometimes we even gain a measure of it. We fill the roads going north, south, east, and west because we want happiness and don't want suffering. Why in the world do your mother and father do what they do? Because they want happiness and don't want suffering. Why are your friends doing what they do? Because they want happiness and don't want suffering. Why do people lie, cheat, steal, and even kill? Because they want happiness and don't want suffering. No matter what, we are always seeking to find happiness and avoid suffering. Sometimes, we are drawn to what we think will make us happy or at least alleviate our suffering, even when it is the worst possible thing for us. It's more than just crazy human high jinks. Indeed, the impulse to seek happiness and avoid suffering seems to be universal for all conscious beings. Why do the squirrels hop about in the yard? Because they want happiness and don't want suffering. Why does the spider weave her web? Because she wants happiness and does not want suffering. Why do the chickens cross the road? Because they want happiness and do not want suffering. No matter what, that game is always in play. Look into others' eyes, and you will know the truth of this. Look at your own eyes in the mirror.

Now, given that people want happiness and do not want suffering, the challenge becomes how to play to win. That is, the question before us is not whether or not we will be in the game, but how we can possibly participate in life to achieve our wish to gain happiness and avoid suffering. That is the real rub! It seems to me that it is not so much death itself that is the rub, but the constant chafing of the wish to find happiness and avoid suffering— moment by moment, hour after hour, day after day, year after year, and perhaps even life after life. Why would we fear the rub of death if life were only suffering? Indeed, death might bring a great relief, a solace from suffering. We are constantly in motion, seeking to find happiness and avoid suffering.

Why are you reading this book? It is this push to find happiness and avoid suffering that disturbs our peace, and death is only a part of that rub.

Thus, what are the strategies for responding to events to improve our chances to gain happiness and to avoid the difficulties that bring us suffering, or at least to limit the amount and duration of the difficulties? You may consider this within the context of this life alone or, if you suspect that there will be continued life after this one, you may consider this within a broader context. In either case, the more you can discover by your wit and observation, the better off you are. I recognize that sometimes we need the comfort of not knowing. For example, it may be that you need to allow the deceit, and perhaps even believe, that your partner is faithful in order to continue on. I don't know. You two work that out. But in general, the more you know and the more clearly you know, the better off you are.

Here's a story that seems to relate. One time in Charlottesville, not too long ago, I ran into a graduate student working in theoretical physics. I always carry around a collection of questions for people who might know about a particular topic—for scientists, doctors, lawyers, police, priests, ministers, accountants, and so on. The list of questions for physicists is a long one, and often I will ask the same questions over and over to different people. I ask physicists how it can be that there is no center to the universe. Wouldn't there have been a place in space where the big bang happened, and since matter moves away from that space, wouldn't that be the center? The answers are generally consistent. It is my understanding that is faulty. Well, this physicist in Charlottesville was particularly good at the answers, I thought. What I always like, and this fellow was very good about this, is the commitment to move closer to understanding, even if it seems to contradict what we had formerly believed to be the case. This shows real integrity, an admirable open-mindedness. People wonder why we should care about such things as physicists routinely investigate—dark energy, dark matter, and so on—but what comes through is that *they can think of no advantage in not knowing* how things are. That leads them to seek to know how things are.

Buddhists are like that too, and that particular physicist confirmed this as well, as Buddhism is one of his interests. Now, Buddhism is not science; however, they both share a strong commitment to understanding how things are and a belief that there will be advantages to understanding. If something is real, we can think of no advantage in not knowing about it. It may not matter too much or it may take a very long time to figure out how to gain advantage out of knowing, but there is no advantage in not knowing what is real. Think of the microbes on your cup or the DNA in our bodies. These kinds of things have always been there. They are real. So it is better to know about them.

The Buddhists are like that in regard to death and impermanence. With every breath, we draw closer to death. Buddhists do not focus on this point because they are morbid or because they want to scare people. They focus on it because it is real. Death has always been so. It is real. So it is better to understand that clearly. That's why they talk about it so much, especially in the beginning.

You may rightly say that there are many things that are real, but there is no clear advantage in meditating on them. So why do Buddhists emphasize meditating on death and impermanence? The context of this narrative is as a motivator for religious practice.

In contemplating the human condition, what comes home to us is that our time is fleeting—time for all of our activities—finishing college, speaking to an old friend about what happened, going to visit a place that you long to see, whatever. Our time is fleeting. In this regard, I always remember that my father, who died at the age of eighty-one, said several times that he wanted to visit England and Ireland, but he never did. He had the time for that. There was even money for that. But he never went, and now he has passed away. And now I have lost my chance to help him do what he wanted.

The Buddhists offer a three-point contemplation of death:

1. Death is definite.
2. The time of death is indefinite.
3. At the time of death, the only thing that claims to help (in any life that may come after this one) is religious practice.

The purpose of this meditation is to increase a person's enthusiasm for, and effort in, religious practice, for now is our only chance to practice it. Of all the motivators for religious practice, awareness of death and impermanence is the most effective.

The contemplation of our human situation—the certainty of death and unstoppable impermanence—is profound and compelling. Thinking of this helps energize us to do whatever it is we think we need to do to move toward having happiness and avoiding suffering. Whatever it is. It is not necessarily limited to motivating our spiritual practices. Now, for a few moments, we have the opportunity to stand between the earth and the sun, so let us please move with intent and appreciation for these moments to do what we need to do to find happiness.

> Prepare a noble death song for the day when you go over the great divide. . . . When it comes your time to die, . . . sing your death song and die like a hero going home.
>
> —TECUMSEH, SHAWNEE WAR CHIEF (1768–1813),
> *Shawnee History*

3. Reasoning within the Buddhist Context

The human situation—constant vulnerability to death and impermanence—is the backdrop in front of which we all perform. We want happiness and don't want suffering, but the vulnerability to death and suffering that is imposed on us by the reality of impermanence often frustrates our wishes. Awareness of death and impermanence is the first essential and a constant point of emphasis for reasoning within the Buddhist context.

We must always understand Buddhism in the context of Indian spirituality. The Indians focused on the verifiable fact that it is difficult to find a lasting peace and comfort in this life. We occasionally find a measure of it, but it is always fleeting. When we get hungry, it's nice to have a good meal. But, after a while, we get hungry again. What food can we eat that satisfies our hunger in a final way? When we are thirsty or tired, it is the same story. And so on and on. Thus, the Indians concluded that we will never find a final and stable peace in these temporary things. Even so, it is true enough that we do find a temporary peace in these temporary satisfactions, and though it can never last, we cannot just give up eating and so on.

The Buddha was born a prince and lived a life of plenty for his first three decades. But, he did not find satisfaction in the royal life of plenty, so he fled into the forest in search of a more stable peace. In his efforts, he adopted the time-honored Indian tradition of denial of the senses. The legend is that he lived for six years on a daily diet of just one sesame seed, one grain of rice, and one jojoba bean, along with water. It seems his efforts in this period were directed toward controlling the sensual impulses. We can see that our sensual needs often draw us into many activities that ultimately harm us, such as stealing, killing, lying, and so on. At the very least, even if we control our sensual needs, they cannot be permanently satisfied. So the denial of the senses is probably an effort to finally subdue the impulses themselves. Ultimately, the Buddha-to-be decided that the denial of the senses too would not work, and he gave up that constraint. He returned to eating more normally, forging a middle way between indulgence and denial. It is the sensible approach of using the world rather than letting it use us. Whether or not you believe in a round of rebirth, you have to see that having bodies such as we do puts us in a position of vulnerability. And, so long as we have this vulnerability, we cannot have a stable peace.

This is the heart of the Indian context of Buddhism—the search for a stable state of peace. I see an ordinary analogue to this wish for peace and stability in our attachment to the digital world. In the digital world, everything is perfect and predictable. Things happen as they are supposed to happen. At least that's the way we think of it, and we lose it, even get angry, when things do not operate as they are supposed to. One day, walking in a beautiful country estate with a friend who is a longtime computer geek, we came up to an extraordinary, Monet-like pond with cattails, reeds, and lotus flowers, all with a Japanese-style wooden bridge in the background. I said, "See? The carbon-based world! It's pretty great, right?" And he said, "Yes, but the silicon-based world is better." We all have this longing for stability and predictability. Some philosophers, mathematicians, and scientists find an unearthly beauty in the world of mathematics, where everything is perfect and precise. Some even conclude that nothing is real but numbers.

Though we may all long for it, it is very difficult to see any measure of peace and stability in this world. There is no one who is evidently beyond suffering. Even the most beautiful, powerful, and wealthy lose it all in the end. We just do not see anyone who clearly enjoys a state of stable peace. At least initially, it is a leap of faith to believe that such a state of lasting peace is even possible. There is just no evidence for it. There is only the *illusion* of peace and stability. And, we conspire together to believe in this illusion and to find evidence for it. As an illusion-based life-form myself, it is hard for me to believe that there could be a world where the skies are forever unclouded, though I want to believe it.

Indeed, Buddhists make the claim that there is a state of stable peace and that it is possible for any of us to reach it. The fourth of the four "seals" that mark an assertion as a Buddhist one is that *nirvāṇa** is peace. This mainly

---

*Remember that the line over the *a* (*ā*) in *nirvāṇa* marks it as a long *a,* an *a* with a double-beat, and the dot under the *n* (*ṇ*) means that it is retroflexed, the *n* sound made while bending the tip of the tongue back toward the top of the head. Please say it aloud.

means that if you achieve *nirvāṇa,* you will not fall from it. From the beginning, this was my main concern. I could not believe that any state could be stable. Since I had these doubts, it was hard for me to make any effort to achieve it. Maybe my concern was due to countless unstable lives in the round of rebirth, or maybe it was just due to the observation of inevitable decay in this lifetime. I thought that if we are all born but inevitably die, everything seems to go in cycles, and we see everything come to an end, how could it be that any of us could achieve an understanding, find a state of peace, and never fall from it? When I first met with the Dalai Lama in India in 1979, this is exactly what I asked him. As I understood his answer, and I have reflected on it for decades since, he said that *nirvāṇa* is an utter eradication of suffering and the causes of suffering, such that they can never arise again. Thus, it is not simply that you have understood something and it's so great you will never forget it. People forget all the time, even important stuff. It is that you have cured the condition completely, and there is no chance for it to develop again.

The most important topic of Buddhist philosophy is cause and effect. The Buddha is respected as one who discovered the causes of suffering and the causes of happiness. In his first sermon after the awakening/enlightenment experience, this is exactly what he lays out in the teaching of the four noble truths. He identified suffering and the causes of suffering and made the extraordinary claim that there is a state beyond suffering and that there is a path leading to that state beyond suffering. The basic procedure is that *if you do not want the effect* of suffering, *do not engage in the causes* of suffering. And *if you do want the effect* of a life free of suffering, *engage in the causes* of such a life.

What is the cause of suffering? According to the Buddhists, the cause of suffering is ignorance. This means especially ignorance about your own true nature. The guiding thought in South Asian spirituality, at least since the time of the Hindu Upanishads, is that we will be liberated by understanding our own nature as it is:

> The Self-existent [soul within]* pierced sense openings outward; therefore, a man looked out, not in.
> But a certain wise man, in search of immortality, turned his gaze inward and saw the Self within.

*Generally, Hindus assert an unchanging soul within, whereas Buddhists deny such a soul exists. Still, both look for peace within.

The foolish go after outer pleasures and walk into the snare of all-
  embracing death.
The wise, however, discerning immortality, do not seek the
  permanent among things impermanent.[1]

It is a truth of psychology and sociology that we are very much under the
influence of how we view ourselves. To a great extent, Indian spirituality
is in line with this thought. Both Hindus and Buddhists determine that
ultimately our natures are free of fault and to realize this is to become free.
What Buddhists identify here as ignorance, the source of all suffering, is *not
simply not knowing something but actively believing in the opposite of what
is true*. If you know you don't know something, then you are aware of that,
and you may try to learn the truth of the matter. If you do not actually know
something but think you do, you will proceed confidently without searching for the real truth. That can get us in trouble. As Josh Billings (aka Henry
Wheeler Shaw, 1818–85) said,[2] "It is better to know nothing than to know
what ain't so."* Thus, initially, the challenge is to try to discover your own
nature as it is, while keeping a wary eye on how you presently view yourself.

In the same way that it is a belief that it is ignorance that gives rise to all
suffering, it is another article of belief that the wrong understanding of your
own nature can be completely eradicated. But that is easier to believe than
the assertion that, once eradicated, the wrong understanding cannot ever be
reseeded. We all have experiences of overcoming misunderstandings, so it
is not too hard to imagine overcoming even this challenging and persistent
misunderstanding. However, we all know stories or have had the experience
ourselves of forgetting what we formerly knew.

So how would such a permanent eradication of ignorance be possible?
Wisdom is the actual antidote to ignorance. And wisdom is the heart of
the Buddhist path. Wisdom, and the liberation it induces, does not just
arise spontaneously but arises as an effect of effort. It is a gradual process.
It usually takes a week or two just to get over a cold, so we would certainly
need to be patient with ourselves in trying to get over lifetimes of sickness
in a round of rebirth.

The gradual buildup to the wellness of liberation depends on training in

---

*There is a similar line often attributed to Mark Twain, though it is difficult to find the
citation: "It ain't what you don't know that gets you into trouble. It's what you know for
sure that just ain't so."

three areas: ethics, meditative stabilization or concentration, and wisdom. Sometimes it seems so "pie-in-the-sky" to hear the Buddhists talking about the development of wisdom. I mean, it just seems so lofty and unimaginable that it is, at the least, discouraging and, at the worst, impossible. However, the description of these three areas of training indicates an integrated path that begins with the simplest efforts and culminates in the final healing. Again, if it takes a week or so just to get over a cold, why would anyone think that we could destroy all of our problems in a wink? If the process is possible at all, it would require patience. As Lama Yeshe said, "Be wise. Treat yourself, your mind, sympathetically, with loving-kindness. If you are gentle with yourself, you will become gentle with others, so don't push."[3]

Since the goal of *nirvāṇa* is described as a state of peace, it is helpful to think of the whole process as one of pacifying the mind or one of healing the mind. Don't think of this as dulling out but as calming down. The thought is that the mind in and of itself is free of fault; thus, on its own, it illuminates perfectly. The mist that obscures it is the fault of ignorance. In another way, think of the status of ordinary life as like living in a constant fever, suffering hallucinations due to ignorance.

The first of the three areas of training is the practice of ethics. Like the physician's procedure of first removing what should not be there and then building up what should be there, cultivating the Buddhist virtues is characterized as abandoning one thing and then adopting another. Ethics begins with the practice of the "ten virtues," such as abandoning killing and adopting a practice of sustaining life. It is a process of building something up, and as in most of our undertakings, it is important also to admire the abilities and skills of those who are better than we are. Ethics is described as the admiration of virtue. It is not just what you do but also what your attitude is. Faith is described as an appropriate response to virtuous objects, and ethics is an admiration of virtue. It is a type of natural ethics. Buddhist ethics is not so much behaving in obedience to another or behaving in a certain way because it is prescribed. Buddhist ethics is behaving in a way that supports our natural wish to have happiness and avoid suffering. In terms of healing, the first procedure is to remove what does not belong—foreign objects, toxins, and so on. Ethics means to turn away from nonvirtuous behavior, which is harmful, and to adopt virtuous behavior, which is helpful. Just as we would hope that you would get better after the bullets were removed or the invading viruses had been defeated, so with ethical behavior, the mind becomes calmer and more peaceful. Ethics is compared to the earth: just as all structures depend on the earth as their foundation, so all spiritual development depends on ethics as its foundation.

Based on ethics, a person now has a chance of developing a stable mind. One of the two types of meditation is concentration meditation, also known as meditative stabilization. Buddhists describe vast realms of higher levels of concentration,[*] but they say that all that is required to pacify the mind adequately to achieve *nirvāṇa* is a level called "calm abiding."[†] Without ethical behavior, a meditator cannot develop adequate concentration because the mind is too stirred up. Think of how shaky and disturbed you become when you are angry or if you have just stolen something, if you have ever had that experience. So, concentration to the point of calm abiding represents another level of pacifying the mind. Concentration is compared to the stability of a flame. Imagine that you are in a dark room with nothing but a single candle. Then a breeze comes in through an open window, and the flame begins to flicker. When this happens, it doesn't show the objects in the room as clearly. When the flame is stable, it illuminates to its full power, whatever the measure of that power may be. So, when the mind is stable—not flickering with distraction—it too illuminates to its full power, whatever the measure of that power.

Based on ethics and meditative stabilization, we have a chance of developing the wisdom that is the final antidote to ignorance.[‡] Since Buddhists describe karma and life in the round of rebirth as invariably linked with ignorance, when a person achieves wisdom, that person will no longer create karma. In addition, Buddhists believe that the power of wisdom burns out all of the old karmic seeds, like exposing photographic film to a bright light. Then, having no karma left, that wise person will no longer be subject to rebirth. They believe that such persons could appear again in the round of rebirth, but they would not be reborn under the power of karma, as is an

[*]For a full description of these realms and meditative stabilization, including calm abiding, see Lati Rinbochay and Denma Lochö Rinbochay, *Meditative States in Tibetan Buddhism,* trans. Leah Zahler and Jeffrey Hopkins (London: Wisdom Publications, 1983).

[†]See also B. Alan Wallace's explanation of how to achieve calm abiding in his writings on *śhamatha* and calming the mind.

[‡]There are many sophisticated descriptions of the content of this Buddhist wisdom. For instance, see Jeffrey Hopkins, *Meditation on Emptiness* (London: Wisdom Publications, 1983); Elizabeth Napper, *Dependent-Arising and Emptiness* (Boston: Wisdom Publications, 1989); and William Magee, *The Nature of Things: Emptiness and Essence in the Geluk World* (Ithaca, N.Y.: Snow Lion Publications, 1999).

ordinary person. Wisdom is compared to the brightness of a flame. If the flame is bright enough, you can see all that is around you. In the same way, increasing your wisdom is like illuminating your world. You see the nature of things.

Why would such wisdom be stable? In the Buddhist way of thinking, *nirvāṇa* is not a created state. If it were, it could decay and reverse. Rather, it is a mere absence. It is a stable state of mind free of suffering and the causes of suffering. Think of it like a room free of elephants, probably like the one you are in now. The absence of elephants in that room was not created, and it abides unchanging. Now, it could be that someone came in and shooed all the elephants out before you came in, and by that effort created *a room free of elephants.* However, the mere absence of elephants in the room was not created, and it abides without disintegration. It may happen that the absence of elephants in that room will go out of existence if someone brings in an elephant or two, but while there were none, the absence of elephants in that room was stable.

Well, just as someone could bring elephants back into your big room, couldn't ignorance come back into your consciousness? *Nirvāṇa* is compared to a candle that has burned out completely, so that the flame is extinguished and the wick and wax are gone. The image is that the flame is like suffering and the wick and the wax are like the origins of suffering. When the candle has burned out completely, there is nothing left to relight. This is the image. This is the thought. It requires some faith to believe it since it is not an obvious possibility. However, you don't need to believe it in order to get on with Buddhist debate. Just store it away for possible future consideration.

Since ignorance is the cause of suffering, once ignorance is removed, suffering will not arise. Thus, the central concern of Buddhism is to defeat ignorance. Remember that the most important topic of Buddhist philosophy is cause and effect, and the strategy is that if you do not want the effect, do not engage in the causes of that effect, and if you do want the effect, engage in its causes. Buddhists say that we may be able to achieve our wish to have happiness and avoid suffering by a process of pacifying and harmonizing the mind. So this is why the procedure is a combination of ethics, concentration, and wisdom. The mind is initially calmed by ethics, then stabilized by concentration, then brightened by wisdom. With this harmony, peace unfolds. At least initially, it is a matter of faith to believe. If it is true that this is a real possibility, it would happen slowly. It would be a gradual process.

What is the content of this wisdom that liberates? Buddhism presents itself as a middle way between two extremes. We can see this in the life story of the Buddha, who went from a life of indulgence as a prince to a life of sensual denial as a renunciant in the forest, before he struck a middle way of sensible moderation adequate to sustain life. However, the more important sense in which Buddhists speak of their religion as a middle way is in reference to their theory of what exists, their ontology. That is, the Buddhists seek to avoid the two extremes, the extreme of existence and the extreme of non-existence. The extreme of existence is the false belief that something exists, when in fact it does not. The extreme of non-existence is the false belief that something does not exist, when in fact it does.

In terms of the Buddhist theory of what exists, an example of the extreme of existence is the false belief that there is a permanent, unitary, independent self that is the core of who you are. This they deny, and in denying it, Buddhists are claiming ground specifically at odds with the Hindus, who very clearly assert a permanent, unitary, and independent aspect of the personality that is the core of you. "Permanent" means something that exists but is not changing moment by moment. "Unitary" means something that is indivisible, so that the thing does not depend on its parts to exist. And "independent" means something that exists apart from depending on other things, such as causes and conditions, that bring the person into being. An ethical example of the extreme of existence is the belief that if you have some measure of wisdom, then it does not matter what you do—so called "crazy wisdom." A limited measure of wisdom does not put you beyond karma, Buddhists say, any more than authority would put you beyond the law. Moreover, if a person becomes fully realized, as the Buddha is said to be, then such a person would not be immoral. As Padmasambhāva, also known as Guru Rinpoche, said in regard to wisdom and ethics, "Though your view may be as high as the sky, your ethics must be as fine as flour."[4]

For the Buddhists, the prime example of the extreme of non-existence—the false belief that something does not exist when in fact it does—is the false belief that the person does not exist. That is, according to their way of thinking, if we think that there is no person at all, then we have fallen to the extreme of non-existence. Many people think that this is what Buddhism teaches. They believe that, since Buddhists assert the selflessness of persons—meaning the emptiness or lack of a self of persons—then they deny there is any person at all. This is not their position. Though Buddhism is not monolithic, for there are many differing positions and points of view, all

Buddhists agree that at least there is no permanent, unitary, independent self. Still, at the same time, they all agree that there is a person. Otherwise, Buddhism would fall to nihilism. The prime ethical example of the extreme of non-existence is the false belief that there is no effect of actions. Clearly, this false belief refers to the moral effects of actions. In practical matters, we can all see that, for instance, when we wash a car, it gets cleaner, or when we gather the workers and the materials, we can build a house. The Buddhist moral belief here is that there is karma, so what they are characterizing as the extreme of non-existence is the idea that there will be no negative effects of what we do—killing, raping, stealing, and so on—so long as it does not bring any retribution in this life, for example, from legal authorities or vengeful relatives. Such a view, that there is no moral or spiritual effect of actions, is fertile ground for bad behavior. Unfortunately, it is a view that is held by many.

So, if you eliminate the extreme of existence, the false belief that something exists when in fact it does not, and the extreme of non-existence, the false belief that something does not exist when in fact it does, what are you left with? A correct understanding of what exists. This is the goal. This is the intent. You no longer believe something exists when it doesn't, and you no longer believe something does not exist when it does. You've got it right. One of my teachers, Kensur Yeshi Thupten, a renowned scholar, who was said to be especially skillful in topics of valid cognition (Skt. *pramāṇa*, Tib. *tshad ma*), which is the general area of Buddhist reasoning and debate, said that valid cognition is "the measure of what exists and what does not exist."[5] In Tibetan, the topic of valid cognition is pronounced as "*tshe ma.*" The syllable "*tshe*" (spelled in Tibetan as *tshad*) occurs in the interrogative "*ka tshe,*" meaning "how much" or "what measure." According to Kensur Yeshi Thupten, "*tshad ma*" means "measure," and the Sanskrit "*pramāṇa*" originally referred to balance scales, like the Scales of Justice, the kind used in the Indian marketplace. So the intent of the study of valid cognition, which is the starting point for all Buddhist philosophy, is to supply a tool that enables us to measure what exists and what does not exist.

Buddhist reasoning and debate is not logic, though logic is involved. Logic undertakes an investigation of the formal validity and invalidity of arguments. Logic focuses primarily on the form of the arguments to determine whether or not the argument works. Within Buddhism, reasoning and debate are not ends in and of themselves. Rather, they are respected as tools for approaching a final understanding. In Buddhist thought, reasoning and logic are included in the topic of valid cognition, which is focused on what are reliable consciousnesses and what are not reliable consciousnesses. Valid cognition includes perception as well as rational discourse, but the intent is to establish a few reliable procedures and then move toward understanding the measure of what exists and what does not exist.

Of course, most people are not trying to sort out the mode of existence of phenomena. Even so, clearly our beliefs and assumptions about how things exist strongly influence what we do in life. Without saying how things actually exist, since I don't know, we can note that many people proceed in life in fervent commitment to one or another view of how things exist. And, sometimes they switch around. Sometimes people will deny all spiritual beliefs for years and then suddenly make a commitment to Jesus as their Lord and Savior. Sometimes faithful people will give up and deny all their old beliefs. In fact, people very often flip back and forth. Some people spend a lifetime ramped to one side or the other, but there is also a lot of flipping around. This is what I call "ontological bipolarism," going back and forth between the extreme of existence and the extreme of non-existence. It is easy to see this unsteadiness in our emotional relations. Maybe there was someone you used to be willing to drive five hours just to have a day with, but now, if you see that person coming your way, you will duck into a shop and wait until that person passes. You all must have heard stories of people who used to be very close but now never speak. I think this emotional unsteadiness is related to our ontological unsteadiness, so it will be helpful to try to sort it out.

There is a saying from the Japanese Zen tradition of Buddhism that seems to express well this ontological bipolarism. It is drawn from a discourse attributed to Ch'ing-yüan Wei-hsin of the T'ang Dynasty, a master of the Chinese Ch'an predecessor of Zen Buddhism, who said:

> Thirty years ago, before I began the study of Zen, I said, "Mountains are mountains; waters are waters." After I got insight into the truth of Zen through the instruction of a good master, I said, "Mountains are not mountains; waters are not waters." But now, having attained the abode of final rest [that is enlightenment], I say, "Mountains are really mountains; waters are really waters."*

---

*Masao Abe, *Zen and Comparative Studies*, ed. Steven Heine (Honolulu: University of Hawai'i Press, 1997), 32. This passage is often remembered as the aphorism, "At first, I saw mountains as mountains and rivers as rivers. Then, I saw mountains were not mountains

Imagine a new monk going to the monastery in the mountains. He looks out with untrained eyes and sees the mountains and waters nearby. Then he sits in *zazen* meditation daily for years, and then it is as if there were no mountains and waters. What had appeared so real upon first arrival in time began to seem devoid of real existence, nothing. Then, after more years of sitting meditation, once again there are mountains and waters. Again the monk affirms the presence of the mountains and the waters, but he does not see them in the way he did when he first arrived. They are indeed there, but now he knows the measure of how they exist.

His view has changed. This change is the essence of meditation and debate as well. The Buddha is quoted as saying, "To children I speak advice/And to *yogīs*, tenets."[6] All of us have difficulties, and the Buddha offers advice to those who need it but look for nothing more. The Buddha advises us to avoid killing and stealing and reminds us to be kind and skillful in our activities. *Yogīs*, practitioners of yoga, have undertaken to see the nature of things. So, to them, the Buddha offers tenets.

Probably the single best English word for "yoga" is "union." It has the sense of "union with the Divine," "union of the sun and the moon," and so on. The word "yoga" is cognate with, that is, a word known together with, the English word "yoke," the wooden mantle placed on the necks of two oxen so they can work together. Of course, it also works to translate "yoga" as "yoking with," for example, "yoking the mind of the practitioner with the Divine" or "yoking together the sun and the moon," which refers to the vital force and the mental energy or even to Śhiva and Śhakti, within a Hindu context. Within a Buddhist context, we may speak of a "union of the mind of a *yogī* with the mind of a buddha" or "yoking the mind of the practitioner with the mind of a buddha."

The ideal practitioner of South Asian spirituality is the *yogī*, a male practitioner, or the *yoginī*, a female practitioner. We normally picture a practitioner of yoga in some sort of stretching pose, and, if we are looking from the outside, we think of yoga as a sort of physical discipline. Indeed, that is part of it. The purpose of the physical postures is to adjust the internal channels and the flow of the vital energy inside. This is all for the sake of increasing the yoga practitioner's clarity of understanding. Thus, the ideal practitioner does not practice just physical discipline but also practices mental discipline,

and rivers were not rivers. Finally, I see mountains again as mountains, and rivers again as rivers."

in meditation and in analytical investigation. For thousands of years, the *yogīs* and *yoginīs* of India, and all of South Asia, have investigated the nature of existence as part of their spiritual practice. Their efforts are rooted in the view that ultimate reality is always right at hand, and we can be liberated by seeing it. Beyond the physical and mental disciplines of the *yogīs* and *yoginīs,* there is the discipline of the heart, which is most clearly laid out in Mahāyāna Buddhism, also known as Great Vehicle Buddhism.

When the Buddha said that he speaks tenets to *yogīs,* he was appreciating the mental discipline of the *yogīs* in their undertaking to perceive the nature of reality and supporting them in that. "Tenets" (Skt. *siddhānta,* Tib. *grub mtha'*) means "established conclusions." This means that a person has settled on that tenet as final. This points at an important aspect of religious systems—that they supply a worldview for their followers. When an event occurs, we may think that it happened due to karma, God's will, Satan's interference, natural forces, or something else. We see the world in accordance with our beliefs. That is why it is called our "view." Now, Buddhism is not a monolithic view, nor is Hinduism. In fact there are several Buddhist tenet systems. In India, for thousands of years there has been lively debate between different groups—Hindus, Buddhists, Jains, and then later Muslims, Sikhs, and Christians. Though there have been skirmishes over the years, in general the Indians deserve a lot of credit for open-minded inquiry free of violence. Their affirmation of the place of reasoning in the spiritual process is one of the reasons that peace has generally prevailed.

Since there are several tenet systems, at its best, Buddhism is not a tradition in which you learn just the assertions of your own school and put them forth. Rather, at its best, this is a story of the evolution of your own view. So, what is the sense of calling a tenet system an "established conclusion" if it is not final and definitive? It is because that view is final and definitive *for the one who has settled on it.* It does not necessarily mean that the person will never abandon that view, but for now that person thinks it is final.[*] So, the Buddha says for *yogīs,* he has tenets. He is indicating that the serious practitioners are those who have gone beyond just needing advice and

---

[*]For a thoroughgoing explanation of the Buddhist and non-Buddhist tenet systems, see Jeffrey Hopkins, *Maps of the Profound: Jam-yang-shay-ba's "Great Exposition of Buddhist and Non-Buddhist Views on the Nature of Reality"* (Ithaca, N.Y.: Snow Lion Publications, 2003).

now seek settled conclusions. *Buddhist reasoning and debate grows out of this investigation into the nature of reality.*

In the scholastic literature of Tibet, philosophical tenets are explained in three areas—the bases, the paths, and the fruits. These are the existent bases of reality, the paths leading to a state of freedom, and the fruits of practice—the attributes of those who are progressing on the path to freedom. In this course, we pretty much look only at the bases. The introduction to Buddhist reasoning and debate is explained from the point of view of the Buddhist philosophical tenet system known as the Sūtra School Following Reasoning (Sautrāntika). This system of Buddhist thought asserts that there are truly existent external phenomena. Though the Tibetans do not consider the Sūtra School to be the final and highest tenet system, it is the place to begin, for it is easy to see that it describes the way the world appears to be. Also, for the vast majority of assertions on the bases put forth in the Sūtra School, the other Buddhist systems do not disagree with them except in their refined descriptions of the way in which these phenomena exist.

You may wonder: if they do not consider the Sūtra School to be the final and highest system, why don't they just go immediately to the view they do consider the highest and focus on that? I think the answer is that it is a graded path of learning. You start where you are, and according to all appearances, there is a truly established external reality. Apart from serious training and investigation, who would hold a view, as is found in the Chittamātra tenet system, that all that exists is of the same nature as your own mind and not actually external as it appears to be? The process begins with analysis of what is at hand—colors, sounds, tastes, and so on—and draws a distinction between what appears and that which apprehends what appears—one's own consciousness. From there, the graded path of analysis goes through several conflicting descriptions of what exists and how it exists. Only then can a person begin to understand and appreciate what the Tibetans generally consider to be the final established conclusions.

Thus, in this course, the description of basic Buddhist ontology, perceiving consciousnesses, the person, and so on, is made from the point of view of the Sūtra School Following Reasoning. This particular explanation of the Sūtra School is drawn from a genre of literature referred to as "The Collected Topics of Valid Cognition" (*Tshad ma'i bsdus grva*). Thus, in this book, I will often say, "In the Collected Topics tradition . . ." The Collected Topics texts are so called because of being presentations of assorted central points collected from many Indian Buddhist sources. They draw their information and style of reasoning especially from the works of Dignāga (Phyogs glang) (480–540 CE), Dharmakīrti (Chos kyi grags pa) (600–660 CE),[7] and Vasubandhu (dByig gnyen) (316–96 CE).[8] The topics collected by Tibetan authors are what they see as essential introductory material for those seeking to learn Buddhist logic and epistemology. Rather than being a single work, the Collected Topics of Valid Cognition refers to any of a number of debate manuals written in Tibetan for the sake of introducing new students of Buddhist philosophy to a wide range of topics presented within a rigorous logical framework. Having completed the Collected Topics, a student is then able to study and understand the higher topics of Buddhist philosophy.

Although debate has been a part of Tibetan Buddhism from the beginning, since it was inherited from Indian Buddhism, and although it is present in every sect of Tibetan Buddhism, the point of view of this book mainly follows teachers of the Ge-luk-ba order of Tibetan Buddhism. I worked with teachers from the Ge-luk-ba order while still in graduate school at the University of Virginia, during research travel in India, and in the years that followed. All of this was set in motion by the efforts of Professor Jeffrey Hopkins, who established the Program in Buddhist Studies at the University of Virginia.

Although I have discussed these topics with, and asked questions of, scores of Ge-luk-ba teachers and ordinary monks, I would point especially to three of them. My first Tibetan teacher of Buddhist reasoning and debate was Lati Rinpoche (Bla ti rin po che). Beginning in 1976, for a period of about fifteen months, Lati Rinpoche taught at the University of Virginia as a visiting lecturer in the Department of Religious Studies. He generously instructed us in the procedure in debate, explained the topics, and supervised our practice sessions. Lati Rinpoche was something of a joker and had a playful energy. He would give us an answer or tell us something and then stand back and sort of leer at us and laugh. We would not know whether he was saying it straight or not. When we went wrong, he would give us unwanted consequences of our views. If we figured out the first one, he would give us another wrong answer, and so on. This style is part of the traditional way of teaching debate. You have to be able to think on your own. Of course, when Lati Rinpoche would see that we were stuck, he would explain the matter, and his answers were always full. He was one of the very few Tibetan teachers I have ever known who could lecture in the style we are used to here, rather than just giving explanations from a text.

In 1978, after Lati Rinpoche had left, Denma Lochö Rinpoche (lDan ma blo chos rin po che) came to the University of Virginia. Rather than teaching from a text, he gave a summary overview of the whole of the Collected Topics. Teaching from amazingly detailed memory and a surpassing grasp of the material, he explained the procedure and content of debates and revealed the level of complexity that can be brought to even the most introductory material. Lochö Rinpoche was renowned for his abilities with memorization. He said that, as a child, before he began his formal study of the Collected Topics, he memorized about half of the four hundred pages of the Ra-dö *Collected Topics* (*Rva stod bsdus grva*) by Jam-yang-chok-hla-ö-ser ('Jam dbyangs phyogs lha 'od zer), which his teacher was going to use for instruction.

In India, I met Kensur Yeshi Thupten (mKhan zur ye shes thub bstan) and studied Buddhist reasoning and debate with him. Unlike the other two Ge-luk-ba teachers I have mentioned, Kensur Yeshi Thupten was not a found reincarnate lama, but a good monk who rose through the ranks and became a scholar/practitioner of the highest order. After I worked with Kensur Yeshi Thupten in India, he too visited the University of Virginia during 1981–82 and continued to train us in topics of reasoning and valid cognition. Like some lamas, Kensur Yeshi Thupten was always very grandfatherly. One Western disciple I met in India said of him that he so clearly showed kindness that he showed you who you are by contrast.

It was an extraordinary fortune to be able to learn from these great teachers. As a result, this course on Buddhist reasoning and debate is based on my study, my experiences with practicing debate, and the words of my teachers.

One of the purposes of debate is to broaden and mature our view, so that we see the world more clearly. Our view influences all. We act as we act and we feel as we feel because we believe as we believe. If we wish to change how we act and how we feel, we have to change how we believe. Thus, the battleground is always internal. It is a shared tenet of the classical South Asian religious systems that the thing that keeps us bound in a round of rebirth, subject to death again and again, is internal and that what will liberate us from this bind is also internal. That is, what keeps us bound is ignorance and what will liberate us is wisdom. For example, it is the opinion of Mahātma Gandhi and many others that this is the imagery of the *Song of the Lord* (*Bhāgavād-Gītā*) of the Hindus. The form of the *Bhāgavād-Gītā* is a dialogue between the god Krishna (Kṛṣṇa or Krishṇa), who is the eighth of the ten full avatars of Lord Viṣṇu, and his earthly cousin, the prince Arjuna. The setting is a very dramatic one—a battlefield where the Pāṇḍavas and their allies are preparing for battle against an army led by their cousins, the Kauravas. The battle is for possession of the family kingdom claimed by both. Commentators see this setting, a battlefield where a battle between relatives is about to start, as representing the internal, spiritual battle that rages in each of us. Correctness of view is part of this battle.

Buddhist reasoning and debate begins with disassembling what appears to us, breaking down and labeling everything so that we begin to see appearances and phenomena for what they are. One way of learning is to build up a quantity of facts so that you will have ready access to many things. Since this is an internal collection, we have governance over these facts and, in time, you will also see the patterns in things. If we see that this thing was produced from causes and conditions, and it disintegrates in time, and we see that this other thing was produced from causes and conditions, and it too disintegrates in time, we will come to see the pattern that all things produced from causes and conditions disintegrate in time. Buddhist debate includes both sides of this process, building up the facts one by one and seeing the patterns.

You will find two approaches to understanding in Buddhism, the more rational style and the more intuitive style. Although both of these are found in every region in which Buddhism is practiced, generally, in the practice of Buddhism as seen in India and South Asia, including Tibet, there is a high cultural value placed on an approach that is *rational and sequential.* More typically, in the practice of Buddhism as seen in China and East Asia, we often see a higher cultural value placed on an approach that is *intuitive and holistic.* These are differing pedagogical approaches intended to help us reach new knowledge. In the case of the rational and sequential approach, it is as if we are building up something new, something that we have never had before. In the case of the intuitive and holistic approach, it is as if we are revealing what has always been there, but that we did not know. Clearly, the practice of Buddhist reasoning and debate is more on the side of the rational and sequential.

What's more, all of these religions indigenous to South Asia say that it is possible for wisdom to arise in each and every one of us. They hold that we all have the capacity to gain the same realizations as the former great persons in that tradition and to become the equal of those great persons. For instance, generally, Buddhists say that it is within the capacity of each and every one of us to become a buddha. This is because we each have the ability to abandon ignorance and cultivate wisdom. Whether you are bright or not, within each of us is fertile ground for the seed of buddhahood, which the Buddhists believe already exists in every one of us. However, such wisdom arises only as an effect of effort. Wisdom is not limited to persons who are special by fate or to those of a certain class. Rather, it is limited to those who develop it.

OVERAPPLICATION OF THE PRINCIPLE
Photograph © User: 4028mdk09/Wikimedia Commons/CC-BY-SA-3.0.

The following joke, which I call "overapplication of the principle," was originally told to me by Professor Bill Knorpp, who teaches philosophy at James Madison University. It is a joke on philosophers and, to a lesser extent, on engineers.

At a university in America, there were three friends who taught in different departments. One was an engineer, one was a theoretical physicist, and one was a philosopher. Though their fields of study were very different, they all shared a love of single-malt Scotch whisky. So, they decided to take the single-malt tour of Scotland together one summer. Pretty soon after they arrived, they went out for a hike in the countryside. As they came up to the top of a hill, they encountered a single black sheep.

The engineer said, "Huh! The sheep in Scotland are black!"

The physicist said, "Well, at least one sheep in Scotland is black."

And the philosopher said, "Well, at least on one side."

I call this joke "overapplication of the principle" in reference to the philosopher's mistake. The engineer did not apply adequate reason and reserve to the evidence, the physicist got it about right, and the philosopher went too far. It is true that we should seek to be rational and proceed on the evidence. However, in simply trying to ascribe the presence of a person, if we were like the philosopher, we would have to see the whole body, perhaps turning the person around and maybe even taking off the clothes, before we could say who it is. For now, the point of the joke is to be aware that we project a great deal based on little evidence. It will be helpful to notice what you do observe and what you conclude from your observations.

PART ONE

Basic Theory and Procedure in Buddhist Debate

Few persons care to study logic, because everybody conceives himself to
be proficient enough in the art of reasoning already.

—CHARLES SANDERS PEIRCE (1839–1914),
"THE FIXATION OF BELIEF"

4. The Comparison of Phenomena

THE MOST IMPORTANT framework for Buddhist debate is the comparison of phenomena. Thus, it is the first skill to acquire. One of the main characteristics of our knowledge is understanding the boundaries of pervasion (*khyab mtha'*) between phenomena. For instance, we find it interesting that all spiders are arachnids, but there are arachnids that are not spiders, such as ticks. The boundaries of pervasion or the extension of a phenomenon is its range—what it includes and what it excludes. By understanding clearly a phenomenon's boundaries of pervasion, we are able to ascertain the scope of that phenomenon. As practiced in this system, when comparing two things such as arachnids and spiders, the question is not whether or not the one thing is the other; rather the question is whether or not there are things that are both and whether or not there is anything that is one but not the other. It may be helpful to think of this as class inclusion. The focus is on the members of the class that together characterize the class. By comparing two phenomena and establishing their relative boundaries of pervasion, the limits of each phenomenon in relation to the other, we come to understand the points of similarity and dissimilarity between them.

The philosopher Ludwig Wittgenstein is often remembered for saying, "For a large class of cases—though not for all . . . the meaning of a word is its use in the language."[1] The comparison of phenomena as practiced here explores the ways that terms are used. However, do not think that this process of comparison is directed solely at discovering the limits of how a word is used. Rather, since Buddhists believe that we are liberated through understanding the nature of things, for them the process of reasoning and debate is intended to serve as a tool for understanding how the phenomena being referred to actually exist in the world, not just how words are used. Still, because word symbols are of such critical importance, the Buddhists do present extensive thought on language as well.

This style of comparison assumes three things to work: (1) there can be only two things being compared, (2) those two things must be existent, and (3) those two things must be different.

1. Only two things may be compared at a time, so, for instance, "How do fruits and citrus fruits compare?" Even though only two things may be compared at a time, like anyone else, a Buddhist thinker might bear multiple things in mind at the same time, but the procedure in debate is to assess the comparison of things two by two. We might understand how p and q compare, then how q and r compare, then how p and r compare. By this technique, in the end, the understanding is complete.

   It is okay to have a disjunctive grouping on one or both sides—a group of *either* this *or* that, such as, "How do fruits and either citrus fruits or berries compare?" It is also okay to have a conjunctive grouping on one or both sides—a group of *both* this *and* that, such as, "How do (1) fruits and (2) things that are both citrus fruits and oranges compare?" Since oranges are always citrus fruits, this last one is no different from asking how fruits and oranges compare, so there is little point. However, bear in mind that it is preferred to compare just two things, not groups. That is usually challenging enough.

2. The two things being compared have to be existent. It would be possible to compare apples and oranges by this process, but how does the horn of a rabbit compare to apples? Well, that does not work in this system. The horn of a rabbit does not have any qualities because it does not exist.* Thus, there is nothing in the group. Empty sets, sometimes called null sets, are out of this game because there are no members having any qualities that may or may not overlap with another group having members. Still, something such as non-cow, which applies as well to the horn of a rabbit as it does to a horse (in that the horn of a rabbit is a non-cow and also a horse is a non-cow), may be compared to other existents. So every non-existent is a non-cow, but there are existent members of the class of non-cows too such as a horse. So, non-cow is not an empty set.

---

*The horn of a rabbit is the stock example of a non-existent, but you can use a square circle, the ruling King of France, a unicorn, or whatever you like.

3. The two things being compared must be different. It would be sense-less to ask, "How do colors and colors compare?" They don't compare in any way because they are only alike, not different at all. Everything that exists is self-identical. Everything is itself. So, there is no comparison between colors and colors. Colors are identical with colors. In this process of comparison, the two things being compared may be different in no other way than just being different names for the same thing, or they may be entirely separate phenomena. We often say, "You have to compare apples to apples." We usually understand this to mean that the things being compared have to be comparable, that is, similar in some way such that they can be compared. In addition, one implication of that saying is that you do not look at just one type of thing only and speak of it. You have to have at least two types of things to compare. The sense of the saying is that the same standards of analysis have to be applied on both sides. Anyway, any two types of things that exist are comparable as "apples to apples" because both are existents. They share that common ground and more.

Actually, in this system of reasoning, being different implies being existent. This is because non-existents do not have any qualities at all, so, for instance, we may not say that the horn of a rabbit is different from a diamond. By the same token, we cannot say that it is the same as a diamond either. Since being different implies being existent, it would be suitable to drop existence as the second requirement in this list and just say that there are only two requirements for the comparison to work: (1) only two phenomena may be compared at a time, and (2) those two phenomena must be different.

There are a couple differences from the phrasing used in this book and what is in *Debate in Tibetan Buddhism.* In the earlier book, the introductory question of comparison is phrased: "What is the difference between the two, existent and hidden phenomenon?"[2] First, rather than "what is the difference between these two?" the question has become "how do these two compare?" The old way is very close to the Tibetan; however, the new way is more in line with how we would say it in English. Typically, when you ask people about the difference between this and that, they will seek to give a descriptive response. This might go along the lines of: "Well, this is more such and so, and that is more such and so." For instance, if you ask someone,

"What is the difference between a parolee and a person on probation?" the person will describe the qualities of a parolee and the qualities of a person on probation. This is not what the Tibetan question is meant to get at. Rather, the question in debate is intended to address whether or not there could be someone who is both a parolee and on probation, whether or not all parolees are on probation, and whether a person on probation would have to be a parolee.

The second big change in this question from *Debate in Tibetan Buddhism* is the change from always referring to the entire group, the class, in the singular to generally referring to the entire group in the plural. For example, in *Debate in Tibetan Buddhism*, a question might be phrased as "What is the difference between the two, existent and hidden phenomenon?" But now, after considerable experience going over this stuff in the classroom with English speakers, I find the use of the plurals for comparisons is just irresistible. That seems to be how we refer to the entire group. So, now the question is most often stated using plurals, for example, "How do existents and hidden phenomena compare?" This works better. The plurals tip us off that we are talking about the entire group.

However, changing over to plurals is not universally better. For instance, if the question is "how do blue and the colors of cloth compare?" it is better to use "blue" rather than "blues" because "blue" in the singular seems to refer to the general class. There are several occasions where it remains better to use the singular.

What are the ways that any two different, existent phenomena may compare? It is easy to visualize the possible comparisons using Euler diagrams. As represented on the facing page, there are four ways the two circles may compare. Look at the way the circles relate. In the top one, which is called "three possibilities," one circle is entirely inside of the other. In the second one from the top, which is called "four possibilities," the two circles overlap, but neither is wholly inside the other. In the third one, which is called "mutually exclusive," the two circles are entirely separated with no overlap at all. In the bottom one, which is called "mutually inclusive," the two circles overlap completely. There is no other way these two circles can relate.

The focus of this procedure is not on the characteristics of the circle as a whole, the characteristics of the class p or the class q. This fact will become clear with experience. Rather, the focus is on the members inside of each circle—those things that are p and those things that are q.

The Comparisons of Phenomena

1. Whatever is a *p* is necessarily a *q*, but whatever is a *q* is not necessarily a *p*.

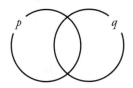

2. It is not the case that whatever is a *p* is necessarily a *q*, and it is not the case that whatever is a *p* is necessarily not a *q*. Also, it is not the case that whatever is a *q* is necessarily a *p*, and it is not the case that whatever is a *q* is necessarily not a *p*.

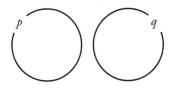

3. Whatever is a *p* is necessarily not a *q*, and whatever is a *q* is necessarily not a *p*.

4. Whatever is a *p* is necessarily a *q*, and whatever is a *q* is necessarily a *p*.

The information that some *p*'s are *q*'s but some are not is communicated by either the first or second cases above. For instance, the information that some impermanent phenomena are sounds and some are not is handled by stating their relative boundaries of pervasion. Whatever is a sound is necessarily an impermanent phenomenon, but whatever is an impermanent phenomenon is not necessarily a sound. Sounds would be represented by the smaller circle inside the larger circle of impermanent phenomena.

If we factor in whether or not there is anything outside of the two circles, there come to be eight separate cases—four with at least one thing outside of the two circles and four for which you cannot give an example of anything outside of the two circles. If there is nothing outside of the two circles to speak of, the two circles would still be drawn the same way; however, for some of these comparisons, the fact that nothing is outside is noted as a separate case. To say that "nothing is outside" is not to say that only non-existents are outside the two circles, but that there is nothing you could speak of—be it existent or non-existent—that is outside the two circles. If the two circles were p and ~p (read "not p"), it would be the case that there is nothing to speak of outside the two circles. If p represents all cows, then everything other than a cow, existent and non-existent alike, would be ~p. In whatever way p is identified, what is other than p would be ~p, so there would be nothing at all left over.

In this system of Buddhist reasoning and debate, for only two of the four cases in which there is nothing left outside the two circles do they make a separate answer. Thus, there are six possible answers to the question of how two phenomena compare.

THREE POSSIBILITIES

3P

Three possibilities (*mu gsum*) might be more literally translated as "three corners." In this case, there are usually three things to point to in the discussion of the comparison. However, this is one of the two comparisons for which the debaters make a difference between (1) the case of three possibilities for which there is something outside the two circles that is neither a p nor a q and (2) the case of three possibilities for which there is nothing outside the two circles that is neither a p nor a q. In the second case, there is not a third thing to point to.

In both of these cases,* as represented in the diagram above, there is a unidirectional pervasion between the two, for whatever is a p is necessarily a q, but whatever is a q is not necessarily a p. That is, if something is one,

---

*Here I am following the system of Kensur Yeshi Thupten in the way he designated these cases rather than the system of Lati Rinpoche, whose system I laid out in *Debate in Tibetan Buddhism*. See Perdue, *Debate in Tibetan Buddhism*, 162–63.

then it is necessarily the other in one direction between p and q but not in both directions, as is the case of two things that are mutually inclusive. This fact is represented by the smaller circle p being wholly included within the perimeter of the larger circle q. There is something (inside the smaller circle) that is both a p and a q, and there is something (inside the larger circle but outside the smaller) that is a q but not a p. Be aware that the relative sizes of the circles may or may not be proportional; they may or may not represent the relative extensions of the two principals being considered. What is being shown is that the larger circle includes at least one phenomenon the smaller does not.

Three Possibilities including Something That Is Neither

Answer in debate: There are three possibilities between p and q.

This is the more typical case of three possibilities, and here there is (1) something that is both a p and a q, (2) something that is a q but not a p, and (3) something that is neither a p nor a q. For example, this is the comparison between sounds (p) and impermanent phenomena (q). Every sound is impermanent, for it only lasts a short while, but not every impermanent phenomenon is a sound. For instance, a car is impermanent, but it is not a sound.

sounds *(p)* and
impermanent phenomena *(q)*

① is something that is both a sound and an impermanent phenomenon, like the sound of thunder.
   Whatever is a sound is necessarily an impermanent phenomenon, but whatever is an impermanent phenomenon is not necessarily a sound. So, for instance:
② is something that is an impermanent phenomenon but not a sound, like a car.
③ is something that is outside of the circles of sounds and impermanent phenomena, like a permanent phenomenon, which is an existent but not impermanent.

It is helpful to see these points displayed in a checklist. The table below has three columns: impermanent phenomena, sounds, and subjects. There are three rows, one for each of the three possibilities. The subjects are given in the right column, and under the headings of "Impermanent phenomena" and "Sounds," checks (✓) and Xs represent, respectively, whether the subject is or is not an example of that phenomenon

IMPERMANENT PHENOMENA	SOUNDS	SUBJECTS
✓	✓	the sound of thunder
✓	X	a car
X	X	a permanent phenomenon

The table shows that the sound of thunder is both an impermanent phenomenon and a sound, that a car is an impermanent phenomenon but not a sound, and that a permanent phenomenon is neither an impermanent phenomenon nor a sound.

EXERCISE 4.1

1. Work with your debate partner* to verbalize the examples for each of the following pairs.† Take turns playing the role of the Challenger, the one who asks the questions, and the Defender, the one who gives the answers. Give specific examples for each point. Here are several pairs, all of which compare as three possibilities including something that is neither:

   spiders and arachnids
   apples and fruits
   impermanent phenomena and matter
   women and human mothers
   shapes and visible objects

---

*You may be able to do these exercises by yourself, but in the long run it will be essential to debate with another live human since that is what you will have to do in the real world.
†Before you start this exercise, you will find it helpful to look at the advice at the end of this chapter.

numbers and whole numbers
men and U.S. presidents

Here is the narrative:

Challenger: How do the two, *p* and *q*, compare?
Defender: There are three possibilities between *p* and *q*.
C: It follows that there are not three possibilities between *p* and *q*.*
  Give an example of something that is both a *p* and a *q*.
D: There is something. The subject,† an *x*.
C: Now, which way does the pervasion go?
D: Whatever is a *p* is necessarily a *q*, but it is not the case that whatever
  is a *q* is necessarily a *p*.
C: Give an example of something that is a *q* but not a *p*.
D: There is something. The subject, an *x*.
C: Give an example of something that is neither a *p* nor a *q*.‡
D: There is something. The subject, an *x*.

Please use the pairs above and speak out the lines giving the examples
and the pervasion. It is a very simple exercise, but it will help you to
prepare for coming exercises. There will be moments when you wonder, for instance, whether or not something fits as an arachnid. For
now, the main thing is just to notice where the debates would go, but
look into the answers too.

2. Make up some more examples of pairs that will fit into this type of
comparison and speak out the narrative for them. (In the process, you
will discover pairs that do not fit into this type of comparison. Of
course, these will be useful later.)

---

*This is not something that is actually true here. The Challenger is just seeking to confuse
the Defender and refusing to give positive feedback.
†The Defender always frames the example as "the subject." This sets it off and makes it clear
exactly what is the subject for discussion, the subject of the debate.
‡There are a couple of rules of etiquette that apply when you posit an example of something
that is neither. First, if possible, give an example that is an existent. Second, it is always
better to give a clever example, when possible, of something that is close and may prompt
more debate or of something that shows your control of the material. Most important, it is
always best to give an example that is right.

Three Possibilities without Anything That Is Neither

Answer in debate: There are three possibilities between *p* and *q*, without anything that is neither.

In the less frequent case of three possibilities, (1) there is something that is both a *p* and a *q*; (2) it is the case that there is a pervasion in one direction but not the other, so whatever is a *p* is necessarily a *q*, but whatever is a *q* is not necessarily a *p*, so there is something that is a *q* but not a *p*; but (3) there is nothing you can point to that is neither a *p* nor a *q*.* This is the way that the selfless (*p*) and existents (*q*) compare. The broadest possible category in the Buddhist theory of what exists is called "the selfless" (Skt. *nairātmya,* Tib. *bdag med*). It refers to all that is free of a permanent, unitary, partless self. The Buddhists say that everything that exists is free of, lacks, or is empty of such a self. This is so, they say, because such a self simply does not exist. They also point out that non-existents too are free of such a self. Of course, it has to be so, for non-existents would have no self of any sort. You may find it helpful to think of this category as "everything that exists as well as everything that does not exist" or "that which may be referred to."

the selfless (*p*) and existents (*q*)

① is something that is both selfless and an existent, like a chair.
Whatever is an existent is necessarily selfless, but whatever is selfless is not necessarily existent.
② is something that is selfless but not an existent, like a unicorn.
There is no possible example of a ③, something that is neither selfless nor existent.

*Of course, I asked Lati Rinpoche if this shouldn't be called "two possibilities." He just laughed at me and said that there is no answer of "two possibilities."

The table for this case looks like this:

THE SELFLESS	EXISTENTS	SUBJECTS
✓	✓	a chair
✓	X	a unicorn

The subject of the selfless and the description of the nature of existent phenomena as well as non-existents will be taken up in the presentation of Buddhist ontology, or the theory of what exists, in chapter 9.

This type of comparison, three possibilities without an example of something that is neither, happens rarely. It has to be a comparison of two existents that together take in every existent and every non-existent as well. It cannot be between something such as objects of knowledge (which is mutually inclusive with existents) and non-existents because we cannot compare non-existents to anything. This rare comparison is noted as a separate case because, even though it is called "*three possibilities,*" there is no "possibility" of something that does not have the quality of p and also does not have the quality of q. There is no third point to hit, which is pretty odd for "three possibilities" of any sort. Remember, in this context, "possibility" does not mean something that exists. Rather, it means something that either has or does not have the qualities of the two phenomena being compared. The description of this sort of comparison as "three possibilities" seems to suggest that the heart of such a comparison is that there is something that is both and that there is a relationship of pervasion in one direction but not in both directions.

EXERCISE 4.2

1. Work with your debate partner to verbalize the examples for each of the following pairs. As before, take turns playing the roles of Challenger and Defender. Give specific examples for each point. Here are a couple pairs that compare as three possibilities without the possibility of something that is neither:

   the selfless and matter
   either existent or non-existent and chairs
   anything that may be referred to and chairs

Follow this narrative:

C: How do the two, *p* and *q*, compare?
D: There are three possibilities between *p* and *q* without anything that is neither.
C: It follows that there are not three possibilities between *p* and *q* without anything that is neither. Give an example of something that is both a *p* and a *q*.
D: There is something. The subject, an *x*.
C: Now, which way does the pervasion go?
D: Whatever is a *p* is necessarily a *q*, but whatever is a *q* is not necessarily a *p*.
C: Give an example of something that is a *q* but not a *p*.
D: There is something. The subject, an *x*.
C: Give an example of something that is neither a *p* nor a *q*.
D: There is no example of anything that is neither a *p* nor a *q*.

Please use these pairs and speak out the lines giving the examples and the pervasion. Remember that if something is unclear, notice where the uncertainty is and look into the answers, to the extent that you wish.

2. Make up some more examples of pairs that will fit into this type of comparison and speak out the narrative for them. (Write out or make a mental note of pairs that do not fit into this type of comparison, and plan to use them later.)

FOUR POSSIBILITIES

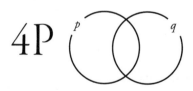

4P

Just as in the case of three possibilities, "four possibilities" (*mu bzhi*) might be more literally translated as "four corners." In this case, there are usually four things to point to in the discussion of the comparison. Also, as in the case of three possibilities, this is one of the two comparisons for which the debaters make a difference between (1) the case of four possibilities for which there is something outside the two circles that is neither a *p* nor a *q* and (2) the case of four possibilities for which there is nothing outside the two circles that is neither a p nor a q.

In either of the two types of four possibilities, this is the comparison where "some are and some are not," in both directions, like happy people and smart people. Some happy people are smart and some are not, and some smart people are happy and some are not. In both of the cases of four possibilities, there is no pervasion between the two things being compared, not in either direction. Whatever is a p is not necessarily a q, and whatever is a q is not necessarily a p. For example, it is not the case that all happy people are smart people, and it is not the case that all smart people are happy people. Some are and some are not.

The comparison of four possibilities is represented by the two circles overlapping. It is essential that there must be at least one thing that is both a p and a q (inside the overlap of the two circles). Also, whether or not there is anything that is neither, there must be something that is a p but not a q (inside the p circle but outside the q circle), and there must be something that is a q but not a p (inside the q circle but outside the p circle). You can understand from this that it is also not the case that whatever is a p is necessarily *not* a q, and it is not the case that whatever is a q is necessarily *not* a p. That is part of being "some are and some are not."

Four Possibilities including Something That Is Neither

Answer in debate: There are four possibilities between p and q.

The classic case of four possibilities has all four points to touch on. These four are:

1. There is something that is both a p and a q.
2. There is something that is a p but not a q.
3. There is something that is a q but not a p.
4. There is something that is neither a p nor a q.

Here too, the relative sizes of the circles may or may not represent the relative extensions of the two principals being considered.

For example, this is the comparison between blue $(p)^*$ and the colors of

---

*It is fine here to say "blue colors" rather than "blue," though it is redundant. It would not work here to say "blue things" because, for instance, a blue car is a blue thing, but the car itself is not a color but a thing that has a color. In this system, a car is a tangible object, not

cloth (q). Some blues are the color of cloth and some are not, and some colors of cloth are blue and some are not.

blue (p) and the
colors of cloth (q)

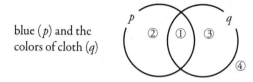

① is something that is both blue and a color of cloth, like the color of a blue cotton shirt.
② is something that is blue but not a color of cloth, like the color of a blue sky.
③ is something that is a color of cloth but is not blue, like the color of a white shirt.
④ is something that is outside of the circles of things that are blue and the colors of cloth, like the color of a ruby.

The table for this comparison looks like this:

Blue	The colors of cloth	Subjects
✓	✓	the color of a blue cotton shirt
✓	✓	the color of a blue sky
X	✓	the color of a white shirt
X	X	the color of a ruby

The chart shows that the color of a blue cotton shirt is both blue and a color of cloth, that the color of a blue sky is blue but is not a color of cloth, that the color of a white shirt is a color of cloth but not blue, and that the color of a ruby is neither blue nor a color of cloth. In this case, there are examples of all four of the possibilities.

---

a color. Rather, the color of a blue car is a color, and nobody can dispute that. There will be more on this in chapter 10, "Basic Buddhist Ontology 2." The point here is that it is always better to be precise. What you said, that is what we are talking about.

EXERCISE 4.3

1. Work with your debate partner to verbalize the examples for each of the following pairs. Give specific examples for each point. There are limitless pairs of phenomena that compare as four possibilities including the possibility of something that is neither. For instance:

   money and things of value
   women and college students
   females and humans
   green and the color of grass
   odors and things that may be sensed
   things that have lights and vehicles
   men and state governors in the United States

   Follow this narrative:

   C: How do the two, *p* and *q*, compare?
   D: There are four possibilities between *p* and *q*.
   C: It follows that there are not four possibilities between *p* and *q*. Give an example of something that is both a *p* and *q*.
   D: There is something. The subject, an *x*.
   C: Give an example of something that is a *p* but not a *q*.
   D: There is something. The subject, an *x*.
   C: Give an example of something that is a *q* but not a *p*.
   D: There is something. The subject, an *x*.
   C: Give an example of something that is neither a *p* nor a *q*.
   D: There is something. The subject, an *x*.

   Please use these pairs above and speak out the lines providing the examples. Take turns being the Challenger and being the Defender and try to come up with new examples every time.

2. Make up some more examples of pairs that will fit into this type of comparison and speak out the narrative for them.

Four Possibilities without Anything That Is Neither

Answer in debate: There are four possibilities between *p* and *q*, without anything that is neither.*

---

*As mentioned earlier, in *Debate in Tibetan Buddhism,* following the system of Lati Rinpoche, I called this alignment of points of comparison "three possibilities without there

Some pairs of phenomena compare in a similar way to the classic case of four possibilities, but for them there is nothing that you can posit as anything that is neither. As in the case of three possibilities without the possibility of something that is neither, in Buddhist reasoning and debate, this is marked as a separate case. Here the three points are:

1. There is something that is both a p and a q.
2. There is something that is a p but not a q.
3. There is something that is a q but not a p.

In this case, there is nothing one can posit which is neither a p nor a q. As in the normal case of four possibilities, we can still say "some are and some are not." Comparisons of this type necessarily involve two phenomena that together include all existents and non-existents as well. An example of this type of comparison is the comparison of existents (p) and non-(impermanent phenomena) (q), which includes all existents other than impermanent phenomena as well as all non-existents.

existents (p) and
non-(impermanent phenomena) (q)

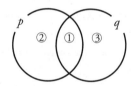

① is something that is both an existent and a non-(impermanent phenomenon), like a permanent phenomenon.
② is something that is an existent but is not a non-(impermanent phenomenon), like a pot.
③ is something that is a non-(impermanent phenomenon) but is not an existent, like the horn of a rabbit.

The table for this comparison looks like this:

---

being something which is neither." However, here I am following the system of Kensur Yeshi Thupten in the way he designated these cases. For more details, see Perdue, *Debate in Tibetan Buddhism*, 162–63.

Existents	Non-(impermanent phenomena)	Subjects
✓	✓	a permanent phenomenon
✓	X	a pot
X	✓	the horn of a rabbit

A fourth possibility, something that is neither, is inconceivable. Something which, on the one hand, is not an existent and, on the other, is a non-(non-[impermanent phenomenon]), that is, an impermanent phenomenon, cannot be posited. As indicated by the use of the horn of a rabbit as the subject in the third point above, it is not necessary that the individual "possibilities" be existents. It is only necessary that there be a subject that exemplifies the two qualities of the individual point. So, in line with this sense of a "possibility," something that is not an existent but is an impermanent phenomenon is not possible.

EXERCISE 4.4

1. Work with your debate partner to verbalize the examples for each of the following pairs. Give specific examples for each point. There are limitless pairs of phenomena that compare as four possibilities including the possibility of something that is neither. For instance:
   impermanent phenomena and non-(material forms)
   material forms and nonchairs
   objects of knowledge and non-cows
   the color of cloth and what is not blue

Follow this narrative:

C: How do the two, p and q, compare?

D: There are four possibilities between p and q without anything that is neither.

C: It follows that there are not four possibilities between p and q without anything that is neither. Give an example of something that is both a p and a q.

D: There is something. The subject, an *x*.
C: Give an example of something that is a *p* but not a *q*.
D: There is something. The subject, an *x*.
C: Give an example of something that is a *q* but not a *p*.
D: There is something. The subject, an *x*.
C: Give an example of something that is neither a *p* nor a *q*.
D: There is no example of anything that is neither a *p* nor a *q*.

Please use these pairs above and speak out the lines providing the examples. You will find yourself looking ahead to see, for instance, what the Buddhists would consider to be something that is a non-(impermanent phenomenon) and is a non-(material form). That is, do they believe in impermanent things that are not material forms? What would they be? It will be helpful to take an interest.

2. Make up some more examples of pairs that will fit into this type of comparison and speak out the narrative for them.

MUTUALLY EXCLUSIVE

MX

Answer in debate: The two, *p* and *q*, are mutually exclusive.

In order to establish that two phenomena are mutually exclusive, there are two requirements: (1) the two must be different and (2) whatever is a *p* is necessarily not a *q*, and whatever is a *q* is necessarily not a *p*. The first requirement, that they be different, implies that mutually exclusive phenomena must be existents and that they are not exactly the same in name and meaning. Recall that for all the comparisons, the two principals must be different. The second requirement implies that there is nothing that is both a *p* and a *q*. For such phenomena, their boundaries of pervasion do not meet at all. The two range over completely different groups of phenomena. There is neither any pervasion between the two nor is there any overlapping at all. Thus, there is no common locus (*gzhi mthun pa*) between them. A "common locus" is a locus, or a basis, or an existent that demonstrates two qualities. Everything that exists is a common locus of some sort. For instance, a dog is a common locus of a person* and an impermanent phenomenon. A table is a common locus of an existent and a material phenomenon. However, some qualities of existent things are never seen together, so they are mutually exclusive. Thus, this comparison is represented by two separate circles. Whenever two phenomena are different existents and whatever is a p is necessarily not a q and whatever is a q is necessarily not a p, there can be no common locus of them. An example of two phenomena that are mutually exclusive is permanent phenomena and functioning things. ("Functioning things" is another way of saying "impermanent phenomena.")

Do not think of two principals that are mutually exclusive as just contradictory terms. It is possible to compare terms, but that is not the intent here. For instance, the term "man" and the term "*hombre*" are mutually exclusive, but they mean the same thing ("*hombre*" is the Spanish term for man). The two phenomena, man and *hombre,* would be mutually inclusive because they are just different names for the same things. Whoever is an *hombre* is a man, and whoever is a man is an *hombre*, dude. But the words are not at all the same, and thus they would be mutually exclusive, as there is nothing that is both the term "man" and the term "*hombre*." So, mutually exclusive phenomena may or may not be contradictory terms. The process of comparison is more like a consideration of class inclusion than a consideration of words. Even though debate is often wordy, always bear in mind that the focus of the system is on understanding the nature of the world, not mastering word usage.

Of course it is possible that the two phenomena being compared have nothing left over so that there is nothing that is not one or the other of them. Evidently, for a pair to be a true dichotomy, they must be two mutually exclusive things that together are exhaustive of all. Such is the case with a and $\sim a$. Whatever you take a to be, $\sim a$ would have to include all else; thus, a and $\sim a$ would be a proper dichotomy such that they are mutually exclusive and together exhaust all possibilities. So, as above, permanent phenomena and functioning things are mutually exclusive but leave over non-existents, which could be mentioned as "possibilities," in the sense of being subjects that are neither permanent nor functioning things. A similar example of a

---

*Generally in English, the word "person" is reserved for humans, but in a system such as Buddhism that asserts rebirth, there is no hard and fast barrier between animals and humans, or between us and them for any two groups. Thus, I refer to dogs as persons.

pair that forms a proper dichotomy would be permanent phenomena and non-(permanent phenomena), for all non-existents are non-(permanent phenomena) and the two members of the pair are together exhaustive of all that could be mentioned.

Even though this case is interesting, a true dichotomy is not noted as a separate case in this system of debate. The way of debating a comparison like this is the same as that for the type of mutually exclusive comparison in which there is something that is left over that is neither p nor q. The reason that it is not noted separately is probably that the two may be proven to be mutually exclusive without considering whether or not there is anything left over. In the cases where the absence of a possibility that is neither is noted—three possibilities without anything that is neither and four possibilities without anything that is neither—there is no third or fourth thing to point to; thus, they have to be explained as separate cases.

In line with a central focus in Buddhist reasoning and debate, an example of two phenomena that are mutually exclusive are the two, permanent phenomena and functioning things. (This is effectively permanent phenomena and impermanent phenomena, which cannot abide together in any one locus, as you can easily see.)

permanent phenomena (p)
and functioning things (q)

Permanent phenomena and functioning things are totally separate phenomena, and there is no common locus of the two.
Whatever is a permanent phenomenon is necessarily not a functioning thing.
Whatever is a functioning thing is necessarily not a permanent phenomenon.

Of course there are countless examples of such mutually exclusive phenomena. Practically any two things you may observe are mutually exclusive. Chairs and tables are mutually exclusive. Two trees are mutually exclusive. Romeo and Juliet would have been mutually exclusive, if they had existed. Your left hand and your right hand are mutually exclusive.

EXERCISE 4.5

1. Work with your debate partner to verbalize the narrative for each of
   the following pairs. There are limitless pairs of phenomena that are
   mutually exclusive. For instance:
     your left hand and your right hand*
     apples and oranges
     matter and consciousnesses
     even numbers and odd numbers
     Matt and Jenn†
     square things and round things
     the number 2 and the number 3
     eight-legged creatures and two-legged creatures

   Follow this narrative:

   C: How do the two, *p* and *q*, compare?
   D: The two, *p* and *q*, are mutually exclusive.
   C: It follows that *p* and *q* are not mutually exclusive. Wouldn't that
      mean that there is nothing that is both a *p* and a *q*?
   D: Right!
   C: Why do you say that there is nothing that is both a *p* and a *q*?
   D: Because no *p* is a *q*, and no *q* is a *p*, so there could not be anything
      that is both a *p* and a *q*.

2. Make up some more examples of pairs that will fit into this type of
   comparison and speak out the narrative for them.

---

*Is your left hand your left hand and your right hand? If it is, then it would seem that your
right hand is neither your left hand nor your right hand because your left hand is your left
hand and your right hand. If your left hand and your right hand are your left hand and your
right hand, wouldn't it be the case that your left hand is your left hand and your right hand
and also your right hand is your left hand and your right hand? Would that mean you now
have four hands? That should make your work easier.
†If Matt were transgender and became Jenn or if Jenn were transgender and became Matt,
there would still not be a common locus of Matt and Jenn because at no point would the
person be both Matt and Jenn. The mother might say something like, "She will always be
my Jenn," but meanwhile, old Jenn/new Matt is going around introducing himself as Matt
and asking old friends to call him Matt now.

MUTUALLY INCLUSIVE

MI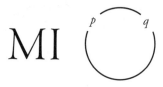

Answer in debate: The two, *p* and *q*, are mutually inclusive.

For two phenomena to be mutually inclusive, the two must be different existent phenomena, just as it is with all the comparisons. In addition, in the case of mutually inclusive phenomena, the relative boundaries of pervasion or the extensions of the two completely overlap. The extension of *p* is precisely equivalent to the extension of *q*. Whatever is a *p* is necessarily a *q*, and whatever is a *q* is necessarily a *p*. Thus, they range over or pervade exactly the same things. Their equality is represented by two circles being combined into one—one circle is superimposed over the other circle of equal size.

In this comparison, the two are just different names for the same thing. The Sanskrit and Tibetan terms translated here as "mutually inclusive" (Skt. *ekārtha,* Tib. *don gcig*) literally mean "the same meaning." There is the term for something, the sound representing that thing, and the referent or meaning of that term. Mutually inclusive phenomena are different only in the sense of not having exactly the same name, for their meanings—the objects that are included within the extension of each—are exactly the same.

We tend to think of the sameness of two things that are alike. When it comes to naturally produced things, we can imagine that there is a little bit of difference between this apple on the left and this one on the right. However, when it comes to manufactured products, we tend to think that they are indistinguishable. However, though they are basically all the same, and to choose one is just the same as choosing another, each bottle of Omnicorp Cola is different and mutually exclusive from all the others. Look at two bottles of Omnicorp Cola or any other products that look alike and understand that they are different and there is nothing that is both of them.

Even though two mutually inclusive phenomena are "just different names for the same thing," it would be a mistake to think of them as synonyms. Again, just as above, noting that two phenomena are mutually exclusive is not the same as saying that they are contradictory terms, in the same way, noting that two phenomena are mutually inclusive is not the same as saying that they are synonyms.* It is about the phenomena rather than the terms. For instance, the comparison below used to exemplify mutually inclusive phenomena is impermanent phenomena and functioning things. Thus, of course, the term "impermanent phenomena" and the term "functioning things" are synonyms, but in this process of the comparison of phenomena, the terms are mutually exclusive, for the terms are different existents and there is nothing that is both the term "impermanent phenomena" and the term "functioning things." Again, the comparison of phenomena is more like a consideration of class inclusion than a consideration of just the words. The point is that each and every thing that has the quality of being an impermanent phenomenon is also a functioning thing and that each and every functioning thing is also an impermanent phenomenon. Remember that a school of debate is called a "school of definitions" or a "school of qualities," for they are trying to sort out just what does exist and how it exists.

Again, there are two cases here, one for which there is something that is neither of the two phenomena and one for which there is nothing that is neither, though these two cases are not noted separately in this system of debate and they are debated and proven in the same way.

An example of two mutually inclusive phenomena is impermanent phenomena and functioning things. These are two ways of referring to everything that is produced from causes and conditions, so they both include all the same things but neither includes permanent phenomena nor non-existents.

impermanent phenomena (*p*)
and functioning things (*q*)

Impermanent phenomena and functioning things range over exactly the same phenomena.

Anything that is one of them is also a common locus of both of them.

*This error was first brought to my attention by Georges Dreyfus (aka Ge-shay Sang-gyay-sam-drup) who advised me that it is not correct to describe these comparisons as "mutually inclusives or synonymous" and "mutually exclusives or contradictories," as I did in Daniel Perdue, *Debate in Tibetan Buddhist Education* (Dharamsala, India: Library of Tibetan Works and Archives, 1976).

That is, whatever is an impermanent phenomenon is necessarily a functioning thing, and whatever is a functioning thing is necessarily an impermanent phenomenon.

EXERCISE 4.6

1. Work with your debate partner to verbalize the narrative for each of the following pairs:
    existents and phenomena
    matter and form
    women and adult female humans
    2 + 2 and 4
    cows and non-(non-cows)
    the number 3 and prime numbers greater than 2 and less than 5
    phenomena and that which holds its own entity*

Follow this narrative:

C: How do the two, p and q, compare?
D: The two, p and q, are mutually inclusive.
C: It follows that p and q are not mutually inclusive. Wouldn't that mean that everything that is a p is also a q?
D: Yes.
C: Give an example of something that is both a p and a q.
D: There is something. The subject, an x.
C: Are you saying that the subject, an x, is a p?
D: Yes.
C: Are you saying that the subject, an x, is a q?
D: Yes.[†]

2. Make up some more examples of pairs that will fit into this type of comparison and speak out the narrative for them.

---

*The definition of a phenomenon is that which holds its own entity. Every definition and its definiendum, the handy name we call that thing by, are mutually inclusive.
[†] I know the exercises can seem silly, but you are already developing new neural connections.

EXERCISE 4.7

1. Work with your debate partner to figure out the way the following
   pairs of phenomena compare. You will find it helpful to draw out the
   circles and figure out examples for each point.
   prime numbers and even numbers
   numbers and integers
   whole numbers and natural numbers
   eight-legged creatures and arachnids
   things that have doors and vehicles
   things that are red and cars
   green and the color of money
   stars in our solar system and stars in the Milky Way
   planets in our solar system and rocky planets in our solar system
   satellites of the Earth and natural satellites of the Earth
2. Now make up your own. Take turns as Challenger and Defender and
   follow the bits of narrative that are provided for the six answers. You
   get extra credit for using examples from Buddhist ontology, if not in
   this life, in the one that comes after.

Comments: Analytical thinking of all sorts depends on this comparative
approach to learning. Knowing the boundaries of pervasion of a thing, its
range in the world, informs us about what is possible. You may think of it as
learning the meanings of words, but the light of learning illuminates more
than semantics. Analytical understanding begins with observation, then
we learn the details, and then we see the patterns. Understanding this in
distinction to that and understanding that this and that are alike in some
way are essential tools in this investigation.

But are these real things that are being compared or is this just some
intellectual sleight of hand? The things that are being compared are as real
as you are and as close as your breath. How far do you have to reach out to
contact something that is impermanent? And what would you reach with
other than something that is impermanent? It's about these things.

So, exactly what is being compared in this process? In the analytical comparison of two phenomena, p and q are predicates or qualities, as a man has
the quality of being a person. The question is about what subjects have p
as a predicate and what subjects have q as a predicate. Thinking of the full
range of things inside the bubble of p and the full range of things inside the

bubble of *q,* the process is to consider how these two spheres of phenomena compare to each other. Is one wholly included in the other? Are they exactly the same? Do they overlap at all? The answer has to be one of the ways shown above.

The principals being compared are collective entities. We figure out how the spheres relate by testing particular examples of things that have the *qualities* of the two circles. We ask whether or not there is anything in the real world that may accurately be said to have both qualities. The answer to that then implies whether or not we may accurately use those terms as predicates in a sentence such as, "The subject, an *x,* is both a *p* and a *q.*" Thus, the point of comparison between two principals is those two as *predicates* of real things in the world, and the comparison is verified by testing exemplifications of those qualities.

The process is not at all strange. It is something people do the world over. It is just one of the ways we learn. However, this process in Buddhist reasoning and debate gives imagery to the learning in a very natural way.

So, if we are doing this all over the world, how have we traditionally done it in English? I have listened for years trying to capture native specimens. I think that generally we do this using plurals.

> "I don't think dinosaurs and birds are at all alike."
> "Some teas are more aromatic than others."
> "Russians don't necessarily live in Russia."

Therefore, I have switched to the use of plurals for the analytical comparison of phenomena. In *Debate in Tibetan Buddhism,* I expressed the two principals of a comparison with singular terms, saying, for instance, "How do functioning thing and existent compare?" However, years of instructing new debaters in English have shown me that this is not the natural way we tend to pose a question of the comparison of phenomena. Rather, we tend to express the principals as plurals and say, for instance, "How do functioning things and existents compare?" In the earlier book, I did not use the plurals because I feared that they would imply that there would be three possibilities between *each and every* functioning thing and *each and every* existent. However, that is not true because, for instance, there are not three possibilities between impermanent phenomena and functioning things. So, in practice on the ground, I have discovered that the use of plurals to express the two principals in a comparison of phenomena does not convey what I feared and what I sought to avoid. Using what is natural speech in English trumps this qualm I had earlier.

Exercise 4.8

1. Listen quietly to people talking and try to capture whether or not they are ever engaged in the process of comparing phenomena in any way similar to this process. Pay attention to what you read and to what you are saying to see if this process applies.
2. Find at least one natural speech specimen where someone, including yourself, makes a mistake in the comparison of phenomena. Listen for it in films, television, music, and speech. Capture that specimen and write it down on a sheet of paper. Draw the circles and explain the mistake.

Advice: The comparison of phenomena is probably the single most important tool in Buddhist reasoning and debate. Here are some guidelines.

1. What is the internal procedure for thinking about how two things compare? It seems that the internal procedure is not codified. Although, in such a broad tradition, many must have given advice over the years, I do not recall ever getting any instruction myself. Even so, here is what seems a rational procedure. First, spend just a moment pondering the p-phenomenon, thinking of all the things that may be said to have that as a quality, then do the same for the q-phenomenon. These reflections should rough in the boundaries of pervasion for each of the two. I think of these "boundaries of pervasion" as like circles that contain all the p-phenomena or q-phenomena rather than as borders like the one between the United States and Mexico.

   Next, look to see if these two circles overlap at all. That is, is there anything at all that is both a p and a q—a common locus of the two phenomena? If not, you know that the two phenomena being compared are MX.

   If they do overlap, then wonder whether or not the circle of one of the two phenomena is wholly included in the circle of the other phenomenon. If the inclusion goes both ways, so that every p is a q AND every q is a p, then the two phenomena are MI.

If the inclusion goes only one way, so that every *p* is a *q* BUT it is not the case that every *q* is a *p*, then the two are 3P. (At this point, you almost never need to wonder if there is something that is neither, unless one of the principals is the selfless or something else that refers to everything imaginable.)

If the boundaries of pervasion of the two phenomena overlap so that there is a common locus of the two but there is no pervasion between *p* and *q*—that is, if it is not the case that whatever is a *p* is necessarily a *q* AND it is also not the case that whatever is a *q* is necessarily a *p*—then the two compare as 4P. At this point, the wise will glance to see whether or not there is something that is neither a *p* nor a *q* to determine if the answer should be 4P without neither. I never seem to be able to remember to do this.

2. Avoid the error of thinking that the process is about a shared attribute of the two principals. Rather, it is about whether or not *there is something that is* both of them. Very often, for beginners first exposed to this way of thinking, what they need to be thinking about seems to come into and go out of focus. They will think, for instance, that permanent phenomena and impermanent phenomena have a common locus because both are existents. No, there is no common locus of permanent phenomena and impermanent phenomena because *there is nothing that is* both permanent and impermanent. Or, they will think that there is an overlap between humans and cats because they are both carbon-based life forms, for instance. But there is no overlap because there is nothing that is both a cat and a human. You see, the problem here is that if you think like this, then you have three circles—cats, humans, and carbon-based life forms—rather than the required two circles. Cats and humans would be little circles inside of the larger circle of carbon-based life forms.

Recall that in my comments above, in the issue of what is being compared in the comparison of phenomena, I settled on saying that it is the qualities of the individuals within the collective entities. The issue is not about the class *p* as a whole but about all of the individual members that are *p*. As I will show later, it may be that the group as a whole has a quality that is not shared by every member of the group. Indeed, it even occurs sometimes that the group as a whole has a quality that no member of the group has.

Inside of each circle *p*, imagine a thousand little circles or little points, each of which stands for something that is a p. (In some circles, there would be far more than a thousand. In some, there would be only one.) Among all those things that are p's, are there any that are also q's? If so, that is what you need to focus on, not whether or not there is anything that p and q have in common.

3. Don't worry about being wrong. It is to some extent: nothing ventured, nothing gained. You have to try, and you have to be brave. Of course, if you are just firing off into the night, just to have something to say, no one will want to debate with you or even pay attention to you. However, if you are so afraid to be wrong that it blocks you, you will not progress well. Just let the barriers down.

   One of the things I most like about debate classes is that the pretense has to drop away. After a while, in every debate class, we all know the relative rankings of every student in the class, at least into three to five groups. I think that the number one obstacle to learning is the refusal to admit that you do not know. If a cup is already full, you cannot pour anything into it. If everybody in the class knows how much or how little you know, there cannot be any pretense. One time, as a first-year undergraduate at the University of Virginia, I was waiting at a bus stop with a friend from the dorm. As people passed by, I greeted several of them. My friend asked me how I knew so many people, and I told him they were acquaintances from my German class. (I subsequently got a big, fat F in German.) I knew those kids because in language classes like that, everybody knows each other, and everybody knows how much you know. You have to drop your pretense that you know something because your ignorance is going to be on full display. Debate classes are like that too. What I'm saying is that, in the long run, you will learn more if you treat all of life like one of those language classes.

4. Don't worry about being profound. Hopefully, that will come in time. Just be right. Just say things that are defensible.

5. When you give an example of something, be precise. Do not say that a blue car is something that is blue but not a color of cloth. That is not at all clear. It is the color of a blue car that is blue but not a color of cloth. A blue car is a big chunk of metal, glass, plastic, and so on. And, though it *has* color, it is not a color. You may continue to wonder whether or not a blue car is blue, but who could question whether or not the *color* of a blue car is blue? That would be ridiculous.

6. Develop the habit of giving very specific subjects. This is somewhat different from being precise. What I mean is, give a subject such as "the color of my father's old blue car" or "the color of my blue T-shirt." The reason for this is that it will be easier in the long run to give reasons that justify your assertions. For instance, why is the color of my blue T-shirt a color of cloth? Why? Because of being the color of a blue T-shirt. This habit will prove to be helpful down the road, round the way.

7. Finally, remember to be consistent in what you are talking about. Most words have multiple meanings, but, when you are comparing two things, you cannot surf between the different meanings. If you do, you end up with too many balls in the air, and it will not be manageable. For instance, suppose you are talking about "the subject, coke" and considering whether or not it is a mineral. Just hearing the sound "coke," it is not clear exactly what is being referred to—the popular soft drink, cocaine, or the carbon material that is a by-product of coal. Suppose you make it clear that you are talking about the coal by-product. Then, what happens is sometimes people will be sly and say something such as, "Coke is not a mineral. It is a powdery, plant-based substance." Then what are you supposed to do—try to argue that cocaine is a mineral? Of course not. This is just a sleight of hand. The only possible purpose of such statements is an attempt either to derail the conversation or to be funny.

LATI RINPOCHE

Lati Rinpoche said, "There is no phenomenon that cannot be understood. There is no doctrine that, if studied well, cannot be learned. And there is no person who, if he or she studies well, cannot become wise."

Photograph by author.

5. Two Kinds of Statements

───────

Though Buddhist reasoning and debate are directed toward the goal of understanding the nature of things in the world, they depend on words. One may think internally in a rational way while considering the different sides of a question, and that internal investigation may or may not be dependent on words,* but if you wish to state an argument to another in speech or in writing, you will have to depend on words and statements. In Buddhist reasoning and debate, the elements of an argument consist of two types of statements: (1) statements of qualities† and (2) statements of pervasion. These are not the argument forms themselves but the elements of those forms, which can work together to make an effective argument. The best approach to building up any new skill is to take it a little bit at a time, step by step, so it will be easier to understand the argument forms once you are familiar with how these two types of statements are understood in this system.

Buddhist debate as practiced in Tibet is hardly ordinary speech. It is a kind of jargon for those who are trained in it, like computer-speak or medi-calese. Lati Rinpoche told a joke along these lines. In old Tibet, each year at the time of Losar, the Tibetan New Year, which falls somewhere between about January 15 and March 15, depending on the year, there would be the annual gathering called "Monlam Chenmo," the Great Prayer Festival, in the capitol of Lhasa. Part of the festivities included the final examination debates for the monks from different monasteries. Many thousands would gather, and, wherever monks would gather in great numbers, there would

───────

*Thoughts are not necessarily bound to words. For instance, consider a chimpanzee using a stick to fish ants out of a hole. Probably the chimps do not have a word for a stick, and, if they do, they do not voice it. Even so, probably a chimp could be taught to sign "stick."
†In Perdue, *Debate in Tibetan Buddhism,* I called this type of statement a "copulative association." See, for instance, pages 795ff.

be prayers, rituals, and debates. Two monks sat in a tea stall debating, and they were using "a golden pot" as the subject of their debate. The owner was disturbed to hear the monks "arguing." The next year, during the Monlam Chenmo, the very same thing happened in the same place, the two monks sat together in the tea stall arguing about a golden pot. This time the owner decided to speak up and said, "Last year you were here arguing over this golden pot, and here you are again this year still arguing over this golden pot. Monks should not be so greedy. I will give you each a golden pot, if you will just stop arguing."* The poor fellow just did not understand them. If he had been able to understand their words, he would have known they were not arguing over a golden pot but were arguing about the nature of a pot. Doubtless neither of them ever owned a golden pot.

Even though formal debate is not ordinary speech, the predominant need for analytical thinking is for ordinary encounters in the world. Thus, part of the job here in developing this style of analytical thinking is to be able to apply it to ordinary speech. This begins with spotting the many ways that the two main kinds of statements are expressed in ordinary English and understanding what that person means to say. So here I will display a few specimens. I do not think that these lists of the two types are complete, though they do pretty much cover it. Keep in mind that sometimes you may need to ask people exactly what they mean by what they are saying. That is, you may have to ask them if they intend to say such and so, something you can understand clearly. Often I wonder if what the person is saying is intended to be a statement of a quality or a statement of pervasion. This is usually easy enough to sort out with a question.

STATEMENTS OF QUALITIES

p is a q.

A chair is an impermanent phenomenon.†

---

*I know! Why is it that humor is so culturally bound?

†It must be noted clearly that a statement such as "A chair is an impermanent phenomenon" usually means in ordinary English that each and every chair is an impermanent phenomenon, and in modern Western predicate logic, that is indeed how such a statement is interpreted. Thus, it would be a universal statement or a statement of pervasion rather than a statement of a quality. (When we say something like "Unhappily, my favorite chair is impermanent," that is just a statement of a quality and not meant as a universal statement, even though everyone's favorite chairs are impermanent.) Because the Buddhist debaters

The Statue of Liberty is something that was produced from causes and conditions.

Professor Perdue is an American.

p is *q*.

The color of a blue shirt is blue.

The color of my car is white.

This coffee is bitter.

In statements of qualities, there is a subject, a linking verb or a "copula," and a predicate. These sorts of statements may be represented as above with the star ☆ representing the subject, and it is inside the world of *p*-phenomena, which is the circle, meaning ☆ has the quality of a *p*. The statement says that the predicate is a quality of the subject or, at least, that the predicate is something that can be ascribed to the subject. The predicate may be a predicate nominative or a predicate adjective. The form "*p* is a *q*" looks more like a predicate nominative, and the form "*p* is *q*" looks more like a predicate adjective. Either way is fine. A predicate nominative just means that the predicate following the linking verb is a noun, for example, "an impermanent phenomenon" or "something that was produced from causes and conditions." A

---

always identify a sentence of this form as a statement of a quality about some individual subject and never as a universal statement about each and every instance of that subject, we have a remarkable difference between ordinary speech and modern predicate logic on the one side and Buddhist reasoning and debate on the other. It is startling that the Buddhist logicians stake out this different interpretation. It must be, at least in part, because the argument forms—syllogisms and consequences—are a combination of statements of qualities and a pervasion. These argument forms would not work as they do if they consisted of only statements of pervasion. Perhaps more importantly, we are left wondering just what is the nature of the subject in a statement of a quality. This issue feeds into the study of the nature of every phenomenon, and understanding the ultimate nature of every phenomenon is one of the main goals of Buddhist reasoning and debate.

predicate adjective means that the predicate is not a noun but an adjective, for example, "white" in "white car." So in the statement "The color of my car is white," "white" is a predicate adjective. In the same way, "bitter" is used as an adjective describing a quality of "this coffee" in "This coffee is bitter." Even when the predicate is an adjective, it means essentially the same thing as the predicate nominative. That is, the sentence "This coffee is bitter" has the sense of "This coffee is a bitter thing," implying that among bitter things, this coffee is one of them.

Our usual impulse is to take such a statement as the equivalent of a pervasion or a universal statement, such as taking "A chair is an impermanent phenomenon" to mean that *each and every chair is an impermanent phenomenon.* Though that is certainly true, or else chairs would not fall apart, that is not how the statement of a quality is understood in Buddhist reasoning and debate. When we want to say that *each and every chair is an impermanent phenomenon,* we say, "Chairs are impermanent phenomena" or the usual expression of a pervasion, "Whatever is a chair is necessarily an impermanent phenomenon." Both of these are universal statements with regard to all chairs.

Of course, we would not tend to think that a statement such as "The Statue of Liberty is something that was produced from causes and conditions" would apply to a group of things because the statue is unique. So, for this sort of statement, whether it refers to the Statue of Liberty in and of itself or to each and every Statue of Liberty is indistinguishable because there is only one.

Someone might take a statement such as "Professor Perdue is an American" to mean that *each and every Professor Perdue is an American.* But clearly that goes too far. There must be at least one Professor Perdue who is British or French or Canadian or something other than American. However, I would say that reading this sentence as applying to each and every Professor Perdue is not the meaning of this sentence in ordinary English. Still, many times people will surf on that way of reading such sentences to try to refute the other person's sensible statements. It is not necessary to tack the sentence down so that the subject could refer only to one person, by listing the full name, the date and place of birth, the parents' names, and so on. It is a concrete example, and which Professor Perdue is being referred to may be easily understood by the context.

How are these simple sentences supposed to be understood in this system of Buddhist reasoning and debate?* The subject portion of such a sentence may be a *concrete singular term* or an *abstract singular term*.[1] The subject is singular because it refers to just one thing, even when there are many examples of that thing. In the case of "Professor Perdue is an American," the subject is something concrete, a thing you can point out in the world. Very often in ordinary discourse and in debate, we make statements about concrete singular things in the world: "I like this chair," "This chair is heavy," and so on. What good would debate be if we could not speak of these things around us?

In a case such as "A chair is an impermanent phenomenon," when we are not talking about a chair in the room, the subject is abstract. Speaking in the abstract, "a chair" in this sentence does not refer to any particular chair or to each and every chair. It is true that each and every chair is an impermanent phenomenon, but that is not the intent of the statement in Buddhist reasoning and debate. Neither does it refer to the collection of all chairs as a gross gathering of all chairs in existence, as if we were to pile them all up together. Also, here "a chair" does not refer to the *idea* of a chair, for an idea is a mental abstraction and you cannot sit on a mental abstraction. And "a chair" here is not some *ideal* chair, like a Platonic form of the perfect chair. Rather, in this sentence, "a chair" refers to a chair as such, the abstract singular chair— chair in and of itself, chair in isolation from all that is different from chair in either name or meaning. This use of "a chair" as an abstract singular term is comparable to the use of the phrase "the triangle" in the sentence:

The triangle is the principal figure of Euclidean geometry.

Here "the triangle" serves as an abstract singular term, referring to the triangle as such, not to each and every triangle.

Usually, when the subject is singular, either a concrete singular or an abstract singular, the grammatical predicate says something about the subject as a collective whole, considered alone in its own specific nature and apart from the many things that exemplify it. This is called *collective predication*. It is not that weird of a reading really. Imagine, if someone came into your home, put her hand on the back of a chair, and said with a smile, "This

---

*For the full discussion of each element of a statement of a quality (or copulative association), see Perdue, *Debate in Tibetan Buddhism*, 775–89.

is a nice chair." You would not respond, "What part of the chair do you mean is nice?" She means the chair as a collective entity, the chair as a whole. It is the same for abstract singulars.

I am providing this information on how to understand statements of qualities in this system of debate even before introducing the argument forms mainly because they must be understood in a way that is different from the way they are understood in ordinary English. Thus, it is a sort of warning to the students in this course and an important early lesson. However, even with the lesson given early and up front, sometimes the lesson alone is not enough, and we have to express the sentence in a way that is at odds with ordinary English.

For instance, even though everything that exists is exactly identical with itself, not everything is an exemplifier of itself. Is the empty set (sometimes called a "null set") an empty set or are there sets that are empty sets and, thus, are members of the empty set, so the empty set itself is not an empty set? In Buddhist debate, a good example of a phenomenon that does not exemplify itself is definition, which is not itself a definition, not an exemplifier of itself. In order to mark clearly that it does not exemplify itself, we have to express this oddly as:

Definition is not a definition.

The odd part is that it is not expressed with an article before the subject as it would normally be in English:

A definition is not a definition.

This way of trying to express the fact that definition does not exemplify itself is more than curious because *a* definition would have to be a definition. If something qualifies as a subject in this sentence—as a definition— then it would have to be a definition. Thus, sometimes, just knowing how statements of qualities must be understood in this system of debate is not enough. We have to go against ordinary English to avoid saying something that is senseless. The only oddity is in dropping the articles—"a," "an," and "the"—from the subject. They may be used in the predicates of such statements without affecting the required way of reading the statements. There will be more explanation of why definition is not a definition a little later.

Since the predicate of a statement of a quality always says something about the subject as a collective whole, the subject is singular and the predicate says something about that single subject. So:

A chair is an impermanent phenomenon

means that "chair" or "a chair," understood as an abstract singular entity, chair in and of itself, is *an* impermanent phenomenon, one among many.

As opposed to collective predication, with *distributive predication* the grammatical predicate is applied to the subject distributively; that is, the predicate says something about the subject distributively, about each and every occurrence of the subject. We sometimes read a statement of a quality in English as involving distributive predication, but that is not the intent of the statement of a quality *in this system of reasoning.** Indeed, sometimes in English, even when the subject is grammatically singular, we can easily see that the intent is distributive. For instance:

A man is a mysterious thing.

This is a poetic expression that clearly means that each and every man is a mysterious thing. It is singular, but the flourish sets it apart, and we understand it applies to all of us—women and children as well, presumably.

When we want to be clear that we mean to use distributive predication, we tend to state the subject in the plural, like "Men are mysterious" or "Chairs are impermanent." However, such statements have to be understood not as statements of qualities but as statements of pervasions, for that is their intent. They intend to say something about each and every man and each and every chair.

Of course, sometimes the subject may be pairs or groups of things, but even then—as the statement is understood in Buddhist reasoning and debate—the subjects are abstract singulars, a collective group, and the predicate is not to be understood as distributive. For instance, you can say:

A table and a chair are material phenomena (or even, "are a material phenomenon").

---

*I say "sometimes" because for statements such as "this cat is a mammal" or "my car is red," we always read them as involving collective predication.

and

A table and a chair are impermanent phenomena (or "are an impermanent phenomenon").

Since both of these things are true, you can say:

A table and a chair are material phenomena and impermanent phenomena.

However, as the sentence is read in this system of thought, it is not suitable to say:

A table and a chair are a table and a chair.

This is because a table and a chair—taken together—are not a table, and also a table and a chair—taken together—are not a chair. Why not? Because the subject must stand together as one collective whole.

In a statement of a quality such as "*p* is a *q*," the subject is always a concrete or abstract singular, and the predicate always says something about the subject or subjects as a collective whole. In addition to the subject and the predicate, a statement of quality must have a linking verb or copula that means "has [or have] the quality of being" or "has [or have] the nature of being." Thus:

p has the quality of being a *q*.
A chair has the quality of being an impermanent phenomenon.

A statement such as "*p* has the quality of being a *q*" is a bit formal, not very likely in ordinary speech.

In the end, I think that this sort of statement should apply only to existents. A chair has the quality of being an impermanent phenomenon, but the horn of a rabbit does not have the quality of being a non-existent because the horn of a rabbit does not have any qualities.* So, it is suitable to say that the linking verb may also mean "may be said to be," as in:

---

*I am going against the blanket statement in Perdue, *Debate in Tibetan Buddhism,* 787, where I said that "is" or "are" always mean "has [or have] the quality of being" or "has [or have] the nature of being."

p may be said to be a *q*.
The horn of a rabbit may be said to be a non-existent.

Even though the horn of a rabbit does not have any qualities, it is suitable
to say, "The horn of a rabbit may be said to be a non-existent." It is suitable
to say anything about the horn of a rabbit, though it is a non-existent. This
backs off a little from the earlier explanation of the linking verb required
by statements of qualities, but don't throw out "*p* has the quality of being
a *q*" because it works predominantly. To gloss the linking verb as "may be
said to be" is very weak, defensible but weak. It could be seen as suggesting
some sort of nihilism. Still, it should be okay to use it in reference to things
we know are non-existents.

The subject is always a concrete or abstract singular, so it is best to use
the indefinite article "a" or "an" in both parts of the sentence when possible.
That is just better English. It may take some mental force to hear "A chair
is a material phenomenon" and keep in mind that the subject is understood
as an abstract singular, but it is always better to use normal language when
possible. But that is not always possible. Remember that above I gave definition as an example of something that is not an exemplifier of itself. This is
because definition in and of itself, the collective entity, is not a definition
but a definiendum, something that is defined. It is probably correct to say
that

A definition is a definition.

That is sort of irresistible because whatever qualifies as "*a* definition" must
be a definition. However, definition itself is not *a* definition because it is
something that is defined. Thus, to point out that a definition is a definition
does not say anything about the collective whole, definition in and of itself,
because definition itself is *not* a definition. So, sometimes the indefinite
article before the subject has to be dropped in order to express the meaning
correctly.

So, how does this work?* The two players here are definition and definiendum, literally meaning the thing defined. Generally we think of a definition as a string of words that describes something, identifying the essential

---

*There will be a fuller explanation of this topic in this book, chapter 20, "Definitions, Divi-
sions, and Illustrations."

characteristics of that thing. Many people are not familiar with the word "definiendum," but you can tell from the structure of the word as derived from Latin that it refers to that which is defined. So we tend to think of both of them as words. However, in the Buddhist system, the definition is the actual object, and the definiendum is the name designated to that object. The definition is not just a word or string of words, not a mere description, but the object itself. For instance, the definition of a phenomenon (another name for an existent) is

that which holds its own entity.*

Thus, what this means is that the Buddhists are identifying this as the essential characteristic of a phenomenon. This does not mean that it is a string of words describing the character of a phenomenon, but that all of these things that have the character of holding their own entities are suitable to be called "phenomena."† The definition is the actual thing, and, for the sake of convenience, we designate that which holds its own entity with the name "phenomenon." Thus, the way we understand a term is by first becoming familiar with the actual objects that illustrate its definition. Only then may we understand the definiendum, the mere conventionality, the handy name that we use to designate those sorts of objects, things that hold their own entities and so forth.

Next, understand that a definition is not in turn defined. That is, there is no definition of any particular definition. The character of a thing is its character, and nothing more defines it. Definitions may be described or explained, but they are not defined by their own definitions. Though any particular definition is never defined in turn, this is not true of definition in and of itself, for definition in and of itself is not a definition but a definiendum. This is so because there is a definition of definition, for definition is defined as

that which is a triply qualified substantial existent.

A definition is called a "substantial existent" (Skt. *dravya-sat,* Tib. *rdzas yod*) because it is the actual object, the meaning or referent of its definien-

---

* There is some explanation of the definition of a phenomenon in this book, chapter 9, "Basic Buddhist Ontology 1." Also, see Perdue, *Debate in Tibetan Buddhism,* 271.
† Bear in mind that "phenomena" is the plural of "phenomenon." Right?

dum. But definition itself is not a definition but a definiendum. In order to mark that clearly, the subject is stated without an article:

Definition is a definiendum,

and

Definition is not a definition.

Thus, sometimes the indefinite article "a" or "an" must be left out of the subject in order to alert the reader to the fact that the subject can only be understood as the abstract singular, the thing in and of itself, even though including the indefinite article would be more grammatical English. This does not mean we need to speak "Tibenglish" now, English spoken in the mold of Tibetan, which does not typically use indefinite articles. Rather, we should always try to use ordinary English when possible and bear in mind how statements of qualities are understood in the system.* What's more, the way the statements are understood is not that unusual.

Of course, though everything that exists is a common locus of multiple qualities, nothing is a common locus of all qualities. Thus, some statements of qualities are negative.

> p is not a q.
> Professor Perdue is not British.
> p does not have the quality of being a q.
> Professor Perdue does not have the quality of being British.
> Definition does not have the quality of being a definition.

For these "is not" or "are not" statements, it is suitable to consider the meaning of the linking verb to be

does not have the quality of being

---

*I provide this advice because I have found that students learning Buddhist reasoning and debate sometimes start inappropriately dropping the indefinite articles from the subjects, perhaps overcorrecting for the times in which using the indefinite articles would be misleading, such as saying "A definition is a definiendum" rather than "Definition is a definiendum." Under the influence of this oddity, even native English speakers start saying things like, "Chair is a functioning thing." They know better, but . . . bless their little hearts.

or

does not have the nature of being.

Even for non-existents, which do not have any qualities at all, a statement denying it has such and such quality works. Thus:

The horn of a rabbit does not have the quality of being an existent.

In sum, in the Collected Topics tradition of Buddhist debate, for a statement of qualities, (1) the subject is either a concrete singular, when the statement is about something clear and concrete like the White House or my favorite chair, or it is an abstract singular, and (2) the predication is always collective, never distributive. The qualities of a phenomenon as a singular entity may be distinct from the qualities of the illustrations of that phenomenon, in the way that definition itself is a definiendum, but no definition is a definiendum. It is easier to understand the collective whole, the thing in and of itself, when the subject is a concrete singular thing, like a chair in the room, but trying to understand the nature of an abstract singular subject is important too. The issue of the nature of the subject goes to questions of generalities or universals, the bases of designation of phenomena in a consideration of the selflessness of phenomena in Buddhism, and so on. However, we cannot sort out everything up front. Rather, it is best to figure out a rational procedure and then use that to settle questions. For our philosopher friends, let your epistemology inform your ontology, not the other way around.

Still, we do know these things about how the abstract singular subject is considered in the Collected Topics system:

1. If anything in the subject is existent, then the subject is existent. For instance, the selfless, which takes in all existents and non-existents, is itself existent because among the things that may be properly referred to as selfless, there are existent things. In the same way, the pair, a chair and the horn of a rabbit, is existent simply because part of the pair is existent.

2. If anything in the subject is permanent, then the subject is permanent. For instance, existent itself includes all permanent and all impermanent phenomena, and for this reason existent itself is considered to be

permanent. This has to be because, in order to understand existent as a whole, one must understand that permanent factor.

These two points are based on the consideration of what is in the subject. These points do not mean that the subject is being thought of distributively but that the nature of the subject and the possible ways to perceive it are influenced by what is meant by the subject collectively.

STATEMENTS OF PERVASION

In this system of debate and reasoning, statements of qualities are never intended to say something distributively about a subject, about each and every occurrence of that subject. On the other hand, statements of pervasion always say something distributively, about each and every occurrence of a phenomenon.

The word "pervasion" is a time-honored translation of the Sanskrit *vyāpti* and the Tibetan *khyab pa*. These words convey the sense that something is spread throughout, covered by, filled with, completely occupied by, or universally penetrated by another thing or quality. It is used to state that every member of a group of phenomena is completely occupied by some quality. For instance, here is a statement of pervasion:

Whatever is a material phenomenon is necessarily impermanent.

This statement means that spread throughout the group of material phenomena is the quality of being impermanent, that the entire group of material things is covered wall to wall, as it were, with impermanence, that the entire group is filled with impermanent things, that the entire group is fully, completely, universally occupied by impermanent things. Of course, this does not say that each and every impermanent thing is a material phenomenon, which would be false because time, for instance, is impermanent but not material. You may prefer to think of these as universal statements, but "pervasion" is truer to the original words. In this course, there are two main ways of stating a pervasion:

Whatever is a p is necessarily a q.
Whatever is a cat is necessarily a mammal.

If something is a p, then it is necessarily a q.
If something is a cat, then it is necessarily a mammal.

The sense of these statements is clear enough. The second and fourth sentences state that each and every cat is a mammal. They do not say that every mammal is a cat, which would be false, since dogs are mammals, but they are not cats. So, a correct statement of pervasion always says something about each and every p-phenomenon, the phenomenon referred to in the first part of the sentence, the antecedent. As that implies, a correct statement of pervasion will never say something about some but not all of the p-phenomena. To appreciate why these statements are called "pervasions," the statement that whatever is a p is necessarily a q may be understood as saying that p's are pervaded by being q's. For example, the statement that all cats are mammals may be understood as saying that cats are pervaded by being mammals.

For any correct pervasion, the range of the p-phenomenon must be equal to or smaller than the range of the q-phenomenon.* For instance, there is the correct pervasion:

Whatever is an impermanent phenomenon (p) is necessarily a functioning thing (q).

---

*The range of a phenomenon is all the things that have the quality of that phenomenon. For instance, the range of cats is all the things that have or are pervaded by the quality of catness. When I say that the range of the p-phenomenon must be equal to or smaller than the range of the q-phenomenon for there to be a correct pervasion of the form "Whatever is a p is a q," I mean the following: The range of the p-phenomenon is *smaller* than the range of the q-phenomenon if each thing in the range of the p-phenomenon is in the range of the q-phenomenon, but there is at least one thing in the range of the q-phenomenon that is *not* in the range of the p-phenomenon. The range of the p-phenomenon is *equal to* the range of the q-phenomenon if each thing in the range of the p-phenomenon is in the range of the q-phenomenon *and* each thing in the range of the q-phenomenon is in the range of the p-phenomenon.

As you know, these two are MI, mutually inclusive, so it is also the case that whatever is a functioning thing (*q*) is necessarily an impermanent phenomenon (*p*). Thus, in this case, the *p*-phenomenon and the *q*-phenomenon are equal in extent, that is, everything that is a *p*-phenomenon (impermanent) is a *q*-phenomenon (a functioning thing) and everything that is a *q*-phenomenon (a functioning thing) is a *p*-phenomenon (impermanent). For the only other possible correct pervasion, the range of the *p*-phenomenon must be smaller than the range of the *q*-phenomenon. For instance, there is the pervasion:

Whatever is a cat (*p*) is necessarily a mammal (*q*).

Cats and mammals are 3P, three possibilities, such that whatever is a cat (*p*) is necessarily a mammal (*q*), but it is not the case that whatever is a mammal (*q*) is necessarily a cat (*p*). Thus, the range of the *p*-phenomena (cats) is smaller than the range of the *q*-phenomena (mammals) because there is at least one thing that is a mammal but not a cat. These are the only two patterns of pervasions that can work in an accurate statement of pervasion.

There is nothing particularly surprising about statements of pervasion in this system as opposed to universal statements in other systems. The greatest challenge is in learning to recognize the many ways that people express these sorts of statements in the real world. Here are some:

If something is a *p*, then it is a *q*.
If something is a cat, then it is a mammal.

All *p*'s are *q*'s.
All cats are mammals.

That something is a *p* implies that it is a *q*.
That something is a cat implies that it is a mammal.

p's are *q*'s.
Cats are mammals.

A *p* is a *q*.
A cat is a mammal.*

Whatever is a *p* is a *q*.
Whatever is a cat is a mammal.

Every *p* is a *q*.
Every cat is a mammal.

Everything that is a *p* is also a *q*.
Everything that is a cat is also a mammal.

For every *p*, it is a *q*.
For every cat, it is a mammal.

Each thing *p* is such that it is a *q*.
Each cat is such that it is a mammal.

It is a *q* because it is a *p*.
It is a mammal because it is a cat.

Because it is a *p*, it is a *q*.
Because it is a cat, it is a mammal.†

---

*It is potentially confusing to offer here, in the list of ways statements of pervasion are spoken in English, a form of statement that has already been identified as a statement of a quality. However, it is clear that in normal English a statement such as "A cat is a mammal" is meant to convey that each and every cat is a mammal. The statement means that it is in the character of a cat to be a mammal, and that is true for every cat. Moreover, this sort of statement is identified in modern Western predicate logic as meaning just that: that each and every cat is a mammal. Thus, despite the possibility of confusion, this type of universal statement has to be on this list so that you will know what it means when someone says it.

†These two statements and the two just above it are really enthymemes (arguments with an implicit or suppressed premise), where the suppressed premise is "all cats are mammals" or "all *p*'s are *q*'s." The singular premise is "it is a cat" and the conclusion is "it is a mammal." I have included them here because you hear people say them very frequently and they are a way of expressing a pervasion in that they cause a person to think the suppressed pervasion.

Each and every *p* is a *q*.
Each and every cat is a mammal.

Anything at all that is a *p* is also a *q*.
Anything at all that is a cat is also a mammal.

For every *p*, [it is also] a *q*.
For every cat, [it is also] a mammal.

When you have a *p*, you have a *q*.
When you have a cat, you have a mammal.

It seems that the most prevalent ways of stating a pervasion in ordinary English are: "All cats are mammals," "Every cat is a mammal," and "Cats are mammals."

WHAT STATEMENTS OF PERVASION IMPLY

Statements of pervasion imply* other statements of pervasion and statements of qualities.†

Statements of Pervasion Imply Other Statements of Pervasion

By performing mere mechanical transformations, we can precipitate several statements from any statement of pervasion that must be true if the initial statement is true. For instance, take our standard:‡

---

*Here the word "imply" does not mean just "hints at" or "suggests" but has the sense of "flows from logically." Of course, this includes hinting at something or suggesting something, but it also includes that, if the original pervasion is true, the implications of it must also be true, and defensible.

†There is a special case here, a case of an accurate implication derived from a statement of pervasion that is neither another pervasion nor a statement of a quality. That is, if it is true that whatever is a cat is necessarily a mammal, then we have to accept that *some* cats are mammals. However, this is not really part of the Buddhist way of doing things, and in ordinary English, to say this or point this out is very often a misdirection that tries to get people to think that there are or might be some cats that are *not* mammals. The special case implication is true, but slippery.

‡These processes can be performed with any of the various ways of expressing pervasion.

All p's are q's.
All cats are mammals.

By a process called "obversion" in which the quality of this positive sentence "all" is changed to the negative "no," the subject remains the same in both statements, and the predicate becomes the contradictory of the original predicate, this statement implies:

No p's are non-q's.
No cats are nonmammals.

Taking the immediately preceding statement and changing it by a process called "conversion" in which we simply reverse the order of the subject and predicate in the statement, the obverted statement above implies:

No non-q's are p's.
No nonmammals are cats.

Even though the process of obversion works for all four types of categorical statements, understand clearly that the process of conversion works for only two of the four; thus, conversion cannot always be applied safely. That is, the truth value is not always preserved when you convert a statement, so only certain types of statements can be converted into an equivalent statement. For instance, if we try to convert our standard "All cats are mammals," we would get the false statement "All mammals are cats." So, be cautious.

Finally, taking the immediately preceding statement and changing it again by obversion, this statement implies:

All non-q's are non-p's.
All nonmammals are non-cats.

It is easier for us to hear this, when it is stated as:

If something is not a q, then it is necessarily not a p.
If something is not a mammal, then it is necessarily not a cat.

The result of the last step is called the "contrapositive" of the original statement. You can directly move from the original to its contrapositive by what is called the "law of the contrapositive." The two earlier steps are indeed logical implications of the original pervasion, and they would routinely be considered in the process of comparing phenomena, but generating the contrapositive directly from the original statement is a standard part of the process of inference itself. Simply put, you switch the places of the *p*-term and the *q*-term and negate them both. You can do this because the contra-positive and the original statement are logically equivalent—one is true if and only if the other is true. So, forming the contrapositive is a handy tool.

It happens quite often in ordinary conversation that people fail in their efforts to generate the contrapositive correctly. You might think that this is an exaggeration, but just listen like a spy and you will hear it. It would be difficult to make this mistake with cats and mammals, but here is how it would go: Someone says, "All cats are mammals." Another person responds, "No, there are mammals other than cats," as if you had said not only that all cats are mammals but also that all mammals are cats. We can take the person's statement to mean, "Some mammals are non-cats." That is true enough, but the full implication of the person's original pervasion is, "For everything that is other than a mammal, in that range of things you will find no cats." That is the correct application of the contrapositive. Here are some other ways of expressing the contrapositive of the original pervasions "all *p*'s are *q*'s" and "all cats are mammals":

If something is not a *q*, then it is necessarily not a *p*.
If something is not a mammal, then it is necessarily not a cat.

If it is not a *q*, then it is not a *p*.
If it is not a mammal, then it is not a cat.

No non-*q* is a *p*.
No nonmammal is a cat.

Non-*q* implies non-*p*.
Nonmammalness implies noncatness.[*]

Every occurrence of something that is a non-*q* is also an occurrence of a non-*p*.
Every occurrence of something that is a nonmammal is also an occurrence of a non-cat.

It is not a *p* because it is not a *q*.
It is not a cat because it is not a mammal.[†]

[*]This is intentionally strange phrasing. In Buddhist logic, they think of these as qualities. So, everything that has true catness also has mammalness.
[†]This form of statement is not an explicit statement of a pervasion, but an implicit one.

Statements of Pervasion Imply Statements of Qualities

How do we know that a pervasion works? We test pervasions by looking at cases. If someone says that every p is a q, we will wonder whether or not there is something that is a p that is not a q. Could there be a cat that is not a mammal? No. So, that pervasion looks good. What this process of verification shows is that statements of pervasion imply statements of qualities. The statement of pervasion, "Whatever is a cat is necessarily a mammal," implies:

> Your cat is a mammal.
> My cat is a mammal.
> Yo' mama's cat is a mammal.
> A lion is a mammal.
> A tiger is a mammal.

And so on—every cat is a mammal. Thus, the statements of pervasion should be understood as saying, for anything at all that has the quality of a p, that thing will also have the quality of a q. For example, for anything at all that has the quality of being a cat, that creature will also have the quality of being a mammal.

STATEMENTS OF PERVASION THAT INCLUDE A NEGATIVE

Of course, as Sportin' Life sings in *Porgy and Bess,* "It ain't necessarily so."[2] So, of course, sometimes in statements of pervasion there is a negative of one sort or another. Over the years, students in this course, including myself when I was new, have had some difficulties in assessing the meaning of these pervasions that involve a negative. This is in part because these statements are almost always bound to the form "Whatever is a p is necessarily a q" or "If something is a p, then it is necessarily a q," whereas these are not always our standard ways of expressing the relations between categories in English. Therefore, it will be helpful to lay out the range of statements of pervasion

---

Actually the statement is a sort of argument that something is not a mammal, and since we know that all cats are mammals, this thing cannot be a cat. The pervasion—that all cats are mammals—is not expressed explicitly, but the statement requires you to perceive the pervasion implicitly. That is, the statement carries that content.

having a negative and then provide for each one some more ordinary equivalents in English.

There are three places where a negative can appear in a statement of pervasion: (1) in the verb, expressed as "is not," (2) in the first clause, the antecedent in a conditional sentence, with the p-phenomenon, expressed as "not a p," and (3) in the second clause, the consequent in a conditional sentence, with the q-phenomenon, expressed as "not a q." So, there are three toggle switches between affirmative and negative, and two cubed is eight, so there are eight possible scenarios. The first of these has all three toggles in the affirmative and that has already been covered. All the other seven have a negative somewhere. The table on the next page shows all eight together:

Going over the table box by box, we can assess some things about how statements of pervasion would normally be expressed in ordinary English. The statement in box 1, a statement of the form "whatever is a p is necessarily a q," has already been explained in full.

In box 2, we have a pervasion of the form "Whatever is a p is necessarily not a q." This pervasion is the equivalent of the more standard English "No p is a q." By a process of simple conversion—by simply trading the places of the p-phenomenon and the q-phenomenon—we get the statement "No q is a p," which is equivalent to the pervasion "Whatever is a q is necessarily not a p." If it is true that no p is a q, then it has to be true that no q is a p. This is not just reading back into the statement from the clear knowledge that no cat is a reptile and no reptile is a cat; rather, it is part of the logic of this type of pervasion. However, understand clearly that not every true statement of pervasion can be converted to yield another true pervasion. For instance, the conversion of the true statement "All cats are mammals" is "All mammals are cats," which is not true. So, be careful about conversions.

In box 3, we have a pervasion of the form "Whatever is not a p is necessarily a q." This sort of pervasion is tricky. Simply knowing that something is not a p does not tell us very much. It is easy to say, for instance, when both parts have negatives, that whatever is *not* a mammal is necessarily *not* a cat, but what can be given as an affirmative in the q-position merely from the fact that something is not a p, or not a cat? It is negative information that yields little positive insight. Imagine this snippet of conversation, "What did you give her?" Answer: "I did not give her a cat." What would you know from that? Certainly not what was given. Not even that anything was given at all. Even so, no matter what, if something is not a p, whatever it is—whether what remains is existent or not—it is selfless. Remember that the selfless is

	Is necessarily	Is not necessarily
First phenomenon: affirmative Second phenomenon: affirmative	**1** Whatever is a p is necessarily a q. Whatever is a cat is necessarily a mammal. (The implications are given above.)	**5** Whatever is a p is not necessarily a q. Whatever is a mammal is not necessarily a cat. It is not the case that whatever is a mammal is necessarily a cat.[1] There is at least one mammal that is not a cat. Some mammals are not cats.[2]
First phenomenon: affirmative Second phenomenon: negative	**2** Whatever is a p is necessarily not a q. Whatever is a cat is necessarily not a reptile. No cat is a reptile. No reptile is a cat.	**6** Whatever is a p is not necessarily not a q. Whatever is a mammal is not necessarily not a cat. It is not the case that whatever is a mammal is necessarily not a cat. There is at least one mammal that is a cat. Some mammals are cats.
First phenomenon: negative Second phenomenon: affirmative	**3** Whatever is not a p is necessarily a q. Whatever is not a cat is necessarily selfless.[3] Even if it isn't a cat, it's still selfless.	**7** Whatever is not a p is not necessarily a q. Whatever is not a cat is not necessarily a mammal. It is not the case that whatever is not a cat is necessarily a mammal. There is at least one thing that is not a cat and is not a mammal. Some things that are not cats are not mammals.

	Is necessarily	Is not necessarily
First phenomenon: negative Second phenomenon: negative	<u>4</u> Whatever is not a *p* is necessarily not a *q*. Whatever is not a mammal is necessarily not a cat. Every nonmammal is a non-cat. Every cat is a mammal.	<u>8</u> Whatever is not a *p* is not necessarily not a *q*. Whatever is not a cat is not necessarily not a mammal. It is not the case that whatever is not a cat is necessarily not a mammal. There is at least one thing that is not a cat but is a mammal. Some things that are not cats are mammals.

1. It is almost always easier to understand "not necessarily" by taking the negative to the front of the sentence to say, "It is not the case that . . ."
2. The particular quantity word "some" has the sense of "at least one."
3. It would seem that this pervasion could never be part of a valid syllogism because the sign would be found in the dissimilar class. See chapter 6.

the most comprehensive category of all, including both all existents and all non-existents, so whatever you can imagine that is not a *p,* it is still selfless. In terms of the boundaries of pervasion, you can think of this as meaning "Whatever is not a *p* is necessarily something that may be referred to."

As mentioned in the note to this table, although it seems that the pervasion statement in box 3—whatever is not a cat is necessarily selfless—is true, it would seem that this pervasion could never be part of a valid syllogism. This is because the *p*-phenomenon, non-cat, would not be found exclusively in the similar class of the selfless but would also—at least in theory—be in the dissimilar class of the nonselfless. Of course, according to the Buddhist presentation, the nonselfless could not possibly exist because all things, existent and non-existent, are selfless. So, is the nonselfless among the non-existents? This is a quandary, maybe a logical paradox. Think more on this point when you read chapter 6, "The Buddhist Syllogism."

Of course, for the box 3 form of a statement of pervasion, you can play some tricks such as saying, "Whatever is not a cat is necessarily a non-cat," but that reveals very little. Also, there is the question about whether or not "is necessarily a non-cat" is affirmative, since it confirms a negative phenomenon. A better use for this form is to use qualifiers that limit the scope. For instance, "Whatever existent is not a permanent phenomenon is necessarily an impermanent phenomenon." That is true enough, and it yields some information. This approach can prove useful. In case you wonder, "an impermanent phenomenon" avoids the fault of "non-cat" mentioned above because it is considered a positive phenomenon, even with the "im-" in "impermanent."

In box 4, we have a pervasion of the form "Whatever is not a p is necessarily not a q." Remember that correct pervasions can only be of two profiles: (a) the p-phenomenon in the first clause and the q-phenomenon in the second clause are mutually inclusive, and (b) the p-phenomenon and the q-phenomenon compare as three possibilities such that the p-phenomenon is smaller in extent than the q-phenomenon. The sort of pervasion as shown in box 4 can work for both of these. For instance, "Whatever is not a cat is necessarily not a feline" or "Whatever is not a mammal is necessarily not a cat."

In box 5, we have a pervasion of the form "Whatever is a p is not necessarily a q." When the verb is negated—when the statement goes from "is necessarily" to "is not necessarily"—the implications are not as clear. The first thing that will help us understand is to rephrase the statement. It is closer to ordinary English and makes the statement easier to understand if we pull the negative from "is not necessarily" and place it up front so the statement becomes "It is not the case that whatever is a p is necessarily a q." If it is not the case that *everything* that is a p is a q, then there must be something that is a p but is not a q. Thus, it is a clear implication of this statement that there is at least one thing that is a p but is not a q. There must be at least one exception or counterexample to the universal generalization that all p's are q's. For example, if it's not the case that all mammals are cats, then there must be at least one mammal that is not a cat. If we want to test whether the statement that it's not the case that all mammals are cats is true, we have to find an exception to the generalization that all mammals are cats. Here, we have to supply more information from offsite. We all know there are mammals that are not cats—like dogs and so on, but just the measure of information that we have before us here—that whatever is a mammal is not necessarily a cat—does not yield the knowledge of which thing or things are mammals but are not cats. What is important right now is to recognize the source of what you are thinking. Is it first-order knowledge drawn from just the information before you? Or is it second-order knowledge drawn from what you have before you as well as other information you have from elsewhere? Of course, it is essential to draw from what you have from anywhere, but you should also appreciate the benefits and the limits of the implications of a statement. The table is intended not only to suggest how we would normally express these statements in English but also to measure the extent of the information that those statements can yield.

In box 6, we have a pervasion of the form "Whatever is a p is not necessarily not a q." Again, it is helpful to take the "not" out of "not necessarily" and place it at the front of the sentence to make it: "It is not the case that whatever is a p is necessarily not a q." The pervasion "Whatever is a p is necessarily not a q" is the equivalent of "No p is a q" (see the discussion of box 2 above). Thus, "It is not the case that whatever is a p is necessarily not a q" is equivalent to "It is not the case that no p is a q." For instance, it is not the case that no mammal is a cat. In addition, by the mechanics of simple conversion as in box 2—by simply trading the places of the p-phenomenon and the q-phenomenon in "No p is a q"—we get the equivalent statement "No q is a p," which would be expressed as the pervasion "Whatever is a q is necessarily not a p." But in this box, there is a lack of this pervasion, so the negation of this statement is "It is not the case that no q is a p." For instance, it is not the case that no cat is a mammal.

In box 7, we have a pervasion of the form "Whatever is not a p is not necessarily a q." This is easier understood as "It is not the case that whatever is not a p is necessarily a q." This is applied to our standard example as "It is not the case that whatever is not a cat is necessarily a mammal." It is a clear implication of this statement that there exists at least one thing that is not a cat and is not a mammal. We can test for the truth of this implication by considering that there is a broad array of things that are not cats—dogs, birds, rocks, perceptions, and so on. Clearly at least one of these, such as a rock, is not a mammal, so the statement is true. However, this is reading back into the statement from what we know. Of course, what we already know may be a valuable source of information because the pervasion makes claims about existents in the world, not just words. Testing whether the statement and its implications are true requires these considerations.

In box 8, we have a pervasion of the form "Whatever is not a p is not necessarily not a q." It is challenging to understand this statement with three negatives in it in any language. It may be converted to the equivalent "It is not the case that whatever is not a p is necessarily not a q." In other words, the statement asserts that it's not the case that everything that is not a *p* is also not a *q*. Therefore, a clear implication of this statement is that there exists at least one thing that is not a *p* but *is* a *q*. Let's use the example of "It is not the case that whatever is not a cat is necessarily not a mammal." This statement implies that there is at least one thing that is not a cat but is a mammal. If we want to know whether the original statement and its implications are true, we need to see whether there is one thing that is not a cat but is a mammal. Of course, there are many. A dog or a mouse or a squirrel is not a cat but is a mammal. Again, when we want to see whether the statement is true, we read back from what we know about cats and mammals. The original statement itself simply implies that there is at least one thing that is not a cat but is a mammal. But we can't tell the statement is true until we look into the world and find something that is not a cat but is a mammal.

Note: If you do not fully understand all of these different kinds of statements of pervasion and their implications at this point, don't worry too much about it. Just keep the chart as a reference page. Some of these occur rarely. With practice, all of them become easy enough.

EXERCISE 5.1

1. There is nothing to do but to think and listen quietly. Think about these two kinds of statements, statements of qualities and statements of pervasion: Listen to people talking in your primary language and "label" the statements of qualities and statements of pervasion. Try to think of or capture an example in which the subject of a statement of a quality is an abstract singular and the predicate says something about that subject in a way that is collective but not distributive. Pay attention to what you read and to what you are saying.

2. Pay attention to what you are saying, what you hear others saying, what you read, and what you are thinking and notice the frequent use of statements of pervasion. Try to find a way that these universal statements are expressed that is not among the ones listed here.

3. Listen to see if you can hear anyone working to verify a statement of pervasion by looking at cases. They will be saying things such as, "Well, I guess a tick is an arachnid, at least they do have eight legs." Do you see?

4. When you encounter a statement of pervasion, try to think of some of the other universal statements that are implied by that statement. Try to catch an example of someone misapplying the law of the contrapositive.

5. Spend some time with the table of pervasions to work with the rephrasings and implications. Substitute things and speak them out loud. By doing this exercise, you are wearing in new connections that will help you think better.

DENMA LOCHÖ RINPOCHE

Denma Lochö Rinpoche once said to me, "People who think to commit suicide don't understand life. When you die, you immediately enter the bardo [the state between lives] and begin searching for a new rebirth. It is frightful in the bardo, and it is very difficult to attain a human life again. Suicide only makes things worse."

Photograph by author.

6. The Buddhist Syllogism

I N Buddhist reasoning and debate, there are two main argument
forms used to defeat wrong conceptions and to support a clear understanding. The first one we should become acquainted with is the syllogism,
which consists of a thesis and a reason stated together in a single sentence.*
Once you are familiar with the Buddhist syllogism, you can understand the
other argument form, the consequence, which is an argument structurally
similar to a syllogism, but it is merely a logical outflow of an opponent's
own assertions. The Tibetan argument forms were brought over with minor
adaptations from the Indian logical forms. The syllogism and the consequence are two different tools, and they operate differently. For a syllogism,
the person who formulates the argument, the one who speaks it or writes
it, is bound to the argument and is responsible for the validity of the argument. The word for the thesis (Skt. *pratijñā,* Tib. *dam bca'*) of a syllogism
has the sense of "a promise." So, for a syllogism, the speaker is always trying
to say correctly how things are. For a consequence, one requirement for the
argument to be valid is that it flows as a logical implication of another's
assertions, but the one who formulates a consequence is not bound to the
validity of the argument, only to the fairness of the connection to the other
person's words. There is no thesis or "promise" for a consequence. In its
place is a point of clarification (*gsal ba*). Both of these argument forms may
provide valid arguments that can effectively clear away wrong ideas and help
a person conceive correct ideas. The syllogism is the basic argument form,
and the consequence plays off of it; thus, it is necessary to learn about the
syllogism first.

---

*For a full and rich explanation of the topic of the Buddhist syllogism and many other sur-
rounding topics, see Rogers, *Tibetan Logic*.

THE ARGUMENT FORM

In the tradition of Buddhist epistemology, syllogisms are not valid arguments in the sense of being valid under all interpretations. Rather, here an argument is determined to be valid only in relation to certain persons at certain times.* This is because the only value of an argument is in its efficacy in bringing forth new knowledge. This implies that the Buddhist logicians assert that an argument is not determined to be valid merely by its form, for validity is inextricably linked with the possibility of epistemological verification of that argument. Thus, a "logical" argument is determined to be valid only in a certain restricted sense. There are four main characteristics involved in determining validity:

1. The property of the subject
2. The forward pervasion
3. The counterpervasion
4. The epistemological requirements

The form of syllogism generally used in the Tibetan philosophical literature and in debate consists of a thesis and a reason, both what is to be proven and the proof, in one sentence. Here this argument form is called a "syllogism," not in the sense of a series of sentences consisting of the premises and a conclusion, but in the sense of an argument form. For example, a syllogism is stated in the style of the Buddhists:

> The subject, sound, is an impermanent phenomenon because of being a product.

The thesis, or what is to be proven, is that sound is an impermanent phenomenon. In this argument form, the thesis is framed: the subject, sound, is an impermanent phenomenon. The reason or proof, in this case, product, is framed: because of being a product. This argument form is called an enthymeme, which is a sort of informal argument with a "suppressed" premise or conclusion. Such an argument is often contained in a single sen-

---

*Recent scholarship suggests that the epistemological restrictions on the validity of an argument may be a unique development of the Ge-luk-ba order of Tibetan Buddhism. See Hiroshi Nemoto, "The Role of an Opponent in Buddhist Dialectic: The dGe lugs pa School's Concept of *phyi rgol yang dag*" (paper, 12th Seminar of the International Association of Tibetan Studies, August 18, 2010).

tence, as is the Buddhist syllogism. The Buddhist syllogism is a first-order enthymeme in which the major premise, that all products are impermanent phenomena, is "suppressed," meaning that it is not stated explicitly. This single-sentence form of the Buddhist syllogism used here is a condensation of a multisentence form used in the works of the Indian Buddhist logicians.[1] Consequently, this terse argument form implies a series of premises and a conclusion, which forms a more recognizable syllogism, as will be shown. As you will see, the single-sentence form is particularly well adapted to flowing debate.

THE ELEMENTS OF A SYLLOGISM

The series of sentences implied by the single-sentence form of the Buddhist syllogism is predicated by cross-relating the three basic units of that syllogism. These three are the subject, the predicate to be proven, and the reason, more typically known as a "sign." In the sample syllogism

> The subject, sound, is an impermanent phenomenon because of being a product,

the subject is *sound,* the predicate to be proven (or the predicate of the probandum) is *impermanent phenomenon,* and the sign (mutually inclusive with reason) is *product.* Here, the term "predicate" is not used just in its grammatical sense, in the sense of a predicate of a sentence as in "sound is an impermanent phenomenon," but means a "quality" or "attribute," in the way that being a material phenomenon is a *property, quality,* or *attribute* of a tree or of paper. Anything, be it existent or non-existent, is suitable to be stated as a subject, a predicate to be proven, or a sign, though they do not always work, of course.

The subject is the basis with respect to which a person is seeking to learn something. According to the tradition, a proper subject of a syllogism, also known as a basis of debate or a basis of inference, must meet two requirements, one formal and one epistemological.[2] First, the subject must be held as a basis of debate in a syllogism, for example, as sound is held as the subject in the proof of sound as an impermanent phenomenon. In other words, a subject must occupy the first position in a syllogism. Second, as in the sample syllogism, there must be a person who has ascertained that sound is a product (that sound has the quality given as the reason) and that person must now be engaged in wanting to know whether or not sound is an impermanent phenomenon. That a person has understood that sound is a product, as argued in the syllogism, indicates that the person is already involved in the reasoning process. The requirement that the person is now seeking to determine whether or not sound is an impermanent phenomenon indicates that the reasoning process is not yet complete, for the person is still seeking to learn something about the basis of inference, sound.

From this epistemological requirement, one can understand that the form of syllogism used in this system is not valid in the sense of being valid for all persons. There must be a person who, within having certain knowledge about the basis of debate, is now seeking to know something further, as guided by the syllogism, that he or she did not formerly know. Thus, although *formally solid* ("solid" or "reliable" in its form), the sample syllogism is not asserted to be valid for all persons in all contexts. For instance, it is not valid for a person who is unable to understand, such as a dog who does not understand language. Nor is it valid for a buddha or anyone else who has already completed the understanding and has not forgotten it. Neither the unprepared person nor one who has already realized this is *seeking to know* whether or not sound is an impermanent phenomenon.

In the sample syllogism, sound is the subject about which one is seeking to know something. What the qualified individual is seeking to know is whether or not sound is an impermanent phenomenon. In this syllogism, *impermanent phenomenon* is the predicate to be proven with respect to the basis of inference, sound. Thus, the thesis or promise of the sample syllogism, that which is to be proven, is *that sound is an impermanent phenomenon*. Anything may be stated as a predicate to be proven. For instance, someone might state a proof of sound as a permanent phenomenon. This does not imply that the person can prove sound as having just any sort of quality at all and certainly not as being a permanent phenomenon, but that someone can *state* anything as a predicate to be proven of sound. You can say anything you want, but that doesn't make it so.

In the proof of sound as an impermanent phenomenon, that which is to be negated is *that sound is a permanent phenomenon*. This is the opposite of the thesis, that sound is an impermanent phenomenon. More precisely, that which is negated is *that sound is a non-(impermanent phenomenon)*. Although the Collected Topics literature consistently reports that that which is to be negated is that sound is a permanent phenomenon, there is a slight verbal fault with this, for this is not the full negation of the predicate to be proven.* The predicate to be negated is *non-(impermanent phenomenon)*, the opposite of the predicate to be proven, not *permanent phenomenon*. A "permanent phenomenon" is something that exists and does not disintegrate moment by moment, so the predicate of being a permanent phenomenon is found only among existents. However, "non-(impermanent phenomenon)" may be ascribed to both permanent phenomena and to non-existents as well, for a non-existent too is a "non-(impermanent phenomenon)." In taking the predicate to be negated as *non-(impermanent phenomenon)*, we are able to explicitly exclude the possibility that the quality of being an impermanent phenomenon, the predicate to be proven, might be found among non-existents. Understand that the grammar here has it that the "non-" applies to "impermanent phenomenon," not just to "impermanent." So, for clarity I write it as "non-(impermanent phenomenon)," with "impermanent phenomenon" in parentheses. In either case, being a permanent phenomenon or a non-(impermanent phenomenon) is to be negated with respect to the basis of inference, sound. In explicitly proving that sound is an impermanent phenomenon, the argument implicitly proves that it is not a permanent phenomenon.†

In the sample syllogism, the sign or reason is *product*. The thesis, sound is an impermanent phenomenon, is justified by the reason, product. Sign is mutually inclusive with reason and proof. Anything may be put as a sign, although it may or may not be a valid reason. In the proof of sound as an impermanent phenomenon by the sign, product, it is product alone that is put as the sign rather than "because of being a product."

Although you may state anything as the sign in the proof of sound as an impermanent phenomenon, only some reasons will justify the thesis. Moreover, certain epistemological requirements must be satisfied in order for a reason to be correct.

---

*For more on this, see Rogers, *Tibetan Logic*, 93–100.
†Bear in mind that this sample syllogism, which is the standard always used to lay out the essentials of the Buddhist syllogism, is quite pointed. The Buddhists do not use the example of sound as an impermanent phenomenon simply because it is easy to understand, because sounds seem to dissipate so quickly. Rather, the Buddhists are making a point of opposing the Hindus who assert that the world is created out of sound generated by the Divine and that the sound is eternal.

CORRECT SIGNS

As in every system of reasoning, there are valid and invalid arguments. In the Buddhist system of logic and epistemology as practiced in Tibet, the definition of a correct sign is

> that which is the three modes.[3]

The three modes are three criteria that a correct sign must satisfy. These are that the sign must be:

1. the property of the subject,
2. the forward pervasion, and
3. the counterpervasion.[4]

An example of a correct sign is *product* in the syllogism:

> The subject, sound, is an impermanent phenomenon because of being a product.

Understand that product itself is the three modes, for it is the property of the subject, the forward pervasion, and the counterpervasion. Of course, there are three sentences implied by the single-sentence Buddhist argument, the two premises and the conclusion, which are created by relating the parts of the syllogism to each other, as you will see. Even so, always bear in mind that it is only the sign that is the three modes. A correct sign is not something that has the three modes, but it *is* the three modes. The definition of the correct sign in the proof of sound as an impermanent phenomenon by the sign, product, is

> that which is the three modes in the proof of sound as an impermanent phenomenon by the sign, product.[5]

This is not the definition of a product, which is *the momentary*. Rather, it is the definition of the correct sign in the proof of sound as an impermanent phenomenon by the sign, product. Just product alone is the correct sign in this particular proof, but product as such is not what is being defined. As you will see, there are definitions of each of the three modes in the proof of sound as an impermanent phenomenon by the sign, product.

The Property of the Subject

The first of the three modes of a correct sign is the property of the subject. Here the term "property" has the sense of a predicate, a quality, or an attribute, and the claim is that "product" or "productness" is a property of sound—that the property of the sign, or the quality of the reason, is present in the subject. It sounds strange to the English ear, but the Sanskrit sort of presents the sign as a quality, for example, "productness," the quality of being a product. In a proof such as this, the subject and the sign must be such that it is accurate to state them together in a statement of a quality, a sentence of the form "That subject is that sign." For instance, sound and product are like this, for it is accurate to say that sound is a product. Sound is a product in that it is produced from causes and conditions. Sounds do not arise just spontaneously and without cause. Thus, "productness" exists with sound, for it is a quality of sound.

The definition of something's being the property of the subject in the proof of sound as an impermanent phenomenon is

> that which is ascertained (by a person for whom it has become the property of the subject in the proof of sound as an impermanent phenomenon) as only existing, in accordance with the mode of statement, with sound.[6]

Product is the property of the subject in the proof of sound as an impermanent phenomenon by the sign, product, because product is ascertained (by a person for whom product has become the property of the subject in the proof of sound as an impermanent phenomenon by the sign, product) as only existing, in accordance with the mode of statement, with sound. The property of the subject is reckoned between the sign and its basis of relation, the subject. Thus, although technically only the sign, product, is the property of the subject in the sample syllogism, the first mode of the correct sign in this syllogism is *formulated*: sound is a product. And, this indicates that this is always the way to check for whether or not a sign has the property of the subject: Is that subject that sign? Does that subject have the quality of that sign?

Reflecting this formulation, the definition specifies the association between the sign and the subject saying that the property of the subject must be "ascertained as only existing, *in accordance with the mode of statement,*

with sound." The mode of statement in the proof of sound as an impermanent phenomenon by the sign, product, is an "is" statement, a copulative
statement or a statement of being. The reason is framed: "because of *being* a
product." Thus, the reason is saying something about the manner of being
of sound. Sound *is* a product. This type of statement is to be distinguished
from "exists" statements, reasons that justify the existence of something by
the sign. For example, in the syllogism

> The subject, on that mountain pass, there is fire because there is
> smoke,

the mode of statement is one of existence. The reason is stated in a manner
to prove the existence or the presence of something, fire, by the existence of
another, smoke. This is not the same as saying, as implied by the definition,
that the sign must *exist with* the subject. For example, in the proof of sound
as an impermanent phenomenon by the sign, product, product exists with
sound in accordance with the mode of statement, for sound has the quality
of *being* a product.[7]

Also, the definition specifies that in order for something to be the property of the subject in the proof of sound as an impermanent phenomenon,
it must be ascertained by a person for whom it has become the property of
the subject in the proof of sound as an impermanent phenomenon. A reason
is not correct, it does not meet even the first requirement of a correct sign,
unless it is ascertained by a certifying consciousness. In this system, a syllogism cannot be valid merely by its form.

The heart of this definition is that the property of the subject is *ascertained as only existing* with sound.[8] The specification that the sign must
be *ascertained* with sound serves to eliminate an indefinite understanding.
Product is *not* the property of the subject in the proof of sound as an impermanent phenomenon for a person who is wondering whether or not sound
is a product and neither is it for a person who firmly holds that sound is
not a product. The person must have ascertained definitely that sound is a
product. Again, this emphasizes that the validity of an argument is bound
up with the epistemological verification of that sign. A sign is the property
of the subject only in relation to individual persons. The requirement that
the sign must *exist* with the subject ensures that the sign is a property of the
subject, as productness is a property of sound. In saying that the property

of the subject is ascertained as *only existing* with the subject, the definition ensures that the sign must exist with the subject, though not exclusively with the subject. That is, the sign must actually be a property of the subject, as sound has the property of being a product. Yet, in order to be the property of the subject, the sign need not exist exclusively with the subject but may apply to other things as well. This is the case here, for it is not the case that product exists as a quality of only sounds, because product exists as well as a quality of other phenomena such as chairs, tables, and so forth.

Note Well: Because of the epistemological requirement of the first mode of the sign—that the sign is a fully qualified property of the subject only for someone who has definitely ascertained the quality of that sign as a property of that subject, that is, that sound is a product—there is an important restriction on how syllogisms may be formulated.* The restriction is that it cannot be a valid argument if there is the same thing in part 2 of the syllogism, the property of the subject, and part 3, the sign. This is because the four ascertainments must be done in sequence—the first mode of the correct sign, the second mode of the correct sign, the third mode of the correct sign, and, only then, the ascertainment of the conclusion. If there is the same thing in both parts 2 and 3, for instance,

> The subject, sound, is a product because of being a product,

then, when a person understands the property of the subject—that sound is a product—that person would have already understood the conclusion— that sound is a product. Do you see? It is suitable to have the same thing in parts 1 and 2 or to have the same thing in parts 1 and 3, but it does not work in parts 2 and 3. It sounds kind of funny to our ears to hear, for instance:

> The subject, an impermanent phenomenon, is an impermanent phenomenon because of being a product.

However, remember from the description of statements of qualities in chapter 5, "Two Kinds of Statements," that not every phenomenon exemplifies

---

*Lati Rinpoche, oral commentary. This was mistakenly not reported in *Debate in Tibetan Buddhism*.

itself. For instance, definition is not a definition. Thus, the information that a thing exemplifies its own quality, in the way that an impermanent phenomenon is an impermanent phenomenon, may be new knowledge.

In summary, product is the property of the subject in the proof of sound as an impermanent phenomenon by the sign, product, because of being ascertained (by a person for whom it has become the property of the subject in the proof of sound as an impermanent phenomenon by the sign, product) as only existing, in accordance with the mode of statement, with sound. The property of the subject in this syllogism is formulated: sound is a product. However, whatever is a property of sound is not necessarily suitable as a correct sign in the proof of sound as an impermanent phenomenon because of the epistemological reasons given above concerning the person for whom the syllogism is stated and because of the requirements of the other two modes of a correct sign, the forward pervasion and counterpervasion.

Forward Pervasion

The second mode of a correct sign is the forward pervasion. Whereas the property of the subject is reckoned between the sign and the subject, both of the required pervasions are reckoned between the sign and the predicate to be proven, also known as the predicate of the thesis. More technically, in the case of the forward pervasion, it is a relationship between the sign and the similar class. The similar class is the basis of relation of the forward pervasion just as the subject is the basis of relation of the property of the subject.

In the proof of sound as an impermanent phenomenon, the class of impermanent phenomena is the similar class. The definition of the similar class in the proof of sound as an impermanent phenomenon is

> that which is not empty of impermanence, in accordance with the mode of proof, in the proof of sound as an impermanent phenomenon.[9]

Anything that is an impermanent phenomenon is a member of the similar class in the proof of sound as an impermanent phenomenon. The mode of proof referred to here is the mode of being or the copulative mode, for the sample syllogism seeks to show that sound *is* an impermanent phenomenon, as opposed to the "exists" mode of proof. Thus, in accordance with the mode of proof, all things which *are* "not empty of impermanence" (that is, *are* impermanent phenomena) are members of the similar class—matter, consciousnesses, and so forth.*

The sign's being the forward pervasion in the proof of something refers to its relating to the similar class in a certain way. For instance, the definition of something's being the forward pervasion in the proof of sound as an impermanent phenomenon is

> that which is ascertained (by a person for whom it has become the second mode of the sign in the proof of sound as an impermanent phenomenon) as existing exclusively in the similar class in the proof of sound as an impermanent phenomenon.[10]

In order for a sign to be the forward pervasion, it must exist exclusively in the similar class, that is, it must be found exclusively in the similar class. In the sample syllogism, this means that product, or productness, if you will, must exist exclusively among impermanent phenomena. According to the tenets of all Buddhists, this is so because there are no products that are not impermanent phenomena.

The heart of the definition of forward pervasion is that the sign is *ascertained as existing exclusively* in the similar class.[11] The requirement of ascertainment serves to eliminate a doubtful cognition or an uncertain cognition. The sign is the forward pervasion only for a person who realizes definitely that the sign exists exclusively among members of the similar class. Again, epistemological verification is required as a component of validity.

That the sign must *exist* in the similar class serves to eliminate contradictory reasons, for example, as in the syllogism:

> The subject, sound, is a permanent phenomenon because of being a product.

Here the sign, product, does not exist at all in the similar class of permanent phenomena, for it exists exclusively in the dissimilar class of impermanent phenomena, or perhaps non-(permanent phenomena). If being the property of the subject were the only requirement of a correct sign, then you could validly prove sound to be a permanent phenomenon by the sign of being a

---

*For more information, see Rogers, *Tibetan Logic,* 79ff.

product. However, since a correct sign must be the forward pervasion and the forward pervasion requires that the sign must *exist* in the similar class, such a proof could never be valid.

Moreover, a correct sign must exist *exclusively* in the similar class and cannot be present in the dissimilar class. The dissimilar class in the proof of sound as an impermanent phenomenon includes the class of permanent phenomena. The requirement in the definition of forward pervasion that the sign must exist exclusively in the similar class serves to eliminate indefinite reasons, for example, as in the syllogism:

> The subject, sound, is an impermanent phenomenon because of being an existent.

Here the reason, existent, exists not only in the similar class as a quality of impermanent phenomena but also in the dissimilar class as a quality of permanent phenomena, for both permanent and impermanent phenomena are equally existents. Thus, the definition of forward pervasion provides that the sign must exist *exclusively* in the similar class.

However, although the sign must exist *exclusively* in the similar class, the definition does not specify that the similar class must exist exclusively in the sign. Rather, there are two types of correct signs in this regard: (1) those such that the sign and the similar class are equal in extent and (2) those such that the similar class is greater in extent than the sign.* In the sample syllogism

> The subject, sound, is an impermanent phenomenon because of being a product,

the sign and the similar class are equal in extent. All products are impermanent phenomena, and all impermanent phenomena are products. There is nothing that is the one but not the other. However, in the syllogism

> The subject, a tabby cat, is a mammal because of being a cat,

the similar class is greater in extent than the sign. There are mammals such as dogs or cows that are not cats. The definition requires that the sign exist *exclusively but not necessarily universally* in the similar class. For example,

---

*See Rogers, *Tibetan Logic*, 142–43.

catness exists exclusively but not universally among mammals. The extent of the sign may be equal to or lesser than the similar class, but it cannot be greater. Consequently, the extent of the similar class may be equal to or greater than that of the sign, but it cannot be less. You should already understand this from what you learned about statements of pervasion.

"Pervasion" means that the reason is *pervaded* by the predicate to be proven, as a floor is pervaded by a wall-to-wall carpet. The extent of the reason is either less than or equivalent to the extent of the predicate to be proven, so the extent of the predicate to be proven is either greater than or equivalent to the extent of the reason. In general, if the subject has the quality of being that sign and whatever is that sign is that predicate to be proven, then the subject must also have as a quality the predicate to be proven. Applied to the sample syllogism, sound has the quality of being a product and whatever is a product is an impermanent phenomenon; thus, sound has the quality of being an impermanent phenomenon as well. In a valid syllogism, the *sign* is the *pervaded,* for its extent is less than or equal to the extent of the predicate to be proven that pervades it, and it is the *proof,* for the sign proves the thesis. Conversely, in such a syllogism, the *predicate to be proven* is the *pervader,* for its extent is greater than or equal to the extent of the sign that is pervaded by it, and it is the *proven,* for the reason proves it as a predicate of the subject.

In this system of translation, pervasion statements are generally formulated: whatever is that reason is necessarily that predicate to be proven. For example, the forward pervasion of the sample syllogism is formulated: whatever is a product is necessarily an impermanent phenomenon. Translated more literally, the general formula would be rendered: if something is that sign, then it is *pervaded* by being that predicate to be proven. If this is applied to the sample syllogism, the pervasion would be: if something is a product, then it is pervaded by being an impermanent phenomenon. For all statements in which the mode of statement is an "is" statement, it is suitable to translate a statement of pervasion into the form of an English conditional sentence, a sentence of the form: if something is a *p*, then it is necessarily a *q*. This conditional form is often relied upon in the translation, though usually pervasions are translated in the form: whatever is a *p* is necessarily a *q*. For syllogisms in which the mode of statement is an "exists" statement, the translation is always of the form: if there is a *p*, then there is necessarily a *q*. Also for syllogisms in which there is a grammatical subject and predicate in both parts of the pervasion, the translation is always of the form: if *p* is a *q*, then *p* is necessarily an *r*. (This would be like the statement, "If this animal is a cat, then this animal is necessarily a mammal.")

As you can understand from what you read in chapter 5, "Two Kinds of Statements," it is important to understand the nature of pervasion as associative and not as a statement of a quality.* Although the sign *exists exclusively* in the similar class in the sense that *whatever is that sign* has the quality of being a member of that similar class, the pervasion is not meant to communicate that the sign itself is that predicate (although it may be). More correctly, pervasion indicates that the sign is *associated* with that predicate. For instance, products exist exclusively among impermanent phenomena. Products and impermanent phenomena are inextricably and necessarily associated. If something is a product, it is necessarily impermanent. In this case, it is also true that since product itself is a product, it is also an impermanent phenomenon. That is, here it may be said that the sign, product, is an example of the predicate to be proven, impermanent phenomenon, in the sense that product *is* an impermanent phenomenon. However, as will be seen, there are many cases for which, although there is pervasion, it cannot be said that the particular sign *is* that predicate in the sense that the sign has the quality of, demonstrates the being of, and exemplifies that predicate. Pervasion does not mean that the sign *is* the predicate to be proven. Rather, the meaning of pervasion is that the predicate to be proven encompasses the sign and is invariably associated with it.

The procedure of translating statements of pervasion into sentences of the form "Whatever is a *p* is necessarily a *q*" serves to express this nature of pervasion. In saying that whatever is a product is necessarily an impermanent phenomenon, the point of emphasis is not so much on product itself but on *those things that are* products. This statement of pervasion says that product is an impermanent phenomenon since product is itself a product, in that it says that *everything that has the quality of being* a product also has the quality of being an impermanent phenomenon. Thus, those things—such as pots, persons, consciousnesses, and so forth, as well as product itself—that are products are also impermanent phenomena. Being a product is invariably associated with being an impermanent phenomenon. In the statement of pervasion "Whatever is a product is necessarily an impermanent phenomenon," the word "whatever" stands in place of the points of emphasis,

---

*The term "associative" is suggested by Gārgyāyana, *The Science of the Sacred Word* (Adyar, Madras, India: The Theosophist office 1910–), 2:168–70n.

these things that are products—pots, persons, consciousnesses, and so on. Ascertaining this is essential for understanding the system of reasoning presented in the Collected Topics texts on Buddhist reasoning.

Counterpervasion

The third mode of a correct sign is the counterpervasion. This type of pervasion is a necessary implication of the forward pervasion because—at least in terms of the form—in all cases in which the sign is the forward pervasion it is also the counterpervasion.

The basis of relation of the counterpervasion is the dissimilar class, which in the proof of sound as an impermanent phenomenon is the class of non-(impermanent phenomena). The definition of the dissimilar class in the proof of sound as an impermanent phenomenon is

> that which is empty of impermanence, in accordance with the mode of proof, in the proof of sound as an impermanent phenomenon.[12]

Anything that is not an impermanent phenomenon is a member of the dissimilar class in the proof of sound as an impermanent phenomenon. Thus, any permanent phenomenon or any non-existent is a member of this dissimilar class.

The dissimilar class is the basis of relation of the counterpervasion, the third mode of a correct sign. The sign's being the counterpervasion refers to its being distinct from the dissimilar class in a particular way. For instance, the definition of something's being the counterpervasion in the proof of sound as an impermanent phenomenon is

> that which is ascertained (by a person for whom it has become the third mode of the sign in the proof of sound as an impermanent phenomenon) as universally absent in the dissimilar class in the proof of sound as an impermanent phenomenon.[13]

If a sign is the counterpervasion in the proof of something, it is ascertained as universally absent in the dissimilar class. For the sample syllogism, this means that product is ascertained as universally absent among non-(impermanent phenomena). This is established, for products exist exclusively among impermanent phenomena. Thus, you cannot find any products in a class that is mutually exclusive with the similar class—there are no products that are non-(impermanent phenomena).

In the definition of counterpervasion, as in the definitions of the other two modes of the sign, there is an epistemological requirement—of how and by whom a sign must be ascertained—and an ontological requirement—of how the sign must exist in relation to its basis of relation. The sign must be ascertained as the counterpervasion by a person who is actively involved in the reasoning process. In this case, the ontological requirement is that the sign must be *universally absent* in the dissimilar class and, although (according to the requirements of the forward pervasion) it must exist exclusively in the similar class, it may or may not be universally present in the similar class.[14] This is to say that the extent of the sign may be less than the extent of the predicate to be proven.

As in the cases of the property of the subject and the forward pervasion, only the sign is the counterpervasion. Still, counterpervasion is *formulated* between the sign and its basis of relation, the dissimilar class. In general, this is: whatever is not that predicate to be proven is necessarily not that sign. Applied to the sample syllogism, the counterpervasion is formulated: whatever is not an impermanent phenomenon is necessarily not a product. Since all products are impermanent phenomena, anything that is not an impermanent phenomenon cannot be a product. Note that this is the contrapositive, properly done by reversing the antecedent, "something is a product," and the consequent, "it is an impermanent phenomenon," and negating both.

The nature of counterpervasion is reflective of, and results from, the nature of forward pervasion. For any syllogism in which the sign is established as the forward pervasion, that sign will also be the counterpervasion. Still, the values of these two types of pervasion are somewhat different. The main requirement of the forward pervasion is that the sign must exist exclusively in the similar class, whereas the main requirement of the counterpervasion is that the sign must be universally absent in the dissimilar class. Also, the ascertainment of the forward pervasion and the ascertainment of the counterpervasion are different sorts of realizations. If a person explicitly realizes the forward pervasion, that person would also implicitly realize the counterpervasion. And if a person explicitly realizes the counterpervasion, that person would implicitly realize the forward pervasion. From this point of view, the two types of pervasions are different requirements. Although they are ontologically concomitant—for if the sign is the one, then it is also the other as well—they are *explicitly* ascertained separately.

Here are the components of a syllogism all together in one place:

Components of a Syllogism

Sample Syllogism:

The subject, sound, is an impermanent phenomenon because of being a product.

          I   2   3

1. Subject (Skt. *dharmin*, Tib. *chos can*): sound
2. Predicate to be proven (Skt. *sādhya-dharma*, Tib. *bsgrub bya'i chos*): impermanent phenomenon
3. Sign (Skt. *liṅga*, Tib. *rtags*): product
4. That which is to be proven (Skt. *sādhya*, Tib. *bsgrub bya*): sound is an impermanent phenomenon
   Formulated in general: that subject is that predicate to be proven
5. Predicate to be negated (Skt. **pratiṣhedhya-dharma*, Tib. *dgag bya'i chos*): permanent phenomenon or non-(impermanent phenomenon)
6. That which is to be negated (Skt. *pratiṣhedhya*, Tib. *dgag bya*): sound is a permanent phenomenon
   Formulated in general: that subject is non-(that predicate to be proven)
7. Similar class (Skt. *sapakṣha,* Tib. *mthun phyogs*): impermanent phenomenon
8. Dissimilar class (Skt. *vipakṣha,* Tib. *mi mthun phyogs*): permanent phenomenon or non-(impermanent phenomenon)
9. Property of the subject (Skt. *pakṣha-dharma,* Tib. *phyogs chos*): product
   Defined: that which is ascertained (by a person for whom it has become the property of the subject in the proof of sound as an impermanent phenomenon by the sign, product) as only existing, in accordance with the mode of statement, with sound
   Formulated in general: that subject is that sign
   Formulated for the sample syllogism: sound is a product
10. Forward pervasion (Skt. *anvaya-vyāpti,* Tib. *rjes khyab*): product
    Defined: that which is ascertained (by a person for whom it has

become the second mode of the sign in the proof of sound as an impermanent phenomenon by the sign, product) as existing exclusively in the similar class in the proof of sound as an impermanent phenomenon

Formulated in general: whatever is that sign is necessarily that predicate to be proven

Formulated for the sample syllogism: whatever is a product is necessarily an impermanent phenomenon

11. Counterpervasion (Skt. *vyatireka-vyāpti,* Tib. *ldog khyab*): product

Defined: that which is ascertained (by a person for whom it has become the third mode of the sign in the proof of sound as an impermanent phenomenon by the sign, product) as universally absent in the dissimilar class in the proof of sound as an impermanent phenomenon

Formulated in general: whatever is not that predicate to be proven is necessarily not that sign

Formulated for the sample syllogism: whatever is not an impermanent phenomenon is necessarily not a product

The Epistemological Requirements

The fourth and final main characteristic required for a valid Buddhist syllogism concerns the set of epistemological requirements. For each of the three modes, there is an epistemological requirement. In relation to the property of the subject, the sign is correct only for a person who has ascertained definitely that sound is a product. In relation to the forward pervasion, the sign is correct only for a person who realizes definitely that the sign exists exclusively among members of the similar class. And, in relation to the counterpervasion, the sign is correct only for a person who realizes definitely that the sign is universally absent from the dissimilar class.

Moreover, remember that the three modes of a correct sign are in set sequence. This is why they are called the "first mode," the "second mode," and the "third mode." When these have been understood in sequence, a fully qualified opponent is then ready to acquire the new understanding that is the conclusion of your syllogism. This is why, in a valid syllogism, there cannot be the same thing in part 2, the predicate of the probandum, and part 3, the sign since once an opponent had understood the property of the subject, that person would have already understood the conclusion, thus breaking the sequence.

One thing we may understand from the criteria for validity is that the premises must be verifiably true, certified as concordant with fact by ascertaining valid cognizers, which are incontrovertible consciousnesses that correctly know their objects. Someone might make the argument "The subject, sound, is a *permanent phenomenon* because of being a product," and the argument may be logically sound in the sense that *if* the premises were true, then the conclusion would be true. However, it is not factually true according to the assertions of this system of philosophy; thus, it is not valid. Here "product" is a *contradictory reason,* for products do not exist exclusively in the similar class of permanent phenomena but are universally absent in the similar class. Emphasizing the imperative in Buddhist reasoning that pervasion must be associative in the real world in the way that productness is always associated with impermanent phenomena, in his commentary on the *Wheel of Reasons,* Den-dar-hla-ram-ba explains that the association of pervasion between the sign and the predicate to be proven "is objectively established, and is not established by one's mere wish. . . . If pervasion were established through one's mere wish, then even contradictory signs would become correct provers."[15] The correct pervasion of the reason by the predicate to be proven is a necessary association of those two phenomena. It is objectively established, from the side of the objects, and is not built up out of one's subjective interpretation or imagination. Pervasion is a necessary association of two related phenomena and predicated from the natures of those phenomena.

Furthermore, even arguments that are formally sound and factually true may or may not be valid, for a valid argument must meet the epistemological requirements concerning the person faced with the argument. The person must be one who is actively seeking to understand the thesis/conclusion of the syllogism. An argument is not valid for all persons at all times. For one who has already ascertained the conclusion or for one who is unable to ascertain the conclusion, the argument is not valid even though it may be sound and the premises and conclusion factually true. Thus, in this system of reasoning, even an argument that is logically sound, in the sense that a true conclusion flows from true premises, is not necessarily valid. A valid argument must be sound, but a sound argument is not necessarily valid.[16]

UNPACKING THE BUDDHIST ENTHYMEME

As described in this chapter, it is easy to understand that the single-sentence syllogism used in the Collected Topics tradition of Buddhist reasoning implies the more familiar syllogistic form consisting of a series of sentences leading to a conclusion. For instance, the sample syllogism

The subject, sound, is an impermanent phenomenon because of being a product

implies a series of three sentences and a conclusion:

Sound is a product.

Whatever is a product is necessarily an impermanent phenomenon.

Whatever is not an impermanent phenomenon is necessarily not a product.

Therefore, sound is an impermanent phenomenon.

Normally the major premise, which is reckoned between the reason and the predicate of the thesis/conclusion, is put first, and the minor premise, which is reckoned between the subject and the reason, is put second; however, here they are stated in the order of the three modes of the sign.

In the Buddhist enthymeme, the minor premise—that sound is a product—and the thesis/conclusion—that sound is an impermanent phenomenon—are stated explicitly. The major premise—that all products are impermanent phenomena—is "suppressed" or merely implied and not stated explicitly.

The first three sentences in this implied syllogism are premises only in the sense that if they are true, then the conclusion too must be true. For any *valid* syllogism, the implied premises are not just assumptions that may or may not be true. Rather, according to the way the three modes of the sign are defined in this system of reasoning, the three sentences implied by any *valid* argument must be true, and a person for whom the argument is valid must ascertain them as true.

EXERCISE 6.1

The following questions pertain to the standard sample syllogism:

The subject, sound, is an impermanent phenomenon because of being a product.

Working with your debate partner, taking turns back and forth, answer the following questions.*

1. What is the subject in the sample syllogism? What is the predicate to be proven? What is the reason? What is the sign? How do the two, reason and sign, compare?
2. What is it that the syllogism is supposed to prove? What is it that the syllogism is supposed to negate?
3. What is the similar class? What is the dissimilar class? Is there a fault in describing the dissimilar class as permanent phenomena? Is it appropriate to describe the dissimilar class as non-(impermanent phenomena)? How do those two compare? Give examples for these and prove them.
4. What may be given as a sign/reason in the proof of sound as an impermanent phenomenon?
5. What may be given as a correct sign for the sample syllogism?
6. What are the three modes of a correct sign for the sample syllogism?
7. What is the property of the subject? What is the heart of the definition of the property of the subject that you should remember? How is the property of the subject formulated in general? How is it formulated here? (Hint: These formulations are how you check to see if the mode is there.)
8. What is the forward pervasion? What is the heart of the definition? How is the forward pervasion formulated in general? How is it formulated here?
9. What is the counterpervasion? What is the heart of the definition? How is the counterpervasion formulated in general? How is it formulated here?

EXERCISE 6.2

There is some quality about this form of argument that does not quite fit in at first. It feels almost as if the connections are backward. I have seen it over and over. Perhaps it is "backward" to the way we normally reason. Still, there is no doubt it works. I have also seen that after a little practice, it becomes very natural.

---

*Yes, at first you can "cheat," but then try to give the answers without looking. Keep doing it until you get a little bored *because you just know them all.*

1. Find some arguments and express them in the form of a Buddhist syllogism. Use just the same words you are hearing or reading, insofar as possible. Listen to yourself thinking and speaking. Listen to the people you are talking with. Listen to lectures and media. Pay attention and look for arguments in your readings. This will help you to better pick up on discourse that has content with logical implications, and it will help you to get used to the Buddhist syllogism.

EXERCISE 6.3

▶ Forge your own syllogisms. Choose one from column A, subjects, one from column B, predicates to be proven, and one from column C, reasons, to make a logically sound argument. Try to make at least twenty.

▶ Choose the verb "is" or "is not" for the predicate to be proven and the verbal "being" or "not being" for the reason, as you need them.

▶ With each one, follow the checking procedure by first checking the property of the subject according to the formula above, then checking the forward pervasion. There is no need to check the counterpervasion separately because if the forward pervasion is there, so is the counterpervasion.

▶ Remember that it is okay to use the same thing in parts 1 and 2 or in 1 and 3, but you cannot use the same thing in parts 2 and 3.

▶ Use this as your frame of reference:
The subject, _____ , is/is not _____ because of being/not being _____ .

COLUMN A SUBJECTS	COLUMN B PREDICATES TO BE PROVEN	COLUMN C REASONS
a cat	an existent	a product
a Persian cat	an impermanent phenomenon	a cat
a chair	a product	a material phenomenon
a permanent phenomenon	a mammal	an impermanent phenomenon
a red car	a non-existent	a mammal
sound	a permanent phenomenon	a reptile

EXERCISE 6.4

1. The freestyle exercise: create at least ten of your own syllogisms in the Buddhist form. Use anything you want, but be sure to use some with the Buddhist terminology. Make up a couple from your own interests. For instance:

> The subject, Monet, was an impressionist painter because of being a French impressionist painter.

Advice: (Some of this is carried over from the advice at the end of chapter 4, "The Comparison of Phenomena," and some is new and particular to making syllogisms.)

1. When you are trying to think of a reason, think categorically, not descriptively. For instance, look at the syllogism about Monet above. Our normal impulse is to try to describe something about his art that justifies calling him an impressionist painter. However, the categorical reason justifying that he was an impressionist painter because he was *a French impressionist painter* is unassailable. It seems unfair to us at first, for it tells so little. But, debate moves in very small increments, best done at a rapid pace. Anyway, this reason is perfectly defensible, whereas descriptions can be challenging.

2. Once you have chosen your reason, employ the checking procedure to see if your argument works, until using this procedure becomes completely automatic:

   ► Ask yourself: is that subject that sign? Fill in the words that you use in your syllogism, not "that subject" and "that sign." For instance, ask yourself, "Was Monet a French impressionist painter?" If the answer to the first check is yes, proceed to the second check.

   ► Ask yourself: is it true that whatever is that sign is necessarily that predicate to be proven? Again, use your words, not the formula words. For instance, ask yourself, "Is it true that whoever is a French impressionist painter is necessarily an impressionist painter?" If the answer to the second check is also yes, then proceed to the final check.*

---

*In terms of the mere mechanics of it, there is no need to check the counterpervasion independently. If the forward pervasion is true, so is the counterpervasion. It may be that we formulate and note the counterpervasion so quickly that it is hard to notice.

► Wonder: well, if it is true that that subject is that sign and that whatever is that sign is necessarily that predicate to be proven, then it must be the case that that subject is that predicate to be proven. Ask yourself: is that subject that predicate to be proven? For instance, wonder, "If it is true that Monet was a French impressionist painter and that whoever is a French impressionist painter is necessarily an impressionist painter, then it must be the case that Monet was an impressionist painter." If so, rejoice in the proven knowledge.

3. Don't worry about being profound. Hopefully, that will come in time. Just be right. Just say things that are defensible.

4. When you formulate your argument, be precise. Do not say that a blue car is blue. Say that *the color of a blue car* is blue. This will save you loads of trouble. You see? Who could possibly say that the color of a blue car is not blue?

5. Develop the habit of giving very specific subjects. This is somewhat different from being precise. What I mean is, don't say, "The subject, a French impressionist painter, is an impressionist painter." Then you must come up with some sort of description of what is required to be an impressionist painter. Start with Monet, and then it's easier. You will see the wisdom of this with practice.

KENSUR YESHI THUPTEN

Kensur Yeshi Thupten once said to me, "Happy people don't drink and take drugs."

Photograph © 1987 Armen Elliott.

7. The Only Two Valid Syllogism Forms

Recall from chapter 5, "Two Kinds of Statements," that there are only two patterns for a correct statement of pervasion. For instance, take the standard expression of a pervasion:

Whatever is a *p* is necessarily a *q*.

If this is true, the range of the *p*-phenomenon must be either equal to or smaller than the range of the *q*-phenomenon. Side by side, these two patterns would look like this:

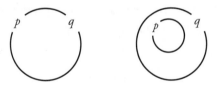

An example of the first pattern, the one on the left, in which the *p*-phenomenon is equal in extent to the *q*-phenomenon, is the pervasion:

Whatever is a product (*p*) is necessarily an impermanent phenomenon (*q*).

Product and impermanent phenomenon are MI; thus, they are equal in extent.

An example of the second pattern, the one on the right, in which the *p*-phenomenon is smaller in extent than the *q*-phenomenon, is the pervasion:

Whatever is a product (*p*) is necessarily an existent (*q*).

Products and existents are 3P such that whatever is a product is necessarily an existent, but it is *not* the case that whatever is an existent is necessarily a product. For instance, a permanent phenomenon is an existent but not a product. Thus, the range of the p-phenomenon is smaller than the range of the q-phenomenon. These are the only two types of pervasions that can work, in the sense of yielding true statements.

The fact that there are only these two patterns for a correct pervasion determines that there can be only two valid forms of the Buddhist syllogism. From what you know from chapter 6, "The Buddhist Syllogism," the basic argument form *coordinates* a statement of a quality (the property of the subject) with the statement of pervasion to lead a person to understand another statement of a quality (the thesis, which should now be your conclusion).

To show how these two types of correct pervasions perform in valid syllogisms one-by-one, the first pattern, in which the range of the p-phenomenon is equal to the range of the q-phenomenon, is shown in the classic syllogism used as the basis for instruction on syllogisms:

The subject, sound (◀≀), is an impermanent phenomenon (q) because of being a product (p).

The second pattern of a correct pervasion, in which the range of the p-phenomenon is smaller than the range of the q-phenomenon, is shown in the correct syllogism:

The subject, sound (◀≀), is an existent (q) because of being a product (p).

Of course, for any sort of valid syllogism, the sign is the three modes. The first of these is the property of the subject, formulated as "that subject is that sign." Side by side, the property of the subject for these two patterns of valid syllogisms would look like this:

The Property of the Subject

The pattern in which the sign and the predicate to be proven are equal in extent

The subject, sound (🔊), is an impermanent phenomenon (*q*) because of being a product (*p*).

1. Sound (🔊) is a product (*q*).

The pattern in which the extent of the sign is smaller than the extent of the predicate to be proven

The subject, sound (🔊), is an existent (*q*) because of being a product (*p*).

1. Sound (🔊) is a product (*q*).

1

Up to this point, the two types of valid syllogism forms are completely alike. In fact, for these two sample syllogisms, they are identical. Their difference in form shows only when the two different pervasion patterns are represented.

The second mode of a correct sign is the forward pervasion, formulated as "Whatever is that sign is necessarily that predicate to be proven." Side by side, the forward pervasions for these two patterns of valid syllogism would look like this:

The Forward Pervasion

The pattern in which the sign and the predicate to be proven are equal in extent

The subject, sound (🔊), is an impermanent phenomenon (*q*) because of being a product (*p*).

2. All products (*p*) are impermanent phenomena (*q*).

The pattern in which the extent of the sign is smaller than the extent of the predicate to be proven

The subject, sound (🔊), is an existent (*q*) because of being a product (*p*).

2. All products (*p*) are existents (*q*).

2

These two are duplicates of the two patterns for correct pervasions.

There is no need to represent the third mode of a correct sign, the counterpervasions, separately for the two valid forms because they would look just the same as the forward pervasions. Only the words would be different. In the pattern on the left, the counterpervasion would be "Whatever is not an impermanent phenomenon is necessarily not a product" and on the right, the counterpervasion would be "Whatever is not an existent is necessarily not a product."

All that remains are the two conclusions, which are compelled by the foregoing premises for an appropriate person ready to understand. The conclusion is formulated as "That subject is that predicate to be proven." Side by side, the conclusions for these two patterns of valid syllogism would look like this:

The Conclusion

The pattern in which the sign and the predicate to be proven are equal in extent

The subject, sound (◀꞉), is an impermanent phenomenon (q) because of being a product (p).

Therefore, sound (◀꞉) is an impermanent phenomenon (q).

The pattern in which the extent of the sign is smaller than the extent of the predicate to be proven

The subject, sound (◀꞉), is an existent (q) because of being a product (p).

Therefore, sound (◀꞉) is an existent (q).

 therefore

Now, putting both of these patterns for valid syllogisms side by side, it is easy to see the system.

The Only Two Valid Forms of a Buddhist Syllogism

The pattern in which the sign and the predicate to be proven are equal in extent

The subject, sound (🔊), is an impermanent phenomenon (q) because of being a product (p).

1. Sound (🔊) is a product (p).

2. All products (p) are impermanent phenomena (q).

Therefore, sound (🔊) is an impermanent phenomenon (q).

The pattern in which the extent of the sign is smaller than the extent of the predicate to be proven

The subject, sound (🔊), is an existent (q) because of being a product (p).

1. Sound (🔊) is a product (p).

2. All products (p) are existents (q).

Therefore, sound (🔊) is an existent (q).

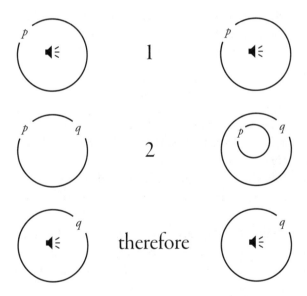

These are the only two patterns for a valid syllogism in Buddhist reasoning and debate. Even if one or both of the sign and the predicate to be proven are negative, the diagrams will still look the same.

EXERCISE 7.1

1. Create valid Buddhist syllogisms, then draw the patterns for each of your syllogisms until the patterns appear to your mind as the visual device. You may want to review the advice that goes along with exercise 6.4 at the end of chapter 6, "The Buddhist Syllogism." Remember to think categorically and to continue to do the checking procedure until it becomes second nature.

2. Run an experiment to check the claim that "even if one or both of the sign and the predicate to be proven are negative, the diagrams will still look the same." Create syllogisms with negatives to see whether or not they do indeed look the same. Remember that the one pattern with an affirmative predicate to be proven and a negative sign is very problematic:

> The subject, x, is a q because of *not* being a p.

Basically, forget about that alignment. (See the discussion of the pervasion in box 3 in the table of pervasions in chapter 5.)

When you are running the experiment, understand that for a syllogism such as this,

> The subject, an octopus, is not a cat because of not being a mammal,

because there are more mammals than there are cats, what is other than mammals includes less than what is other than cats, and so what is other than mammals is smaller in extent than what is other than cats. In other words, there are far more mammals than there are cats, so "all that is other than mammals" is smaller than "all that is other than cats."

Finally, bear in mind that "because of being an existent that is not a form" is not a negative, but "because of not being a form" and "because of being a nonform" are negatives, at least for purposes of this exercise.

8. THREE TYPES OF CORRECT SIGNS

IT WILL BE helpful to understand something more of the range of correct syllogisms as Buddhists understand them. The few comments here are just a gesture toward a topic that is treated in a much vaster way a little later in the traditional study of Buddhist reasoning and debate. This presentation is based in the Collected Topics tradition of Buddhist reasoning as practiced in Tibetan Buddhism. In turn, that is all based in Indian thought.

Rather than being a single text, the Collected Topics texts form a genre of literature in Tibetan, and there are many versions of such texts. The Collected Topics text by Pur-bu-jok Jam-ba-gya-tso (Phur bu lcog byams pa rgya mtsho), known as the *Tutor's Collected Topics* (*Yongs 'dzin bsdus grva*) because he was one of the tutors of the thirteenth Dalai Lama for whom he wrote the text, was the source for *Debate in Tibetan Buddhism*. That text is divided into three major parts consisting of "The Introductory Path of Reasoning" (*Rigs lam chung ngu*),* "The Middling Path of Reasoning" (*Rigs lam 'bring*), and "The Greater Path of Reasoning" (*Rigs lam che ba*). "The Greater Path of Reasoning" contains book-length presentations of "Awareness and Knowledge" (*bLo rig*) and "Signs and Reasonings" (*rTags rigs*)† as well as other collected topics.

The division into introductory, middling, and greater paths of reasoning (*rigs lam*) accords with the capacity of the student. The debaters speak of "gaining the path of reasoning," meaning that the person has developed a certain capacity and facility with the procedure in debate. Those who have the path of reasoning debate without hesitation and indecision, for they know well the implications of both their own and others' assertions and

---

**Rigs lam chung ngu* could be translated more literally as "The Lesser Path of Reasoning" or "The Smaller Path of Reasoning."
†There is some evidence suggesting that *rtags rigs* might appropriately be translated as "Types of Signs."

immediately draw out those implications and possible interpretations of what was said.

One scholar noted that "reasoning" in the expression "The Path of Reasoning" has the same meaning as "correctness" and "suitability."[1] That water flows downhill accords with reasoning, correctness, and suitability. Since we can see strongly billowing smoke on a mountain pass and we know that wherever there is smoke there is fire, we may conclude that fire exists on that smoky mountain pass. By the power of the facts, we are able to establish reasonably, correctly, and suitably that fire exists in that place. By this interpretation, a "path of reasoning" also means a "path of correctness" and a "path of suitability."

This "gesture" to the three types of correct signs is drawn from the "Signs and Reasonings" literature as presented by my old debating partner, Katherine Manchester Rogers, in her work of amazing scholarship *Tibetan Logic*. In that work, correct signs are divided in several ways, but the main division is a division by way of entity into the three:

1. Correct effect signs
2. Correct nature signs
3. Correct signs of nonobservation.*

These three types of correct signs support Buddhist learning and practice because they train a person in cause and effect, the entity or nature of things in the world, and the way of understanding the existence of something by a negative route of reasoning. Cause and effect are of essential importance in Buddhism because from the beginning, the Buddha described a cause and effect link between our sufferings and our actions and a cause and effect link between new actions on the path and the effect of liberation from suffering. Also from the beginning, understanding the nature of things—especially understanding the nature of impermanent phenomena—supports breaking through to "new actions on the path." Correct signs of nonobservation "were set forth for the sake of realizing that all things are selfless."[2] Buddhists describe reality with negative terms such as "selflessness" or "emptiness" and seek to discover the final nature or reality of a thing by eliminating what is not there in the nature of a thing, in order to understand what remains when the "self" that a thing is empty of is eliminated. The great Nying-ma

*For a rich and detailed explanation of this division of correct signs, see Rogers, *Tibetan Logic*, 149–273.

lama Dilgo Khyentse Rinpoche described this approach as like capturing a snake by setting down a cage over it.[3]

CORRECT EFFECT SIGNS

In a syllogism with a correct effect sign, the sign is an effect and the predicate of the probandum, what that sign proves, is the cause of that effect. The classic example of a syllogism with an effect sign is:

> The subject, on that mountain pass, there is fire because there is strongly billowing smoke.

Although many questions arise in our minds, and that is appropriate, you would have few questions if you came home and saw strongly billowing smoke coming out of your house. Inference, the intellectual understanding that can result from reasoning, is a way of understanding the presence of something that is not observed directly. Even without seeing the fire, by the sign of the presence of smoke and the knowledge that wherever there is smoke there is fire, you understand that fire is present.

You can prove the cause by knowledge of the effect, but you cannot reliably prove the effect by knowledge of the cause. For instance, if you come home to your apartment and it was all torn up and your valuable stuff was gone, you would think that someone had robbed you. However, if you are leaving your apartment and you see some shady dude hanging out, you cannot know from that alone that your apartment will be robbed. Still, you ought to be cautious. The more traditional example is that the presence of smoke, an effect of fire, proves the presence of fire, but the presence of fire, the cause of smoke, does not prove the presence of smoke because sometimes there is smokeless fire, such as with the sun.

CORRECT NATURE SIGNS

The second type of correct sign is a correct nature sign. In a syllogism with a correct nature sign, the sign and the predicate to be proven are of the same nature or of the same entity such that you can know that the one is there whenever the other is there. For instance, cats and mammals are like this, at least in one direction. If you have a cat, you have a mammal. However, if you have a mammal, you do not necessarily have a cat. The way this sameness of nature is understood is that for two different phenomena, if the one is absent, then the other is absent by necessity—at least in one direction. This means that, if there were no mammals, there would be no cats; however, if there were no cats, there might still be mammals, such as mice and rabbits and so on. Thus, you understand that the claim that "there was a mammal here because there was a cat here" is irresistible, but the claim that "there was a cat here because there was a mammal here" is not.

When two phenomena of the same nature are MI, when the one is eliminated, the other is eliminated also—in both directions. For instance, if somehow there were no products, there would be no impermanent phenomena. In the same way, if there were no impermanent phenomena, there would be no products. The presence of one proves the presence of the other, and the absence of one proves the absence of the other. The classic example of a syllogism with a nature sign is:

> The subject, sound, is an impermanent phenomenon because of being a product.

Products and impermanent phenomena are of the same nature.

CORRECT SIGNS OF NONOBSERVATION

The third type of correct sign is a correct sign of nonobservation. Whereas you often hear the claim that "you can't prove a negative," as defined in this system of thought, a correct sign of this sort must prove a negative. This type of proof may be in regard to either the natures of phenomena or the causes and effects of phenomena.

A correct sign of nonobservation that is *suggestive* of proving emptiness or selflessness is:

> The subject, sound, is empty of being permanent because of being a product.[4]

The predicate to be proven is a negative: "empty of being permanent." The subject, sound, is the basis of negation (that is, the basis that is empty of being permanent). This sign of nonobservation is in regard to the nature of a phenomenon. It is in the nature of products that they are empty of being permanent.

A correct sign of nonobservation that *explicitly* proves emptiness is:

The subject, the self of persons, is empty of inherent existence because of being a dependent-arising.[5]

The predicate to be proven is a negative: "empty of inherent existence." The subject, the self of persons, is the basis of negation (that is, the basis that is empty of inherent existence). Here the "self of persons" must refer to the existent entity of the person, not to a permanent, unitary, independent self that does not exist. This sign of nonobservation too is in regard to the nature of a phenomenon. It is in the nature of dependent-arisings (MI with existents) that they are empty of inherent existence.

A correct sign of nonobservation with regard to the causes and effects of phenomena is:

The subject, on that island in the river at night, there is no smoke because there is no fire.[6]

Imagine yourself standing on a riverbank on a dark, clear night looking in the direction of a small island in the river that you know is there because you have often observed it during the daytime. You may infer the absence of smoke, an effect of fire, on that island by the absence of fire, which you would see at night. Here, the argument is put forth to prove the absence of an effect—smoke—due to the absence of a cause—fire.

Exercise 8.1

1. Assuming for each argument that there is someone who is actively seeking to know, make your best guess about what kind of correct sign is in each of the following arguments:

   The subject, in this coffee I am drinking, there is no sugar because there is no taste of sugar.
   The subject, a Persian cat, is a mammal because of being a cat.
   The subject, the number 3, is an integer because of being a prime number.
   The subject, here in this cave, there has been fire because there are black smoke smudges on the ceiling.

The subject, at the bank during the robbery, John Q. Citizen was not there because John Q. Citizen was observed elsewhere.

The subject, this male suspect, has recently fired a gun because of the presence of gun smoke residue on his hand.

The subject, the sound of a conch shell horn, is a sound because of being a sound arisen from human exertion.

The subject, a chair, is an existent because of being an impermanent phenomenon.

2. Create your own syllogisms with correct signs. Make up at least three for each of the three types of correct signs.

9. Basic Buddhist Ontology 1

The Selfless, Existents, Types of Existents, and Non-existents

ALL THE BUDDHIST tenet systems are goal-oriented systems of philosophy. They are presented for the sake of laying out clearly a definitive and final explanation of what exists in order to inform practitioners about the nature of things. They do not undertake to discover what exists for the sake of knowledge alone. Rather, they proceed with the assumption that the knowledge of what exists will liberate.

Thus, the first thing to do is to lay out the basic understanding of what exists and what does not exist as described in the system of philosophy that serves as the basis for Buddhist reasoning and debate. However, for our purposes here, remember that you do not have to believe this stuff in order to get on with learning Buddhist reasoning and debate. Of course, I find the descriptions very compelling, I admit, but you do not have to. Rather, you just need to understand how these terms are used in this system of reasoning in order to understand the examples and the entire presentation in this book. Once you have done that, you will be able to apply the style of reasoning to whatever you are interested in. (In fact, the entirety of the analytical system presented here could be expressed in terms of mathematics, biology, law, medicine, or any field in which there are clear definitions.) What's more, if you just take the Buddhist ontology—their theory of what exists—that is presented here to be definitive, that approach is not even in accordance with the advice of the Buddha, who is quoted as saying,

> Like gold [that is acquired] upon being scorched, cut, and rubbed,
> My word is to be adopted by monastics and scholars
> Upon analyzing it well,
> Not out of respect [for me].*

*This is quoted from Jeffrey Hopkins, *Emptiness in the Mind-Only School of Buddhism*

In using the example of checking whether or not a piece of ore is genuine gold, the Buddha is indicating that there is a great deal at stake here. As a person in business is careful about money, so religious seekers must take care about where they put their trust. This means that you should check a person's words—even the words of the Buddha—very carefully, rather than just taking them on faith. Since the South Asian approach to spirituality is that we are liberated through understanding the nature of things, someone else's words can be helpful only if those words are accurate. Moreover, even if the description is completely accurate, merely being able to repeat the words describing reality will not be actual wisdom, so that too would not help. Thus, the Buddha gives a warning. Merely knowing the words of the Buddha is not knowledge. Rather, the advice is to take note of the words and check them closely. Then, you may gain knowledge.

Having said that, it is not necessary to have a full and final understanding of the topics before you can go on. If we get hung up on trying to understand definitively exactly what is meant by "selflessness" or a "permanent phenomenon," we will not get very far. So, the request I have for you here is simply to learn this material and to think about it, and doubtless you will be thinking about it, as it is hard to avoid doing so. The reason I make this request is that it will be impossible to gain the skills of Buddhist reasoning and debate using this book if you do not understand the terminology as it is used in the tradition. So, first develop your skills to make sure you have a good solid procedure in reasoning, and then you can use those skills to figure out what actually exists. Again, let your epistemology inform your ontology, not the other way around. Any other approach is not really sensible.

The Buddhist ontology presented here is reckoned from the point of view of the Collected Topics literature.* The study of the Collected Topics is the general introduction to valid cognition, meaning logic and epistemology, and also includes introductions to several other topics of philosophy such as basic ontology, cause and effect, generalities (or universals) and instances (or particulars), introductory consciousness studies, and Buddhist reasoning forms. Together these introduce students to the study of Buddhist and

(Berkeley: University of California Press, 1999), 71. Hopkins notes that, "Gung-tang's *Difficult Points* (29.1/13a.5) identifies this version of the stanza as being like that found in the translation of Kalkī Puṇḍarīka's *Great Commentary on the 'Kālachakra Tantra', the Stainless Light*." Ibid., 367n.

*See Perdue, *Debate in Tibetan Buddhism*, xiii–xxiii.

non-Buddhist systems of tenets in support of developing wisdom on the spiritual path.* As mentioned earlier, this Collected Topics ontology is based on the Buddhist philosophical system/tenet system known as the Sūtra School Following Reasoning (Sautrāntika). But rather than trying to learn much about the tenet systems here, gain a familiarity with this basic debate procedure first, and then look into those topics to the extent you wish.

In the Collected Topics tradition of Buddhist reasoning and debate, the usual way of explaining a topic includes presentation of the definitions, the divisions of the phenomenon, and illustrations (*mtshan gzhi*) or examples (*dpe*).† It is essential to put these in mind in order to be able to understand the few topics introduced here, practice the debates, and gain the skills. Think of this approach as looking for the essential characteristics of things. In fact, in Tibetan, the study of philosophy is known as *mtshan nyid,* meaning definitions, characteristics, or qualities. If you think that seems a quaint way of studying philosophy, think of the analysis of whether or not a tomato is a fruit, whether or not glass is liquid, and whether or not Pluto is a planet. Thinking about the divisions of things can be very elucidating. For instance, in thinking of the students in a university, it tells us a lot about the school when we consider the different ways that the students in that school may be divided. First we might divide the students into males and females. Then we might divide them into graduate students and undergraduates, in-state students and out-of-state students, US citizens and foreign visitors, and so on. We might divide them by majors, by ethnic groups, by sexual orientation, and so on. When we look at these many divisions, it certainly helps to build up an image of the school. This is true for all groups of phenomena. If you are trying to discern the essential characteristics of things, it is important to sort out what is included and what is excluded. Finally, the presentation of topics in the Collected Topics literature will always

---

*For a thoroughgoing explanation of the Jaina, Hindu, and Buddhist tenet systems, see Hopkins, *Maps of the Profound.*
†There is a technical difference between an illustration and an example. An illustration is spoken of mainly in reference to a basis (*gzhi*) or existent that illustrates a definition or the definiendum, the name imputed to that definition. See Perdue, *Debate in Tibetan Buddhism,* 68–72. An example is spoken of mainly in reference to a syllogism, for which an example is offered to give an easier approach to understanding the conclusion of the argument. See Rogers, *Tibetan Logic,* 103–7. An example may be anything existent or non-existent, whereas an illustration must be existent.

include examples or illustrations, that is, things that are that thing, as a spider is an arachnid.*

I have written this chapter according to an outline. Basically it tracks alongside the definitions, divisions, and illustrations/examples of the phenomena discussed. This style of presentation follows the Indian and Tibetan style, but it may seem obscure if you are not used to it. There is a scheme for formatting headings differently at different levels, but I know from experience that formatting different heading levels distinctively by itself is not usually enough to tip off the reader where we are. You would have to read as closely as a Talmudic scholar to sort out the different heading levels based simply on their appearance. And, if you cannot do that, it sometimes seems to the reader as if the text is jumping around and is disconnected. So, rather than trying to make all the heading levels different in appearance, I have taken two steps to make the organization more accessible. First in this chapter and the next, I have marked the headings with their levels (1–7) noted as "HL1," "HL2," and so on. Second, in each of these two chapters, I also present the outline the chapter follows, as an easy guide for the reader. Here's the outline for this chapter:

I. The Selfless [HL1]
   A. The Definition of the Selfless [HL2]
   B. The Divisions of the Selfless [HL2]
      1. Existents [HL3]
         a) The Definition of an Existent [HL4]
         b) The Phenomena Mutually Inclusive with Existents [HL4]
         c) Seven Divisions of Existents [HL4]
            (1) The Division of Existents into Impermanent Phenomena and Permanent Phenomena [HL5]
               (a) Impermanent Phenomena [HL6]
                  i) The Definition of an Impermanent Phenomenon [HL7]
                  ii) Examples of Impermanent Phenomena [HL7]
               (b) Permanent Phenomena [HL6]
                  i) The Definition of a Permanent Phenomenon [HL7]

---

*For more details on these areas of study, see chapter 20, "Definitions, Divisions, and Illustrations."

THE SELFLESS [HL1]

In every Buddhist tenet system, ultimate reality is described as selflessness or emptiness. By either name, this refers to an absence, a lack of a self or being empty of a self.

THE DEFINITION OF THE SELFLESS [HL2]

The definition of the selfless is

that which is without a self.

Exactly what is referred to as the "self" varies from system to system, but at the very least, all Buddhist tenet systems agree that everything, every object and every person, is free of being a permanent, unitary, and independent self. Beyond that, they also agree that not only every existent but also every non-existent too is free of being a permanent, unitary, and independent self. Thus, everything existent and non-existent alike is included in the selfless, and so it is the broadest category.

The Buddhist agreement that everything is selfless does not mean that I am not myself, that you are not yourself, and that a chair is not itself. Of course, I am myself, and you are yourself. Clearly, Buddhists should and do affirm self-identity. Also, the idea of selflessness is not meant to imply that there is nothing. Such a view falls to the extreme of non-existence. Very often people think that is what Buddhists are saying—that there is nothing at all. That's not it. Selflessness means that all that exists arises dependently. All phenomena, all existents, are dependent-arisings. If a thing is impermanent, it is easy to see that it arose in dependence on its causes and conditions. You have the body you have in dependence on your mother and father, all the food you ate, and so on. For permanent phenomena, which do not arise in dependence on causes and conditions as do our bodies, chairs, and so on, they too are not independent entities because they depend on their parts and on the consciousnesses that perceive them and impute them. "Impute" means to "attribute" or "ascribe," and in this case it means that the perceived phenomenon arises in dependence upon being imputed. Thus, simply, Buddhists are saying that everything that exists and that which does not exist too are empty of being independent, self-arisen entities.

Selflessness is such a point of importance for the Buddhists, at least as laid out in this system of debate, that they mark it as the most inclusive term, taking in everything. Clearly, they are making a point about the nature of things and the emphasis of the system. It would be like a Christian categorization of things, with the broadest term being "the God-created," for Christians assert that all that exists was created by God, and God too is God-created, for He is asserted to be self-arisen. God alone is said to have what the German philosopher Gottlieb von Leibniz called "aseity," or self-being.

THE DIVISIONS OF THE SELFLESS [HL2]

The selfless is divided into existents and non-existents. The traditional division is into established bases, which is mutually inclusive with existents, and non-existents; however, since we all understand "existents," though maybe not profoundly, it's easier just to use "existents" here.

You may wonder: if the selfless includes both existents and non-existents, is the whole category of the selfless itself existent or non-existent? It is one of the guidelines of Buddhist epistemology that a group that includes both existents and non-existents is itself considered to be existent. Thus, of course, the selfless is considered to be existent. If the selfless were non-existent and anything that is a self is unimaginable, that would imply that nothing at all exists. Then Buddhists would be radical nihilists. Thus, the selfless exists. In another way, following this guideline that a mixed group of existents and non-existents is itself existent: if a class contained only non-existents, it would perhaps be a null set; however, if this class has existent members, it would certainly not be a null set. If there are existent members, then these existents show the quality of being selfless and may be observed by a valid cognizer, an accurate consciousness certifying existence. In a similar way, a group that includes both permanent phenomena and impermanent phenomena is itself considered to be permanent. As the selfless includes all types of existents, it is considered to be permanent.

The selfless is 3P, without anything that is neither, with practically any existent for which there is something that is that existent,* from existent itself to a chair. Other than the existents of which being them is not possible, as mentioned below, with which it would compare as MX, the only other comparison with the selfless would be with those things it is MI with, such as its definition above and things like non-(non-selfless). Of course, it does

---

*Note that the description of "an existent for which there is something that is that existent" is different from an existent that exemplifies itself. As was mentioned in chapter 5, "Two Kinds of Statements," although all phenomena are identical with themselves, some phenomena do not exemplify themselves. The example there is that definition, for instance, is not a definition. Here, the restriction of "an existent for which there is something that is that existent" is meant to exclude the existents of which being them is not possible. The stock example of this is the two—a pillar and a pot. There is nothing that is both a pillar and a pot; therefore, in a comparison of the selfless and the two—a pillar and a pot—there is nothing you could put as both selfless and the two—a pillar and a pot. So the selfless and the two—a pillar and a pot—would be MX. This does not say that the two—a pillar and a pot—are not selfless, for they are—individually and as a pair, just that there is nothing that is the two—a pillar and a pot. However, the two, the selfless and definitions, would compare as 3P without something that is neither. Even though definition does not exemplify itself, there are things that are definitions. See Perdue, *Debate in Tibetan Buddhism,* 327–42.

not compare at all with non-existents because the process of comparison requires two existents.

EXISTENTS [HL3]

Recall that Buddhism describes itself as a middle way between the two extremes, the extreme of existence—the false belief that something exists when in fact it does not—and the extreme of non-existence—the false belief that something does not exist when in fact it does. If we avoid these two extremes, what is left over is the belief in what does in fact exist. Also, recall the commentary of Kensur Yeshi Thupten, who said that valid cognition—a true understanding of any existent—means the measure of what exists. So, according to the Buddhists, what does exist?

THE DEFINITION OF AN EXISTENT [HL4]

The definition of an existent is

that which is observed by a valid cognizer.

"A valid cognizer" is a certifying consciousness. Whatever it observes must exist. (This is in line with the principle that you cannot know that which does not exist.) This seems rather circular on the face of it. An existent is what is observed by a valid cognizer, and a valid cognizer observes existents. (In this system of thought, they hold that a valid cognizer cannot be wrong in regard to the object it understands.) Even though it does seem rather circular, it does not bother me as much as it used to. It seems that the point of it is to affirm the certainty of knowledge, as opposed to mere belief, and, in this meditative tradition, to affirm the priority of consciousness, rather than the outer world.

THE PHENOMENA MUTUALLY INCLUSIVE WITH EXISTENTS [HL4]

Initially, it is helpful to understand the eight names given to existents and the characteristics noted for each of these. There are other names too, but these are primary. As already mentioned, existents are also called established bases. The definition of an established base is that which is established by a valid cognizer.

This means that every existent is an established base, a *basis* the existence of which is certified by a valid cognizer. This is in line with the definition of an existent as *that which is observed by a valid cognizer.* Also, very closely in line with the characterizations of an existent and an established base is that everything existent is an object of comprehension, defined as

that which is realized by a valid cognizer.

Thus, in three ways, all existent things are characterized as those things that are established, observed, and realized by valid cognizers. That is, Buddhists are emphasizing the issue of what is a reliable consciousness and affirming that what those consciousnesses understand must be existent bases of reality. Along the same lines, everything that exists is an object, defined as

that which is known by an awareness.

Also, everything that exists is an object of knowledge, defined as

that which is suitable as an object of an awareness.

In this epistemology, awareness (*blo*) goes along with knower (*rig pa*) and consciousness (*shes pa*). If something is one of these, then it must also be the others as well. An awareness is not the same as a valid cognizer, which is a correct, certifying consciousness. Rather an awareness is any sort of consciousness, right or wrong, reliable or not. However, the bit in the definition of an object as "known by" an awareness limits the types of awarenesses that might know an existent to those that are correct and reliable. (Remember again that in this system, as in standard epistemology, you cannot know something that is not true, not real, not accurate, not existent.) Similarly, in the definition of object of knowledge, the bit that specifies that an object of knowledge is "suitable as an object" limits them to objects, which are already defined as things that are *known by an awareness;* thus they must be existent for the same reason.

Next, Buddhists say that everything that exists is an object of comprehension of an omniscient consciousness, which is defined as an object realized by an omniscient consciousness.

Here the requirements are that an existent must be an object and must be realized. "Realized" means "realized by a valid cognizer," so that alone limits the objects of comprehension of an omniscient consciousness to actual existents. Anyway, it would be ridiculous to think that an omniscient consciousness would "know" something non-existent. Obviously, the more important point here is the assertion that there are omniscient consciousnesses. The Buddha is said to be omniscient or all-knowing. (A buddha is also said to be omnibenevolent or all-loving and sometimes said to be omnipresent or present everywhere; however, Buddhists do not assert that a buddha is omnipotent or all-powerful.) It is quite a claim that anyone could be omniscient, and all Buddhists think that the Buddha is omniscient. Moreover, the Tibetans generally agree that it is within the capacity of each and every one of us to become omniscient, as the Buddha did. What's more, they generally agree that in time we will all do so. Sometimes, when I can't figure something out, I think that in time I will know, but, from my present perspective, this is just an article of faith and may not turn out to be so. Just on its own though, the very idea that anyone who is a normal person trying to deal with life, as the Buddha was, could become omniscient is a startling assertion. But that is the system. In fact, that is the goal. Recall that Lati Rinpoche said, "There is no phenomenon that cannot be understood. There is no doctrine that, if studied well, cannot be learned, and there is no person who, if he or she studies well, cannot become wise."[1]

Next, every existent is a hidden phenomenon, which is defined as

an object realized in a hidden manner by a thought consciousness apprehending it.

The heart of this definition is that each and every existent is *realized in a hidden manner by a thought consciousness* apprehending it. It is an existent object, and, if it is understood by a thought consciousness, it must be understood in a hidden manner. The point here is about how thought works. That is, thought/conceptuality/a thinking consciousness/a conception of anything—here limited to the existent—understands that thing by a "hidden" technique, in a representative way by the appearance of an internal image of whatever you are understanding. According to the explanation of conceptuality in this system, when we think of things we know, we proceed by observing an internal mental image of that thing and that internal mental image *stands in place of* or *represents* what we are understanding. You can kind of catch yourself doing this when you think of something you learned very early on, like dog or cat or ice cream. Those internal images seem strong and vivid. Just two more points here: (a) Buddhists say that such an internal image is static and permanent, and (b) though they do affirm certain thoughts as valid and reliable, they find the avenue of reliance on internal images to be somewhat less preferred than the avenue of understanding an existent directly. There is more on this coming later. Just remember here that Buddhism is a meditative tradition, not just a system of reasoning and debate, so they emphasize the priority and superiority of direct perception over thought.

The eighth and last one here is that every existent is a phenomenon, defined as

that which holds its own entity.

This is entirely different from the other definitions, for it emphasizes the character of the thing itself, not the consciousness perceiving it. It affirms self-identity, that a thing is identical with itself, and in its own way, understood variously by different Buddhist tenet systems, it affirms the world.

These are eight characterizations of what exists. There are more, such as basis (*gzhi*) and common locus (*mtshan gzhi*), not explained here. There is a table in the appendix that gives all the definienda* and definitions together. Each of these eight compare to the selfless as 3P without something that is neither. They are all MI with each of the others—with both the definitions and the definienda. Within the restriction mentioned above that excludes objects of knowledge of which being them is not possible, they are 3P with any particular impermanent phenomenon. Practically anything may be provided as illustrations or examples here because anything, from a pot to a pillar to a post to a person, is an existent. Just use what is at hand, even your hand. These eight are 4P with many permanent phenomena, such as definition.

---

*"Definienda" is the plural of "definiendum" and refers to the things that are defined, the handy names for that which is observed by a valid cognizer, that which holds its own entity, and so on. Keep in mind that, whereas the Buddhist system is in accord with the regular system we know in holding that the definiendum is a name or a word, in this system the definition is not a string of words but the actual phenomena, such as these that are observed by a valid cognizer.

SEVEN DIVISIONS OF EXISTENTS [HL4]

Existents are divided into seven main pairs that together serve to illustrate the Buddhist understanding of phenomena. These are:

> impermanent phenomena and permanent phenomena
> functioning things and phenomena that are nonthings
> products and nonproduced phenomena
> composed phenomena and uncomposed phenomena
> ultimate truths and conventional truths
> specifically characterized phenomena and generally characterized phenomena
> hidden phenomena and manifest phenomena

THE DIVISION OF EXISTENTS INTO IMPERMANENT PHENOMENA AND PERMANENT PHENOMENA [HL5]

The most important division of existents is into impermanent phenomena (Skt. *anitya,* Tib. *mi rtag pa*) and permanent phenomena (Skt. *nitya,* Tib. *rtag pa*). (This is traditionally presented as a division of established bases into permanent phenomena and functioning things; however, here "impermanent phenomena" is paired with "permanent phenomena" because it is easier to grasp initially.) It is better to explain impermanent phenomena first because we are manifestly surrounded by them.

IMPERMANENT PHENOMENA [HL6]

In trying to understand the nature of existence, the sensible place to begin is with what is all around us and inside of us as well. The single most important clear insight we can develop from the study of Buddhist thought is a pervasive awareness of impermanence.

THE DEFINITION OF AN IMPERMANENT PHENOMENON [HL7]

An impermanent phenomenon is an existent, it is a phenomenon. It is impermanent because it is changing moment by moment. Thus, an impermanent phenomenon is defined as a momentary phenomenon.

This means that it exists for just a moment. The things around us—the book, your body, your room, and so on—appear to be stable and abiding. You know, you walk back into the room a few minutes later, wondering, "Where did I put my phone?" and then there it is. Of course, it appears to be the same phone you put down a few minutes ago, but, the way the Buddhists think of it, the phone in this moment is the result, the later effect of the same type, the descendent of the one you left in the room a few minutes ago. We all know that in time the paint fades in the sunlight, the spine of the book gets broken, and you get lines around your eyes and your hair grays, but we usually don't think too much about these things. Buddhists generally agree that every one of these things that are produced from causes and conditions—such as your body, your room, your phone, the book, and so on—arise, abide, disintegrate, and arise again, over and over, 360 times every moment. (According to one Buddhist tenet system, the rate is 60 times every moment, but the predominant opinion is 360 times every moment.) A "moment" is the time it takes for a person to blink or snap the fingers. Things like that are not stable. They last only for a moment, usually to be created again in the next moment. In any given moment, the thing before you serves as the cause of itself in the next moment.

The reality of impermanence is a constant and driving consideration at all levels of Buddhist practice. Buddhists speak of impermanence in two main ways: as coarse impermanence and as subtle impermanence. Coarse impermanence is easy to see, for example, when someone passes away or a building falls down or a chair breaks or a flower wilts and dies. Don't think of this in terms of ultimate analysis, "When is a chair a chair? When is a thing no longer a chair?" That's not it. When a chair breaks, you cannot sit in it any more. The fact of impermanence implies issues of ultimate existence, but that is not what is at stake here. It's just that things break, and that is obvious for all to see. That's coarse impermanence.

It is harder to see subtle impermanence, though it is said to be going on around us all the time. Subtle impermanence is that change in impermanent phenomena that most Buddhists say happens 360 times every moment. It is subtle in the sense of being other than gross and obvious, but it is also subtle in the sense of being strong, for it is unstoppable. Buddhists say that with a stable mind developed in meditation, we can observe subtle impermanence directly. Until then, we can easily envision it. The traditional Indian example for subtle impermanence is a line of candles that all seem to be lighted at the same time, though they are not. The example goes like this. Imagine a line of candles in front of you or all around you. Imagine that the first one on the left slowly flames up on its own without being lighted. Then the next one to the right slowly flames up, and the first one on the left begins to diminish proportionately. Then after the second candle reaches its peak flame for a moment, the third one—the second to the right of the first one—begins to flame up proportionately as the second one diminishes. Then the fourth one, then the fifth one, and so on, for the whole line, until it comes back around to the first one, which lights up again, stays a moment, and then diminishes away. Now, imagine that once you see the pattern, this magical flaming up and extinguishing away, the sequence starts moving faster and faster until eventually it seems that all the candles are always lighted. Given our tremendous experience in viewing videos, this is easy for us to see.

Sometimes on television, you see the following sort of thing. I'm not fully sure of the technical issues involved here, but you know how sometimes you will see a reporter on television walk into a room where people are looking at computers and the computers seem to be on the fritz because there is a slow wipe from top to bottom? It never seems to bother anybody in the room, and this is because they do not see it. I think it happens only when the monitor uses a cathode ray tube (CRT). (Soon no one will understand this example unless they are looking at old video because CRT monitors have been replaced by other types such as liquid crystal display [LCD] monitors.) The wipe on the screen shows because the monitor is refreshing at a slower rate than the video camera recording what we see, so it catches the "impermanence" that we would not see if we were in the room looking at the monitor.

However, you get it, the example is clear enough. The Buddhists are saying that all these impermanent, unstable things around us are arising and abiding only for a moment but that the "refresh rate" is so fast that we do not see it, at least not without a stable and insightful awareness developed in meditation. The Buddhist example pays homage to the Buddha's fire sermon in which he describes the world as being on fire. The fire is impermanence. The example clearly suggests that our perception of the world as stable is an illusion.

EXAMPLES OF IMPERMANENT PHENOMENA [HL7]

In traditional Buddhist debate, the stock example of an impermanent phenomenon is a pot (*bum pa*). However, it is clear from the use of the word in

Tibetan that what must be appearing to the mind of a Tibetan monk or nun in debate is something more like what we would call a metal vase, the sort of thing used in their initiation ceremonies. The word *bum pa* does apply to ordinary pots like the kind we cook with, but experience seems to show that the metal vase is more on point. Other frequently used stock examples of impermanent phenomena include sound, a pillar, and some categories themselves, especially functioning thing itself. Among Americans debating in English, we prefer examples such as a chair, a table, and a rock. Beyond these, there is no constraint. Practically anything can be appropriate, so long as it is a momentary phenomenon.

THE SUBJECT, A POT
Photograph by Jeremy T. Williams.

PERMANENT PHENOMENA [HL6]

Other than impermanent phenomena, the remaining existents are permanent phenomena. As explained below in the seventh and final division of existents, every existent is a hidden phenomenon, which means that each and every existent may be understood by a thought consciousness. Whereas any impermanent phenomenon like a chair or a table *might possibly* be understood by thought, every permanent phenomenon *can only* be understood by thought. That is, according to the assertions of this particular Buddhist tenet system, the Sūtra School Following Reasoning, permanent phenomena exist and may be known, but they cannot be approached explicitly by anything other than a conceptual consciousness. The thought or conceptual consciousness that knows a permanent phenomenon is itself impermanent—changing all the time, as you have observed—but the object observed by that thought is permanent.

Often people think that if permanent phenomena can be known only by a thought consciousness, then permanent phenomena do not really exist, that they are just imaginary. However, this is not what the Buddhists believe. In this system, they say that permanent phenomena are real and existent, but they are abstract and objects of conceptuality only. For instance, take the simple example of non-cow. "Non-cow" includes everything other than that which is cow. So, a horse is a non-cow, a chair is a non-cow, established base itself is a non-cow. Everything other than cow itself, where cow includes every individual cow as well as the plurality of cows understood as the abstract singular cow, is non-cow. In the Collected Topics system of Buddhist reasoning and debate, non-cow is a permanent phenomenon because it includes everything other than cow. Think about it, and you will see that this is a real abstraction, something you could get only intellectually, conceptually, by thinking about it. Clearly, it does not mean that each and every non-cow is a permanent phenomenon, for a chair is a non-cow, but it is an impermanent, breakable thing, whereas non-cow itself is permanent. So, non-cow is not an imaginary thing. It is easy to see that it is real, for you are surrounded by manifest examples of non-cow. Indeed, you can see a chair that is not a cow—observe it directly—but what they are saying in this system is that you cannot observe directly that chair's absence of being a cow. It is a quality of the chair you are sitting in that it is a non-cow, but it is a static, unchanging quality that was not built into the chair. Please reflect on this.

Recall from the comments above in regard to the selfless that one of the guidelines of Buddhist ontology is that a group that includes both permanent and impermanent phenomena is itself a permanent phenomenon. Non-cow is such a group. The reason such a group is considered to be permanent is because it is an intellectual abstraction, an object of thought only, though still existent. This guideline is reminiscent of the guideline that a group that includes both existents and non-existents is itself existent. (This too came up in regard to the selfless itself.) Like the selfless, non-cow too includes non-existents that are not cows. Still, non-cow is existent. These guidelines are reckoned in relation to the consciousnesses that can perceive the groups. Again, please reflect on it.

I am translating the Sanskrit *nitya* and the Tibetan *rtag pa* as "permanent phenomenon" (singular) and "permanent phenomena" (plural). These are the translations I used in *Debate in Tibetan Buddhism,* and these are the predominant and perhaps exclusive translations for these terms in South Asian epistemology. However, there is an important problem with "permanent" or, at least, there is an unusual understanding of what "permanent" means here. This unusual understanding must be WRIT LARGE and underscored so that the reader will *always bear this in mind.* Unless you have been schooled in Indian thought, you will naturally think that "permanent" means eternal. It might be that you allow for the possibility that some eternal phenomena were not brought into being at the dawn of time, or you might deny that and think that all eternal things not only have no end but also had no beginning. Either way, "eternal" would imply that there is no end to such a phenomenon. However, this is not the meaning of permanent phenomena, as spoken of in Indian philosophy. Here, permanent does not necessarily mean eternal.

THE DEFINITION OF A PERMANENT PHENOMENON [HL7]

Rather, a permanent phenomenon is defined as

a common locus of a phenomenon and the nonmomentary.

"A common locus" is an existent that is a basis or locus of two or more qualities, and everything that exists is a common locus. For instance, the United States of America is a common locus of a nation state and a member of the United Nations. You are a common locus of a human and a person. I am a common locus of a man and a human. On and on infinitely. At the very least, you can see that everything that exists is a common locus of an established base and that which is suitable as an object of an awareness. The definition of a permanent phenomenon specifies that it is a basis or locus of a phenomenon, meaning that it must be an existent and that it is something that is nonmomentary. Recall that impermanent phenomena are always momentary, for that is how they are defined. Permanent phenomena are existents that are not momentary. "Momentary" means that the thing is changing moment by moment. A permanent phenomenon never changes. Now, if it exists and it never changes, one might naturally think that it would be eternal. However, the thought in Buddhist ontology has it that a permanent phenomenon is unchanging for the duration of its existence, though it may not exist forever.

A DIVISION OF PERMANENT PHENOMENA [HL7]

Permanent phenomena may be divided into two types, those that are stable in time (*dus brtan pa'i rtag pa*) and those that exist for an occasion (*res 'ga' ba'i rtag pa*).[2] A permanent phenomenon that is stable in time or an abiding permanent phenomenon is one that is eternal. This includes such things as the selfless, established base, and so on. There can be no time when there is nothing that is selfless, for that would mean that there would have to be a self. Remember that utter non-existence too would be selfless. In the same way, there can be no time when there is no established base, for that would mean that nothing at all would exist.

A permanent phenomenon that exists for an occasion is one that is reckoned in relation to a non-eternal phenomenon. For instance, one of the stock examples of a permanent phenomenon is uncomposed space, which is identified as the absence of obstructive contact.[3] "Uncomposed space" is not the same as created space, like when you step back from someone who is standing too close or when a bottle maker provides a liter of space inside the bottle. Rather, uncomposed space is an abstract absence, a lack of obstructive contact. "Space is all pervading because there is an absence of obstructive contact everywhere, even where solid objects exist, for without an absence of obstructive contact an obstructive object could not be there in the first place."[4] So, uncomposed space itself is an abiding and stable permanent phenomenon; however, the uncomposed space reckoned in relation to a non-eternal phenomenon such as the inside of a bottle is a non-eternal, permanent phenomenon that exists for an occasion. For the duration of the life of the bottle, that uncomposed space within it is stable and unchanging. Once the bottle is destroyed, it is no longer suitable to speak of the space inside the bottle. We can remember it, and our recollection that the bottle had space inside of it is clear, but the bottle is no longer a bottle, and so the uncomposed space inside of it went out of existence when the bottle was destroyed.

Both of these types of permanent phenomena—abiding permanent phenomena and permanent phenomena that exist for an occasion—are stable and unchanging for the time that they exist, but only abiding permanent phenomena are eternal. Always bear this understanding in mind when thinking of permanence in this system: *permanence here does not necessarily mean eternal.*

EXAMPLES OF PERMANENT PHENOMENA [HL7]

In the traditional setting of philosophical debate among the Tibetan monks and nuns, the most popular example of a permanent phenomenon is uncomposed space. What has proven to be the most popular example of a perma-nent phenomenon in my classes is *nirvāṇa,* the state of liberation of one who has left the round of rebirth. Why is *nirvāṇa* considered to be a permanent phenomenon? If it is a permanent phenomenon and permanent phenomena do not arise from causes and conditions, then how could it be that the Bud-dhists make the claim that we can achieve *nirvāṇa* by making effort on the path? It is because *nirvāṇa* itself is not a consciousness but is a condition of a consciousness, the mind free of the causes of suffering—specifically the mental afflictions of desire, hatred, and ignorance that Buddhists say give rise to all suffering. *Nirvāṇa* is not the mind itself, which is an imper-manent phenomenon, but an absence of something in the mind that used to be there. "A nirvana is an analytical cessation that comes into existence upon the abandonment of the last affliction. It is not the act of cessation or the act of passing beyond sorrow but a phenomenon possessed in the con-tinuum of a yogi [that is, a meditator] that is the mere absence of the ceased afflictions."[5] *Nirvāṇa* is called an "analytical cessation" because it is a mere absence that comes into existence due to meditative analysis.*

This *nirvāṇa* is the true cessation that is the third of the four noble truths. The word "cessation," which is the time-honored translation for the third noble truth, is not a very frequent word in English. We see it only in the phrase "smoking cessation programs." It means stopping, ceasing, the state of cessation. *Nirvāṇa* is the state of cessation of the causes of suffering. Now, this is like the absence of elephants in a room, not like shuffling all the elephants out of a room. You know, you can observe directly a room without elephants; however, the absence of elephants in a room would be, to apply the above terminology, "a phenomenon possessed in the continuum of a room that is the mere absence of the exited elephants." That absence is not the act of clearing the room of elephants, which is the effect of the efforts of the elephant wranglers. Indeed, Buddhists claim that we can achieve *nirvāṇa* by making effort on the path, sort of like the efforts of the elephant wranglers, in that we can make efforts to overcome all our harmful emo-tions and attitudes that give rise to suffering. Then, when we have done it, the mind is free of the causes of suffering; thus, suffering will not arise again. *Nirvāṇa* in the mental continuum of one who has left the round of rebirth

---

*See Hopkins, *Meditation on Emptiness,* 217–19 for a description of analytical cessations and the other three types of permanent phenomena—uncomposed space, nonanalytical cessations, and suchness.

is a permanent phenomenon that exists for an occasion, from the time the meditator abandons the last mental affliction and after. It is a central belief of Buddhism that this state of abandonment will not degrade, and one will not be forced to return to suffering. Admittedly, for those of us who have not achieved *nirvāṇa,* this remains an article of faith, but one worthy of reflection.

Not every example of a permanent phenomenon is a mere absence or a negative, as space is a lack of obstructive contact and *nirvāṇa* is an absence of an affliction following a final abandonment. For instance, all of the names that go along with existent—established base, object of knowledge, and so on—as well as all the definitions that go along with them—that which is established by a valid cognizer, that which is suitable as an object of an awareness, and so on—are permanent phenomena. It is certainly not that each and every established base is permanent because, for instance, a chair is an established base but is not permanent. Rather, the reason established base itself is permanent is because of the guideline that a group including both permanent phenomena and impermanent phenomena is itself permanent. You can only understand established base in and of itself intellectually.

Every existent is either a permanent phenomenon or an impermanent phenomenon. Impermanent phenomena and permanent phenomena are MX, so no impermanent phenomenon is a permanent phenomenon and no permanent phenomenon is an impermanent phenomenon. Outside the circles of impermanent phenomena and permanent phenomena are only non-existents. Both of them compare to the selfless as 3P without anything that is neither. They both compare to existents and all of its companions as 3P. Any particular individual impermanent phenomenon such as a chair compares to impermanent phenomena as 3P. The same is true for any particular permanent phenomenon such as *nirvāṇa,* which compares to permanent phenomena as 3P. Since things such as definitions and definienda include both permanent and impermanent examples, they compare as 4P to impermanent phenomena and permanent phenomena.

The Division of Existents into Functioning Things and Phenomena That Are Nonthings [HL5]

The predominant way that impermanent phenomena are referred to in Collected Topics debate is as "functioning things," and functioning things are usually paired with permanent phenomena in the division of established bases into two. Here I have paired functioning things with phenomena that are nonthings and permanent phenomena with impermanent phenomena.

FUNCTIONING THINGS [HL6]

Functioning things are mutually inclusive with impermanent phenomena. Functioning things and impermanent phenomena are just different names for the same things. Each and every impermanent phenomenon is also a functioning thing.

THE DEFINITION OF A FUNCTIONING THING [HL7]

The Sanskrit *bhāva* and the Tibetan *dngos po,* translated here as "functioning thing," do not actually indicate anything about impermanent phenomena as *functioning.* However, a functioning thing or simply a thing is defined as

> that which is able to perform a function (*don byed nus pa*).

Thus, we are reading from the definition back into the name and calling them "functioning things." The Sanskrit and Tibetan terms more literally mean something like "actuality" or even "real things." In American English, we normally call the things in the world "tangible objects," meaning that they are real things at hand—palpable, real things. However, tangible objects are just one of the types of functioning things—along with visible objects, sounds, odors, and so on, as well as things such as consciousnesses and time. Thus, "tangible object" would not work as a translation term here. In this Buddhist tenet system, functioning things/impermanent phenomena/products are also "ultimate truths." They are raised up in some way that permanent phenomena are not, so it is okay to think of these things all around as "real things."

In any case, by any name, all impermanent phenomena are functioning things. The main function of a functioning thing is to reproduce itself in the next moment. If impermanent phenomena are arising, abiding, and disintegrating moment by moment, then the next moment of any impermanent phenomenon depends on the former moment of that thing. A lot of things we have are not very practical, but they perform this function up until the last moment. So these are not "functional things" in the way that a well-maintained, fueled-up plane sitting quietly on a runway is a functional aircraft, even though it is not a functioning aircraft in the sense of logging hours in flight. As an impermanent phenomenon, every part of that plane is functioning to produce the functional plane of the next moment.

THE DIVISION OF FUNCTIONING THINGS INTO THREE [HL7]

The most important division of impermanent phenomena is a division of functioning things into three—matter, consciousnesses, and nonassociated compositional factors. It is essential to take a close look at the many parts of that division—the three main parts and the many subdivisions, so that division will be the topic of the next chapter, chapter 10, "Basic Buddhist Ontology 2: The Division of Functioning Things into Three."

PHENOMENA THAT ARE NONTHINGS [HL6]

Since all impermanent phenomena are functioning things, every permanent phenomenon is a phenomenon that is a nonthing or a phenomenon that is a non-(functioning thing), defined as

a phenomenon that is empty of the ability to perform a function.

Permanent phenomena are stable and inactive. They don't do anything. If an existent performs a function, it is changing. The idea is that a chair, for instance, performs the function of creating itself in the next moment, and then in the next moment, it performs a different function and creates itself in the moment after that. It has changed from a chair that creates a chair in moment n to a chair that creates a chair in moment $n + 1$. Permanent phenomena don't do that. They just sit there.

Every existent is either a functioning thing or a phenomenon that is a nonthing. Each of these compare to the selfless as 3P without anything that is neither, and each compares to existents and its companions as 3P. They are MX with each other. Any particular functioning thing like a chair compares to functioning things as 3P, and any particular phenomenon that is a nonthing like uncomposed space compares to phenomena that are nonthings as 3P. As before with permanent and impermanent phenomena, they are both 4P with definition and many other things.

The Division of Existents into Products and Nonproduced Phenomena [hl5]

Impermanent phenomena are products because they are produced from causes and conditions. A product is defined as

a created phenomenon,

which means that it is created from causes and conditions. It is obvious that the things we think of as products in our commercial world—things such as cereal, soap, silk, and cigarettes—are produced from causes and conditions. Someone has to grow the tobacco and make the paper and put them together to create a cigarette. It is equally true of things that we do not normally call products, like rocks and clouds, that they arise in dependence on causes and conditions. It should also be completely obvious that they cannot last forever. After billions of years, even great galaxies come to an end. Forget about that, they don't even last for a second moment. Linked with monetary value or not, everything we see, hear, smell, taste, or touch is a product.

All impermanent phenomena are also causes and effects. We normally think that whatever is a cause is necessarily not an effect and whatever is an effect is necessarily not a cause. This is true in relation to a particular thing in a particular moment. Your phone of this moment is the effect of your phone in the last moment, and your phone of this moment is the cause of your phone in the next moment; thus, in relation to your phone of this moment, its cause and its effect cannot be the same thing. However, in general—not in relation to any particular thing in a particular moment—all causes are also all effects. A cause is defined as

a producer.

An effect is defined as

an object produced.

Only impermanent phenomena are causes and effects. Every impermanent phenomenon is the effect of its causes of the preceding moment, and every impermanent phenomenon is the cause of what it produces. Of course, since things wear out and show coarse impermanence, the continuum of an impermanent thing might end, like when a pot is broken or a fire is extinguished. So what is produced by the pot, for instance, in its last moment are, for instance, the shards of clay.

Mirroring the assertion that every impermanent phenomenon is a product, every permanent phenomenon is a nonproduced phenomenon, which is defined as

a noncreated phenomenon.

Saying that a permanent phenomenon is "noncreated" is not meant to imply that it is a non-existent. Rather, it implies that permanent phenomena are not created by causes and conditions. In fact, the qualification "phenomenon" is added to "noncreated" in order to exclude non-existents. Any non-existent would have to be noncreated because it never came into existence in any way. Since it does not exist, it would not disintegrate as an impermanent phenomenon would. However, a non-existent is not a nondisintegrating *phenomenon* or a noncreated *phenomenon* because it is not a phenomenon of any sort, for it does not exist.

Since product is MI with impermanent phenomena and functioning things and nonproduced phenomenon is MI with permanent phenomena, they compare to the other phenomena in the same way as do impermanent phenomena and permanent phenomena, as described above.

The Division of Existents into Composed Phenomena and Uncomposed Phenomena [HL5]

Impermanent phenomena are composed phenomena. They are put together or aggregated. A composed phenomenon is defined as

a disintegrating phenomenon

because the essential characteristic of what is composed, caused, put together, or aggregated is that it disintegrates and falls apart. Paralleling that, every permanent phenomenon is an uncomposed phenomenon or an uncaused phenomenon, defined as

a nondisintegrating phenomenon.

As before, since composed phenomena are MI with impermanent phenomena and uncomposed phenomena are MI with permanent phenomena, they compare to the other phenomena in the same way as described above.

THE DIVISION OF EXISTENTS INTO ULTIMATE TRUTHS AND CONVENTIONAL TRUTHS [HL5]

Every one of the Buddhist tenet systems explains a division of existents into the two truths, ultimate truths and conventional truths.* However, only the Sūtra School Following Reasoning, which is the point of view of the Collected Topics system of Buddhist reasoning and debate, equates ultimate truths with impermanent phenomena. In this system, an ultimate truth is defined as

a phenomenon that is ultimately able to perform a function.

This definition is not intended to point out anything special about the function performed. A function performed by an ultimate truth is just the same function performed by any impermanent phenomenon. Rather, the definition is pointing at the type of consciousness that is able to perceive impermanent phenomena. Impermanent phenomena are "truths" because they are existents. They are "ultimate" because they are objects of awareness for an ultimate consciousness, a final, unflawed, defensible, and reliable consciousness—a direct perceiver. In fact, this is the way the division of existents into the two truths tracks in each of the tenet systems—in terms of the consciousnesses that are able to perceive the objects. Conventional truths are perceived by conventional consciousnesses, and ultimate truths are perceived by ultimate consciousnesses. What varies from system to system is what is identified as an ultimate consciousness and what is identified as a conventional consciousness. In each of the systems, an ultimate consciousness perceives an object just as it exists. In the system that is the point of view used in the introductory topics here, an ordinary direct perceiver like an eye consciousness seeing blue as blue is a consciousness free from conceptuality and is not mistaken with respect to what appears to it.

---

*For an excellent treatment of this important topic, see Guy Newland, *The Two Truths in the Mādhyamika Philosophy of the Ge-luk-ba Order of Tibetan Buddhism*, Studies in Indo-Tibetan Buddhism (Ithaca, N.Y.: Snow Lion Publications, 1992).

And the proponents of the Sūtra School Following Reasoning say that what appears to a direct perceiver is always an impermanent phenomenon. There is more on consciousnesses in chapter 12, "Consciousnesses in relation to What They Perceive," but understand right here that direct perceivers are not necessarily any big deal. There are descriptions of extraordinary direct perceivers that are the fruit of meditation, but direct perception can also be completely pedestrian. It includes any ordinary correct perception such as correctly perceiving the smell of coffee as coffee or seeing a patch of blue as blue. (This does not mean thinking something like, "I smell coffee" or "The sky is a pretty blue today," for those would be conceptual consciousnesses, not direct perceivers. This means just smelling coffee as the odor of coffee and seeing blue as blue.) We have direct perception very frequently throughout the day, and here that sort of consciousness is referred to as the most reliable one.

Another way of expressing impermanent phenomena is to call them "existent phenomena that may be known explicitly by direct perception" or "existent phenomena that appear to direct perception." This is why the proponents of the Sūtra School Following Reasoning call impermanent phenomena "ultimate truths." They appear to a direct perceiver *just as they exist,* together with all of their individual characteristics and their subtle impermanence.

A permanent phenomenon is a conventional truth, defined as

a phenomenon that is ultimately unable to perform a function.

Conventional truths are not able to perform any function because they are permanent and static. Since in the system of the Sūtra School Following Reasoning, ultimate truths are equated with impermanent phenomena, conventional truths are equated with permanent phenomena. The very reason that they are called "ultimate truths" and "conventional truths" is because of the consciousnesses that are able to perceive the two truths. We may understand any existent by a thought consciousness, a conceptual knower, but conventional truths *can only* be understood by a conceptual consciousness, and ultimate truths *may* be understood explicitly by a direct perceiver. Ultimate truths are truths for an ultimate consciousness, and conventional truths are truths for a conventional mind or an obscured mind. The main problem identified here for conceptual consciousnesses is *not* that they are unreliable, for it may be that you do indeed perceive something clearly and correctly by a conventional, conceptual consciousness. The problem is that a conceptual consciousness does not perceive its object *directly* but understands it through a representative internal image. Thus, it does not see the thing as it is. The division of existents into the two truths shows the priority given to direct perception.

Again, since ultimate truths, impermanent phenomena, and functioning things are MI and conventional truths and permanent phenomena are MI, they compare to the other phenomena in the same way as described above.

The Division of Existents into Specifically Characterized Phenomena and Generally Characterized Phenomena [HL5]

All impermanent phenomena are specifically characterized phenomena, and all permanent phenomena are generally characterized phenomena. Again, this division and these names showcase something about the types of consciousnesses that are able to perceive these phenomena, and in turn they tell us the extent to which we can know these two types of existents. A specifically characterized phenomenon is defined as

> a phenomenon that is established by way of its own character without being merely imputed by a term or a thought consciousness.

This means that in this system impermanent phenomena are asserted to be truly established phenomena. They exist from their own side without dependence on us to give them a name or think about them. When you turn your back, they are still there. Remember that in this particular Buddhist tenet system, the Sūtra School Following Reasoning, they assert truly existent external phenomena. This does not mean that they deny that impermanent phenomena are dependent-arisings. Clearly they are dependent-arisings because they arise in dependence on causes and conditions. However, they don't exist as mere bases of names or only as objects of thought. This is certainly the way ordinary things appear to be. I mean, when you look at your car or your phone or your beloved, they seem to exist from their own side whether or not you designate them with a name or impute them by thought. See? There is your car just sitting there waiting. Impermanent phenomena are called "specifically characterized" because only impermanent phenomena appear together with all of their own individual and specific characteristics. We are not limited to seeing impermanent phenomena in a vague and general way. We can see them directly, very clearly and very specifically. If you just think "pen," you get an image of a pen. However, if you look at a pen in your hand, it appears completely and nakedly just as it exists. You can see every little detail—the plastic was scratched a little there, there's just a little ink left, it is red ink, it was made by Omnicorp, and so on. Of course, that's very interesting if you ever need to identify your pen specifically, but the most important aspect of this full, naked appearance is that the pen—and every other impermanent phenomenon—shows its subtle impermanence. Remember the line of candles. This is the fullness of its nature, and only a direct perceiver can perceive that full nature. This is not the case for permanent phenomena, which must be known in a vague and general way by a thought consciousness or designated in a general way by a term.

Keep in mind that, however permanent phenomena come to be, they do not arise from causes and conditions, even when they are reckoned in relation to an impermanent basis that did arise from causes and conditions. The names of the permanent phenomena that exist for an occasion and the qualities attributed to them go along with the names and qualities noted for their impermanent bases. For instance, the uncomposed space inside a plastic bottle is designated or named in relation to the impermanent bottle, and that space is known by a thought in relation to that bottle.

As opposed to impermanent, *specifically* characterized phenomena, all permanent phenomena are *generally* characterized phenomena. A generally characterized phenomenon is defined as

> a phenomenon that is merely imputed by a term or thought consciousness and is not established as a specifically characterized phenomenon.

Generally characterized phenomena are not established by way of their own character but must be imputed by a thought consciousness or by a term such as "non-cow." Therefore, they are mere imputations. This does not mean that they do not exist but that they are not established from their own side.

Once again, whereas an impermanent phenomenon such as a chair or a table *might possibly* be understood by thought, every permanent phenomenon *can only* be understood by thought. It is essential to understand this point in the epistemology of this system, for it is such a prominent player in all that is going on. This system's description of impermanent things and permanent phenomena and the consciousnesses that have access to these existents may or may not be accurate, but the descriptions presented here as well as in the other recommended sources are accurate representations of the system.

According to this system that serves as the basis for the introduction to Buddhist reasoning and debate, we are able to apprehend an impermanent object directly and nakedly, to see it in all of its individual and specific characteristics, with direct perception. However, we do not have this sort of access to permanent phenomena, for we can understand them only conceptually, that is, by thought or through reference to them by a term. We can understand them, but we cannot observe them directly. For the Buddhists at all levels, this presents something of a problem because thought and, of course, terminology—names for things—as well are always representational rather than authentic. The sound "chair" is nothing you can sit in. The problem with a representational understanding is that what you are observing (an internal image) and what you are understanding are not the same, even if you are thinking about an internal image. Thus, what the proponents of the Sūtra School Following Reasoning are saying is that when we understand an object by thought, be it permanent or impermanent, we understand it in a general way because we don't "see" the thing directly; we see a representation of the thing. Conceptuality—our thoughts—may be right or wrong, but they are always obscured from seeing their objects of understanding directly. More on this later.*

Again, specifically characterized phenomena are MI with impermanent phenomena, and generally characterized phenomena are MI with permanent phenomena. Thus, they compare to the other phenomena in the same way as described above.

THE DIVISION OF EXISTENTS INTO HIDDEN PHENOMENA AND MANIFEST PHENOMENA [HL5]

The division of existents into hidden phenomena and manifest phenomena is a very unusual sort of division, for all manifest phenomena are also

---

*For more on the topic of specifically characterized phenomena and generally characterized phenomena, see Anne Carolyn Klein, *Knowing, Naming and Negation: A Sourcebook on Tibetan Sautrāntika* (Ithaca, N.Y.: Snow Lion Publications, 1991) and Perdue, *Debate in Tibetan Buddhism*, 284–317.

hidden phenomena. As you may recall from above, all existents are hidden phenomena, but manifest phenomena are equated with impermanent phenomena; thus, all manifest phenomena are hidden phenomena, but not all hidden phenomena are manifest phenomena. A hidden phenomenon is defined as

> an object realized in a hidden manner by a thought consciousness apprehending it.

The point of this is that any existent—permanent or impermanent—that is understood by a thought consciousness has to be understood in a "hidden manner," in a representational way by means of the appearance of an internal image. A manifest phenomenon is defined as

> an object explicitly realized by a direct valid cognizer.

The definition specifies that a manifest phenomenon is one *explicitly realized* by a direct perceiver. This is opposed to an object *implicitly realized* by a direct perceiver. This distinction arises from the assertion that "whatever is known by a consciousness does not necessarily have to appear to it."[6] For instance, a mental direct perceiver developed through concentration and meditative insight may know the selflessness of the person. However, that selflessness does not appear explicitly to the directly perceiving consciousness. Rather, that direct perceiver explicitly observes the mind and body as empty of a self of persons and implicitly knows selflessness. Remember that this system says, though not all Buddhist tenet systems agree, that only impermanent phenomena may appear to a direct perceiver and permanent phenomena do not. Thus, the definition of a manifest phenomenon specifies that it is an object *explicitly realized* by a direct perceiver. Yet, a manifest phenomenon is a hidden phenomenon as well because, when it is understood by a thought consciousness, it is understood in a hidden manner.

This odd division is once again showcasing the consciousnesses that perceive objects. Anything and everything that exists may be known in a hidden manner by a thought consciousness or be designated by a term. Only manifest phenomena may be known explicitly by a direct perceiver. Saying that a manifest phenomenon *may be known explicitly* by a direct perceiver only allows for the possibility that it might be known by a direct perceiver, for it might be known by a thought as well. You can go into your room and look at your bed, feel it, and so on, or you can just think about it and know it in a general, representative way.

Hidden phenomena and manifest phenomena compare as 3P including something that is neither. Both hidden phenomena and manifest phenomena compare to the selfless as 3P without anything that is neither. Hidden phenomena are MI with existents and all of its companions. Manifest phenomena are MI with impermanent phenomena and all its companions. Any particular impermanent phenomenon like a rock is 3P with both. Any particular permanent phenomenon like *nirvāṇa* is 3P with hidden phenomena and MX with manifest phenomena. Both are 4P with definition and so on.

Non-existents [HL3]

Recall that the selfless encompasses both existents and non-existents. Thus, the Buddhists are making the point that everything we can imagine, whether real in any sense or not at all real, is free of a self. It may seem trivial to note that non-existents are free of a self, but it better disposes of the question to note that a permanent, unitary, independent self is not to be found anywhere.

A Proposed Definition of the Non-existent [HL4]

There is no definition of a non-existent because a non-existent does not exist and has no qualities to be characterized. Definitions and definienda are established on the bases of their illustrations, which must be existent; therefore, there can be no definition of the non-existent.* Even so, some say that the definition of a non-existent is

that which is not observed by valid cognition.

According to Denma Lochö Rinpoche, this proposed definition incurs the fallacy of nonoccurrence. A non-existent is not an existent and is not experienced as an existent; thus, it does not occur.[7] A non-existent would have to be established—meaning established by a valid cognizer—with its illustrations, those things that illustrate the quality of a non-existent. However,

---

*For a bit more on the problem with any proposed definition of a non-existent, the fallacy of nonoccurrence, see Perdue, *Debate in Tibetan Buddhism,* 72.

we cannot observe by any reliable consciousness that, for instance, a square circle or any other non-existent has the quality of a non-existent, so there is nothing to illustrate a non-existent and so there is no definition of a non-existent. Also, I know of no division of non-existents, and somehow I doubt there could be one.

EXAMPLES OF NON-EXISTENTS [HL4]

Even though there are no illustrations—which would have to be existent—of a non-existent, there are plenty of things we can say are non-existent, like a square circle, the currently ruling king of France,* and so on, but they do not have the *quality* of being non-existents. They don't have any qualities at all. In American culture, I think the go-to example of a non-existent would be a unicorn. The stock example of a non-existent in Buddhist reasoning and debate is the horn of a rabbit. I know you may have seen those jackalopes in truck stops in Wyoming, but those things aren't real. Rabbits don't have horns, and there is no horn of a rabbit. Other stock examples are the fruit of a dead tree or the child of a barren woman. We can update this last example to the child, son, or daughter of a childless couple. You can make up these nonthings endlessly, but you can't produce a single one.

If some things existed in the past but no longer exist, like presumably dinosaurs, they too would not work as examples of a non-existents, but would be considered to be permanent phenomena, objects observed by thought or conceptuality alone. According to the *Go-mang Collected Topics,* the past of a phenomenon is a nonaffirming negative and a permanent phenomenon.[8] Of course, we can see real dinosaur bones, but dinosaur bones are not dinosaurs any more than your hand is you. If you wonder, look into dependent-arising. If something does not exist now but might in the future, like a poverty-free world, that too would not be a good example of a non-existent. Rather, according to the *Go-mang Collected Topics,* a future phenomenon is a permanent phenomenon, observed by thought or conceptuality alone. If a poverty-free world never comes to be, a safe bet for a future phenomenon might be the next moment of your own consciousness, which you can think about but is not a presently existing, directly observable thing.

---

*This is a popular example among old school British philosophers who take some pride in noting that at least they did not execute their royals.

EXAMPLES OF THE SELFLESS [HL2]

The presentation of examples of the selfless finishes out the consideration of the selfless, which in traditional style is done in terms of definition, divisions, and illustrations. Examples of the selfless would include anything existent as well as anything non-existent, except the selfless itself and all the things MI with it. The selfless is existent and permanent and, of course, selfless. However, the selfless is neither an illustration nor an example of the selfless because what is put forth as either of these should be easier to understand than that which it is meant to illustrate or to exemplify, but of course the selfless is not easier to understand than the selfless.

EXERCISE 9.1

1. Memorize the definition of the selfless: *that which is without a self.*
2. Go to the "Table of Definitions" in the appendix, pick out and memorize three or four pairs of definitions and definienda of existent and its companions—object of knowledge and so on. It will be easier to remember them if you review the descriptions of the definitions in the text above. Also, put in mind some illustrations of existents that you can use in debate.
3. Using the same sources, pick out and memorize three or four pairs of definitions and definienda of impermanent phenomenon and its companions. Also put in mind some illustrations.
4. Do the same with three or four pairs of definitions and definienda of permanent phenomenon and its companions. Also put in mind some illustrations of permanent phenomena.

Just familiarize yourself with the pieces on this chessboard and learn how they move so you can understand the lessons in this book and gain the skills. You will then be able to understand English-language debate videos and check for the mistakes.

10. Basic Buddhist Ontology 2
The Division of Functioning Things into Three

———

T HE BUDDHISTS categorize meditation into just two types: (1) meditative stabilization (Skt. *samādhi*), which is meditation for the sake of
developing concentration and (2) analytical meditation. The broad category
of analytical meditation has two sides, analysis of the nature of phenomena and cultivation of attitudes such as love and compassion. The analysis
of the nature of phenomena is known as special insight (Skt. *vipashyanā*).
Concentration or meditative stabilization is essential for developing special
insight, but in the Buddhist way of thinking, ultimately it is special insight
that liberates a person from the round of rebirth.

Among the differing faces of Buddhism that have taken root in America
is a set of practices known as "vipassana." *Vipassana* is word of the Pāli language, the language of the Buddhist texts of the Theravāda tradition, which
some call "Southern Buddhism," practiced in such countries as Burma, Sri
Lanka, Cambodia, Laos, and Thailand. Pāli is a degenerate form of Sanskrit, a Sanskritic or Prakrit. It is not a language for degenerates but a degen-
erated language, as Italian is a degenerate form of Latin. As languages age,
they get simplified and sort of rounded off. In English, for instance, the
old subjunctive case remains only in certain phrases. We say, "I wish I were
wealthy" rather than, "I wish I was wealthy." Looking at your King James
translation of the Bible, note that we have almost completely lost the second
person familiar pronoun "thou."

So, Pāli is a degenerate form of the more ancient Sanskrit. The Pāli word
vipassana is a simplification of the Sanskrit *vipashyanā*. In both words, the
starting syllable *vi* is what is known as an intensifier, like "super" in "super-
weird." The *passana* or *pashyanā* means "seeing," so vipassana (which is an
English word now) is "superseeing" or "special seeing." Vipassana meditation begins with paying attention to your breath, paying attention to your

movements, paying attention to every step and thought. It proceeds to mindfulness. There has been some good success in using vipassana meditation in prisons in the United States because it helps a person develop better impulse control. The meditator becomes more circumspect and mindful. In my own limited experience, I thought vipassana meditation helped me to distinguish between the consciousness and the object observed.

The point here is that Buddhist reasoning and debate also functions as a sort of basic vipassana, at least in the Ge-luk-ba order of Tibetan Buddhism, the order that is the source for this explanation of Buddhist epistemology. Of course, the main activities of monks and nuns of all orders are prayers, ritual, and meditation, but beyond these activities, the Ge-luk-ba order is famous for its focus on, and skill in, reasoning and debate. Practicing a tradition of wisdom-development that dates back to the time of the Vedas, a time before the Buddha himself, they emphasize the necessity for mindful observation of appearances and reliance upon one's own development of wisdom, in conjunction with reliance on devotion. Their study of basic ontology is their way of getting students to pay attention, to become mindful, and to deconstruct appearances. In fact, if you look at vipassana philosophy in such sources as Buddhaghosa and Mahasi Sayadaw,* you will see that it correlates quite well with the material presented in this Collected Topics tradition of Buddhist reasoning and debate. So, this material is an introduction to the development of insight.

The analysis of functioning things provides guidance to impermanent phenomena. The rest of the game is completely internal, what we think about. In that regard, the challenge becomes sorting out what is a thought about an existent and what is a thought about a non-existent. Here too the clear observation and analysis of ordinary sense perception provides some guidance, for sometimes what appears to the senses is not really there. For instance, for me the odor of fresh-cut grass smells like watermelon. It happens every time. The stock example of a sense misperception in Indian thought is seeing white snow as blue. We all know that in certain lighting conditions, white snow will appear as blue and that this is due to the interplay of light and water molecules. It is not due to pigmentation or anything

---

*See, for instance, Bhadantācariya Buddhaghosa, *The Path of Purification (Visuddhimagga)*, trans. Bhikkhu Ñyāṇamoli (Berkeley: Shambhala Publications, 1976) and The Venerable Mahasi Sayadaw, *The Progress of Insight through the Stages of Purification*, trans. Nyānaponika Thera (Kandy, Sri Lanka: Buddhist Publication Society, 1978).

like that. The snow remains white but because of the structure of its water molecules, it looks blue, like the water of blue seas, which is pretty much clear, handful by handful. Indeed, if you take a photograph of snow when it appears blue to the eye, it will appear blue in the photograph for the same reasons that it appears blue to the eye. But, when you go up into the mountains to get a closer look at this exotic blue snow, you cannot find it. If you do not like this example of a sense misperception, perhaps you have one of your own, such as smelling fresh-cut grass as watermelon. These things happen all the time. It is just important to notice that they do. For instance, if you just move your lower eyelid a little, you can make it appear as if there are two of the single thing that is before you, like a light, not just one.

Thus, Buddhists use basic Buddhist ontology as their introduction to vipassana or special insight training. Do not think that the place of reasoning and debate in Buddhism is merely for intellectual elaboration. The whole system is geared toward developing special insight for the sake of liberating beings from suffering.

Of course, philosophical analysis in debate in support of developing special insight is not employed just to become more mindful about impermanent phenomena/functioning things, but it also applies equally to all phenomena, including the permanent objects of our thoughts. What's more, when we are thinking of a non-existent, like a permanent, unitary, independent self, it is also part of the practice of vipassana to notice that. Still, the place to begin is with functioning things, for we are drawn to functioning things—external and internal—like a moth to a lit candle.

FUNCTIONING THINGS [HL1]

Recall that the predominant way of referring to impermanent phenomena in this tradition is as "functioning things" (Skt. *bhāva,* Tib. *dngos po*),* and a functioning thing is defined as

> that which is able to perform a function.

Remember that the main function of a functioning thing is to reproduce itself in the next moment, or at least to reproduce what remains of it. The list

---

*This description of functioning things is made from the point of view of the Followers of Reasoning in the Sūtra School.

below provides the basic divisions of functioning things* and also serves as the outline for this chapter, including the heading levels [HL1], [HL2], and so on, as was done in the last chapter. Without exception, every impermanent phenomenon is included into one or the other of these categories, and each of the three divisions is mutually exclusive with the other two.

The Divisions of Functioning Things

I. Functioning Things (Skt. *bhāva*, Tib. *dngos po*) [HL1]
  A. Matter (Skt. *kanthā*, Tib. *bem po*) [HL2]
    1. External Matter (Skt. *bahirdhā-kanthā*, Tib. *phyi'i bem po*) [HL3]
      a) Visible Forms (Skt. *rūpa*, Tib. *gzugs*) [HL4]
      b) Sounds (Skt. *śhabda*, Tib. *sgra*) [HL4]
      c) Odors (Skt. *gandha*, Tib. *dri*) [HL4]
      d) Tastes (Skt. *rasa*, Tib. *ro*) [HL4]
      e) Tangible Objects (Skt. *spraṣṭavya*, Tib. *reg bya*) [HL4]
    2. Internal Matter (Skt. *ādhyātmika-kanthā*, Tib. *nang gi bem po*) [HL3]
  B. Consciousnesses (Skt. *jñāna*, Tib. *shes pa*) [HL2]
    1. Mental Consciousnesses (Skt. *mano-jñāna*, Tib. *yid shes*) [HL3]
    2. Sense Consciousnesses (Skt. *indriya-jñāna*, Tib. *dbang shes*) [HL3]
  C. Nonassociated Compositional Factors (Skt. *viprayukta-saṃskāra*, Tib. *ldan min 'du byed*) [HL2]
    1. Nonassociated Compositional Factors That Are Persons (Skt. *pudgala-viprayukta-saṃskāra*, Tib. *gang zag yin par gyur pa'i ldan min 'du byed*) [HL3]
      a) Common Beings (Skt. *pṛthak-jana*, Tib. *so so'i skye bo*) [HL4]
      b) Superiors (Skt. *ārya*, Tib. *'phags pa*) [HL4]
    2. Nonassociated Compositional Factors That Are Not Persons (Skt. *apudgala-viprayukta-saṃskāra*, Tib. *gang zag ma yin par gyur pa'i ldan min 'du byed*) [HL3]

---

*For a fuller explanation of the divisions of functioning things, see Perdue, *Debate in Tibetan Buddhism,* 187–221 and 354–76.

MATTER [HL2]

Matter and form are mutually inclusive. They are different names for the same things, and whatever is one is also the other. Matter is defined as

that which is atomically established.

Indeed, even in ancient India they had an idea of atoms, minute particles that form the basis for all matter. Form is defined as

that which is suitable as form.

The definition is just a gesture toward all this form lying around everywhere.

Matter and form are impermanent, disintegrating phenomena, produced in dependence on causes and conditions. Matter or form is divided into the two, external matter and internal matter.

EXTERNAL MATTER [HL3]

External matter is defined as

that which is atomically established and is not included within the continuum of a person.

The part about being "atomically established" limits external matter to matter. The part about "not being included within the continuum of a person" means that external matter is not appropriated as the body of a person. Examples are the sun and the moon, which presumably are not sentient.

External matter is of five types: visible forms, sounds, odors, tastes, and tangible objects. These forms serve as fields of activity of the five sense consciousnesses—eye, ear, nose, tongue, and body consciousnesses, and they occupy us endlessly. They are known as *objects* or *sources* because they are the objects of sense consciousnesses and the external sources of sense perceptions.

VISIBLE FORMS [HL4]

A form-source or a visible form is defined as

an object apprehended by an eye consciousness.

Form-sources or visible objects are of just two types—colors and shapes.*
The definition of a color is

that which is suitable as a hue.

This definition too is just a gesture toward the many colors around us. The
definition of color serves as the universal template for defining all types
of color, so the definition of yellow is *that which is suitable as a yellow hue,*
the definition of red is *that which is suitable as a red hue,* and so on. Colors
are divided into primary colors and secondary colors. Primary colors are
defined as

that which is suitable as a primary hue.

Secondary colors are defined as

that which is suitable as a secondary hue.

The twelve types of color consist of four primary colors and eight secondary
colors:

1. Primary color
   blue
   yellow
   white
   red
2. Secondary color
   cloud
   smoke
   dust
   mist
   illumination
   darkness

---

*I really had to sit with this for a long time. When I first heard that all we see is divided
into just two types—colors and shapes—it struck me as either outright wrong or amazingly
insightful. Still, I cannot think of anything else I can see.

shadow
sunlight*

Indeed, these eight secondary colors are visible objects, but secondary colors also include combinations of primary colors such as orange, which is a combination of yellow and red.

If colors are divided into primary colors and secondary colors, then what is color itself? It is neither a primary color nor a secondary color. You cannot say that color is not a color, but you also cannot say that it is a primary color or that it is a secondary color. Thus, the division is a non-exhaustive one. (See more in chapter 20, "Definitions, Divisions, and Illustrations.")

Besides colors, the only other visible objects are shapes. A shape is defined as

that which is suitable to be shown as a shape.

The eight types of shape are:

1. Long
2. Short
3. High
4. Low
5. Square
6. Round
7. Level
8. Nonlevel

It is not clear that this list of eight types of shapes is exhaustive of all shapes. Some say it is, and others say it is not. It seems to me to be exhaustive because from whatever your perspective, some shapes are high or above you and others are low or below you. That would include most everything. If not, then certainly the dichotomy of level and nonlevel shapes should include all shapes.

SOUNDS [HL4]

The second of the five types of external form is sound. In this system, they consider sound itself to be a form, rather than a nonsubstantial wave moving

---

*For more detail, see Perdue, *Debate in Tibetan Buddhism,* 194–97.

through a medium like air or water. As a form, it is thought to be atomically established, though in a different, more ephemeral way than ordinary matter.* A sound is defined as

an object of hearing.

Mutually inclusive with sound is sound-source, which is defined as

an object of hearing of an ear consciousness.

The system has a very interesting way of dividing sounds into eight types, beginning with *pleasant articulate sounds caused by elements conjoined with consciousness.* Whether or not something is pleasant is a matter of taste east and west, but sounds are pleasant when they appeal to the listener and are attractive, and sounds are unpleasant when they do not appeal to the listener and are unattractive. "Articulate" means that the sound indicates meaning or reveals meaning. It is an expressive sound. Of course, any sensible utterance is an example of articulate sound, such as the sound expressing "Sound is an impermanent phenomenon." Even if it is spoken in a language you do not understand, it may be articulate. For example, it would seem that the sound of a cat purring or the yelp of a dog after you stepped on a paw would also be articulate, as these are sounds that express meaning.

The last part of the first of the eight types of sound specifies those sounds "caused by elements conjoined with consciousness." The four substantial elements in this ancient system are earth, water, fire, and wind. Sounds are not an element but are caused by the play of the elements, in the same way that colors or shapes or tastes are caused by the play of the elements. Now, when we look around, we can see that some bits of matter, like your hand, are animate, and others, like a rock, are not. That means that your hand, for instance, is conjoined with consciousness and moves by your will. Thus, some elements are conjoined with consciousness, and some are not, or at least that seems to be the case. In regard to sounds, a person's tongue is conjoined with consciousness because it is an internal form, a form held within that person's continuum of consciousness. Thus, the sound of that person's voice—when you hear it directly and immediately—is a sound caused by elements conjoined with consciousness. However, if that person's voice is

*See Perdue, *Debate in Tibetan Buddhism,* 205–6.

conveyed indirectly, like over a telephone or from a recording, the sound you are hearing arises from elements not conjoined with consciousness. Of course, when you talk with somebody on the phone, you can recognize the person's voice, and that voice is caused by the person's vocal chords and so forth, but what you actually hear on the phone is a reproduction of that person's voice accomplished by inanimate matter. A more obvious example of a sound caused by elements not conjoined with consciousness is the sound of a waterfall or the sound of thunder.

By combining the three pairs of pleasant and unpleasant, articulate and inarticulate, and caused by elements conjoined with consciousness and caused by elements not conjoined with consciousness, since two cubed is eight, there is a division of sounds into eight types. Together with examples, these are:

1. Pleasant articulate sounds caused by elements conjoined with consciousness, like excellent words conveying the meaning of the Buddha's doctrine
2. Unpleasant articulate sounds caused by elements conjoined with consciousness, like the sound of harsh, angry words
3. Pleasant inarticulate sounds caused by elements conjoined with consciousness, like (depending on the circumstances to settle whether or not it is pleasant) the sound of snapping fingers, the sound of applauding hands, or the sound of Ella Fitzgerald scat singing
4. Unpleasant inarticulate sounds caused by elements conjoined with consciousness, like the sound of a fist hitting you
5. Pleasant articulate sounds caused by elements not conjoined with consciousness, like a sound recording of a person teaching compassion
6. Unpleasant articulate sounds caused by elements not conjoined with consciousness, like a sound recording of a person speaking hateful, angry words
7. Pleasant inarticulate sounds caused by elements not conjoined with consciousness, like the sound of a gong or the sound of a drum*

---

*Gen-dün-drup-ba lists the sound of a tabor, a small drum, as a pleasant inarticulate sound caused by elements conjoined with consciousness and gives the sound of a gong as a pleasant inarticulate sound caused by elements *not* conjoined with consciousness. It would seem that there is no difference, for each is directly arisen from inanimate matter and indirectly from conscious effort. Perhaps in the case of the tabor, the player slaps the hand directly against the drum skin, whereas in the case of a gong the player uses an inanimate instrument to

8. Unpleasant inarticulate sounds caused by elements not conjoined with consciousness, like the roar of a tornado or the sound of a house falling down[1]

You can generate the definitions of any of these eight by substituting "object of hearing" for "sound." Thus, the definition of a pleasant articulate sound caused by elements conjoined with consciousness would be

a pleasant articulate object of hearing caused by elements conjoined with consciousness.

Odors [HL4]

The third of the five types of external forms is odor. The definition of an odor-source, or a source that is an odor, is

an object experienced by a nose consciousness.[2]

There are several ways to divide odors,* but for our purposes the following division into four is good:

1. Fragrant natural odors, like the odor of sandalwood or of fresh mint
2. Unfragrant natural odors, like the odor of decaying flesh
3. Fragrant manufactured odors, like the odor of fresh bread
4. Unfragrant manufactured odors, like the odor of formaldehyde[3]

A fragrant odor is one that is pleasing to you, and an unfragrant one is one that is other than a pleasing odor, that is, an unpleasant one or a neutral one. Though we may argue about what is pleasant and what is unpleasant, from the point of view of an individual at one time, these four are probably mutually exclusive.

---

hit the playing surface. Still, in both cases the sound is produced directly from inanimate matter. Gen-dün-drup-ba, *Dam pa'i chos mngon pa'i mdzod kyi rnam par bshad pa thar lam gsal byed* [Commentary on (Vasubandhu's) "Treasury of knowledge": Illuminating the path to liberation] (Sarnath, India: Pleasure of Elegant Sayings Press, 1973).
*See Perdue, *Debate in Tibetan Buddhism,* 206–8.

Tastes [HL4]

The fourth type of external form is taste, which is defined as

an object experienced by a tongue consciousness.

Tastes are divided into six types:

1. Sweet, like the taste of sugar, honey, or molasses
2. Sour, like the taste of vinegar, lemons, or yogurt
3. Bitter, like the taste of coffee, celery, or spinach
4. Astringent, like the taste of persimmons, green beans, and unripe bananas
5. Pungent/hot/spicy, like the taste of red pepper or black pepper
6. Salty, like the taste of salt or soy sauce

Tangible Objects [HL4]

The fifth and final group of external forms are tangible objects. A tangible object is defined as

an object experienced by a body consciousness

or

an object felt by a body consciousness.

Tangible objects are divided into two types, tangible objects that are elements and tangible objects that are arisen from the elements. The elements are earth, water, fire, and wind. These four are the bases and causes for all matter—visible objects, sounds, odors, and tastes as well as the other tangible objects. Based on a passage from Vasubandhu's *Treasury of Knowledge,* Buddhists list just seven tangible objects that are arisen from the elements. Thus, together with the four elements, there are eleven tangible objects:

1. Tangible objects that are elements
    earth
    water
    fire
    wind

2. Tangible objects that are arisen from the elements
   smoothness
   roughness
   heaviness
   lightness
   cold
   hunger
   thirst

Certainly the four elements in this ancient system—earth, water, fire, and wind—do not correspond at all with what we in the modern era think of as elements. All of us who have any exposure to science think of all this matter—our bodies and all the rest that surrounds us—as built up out of the elements. Both the ancient and modern systems agree that matter is atomically established. Also, science and the Sūtra School Following Reasoning agree that atoms too may be deconstructed into smaller parts still. Although earth, water, fire, and wind are hardly the same as hydrogen, helium, carbon, and so forth, the point is that all matter is constructed out of the elements. In the Buddhist way of thinking, the elements do not occur in strictly irreducible units but exist as *potencies* within physical particles. Each atom is an aggregate of at least eight components: earth, water, fire, wind, visible form, odor, taste, and tangibility arisen from the elements. Also, if sound is present, in addition to these eight, which exist in all material phenomena, sound is there as a ninth potency.* Thus, like the others, sound too is materially established but not in the same sense that other forms are. Also, sound has an extremely short duration. Thus, in their way of thinking, the four elements provide the bases for all material phenomena. All the rest of matter—visible forms, sounds, odors, tastes, and the other tangible objects such as smoothness—are arisen from the elements. Although I have never seen

---

*Gen-dün-drup-ba explains that, in the Desire Realm, which is where all humans live, an atom located in a place where a sense power and sound are not present is composed of eight particle substances. However, if it is located in a place where a body sense power is present, there are nine (the ninth being the body sense power); if, in addition to that, the atom is in a place where the eye, ear, nose, or tongue sense power is located, then there are ten particle substances (the tenth being the potency of that sense power); and if it is in a place where there is also sound, there are eleven (the eleventh being sound). Thus, if an atom is in a place where there are none of the sense powers and sound is present, then sound is the ninth particle substance. Gen-dün-drup-ba, *Dam pa'i chos mngon pa'i mdzod kyi rnam par bshad pa thar lam gsal byed,* 97.4–9.

it done this way, it seems that it would be suitable to divide all matter into the same two groups as the tangible objects are divided into—the elements and what is arisen from the elements.

Keep in mind that the elements are tangible objects—objects of experience of body consciousnesses only. Indeed, we can see fire, or at least that is what we normally say. To be more precise, we see the color and shape of fire because colors and shapes are all the eye consciousness may perceive. In the same way, we don't smell fire, but we smell the odor of fire. But we can feel fire, and it is shown by the presence of heat. The element of fire has the nature of heat, so wherever there is heat, there is fire. It does not have to be a blazing fire. The warmth in your hot coffee indicates the presence of the fire element there. It may strike you as odd that cold is "arisen from the elements" but heat is not, but any measure of heat that you can feel is the fire element, so cold is a relative absence of that element. It is not that the fire element has become absent within the matter that feels cold, it is that it is no longer dominant.

In Indian-based philosophy, very often definitions are given in terms of the nature and the function of the phenomenon. The definitions of the four elements are all like that. The definition of earth is

that which is hard and obstructive.

The nature of earth is hardness, and its function is to obstruct things. The earth element is manifest as stability or as a basis. The predominance of the earth element in a stone is shown by its stability. However, all material phenomena are constructed of aggregate particles that do not consist of just one element alone but are composites of at least eight potencies including all four of the elements. Thus, the elements are always together and never separated. Indeed, even in a rock the elements of water, fire, and even wind do exist as characteristics of a stone, but the stability of the earth element is manifest predominantly. More broadly, this means that physical stability is a sign of the presence of the earth element, even in a fire, for instance, as seen by the way ashes will dance on the licks of flame. Wherever there is physical stability, there is the earth element. Greater or lesser stability indicates greater or lesser manifestation of the earth element.

We know the presence of water by the sign of wetness, and we see the effects of water in the sign of things getting moist. So, the definition of water is that which is wet and moistening.

The nature of water is wetness, and its function is to moisten things. The water element is manifest as cohesiveness. For example, a wet cloth will pick up dirt better than a dry one. The adherence of dirt to moisture indicates the presence of the water element that manifests as cohesiveness. Still, ordinary water is not the water element separate from the remaining elements, for the other elements also exist in water. For instance, a single drop of water shows greater resistance to one's finger than the same amount would show as internal fluid in a greater volume of water. In this system of Buddhist physics, the ability of water to form drops and its stability in that form indicate the presence of the earth element in water. Also, ordinary water shows the presence of the earth element in it because water is obstructive. If you drop into water from high enough, it is like hitting concrete.

It seems that the presence of fire in all matter is suggested by the power of friction. Even cold water rushing against your skin rapidly enough will feel warm. The friction of wind against matter produces heat. The definition of fire is

that which is hot and burning.

The nature of fire is heat, and its function is to burn things.

To us moderns, the most difficult element to fathom is wind. Wind is defined as

that which is light and moving.

The nature of wind is lightness, and its function is to move things. Wind is shown by movement. Any sign of movement shows the presence of the wind element. Wherever there is wind, there is movement, and wherever there is movement, there is wind. When we see the trees swaying and the leaves blowing, we know the wind is up. But, even within our bodies, all movement from digestion to walking to speech is due to the presence of the wind element in our bodies. So, the wind element is subtle, not coarse. When the wind blows the leaves, the wind element is strongly manifest, but the wind's support for those leaves shows the earth element in that breeze, and landslides show the presence of the wind element in the earth.

The remaining tangible objects are the seven arisen from the elements:

smoothness, roughness, heaviness, lightness, cold, hunger, and thirst. These are tangible objects, objects of experience of the body consciousness. They are not the elements themselves but are arisen from, or caused by, the elements in the same way that colors and shapes, sounds, tastes, and so forth, are arisen from the elements.

Each of the five types of external forms is the domain of one of the five sense consciousnesses, and each sense has dominion over its own field of operation: the eye consciousness is empowered with respect to colors and shapes; the ear consciousness, with respect to sounds, and so forth. However, generally each consciousness is insensitive with respect to the objects of the other consciousnesses. Thus, upon meeting with an object such as a flower, the eye consciousness alone is able to perceive its colors and shape; the nose consciousness, its odor, and so on. In this way we perceive an object through the various doors of perception with each consciousness perceiving one aspect. But what is the object itself? We commonly say that we see, for instance, a pot, but does this mean that a pot is an object apprehended by an eye consciousness? It is the color and shape, the visible form, of a pot that an eye consciousness sees, not the pot itself. Still, the pot itself is not a different entity from the color and shape of that pot because if the color and shape of the pot were destroyed, the pot would be destroyed, and if the pot were destroyed, the color and shape of the pot would be destroyed. In this regard, the Collected Topics debaters make a distinction between what the eye consciousness sees (*mig shes kyi mthong rgyu*) and an object apprehended by the eye consciousness (*mig shes kyi gzung bya*). The former is whatever we normally say we see—a pot, a flower, a person, and so on. The latter is only those visual forms that the eye consciousness has dominion over—the color and shape of a pot, the color and shape of a person's body, and so on.

So, how do the Buddhists think of forms? Some Buddhist thinkers say that ordinary forms are classified as one of the five types of external matter on the basis of its predominant purpose or usage. Thus, a painting is a visible form; bread is an object of the tongue consciousness; flesh and bones are earth and thus tangible objects, and so forth. Others say that pots, bread, flowers, and so forth, are tangible objects because of being objects experienced by the body consciousness. Indeed, the eye consciousness perceives the color and shape of a pot, but by this interpretation, the pot itself is earth and thus a tangible object. Seeing fire is a case of seeing the color and shape of fire, but the element fire, that which is hot and burning, is apprehended solely by the body consciousness. This second position seems more defensible. You can imagine the endless quandaries that would result from trying to sort out the "predominant purpose or usage" of things. Also, the second position, that all these forms are amalgams of elements, is more in accordance with the scientific way of thinking, which fits in for us. This issue is worthy of reflection.

INTERNAL MATTER [HL3]

Remember that matter is divided into external matter and internal matter. Internal matter is defined as

that which is atomically established and is included within the continuum of a person.

Internal matter is included within the continuum of a person in the sense of being appropriated as the body or form of a person. Internal matter includes the fleshy body—though not the hair or nails beyond where they may be felt. Of course, a living body—the body of a bear, the body of a tiger, the body of a human—is both internal matter and external matter because what is internal for one person is external for another. (Presumably, if the body were not the body of a living being, it would not be included within the conscious continuum of a person.) Since internal form has color, shape, and so forth, as does external form, we can see the color and shape of a body. A material phenomenon that is both internal matter and external matter is, for instance, the color of a person's eyes, not the sense power but the color of the eyes that we can see. The color of a person's eyes is an internal form because of being a material phenomenon included within the continuum of a person, and it is an external form because of being matter that is an object of others' sense consciousnesses.[4] The internal forms are the bases of a person's feelings of physical pleasure and pain.[5]

In addition to the fleshy material phenomena within a person's continuum—organs, skin, and so forth—which are technically both internal and external matter, internal forms include the five sense powers. In fact, in the division of matter into external matter and internal matter, internal matter refers mainly to the five sense powers: the eye sense power, the ear sense power, the nose sense power, the tongue sense power, and the body sense power. These sense powers are described as subtle matter located in each of the sense organs—eye, ear, and so on—that empower the sense organs.

Since they are subtle or clear matter, they are not visible to an ordinary being and so are counted as only internal matter, not external matter.

The eye sense power gives the eye consciousness dominion over visible forms, colors and shapes. The three causes of a visual perception are the external visible object, the eye sense power, and the former moment of the eye consciousness. Sense powers themselves are not consciousnesses and cannot know an object. Rather, the eye consciousness, empowered by the eye sense power and observing an external color or shape, is generated in the aspect of that object, and, as a result, the eye consciousness that apprehends the external visible form is produced. The sense powers give their respective consciousnesses dominion with respect to only certain external objects. For instance, the nose consciousness is empowered with respect to odors but not with respect to sounds and so forth.

The definition of an eye sense power is

a clear internal form that is the uncommon empowering condition for its own effect, an eye consciousness.

An illustration of an eye sense power is a clear internal form having a shape like a *zar-ma* flower. This form, which is located within the orb of the eye, is in the continuum of a person. A sense power is *clear internal form* because it is matter within the physical body of a person that cannot be perceived by any sense consciousness. A sense power is an *uncommon empowering condition,* which is a type of cause, because it alone can give its consciousness power with respect to its field of perception. Thus, it is a necessary but not a sufficient condition for its effect, which is an eye consciousness.

The definitions, divisions, and illustrations for the remaining sense powers are similar to those for the eye sense power. The definition of an ear sense power is

a clear internal form that is the uncommon empowering condition for its own effect, an ear consciousness.

An illustration of an ear sense power is a clear internal form having a shape like a cut bundle of wheat, this form being in the continuum of a person. The bundle of wheat is shaped as if it were cut off on one end and has the shafts oriented toward the outside of the ear.

The definition of a nose sense power is

a clear internal form that is the uncommon empowering condition for its own effect, a nose consciousness.

An illustration of a nose sense power is a clear internal form having a shape like two copper needles, this form being in the continuum of a person. The definition of a tongue sense power is

a clear internal form that is the uncommon empowering condition of its own effect, a tongue consciousness.

An illustration of a tongue sense power is a clear internal form having a shape like a cut half moon, this form being in the continuum of a person. The definition of a body sense power is

a clear internal form that is the uncommon empowering condition of its own effect, a body consciousness.

An illustration of a body sense power is a clear internal form having a shape like smooth skin, this form being in the continuum of a person. Unlike the other sense powers, which are located in unique organs like the eyes and ears, the body sense power is all over the body.

We may understand from these explanations of external matter and internal matter that this division is not mutually exclusive. Rather, external matter and internal matter compare as four possibilities (4P):

1. Something that is both external matter and internal matter is, for instance, a person's skin, the color of a person's skin, or the feel of a person's skin.
2. Something that is external matter but not internal matter is the sun or the moon.
3. Something that is internal matter but is not external matter is an eye sense power.
4. Something that is neither external matter nor internal matter is an eye consciousness.

The five internal forms, in combination with the five external forms, are necessary for perception by the five sense consciousnesses—eye, ear, nose, tongue, and body consciousnesses. The sense powers and consciousnesses are always cited in the same order: eye, ear, nose, tongue, and body. Some scholars say that they are given in this order because that is the order of certifiability or reliability. That is, the eye consciousness is the least reliable, and the body consciousness is the most reliable. If you are unable to see the form of a person clearly, hearing that person's voice will reliably inform you that there is a person there. Also, often, when we cannot see a form clearly or when it is shaped in an odd or surprising or beautiful way, we naturally seek to verify that shape with our hands because the sense of feel is more reliable. Other scholars point out that the given order of the sense powers and consciousnesses merely reflects the physical placement of those senses within the body. Roughly, the eye is above the ear, the ear above the nose, and so forth. However, the body consciousness is present throughout the body and may not be said to exist predominantly in any one part of the body as do the other consciousnesses, though it is certainly below the other sense locations. Still other scholars say that the external forms, the sense powers, and sense consciousnesses are listed in that order because that sequence reflects the range of perception, visible objects being perceptible from the greatest distance, and tangible objects being perceptible only in direct contact with the body. We can perceive visual objects as far away as the stars; a sound must be much closer, within a few miles or so; odors must be still closer; and tastes and tangible objects must be in direct contact with the body.

Generally, form or matter is divided into ten types, five types of external matter and the five internal sense powers. However, some Buddhists list an eleventh type of form—nonrevelatory forms, also known as forms for the mental consciousness.* An example of a nonrevelatory form in the system of the Great Exposition School, the point of view of the *Treasury of Knowledge*, is a form arising from promises.[6] Such a form is a subtle physical entity created at the moment of first taking a vow, and it remains with the person until the person loses the vow or until death.[7]

CONSCIOUSNESSES [HL2]

After matter, the second of the three types of functioning things are consciousnesses.† All Buddhists hold that consciousness exists as a separate

---

*For more details, see Perdue, *Debate in Tibetan Buddhism,* 188–89 and 191–92.
†For a fuller explanation of consciousnesses, see Lati Rinbochay, *Mind in Tibetan Buddhism;* Perdue, *Debate in Tibetan Buddhism,* 355–62; and this book, chapter 12, "Consciousnesses in relation to What They Perceive."

entity from the body. This is a clear assertion of dualism that is not at all frequent in current Western philosophy, though it can be found. What is frequent in current Western philosophy and in science is the physicalist view that consciousness arises as an effect of having bodies such as we do and that, when the body is no longer viable, consciousness dissolves and ceases. The Buddhists hold that our consciousnesses survive this life and that the continuum of our consciousnesses moves on as a repository of our karmic seeds. Of course, they do not hold that consciousness is a permanent and unchanging aspect of personality, since consciousness is included here in the division of functioning things into three types. Rather, they hold that consciousness of every type is impermanent and changing, but the continuum of consciousness goes on throughout time, changing moment by moment but remaining of the same type. This is like the scientific principle of the conservation of mass that states that the measure of mass inside a closed system will always remain constant. Though the mass might change state, the measure will remain constant.

Of course, in a meditative tradition that puts forth a theory of epistemology, the topic of consciousness is of essential importance. In the Collected Topics system of Buddhist reasoning and debate, consciousnesses are introduced briefly in the early material and then taken up in more detail in the book-length section called "Awareness and Knowledge" (*bLo rig*), the fourth major section in the Collected Topics and part of "The Greater Path of Reasoning." In those texts, the three—awarenesses, knowers, and consciousnesses—are understood as mutually inclusive.[8] Whatever is one is also both of the others. A consciousness is defined as

that which is clear and knowing.*

Many scholars interpret this definition as referring to the nature and function of consciousness, in the way that "that which is hot and burning" refers to the nature and function of fire. In this understanding of the definition of consciousness, the quality of being *clear* refers to the nature or entity of a consciousness, and the specification of *knowing* refers to the function of consciousnesses. "Nevertheless, there are varying interpretations of [the definition's] meaning. Some say that 'clear' refers to the object's appearing

---

*For more detail on this definition, see Perdue, *Debate in Tibetan Buddhism,* 355–59; and Lati Rinbochay, *Mind in Tibetan Buddhism,* 45–47.

clearly from its own side to the appearance factor of the mind and 'knowing' refers to the subject, the awareness, apprehending or knowing the object. There are others who say that 'clear' and 'knowing' both refer to the subject's perceiving the object and thus the definition means 'that which illuminates and knows'."[9]

In his *Presentation of Types of Awarenesses* (*bLo rigs kyi rnam bzhag*), Losang Gyatso concludes that in the system of the Sūtra School Following Reasoning, the meaning of a knower is that which has the activity of discriminating (*'byed pa*) what are and what are not the qualities of just its own object *or* that which [has the activity of] holding (*'dzin pa*) or apprehending (*bzung pa*) by an awareness.[10] He is taking knower (and by extension awareness and consciousness, since they are mutually inclusive with knower) in the broadest possible sense as that which discriminates or apprehends. Of course, a consciousness does not necessarily *know* its object or there would be no need for epistemology. Rather, a consciousness has the function of *discriminating, holding,* or *apprehending* an object by means of an awareness. It approaches or engages its object. Still, a consciousness does "have the activity" of *knowing.*

The most basic division of consciousnesses is into two types:

1. Mental consciousnesses
2. Sense consciousnesses

There is no overlap between mental consciousnesses and sense consciousnesses. Though they obviously coordinate with each other and support each other, there is no consciousness that is both a mental consciousness and a sense consciousness, and all types of consciousnesses are either one or the other.

MENTAL CONSCIOUSNESSES [HL3]

The definition of a mental consciousness is

> a knower that is produced in dependence on its own uncommon empowering condition, a mental sense power.

Mental and sense consciousnesses are divided in terms of their special bases of dependence, their uncommon (meaning unique or unshared) causes. The uncommon empowering condition of a sense consciousness is its own internal sense power. The eye sense power is the uncommon empowering condition for the eye consciousness, and it is just the same with the other four sense powers and their respective consciousnesses. The uncommon empowering condition of a mental consciousness is the mental sense power, which is *any of the six consciousnesses in the immediately preceding moment.* Thus, the eye consciousness of the last moment can serve as the mental sense power and uncommon empowering condition of a mental consciousness of the present moment. We have these experiences all the time when the eye prompts the mental consciousness. Moreover, as the substantial cause of the eye consciousness of the present moment, the eye consciousness of the last moment is also an empowering condition of the present eye consciousness, although not an *uncommon* empowering condition. Similarly, the eye sense power is an uncommon empowering condition of an eye consciousness, and if that eye consciousness induces a mental consciousness, the eye sense power is also an empowering condition of that mental consciousness, although not an *uncommon* one because the mental consciousness can be prompted by any of the senses. Only mental consciousnesses are produced in dependence on an uncommon empowering condition that is a mental sense power, and this is identified not as subtle matter but as a former moment of consciousness.

Of course, in addition to the mind having the ability to image sensations from any of the sense consciousnesses, it has this amazing capacity for conceptuality, as you have noticed. (Thought, conceptuality, and a thinking consciousness should all be MI with a conceptual mental consciousness.) Our typical way of thinking of the mind is that it always operates by thought. However, in this meditative tradition, the Buddhists assert that the mind, like the sense consciousnesses, is also capable of operating as a direct perceiver, knowing its objects without conceptuality. In fact, the ultimate type of mental knowers are mental direct perceivers, for the Buddhists find some disadvantages with conceptuality. However, they do not showcase mental direct perceivers as always extraordinary, ultimate knowers. For instance, they say that a sense consciousness might be engaged in observing something within its field of operation, such as an eye consciousness noticing the color of a blue sky, and then the eye consciousness prompts the mind, after which there is a moment of mental direct perception of the blue sky, and then the mind slips into the thought of a blue sky.*

---

*See Lati Rinbochay, *Mind in Tibetan Buddhism*, 18, 54, and especially 56–59.

SENSE CONSCIOUSNESSES [HL3]

Sense consciousnesses are produced in dependence on their own uncommon empowering conditions, which are physical sense powers such as the eye sense power. The definition of a sense consciousness is

> a knower that is produced in dependence on its own uncommon empowering condition, a physical sense power.

There are five types of sense consciousnesses:

1. Eye consciousnesses
2. Ear consciousnesses
3. Nose consciousnesses
4. Tongue consciousnesses
5. Body consciousnesses

The definition of an eye consciousness is

> a knower that is produced in dependence on its own uncommon empowering condition, the eye sense power, and an observed-object-condition, a visible form.

As mentioned above in regard to internal forms, there are three essentials required for a sense perception. These are (1) an external form such as a visible form, a sound, an odor, and so on, which serves as the object of the perception, (2) internal matter, one of the sense powers, and (3) the continuum of the sense consciousness.

In this context, external forms are "observed-object-conditions" for the five sense consciousnesses—colors and shapes for the eye consciousness, sounds for the ear consciousness, and so on. A condition is a cause, and a form is a condition for a sense consciousness because, partially in dependence on the appearance of such a material object, a consciousness observing that material object is produced. Thus, the Buddhists put forth a view that consciousness is a different entity from matter, and though it interacts with matter, it is not matter and it does not have matter as its substantial cause. We can all see there's plenty of matter lying about, and given the right conditions like proximity and light, we can perceive it. The individual sense powers give the five individual sense consciousnesses power to perceive their appropriate external objects. The sense consciousness is then generated in the aspect of its object and a sense perception occurs.

The remaining sense consciousnesses are defined similarly in relation to their own special sense powers and the objects that they are empowered to perceive. The definition of an ear consciousness is

> a knower that is produced in dependence on its own uncommon empowering condition, the ear sense power, and an observed-object-condition, a sound.

The definition of a nose consciousness is

> a knower that is produced in dependence on its own uncommon empowering condition, the nose sense power, and an observed-object-condition, an odor.

The definition of a tongue consciousness is

> a knower that is produced in dependence on its own uncommon empowering condition, the tongue sense power, and an observed-object-condition, a taste.

The definition of a body consciousness is

> a knower that is produced in dependence on its own uncommon empowering condition, a body sense power, and an observed-object-condition, a tangible object.

Within Buddhism there is great emphasis on the study and training of consciousness. "Buddhism presents a view of self-creation, that one's own actions create one's life situation. In this light, it has been said that Buddhism is not a religion, but a science of the mind."[11] In Buddhism, the emphasis on study is especially directed at developing wisdom, which is ultimately able to liberate. It is fulfilled in the realization of selflessness but begins with awareness and mindfulness of impermanence and ordinary appearances. The place of epistemology in this process is to establish which consciousnesses are reliable and which are not—that is, which can yield knowledge and which cannot. This topic will be explored in chapter 12, "Consciousnesses in relation to What They Perceive." The other parts of self-creation that the Dalai Lama refers to in the quote above have to do with morality and heart. These begin with overcoming selfishness and developing helpful attitudes such as love and compassion.

NONASSOCIATED COMPOSITIONAL FACTORS [HL2]

The third group of functioning things are nonassociated compositional factors. The definition may be put as

a functioning thing that is neither a form nor a consciousness.

All impermanent phenomena that are neither matter nor consciousnesses are included among nonassociated compositional factors. "They are called 'compositional factors' because of being factors that allow for the aggregation of causes and conditions and for the production, abiding, and cessation of products."[12] They are called "nonassociated" because, unlike minds, they are not associated with minds or mental factors.[13] Nonassociated compositional factors are of two types:

1. Nonassociated compositional factors that are persons
2. Nonassociated compositional factors that are not persons

NONASSOCIATED COMPOSITIONAL FACTORS THAT ARE PERSONS [HL3]

A person is a nonassociated compositional factor because of being an impermanent phenomenon that is neither a form nor a consciousness. This means that you are not your body and you are not your mind. Rather, persons are imputed to a collection of form and consciousness, the body and mind. "Since a person is neither form nor consciousness but impermanent, it can be only an instance of the remaining category of impermanent phenomena, a non-associated compositional factor."[14] Because the person is a collection, a gathering, or a grouping of matter and consciousness, the person is not matter alone nor consciousness alone. Imagine that you have a pile of square things and round things. You cannot say that the pile is a collection of round things, and you cannot say that it is a collection of square things. A person is defined as

> a being who is imputed in dependence upon any of the five aggregates.

A person is imputed to a collection of the bases of a mind and body, the mental and physical aggregates. "Imputed" means attributed or ascribed. Just by encountering some small measure of a person's aggregates, we will *impute, attribute, ascribe,* or *project* that the person is there, based on that evidence. Upon meeting with any of the aggregates of a person, like seeing the person's face or hearing his or her voice, we impute the presence of that person. For instance, coming home, you hear your mother's voice from the front door, and you know she is there. When you see the color and shape of a friend's face, you think, "I see my friend." We do not need to contact all of the mental and physical aggregates of a person before being able to project the presence of a person. Thus, the definition specifies that a person is a being imputed in dependence on *any* of the five aggregates.

So, what are the five aggregates? The story goes that the Buddha explained these bases of the person while sitting on a riverbank. He piled up five clumps or heaps of sand and described the bases to which we attribute the person. The Sanskrit word he used for these piles was *skandha* (evidently this is the basis for the English word "candy," for candy was first made with bits of molasses, boiled sugarcane juice, clumped together). The five *skandhas* are the bases to which persons are imputed. Moreover, the five aggregates together include all impermanent phenomena. In the *Go-mang Collected Topics,* functioning things are divided into the five aggregates rather than into the three listed in this chapter. These are:

1. Forms
2. Feelings
3. Discriminations
4. Compositional factors
5. Consciousnesses

This description of the person as a being imputed to the aggregates is intended to lead us to contemplate exactly what is the nature of the person and to what extent our own intellectual projections are at play in thinking of ourselves and others. All systems of Buddhist tenets assert selflessness.

Even though self in general is a synonym of person, the meaning of "self" in the term "selflessness" is different; thus, this is not a doctrine that persons do not exist. Rather, persons do exist and are impermanent phenomena. The meaning of "selflessness" is variously identified in the different schools of philosophy, but all agree that, at least, the person is devoid of being a permanent, unitary, independent self. It is such a "self" that does not exist. Persons exist, but a permanent, unitary, independent self does not.

As you may have anticipated, given that Buddhism asserts a round of rebirth, shouldn't the status of "person" extend even beyond us humans? That is exactly right. In a round of rebirth, there is no "us and them" like us, the humans, and them, the animals. Rather, there is only us. There is a Tibetan saying, "Which comes first, tomorrow or the next life? Who can say?" Although we tend to imagine what we will be doing tomorrow, given the reality of death and impermanence and supposing there might actually be a round of rebirth, it may be that I would be reborn into the belly of ol' Mother Hamster before tomorrow. Who can say? At any rate, the definition of a person is extended even to those that are not human. For instance, the definition of a bear would be

> a being who is imputed in dependence upon any of the five aggregates of a bear.

You can extend this definition of a person out to any individual, whether human or not, in the same way. Thus, the definition of Dwayne "The Rock" Johnson, one of our favorite nonassociated compositional factors that is a person, would be

> a being who is imputed in dependence upon any of the five aggregates of Dwayne "The Rock" Johnson.

If persons are divided, there are two:

1. Common beings
2. Superiors

On first impression, it seems kind of shocking to note that the Buddhists speak of common and superior persons. Here, common beings and superiors are distinguished by their levels of realization. A superior is one who has had a direct perception of emptiness, or selflessness, which is accomplished as an effect of sustained contemplation and meditation. A common being has not. Thus, one is common or superior not by birth, not by strength, not by wealth, not by fame, not by power, and not by authority, but by a measure of internal development. Of course, knowing who is a superior and who is not is challenging. You would know the truth of it for yourself, but in regard to others, it would be an article of belief.

The Sanskrit name for "superiors" is *Āryans* after the ancient invaders who arrived on the Indian subcontinent by at least 1800 BCE, more than 1,200 years before the time of the Buddha. The imprint of the ancient Āryans on Indian culture is vast, but cultural sharing is shown by more than related words. Here, Buddhists take the historical "superiority" of the Āryans and turn it on its head. Rather than being superior by the power of many soldiers and horses and control of chariot technology, one is a superior by a measure of internal development. I believe the cap with a comb of many threads worn by the Tibetan monks is modeled after the headwear of Āryan soldiers, just as is the familiar bristled helmet of the Roman soldier. Again, rather than being a threatening display, the monks see the symbol this way, as explained by Geshé Rabten:

> The thousands of threads streaming out from the top of the hat represent the full development of wisdom, compassion, and power—the attainment of buddhahood. They also serve to remind us of the thousand buddhas of this fortunate eon. Because these are symbols of the ultimate refuge to which we entrust ourselves, they are worn on the highest part of the body—the top of the head.[15]

COMMON BEINGS [HL4]

The *Treasury of Knowledge* says, "Those who have not attained a superior path are common beings."[16] Common beings are of six types, each having the basis of a migrator (Skt. *gati*, Tib. *'gro ba*) in cyclic existence.* Sentient

---

*For excellent explanations of the process of cyclic existence and the six types of beings who live in it, see Khetsun Sangpo Rinbochay, *Tantric Practice in Nying-Ma*, trans. and ed. Jeffrey Hopkins (Ithaca, N.Y.: Snow Lion Publications, 1982); and Lati Rinbochay and Denma Lochö Rinbochay, *Meditative States in Tibetan Buddhism*.

beings are called "migrators" because, for the most part, they are constantly moving and traveling within cyclic existence. The six types of common beings having the basis of a migrator are:

1. Common beings having the basis of a hell-being
2. Common beings having the basis of a hungry ghost
3. Common beings having the basis of an animal
4. Common beings having the basis of a human
5. Common beings having the basis of a demigod
6. Common beings having the basis of a god

These persons are qualified as *common beings* having the basis of a migrator for the sake of distinguishing them from *superiors* having the basis of a migrator. Since superiors and common beings are differentiated not by body type but by qualities of mind, beings having the bases of migrators are of both types. According to Lati Rinpoche, there are probably no superiors having the basis of any of the three lower types of migrators, but there are cases of superiors having the basis of a human, demigod, or god. These are practitioners who, although they have attained a superior's path, have not attained liberation and still take rebirth in cyclic existence as a person having the basis of a migrator. There are superiors who intentionally take rebirth as, for instance, an animal in order to be able to help others; still, this is not a case of a superior having the basis of an animal because the superior is merely assuming that appearance and is not powerlessly reborn as an animal due to the effects of contaminated actions.[17]

SUPERIORS [HL4]

A superior, sometimes called a "worthy one" or a "noble," may or may not be a liberated person. Rather, a person becomes a superior upon having a direct perception of selflessness, and at the point when this first happens, the person is still on the path. There is no red line that cannot be crossed between common beings and superiors. As the Buddhists tell it, all superiors were formerly common beings wandering in the round of rebirth. What's more, it is within everyone's capacity to become a superior. Remember Lati Rinpoche's advice, "There is no phenomenon that cannot be understood. There is no doctrine that if studied well, cannot be learned, and there is no person who, if he or she studies well, cannot become wise."[18] An example of a superior is the Buddha or a higher-ground bodhisattva.

Nonassociated Compositional Factors That Are Not Persons [HL3]

Other than persons, the remaining nonassociated compositional factors are those that are not persons. Just as with all nonassociated compositional factors, these are impermanent things that are neither matter nor consciousness. Included here is, for instance, any measure of time, which we all know is impermanent. Thus, an hour, a day, a week, a month, a year, and so forth—all times—are nonassociated compositional factors that are not persons. Also, such things as numbers and order are nonassociated compositional factors.[19] "'Number' is designated to a condition of measure. 'Order' is designated to a serial state of former and later, high and low, and so forth."[20] Order, as a mere serial state, is an object of apprehension of any of the six consciousnesses and is something that is produced, abides for some time, and disintegrates.

Also included here as a nonassociated compositional factor that is not a person is functioning thing itself as well as all of the phenomena mutually inclusive with it, such as impermanent phenomenon, that which is able to perform a function, and so on. It is not the case that whatever is a functioning thing is necessarily a nonassociated compositional factor, but functioning thing itself is a nonassociated compositional factor because of its being an impermanent phenomenon that is neither matter nor a consciousness.

You may recall the statement that each of the three divisions of functioning things is MX—mutually exclusive—with the other two. Then, it may occur to you that if functioning thing itself is a nonassociated compositional factor and all forms, for instance, are functioning things, then how can they be MX? It is because there is no form that is a nonassociated compositional factor, so there is nothing that is both. Although both matter and consciousnesses are functioning things, functioning thing as such is neither of them. Since functioning thing is an impermanent phenomenon and is not matter or consciousness, it must be a nonassociated compositional factor. Unlike color which, although a color, is neither a primary color nor a secondary color, functioning thing is itself to be found among its divisions.

Reflection: Remember, this material is one way of approaching vipassana, or special insight meditation. A version of this categorization of phenomena is included as a standard part of the meditative tradition known as Vipassana. In either version, the material is intended to introduce students to the same sort of introspection and mindfulness. Such awareness is basic to Buddhism. Please pay attention to this scheme of categorizing phenomena. Just notice things as they come to mind or as you encounter them with your senses in what William James called "one great blooming, buzzing confusion."[21] Vipassana is a way of sorting out this confusion. As Mahasi Sayadaw said,

> Thus, when seeing a visible object with the eye, the meditator knows how to distinguish each single factor involved: 'The eye is one; the visual object is another; seeing is another, and knowing it is another.' The same manner applies in the case of the other sense functions.[22]

In the same way, I am inviting you to pay attention. Just notice things as they come along: "Now I am smelling a pleasant, natural odor." "This is a sound caused by elements conjoined with consciousness." "This is a secondary color." "This is the tangible object smoothness, which is arisen from the elements." Just practice putting mental labels on things. You will learn the system better by playing this game. You will wonder whether or not something is included here or included there, and that is a beginning on debate.

The purpose of this exercise is not to test the system and discover whether or not it is complete. It is an ancient system. Some things may put you off, such as listing earth, water, fire, and wind as elements. Still, there is hardness, there is moistness, there is heat, and there is movement. Although not included here, there is a division of animals into animals living in the depths (of water and the depths under the soil) and animals scattered about the surface. It is interesting, but it hardly compares to modern biology.

So, remember that the purpose of this reflection is to train your mind. Without regard to whether or not you are a Buddhist, whether or not you have any personal interest in any kind of spirituality, their system begins with observation for the sake of training the mind. The word "vipassana" means "special insight," not "great observer" or "one who is skillful in the system." Classify things as you will, just pay attention. Notice your own consciousness as you go through the day. Again, from Mahasi Sayadaw:

> For, at that time, in each act of noticing, the meditator comes to know analytically the mental processes of noticing, and those of

thinking and reflecting, knowing them for himself [or herself] through direct knowledge, by his [or her] experience.[23]

There will be more information later in this book on the different types of consciousnesses that will support this sort of introspection. For now, please focus on labeling external appearances for the sake of increasing mindfulness and inquiry. Analytical thinking begins with observation.

EXERCISE 10.1

1. Do the mindfulness exercises suggested in the reflection above. Just put labels on things as they pass. Ask yourself such questions as, "Is that voice I am hearing a sound associated with elements conjoined with consciousness or not?" Just pay attention. Then, to the extent you can, notice the noticer. Do you think that consciousness is from a source separate from matter? Or is it an effect of matter in that we have brains and nervous systems such as we do? Is the noticer the consciousness or the person? Are they different?

Selfless

Existents

established bases
objects of comprehension
objects
objects of knowledge
objects of comprehension
    of an omniscient consciousness
hidden phenomena
phenomena

Non-existents

examples: the horn of a rabbit,
    a square circle

Impermanent Phenomena/ Functioning Things

functioning things
products
causes
effects
composed phenomena
ultimate truths
specifically characterized phenomena
manifest phenomena

Permanent Phenomena

phenomena that are nonthings
nonproduced phenomena
uncomposed phenomena
conventional truths
generally characterized phenomena

examples: nirvāṇa, non-cow,
    established base, definition,
    one-with-(a pot)

Matter

visible forms	eye sense power
sounds	ear sense power
odors	nose sense power
tastes	tongue sense power
tangible objects	body sense power

Consciousness

mental consciousnesses	sense consciousnesses
├ conceptual └ mental direct perceivers	├ eye ├ ear ├ nose ├ tongue └ body

Nonassociated Compositional Factors

nonassociated compositional factors that are persons	nonassociated compositional factors that are nonpersons
examples: the Buddha, Thomas Jefferson, a dog	examples: time, order, functioning thing

11. THE PARADIGMS FOR PROVING A COMPARISON OF PHENOMENA

AT THIS POINT, you understand from chapter 4, "The Comparison of Phenomena," the ways that two different existent phenomena may compare. You also understand from chapter 6, "The Buddhist Syllogism," the process for forming a valid syllogism. The paradigms for proving a comparison of phenomena put these two skills together. These paradigms are like skeletons on which would be the flesh of the debates or like outlines of a text. Thus, even though they are not complete, it is essential to put these in mind so you can see the patterns. With the paradigms in mind, everyone can foresee where the discussion will need to go. In this regard, the paradigms are like roadmaps.

Whether in our own personal reflection or in discussion with others, we all seek to discover the truth of the world. As the great American scientist and philosopher Charles Sanders Peirce (1839–1914) said, "Every man is fully satisfied that there is such a thing as truth, or he would not ask any question."[1] According to the guidelines for the comparison of phenomena, we may begin by considering whether or not and in what way things may be distinguished. Beyond that, we will have to verify our assessments by looking to see whether or not our positions may be supported.

The pattern here follows the pattern set forth in the comparison of phenomena—3P, 4P, MX, and MI. There are six paradigms here, two each for 3P and 4P, and one each for the other two. Recall that I am following the descriptions of these comparisons as set forth by Kensur Yeshi Thupten.*

---

*In my *Debate in Tibetan Buddhism,* I followed the style laid out by Lati Rinpoche, who designated as "three possibilities without something that is neither" both (1) the comparison of functioning thing and non-pot, which has three subjects but nothing that is neither, and (2) the comparison of the selfless and the existent, which has two subjects but nothing

Here are the paradigms, one by one, together with notes on what you have to do for each.

PROVING THREE POSSIBILITIES

For both of the 3P paradigms, in order to prove that two things compare as three possibilities in either way, you will have to show that there is at least one subject, *x,* that is both a *p* and a *q;* prove that *x* is a *p* with a valid reason; and prove that *x* is a *q* with a valid reason. Second, you will have to show which way the pervasion runs—is it the case that every *p* is a *q* or is it the case that every *q* is a *p*? Whichever way it goes, you will then have to show that there is at least one subject *x* that is one but not the other, as you indicated in your claim about the way the pervasion runs, and then prove that *x* is the one with a valid reason and that *x* is not the other with a valid reason.

Three Possibilities including Neither

In this case, because it includes the possibility of something that is neither, in addition to the other requirements, you will have to posit some subject, *x,* that is neither a *p* nor a *q* and prove with a valid reason that *x* is not a *p* and that *x* is not a *q*.

Answer in debate: There are three possibilities between *p* and *q*.

1. Something that is both a *p* and a *q* is the subject, *x*.

   The subject, *x,* is a *p* because of [supply a valid reason].
   The subject, *x,* is a *q* because of [supply a valid reason].

2. Whatever is a *p* is necessarily a *q*, but whatever is a *q* is not necessarily a *p*. For example, the subject, *x,* is a *q* but not a *p*.

   The subject, *x,* is a *q* because of [supply a valid reason].
   The subject, *x,* is not a *p* because of [supply a valid reason].

---

that is neither. Kensur Yeshi Thupten designates the former as four possibilities without anything that is neither and the latter as three possibilities without anything that is neither. See Perdue, *Debate in Tibetan Buddhism,* 162–63.

3. Something that is neither a p nor a q is the subject, x.

> The subject, x, is not a p because of [supply a valid reason].
> The subject, x, is not a q because of [supply a valid reason].

This and all of the other paradigms laid out here are sterile specimens, like butterflies pinned to a mat. Do not think that the implied debates will have to follow these sterile patterns. Like the butterflies, they are more marvelous when they have life and flow freely.

Three Possibilities without Neither

Answer in debate: There are three possibilities between p and q without anything that is neither.

1. Something that is both a p and a q is the subject, x.

> The subject, x, is a p because of [supply a valid reason].
> The subject, x, is a q because of [supply a valid reason].

2. Whatever is a p is necessarily a q, but whatever is a q is not necessarily a p. For example, the subject, x, is a q but not a p.

> The subject, x, is a q because of [supply a valid reason].
> The subject, x, is not a p because of [supply a valid reason].

As mentioned before, this comparison should be quite rare. It would have to include the selfless or something mutually inclusive with the selfless such as its definition, that which is free of a self, as one of the two principals. There is nothing else that takes in all existents and all non-existents as well.

PROVING FOUR POSSIBILITIES

For both of these paradigms, in order to prove that two things compare as four possibilities in either way, you will have to show that there is at least one subject, x, that is both a p and a q; prove that x is a p with a valid reason; and prove that x is a q with a valid reason. Second, you will have to show that there is at least one subject, x, that is a p but not a q; prove that x is a p with a valid reason; and prove that x is not a q with a valid reason. And third, you will have to show that there is at least one subject, x, that is a q

but not a *p*; prove that *x* is a *q* with a valid reason; and prove that *x* is not a *p* with a valid reason.

Four Possibilities including Neither

Answer in debate: There are four possibilities between *p* and *q*.

1. Something that is both a *p* and a *q* is the subject, *x*.

   The subject, *x*, is a *p* because of [supply a valid reason].
   The subject, *x*, is a *q* because of [supply a valid reason].

2. Something that is a *p* but not a *q* is the subject, *x*.

   The subject, *x*, is a *p* because of [supply a valid reason].
   The subject, *x*, is not a *q* because of [supply a valid reason].

3. Something that is a *q* but not a *p* is the subject, *x*.

   The subject, *x*, is a *q* because of [supply a valid reason].
   The subject, *x*, is not a *p* because of [supply a valid reason].

4. Something that is neither a *p* nor a *q* is the subject, *x*.

   The subject, *x*, is not a *p* because of [supply a valid reason].
   The subject, *x*, is not a *q* because of [supply a valid reason].

Four Possibilities without Neither

Answer in debate: There are four possibilities between *p* and *q* without anything that is neither.

1. Something that is both a *p* and a *q* is the subject, *x*.

   The subject, *x*, is a *p* because of [supply a valid reason].
   The subject, *x*, is a *q* because of [supply a valid reason].

2. Something that is a *p* but not a *q* is the subject, *x*.

   The subject, *x*, is a *p* because of [supply a valid reason].
   The subject, *x*, is not a *q* because of [supply a valid reason].

3. Something that is a *q* but not a *p* is the subject, *x*.

   The subject, *x*, is a *q* because of [supply a valid reason].
   The subject, *x*, is not a *p* because of [supply a valid reason].

PROVING MUTUAL EXCLUSION

To prove that two phenomena are mutually exclusive, MX, there are three points to touch on. First, you have to show that the two phenomena are different. This implies that they are two existents. In the paradigm, the two are shown to be different "because of being phenomena that are diverse." The definition of different or different [phenomena] is

> phenomena that are diverse.

This is true for any two existents that are not identical, even those that are mutually inclusive. For instance, a product is diverse from an impermanent phenomenon, and an impermanent phenomenon is diverse from a product. They are different in name but not in meaning.

Next, you have to show that whatever is the one is necessarily not the other, going both ways. If the first step of proving them to be different were not included, one might argue that the two, a pot and the horn of a rabbit, are mutually exclusive because whatever is a pot is necessarily not a horn of a rabbit and whatever is a horn of a rabbit is necessarily not a pot. However, though these two pervasions are accurate, it is of no benefit to understand them. Thus, the comparisons of phenomena focus on distinctions and similarities between existents.

There is no separate paradigm for proving that two phenomena are mutually exclusive without anything that is neither because the system does not set that off as a separate case.

Answer in debate: The two, p and q, are mutually exclusive.

1. The subjects, p and q, are different because of being phenomena that are diverse.
2. Whatever is a p is necessarily not a q because of [supply a valid reason].
3. Whatever is a q is necessarily not a p because of [supply a valid reason].

The best sort of reason to give to justify a pervasion is another pervasion. For instance, if we were comparing the two MX phenomena, permanent phenomena and impermanent phenomena, we could say, "Whatever is a permanent phenomenon is necessarily not an impermanent phenomenon because whatever is a permanent phenomenon is necessarily not a momentary phenomenon, but whatever is an impermanent phenomenon is necessarily a momentary phenomenon."

PROVING MUTUAL INCLUSION

There are two points to touch on to prove that two phenomena are MI, mutually inclusive. First, as in the case of MX, you must show that the two are different. For all the comparisons, the two principals must be different. Again, this entails that they must be existent but not identical. Otherwise, one might say that a pot and a pot are mutually inclusive or that the horn of a rabbit and the ruling King of France are mutually inclusive.

There is no separate paradigm for proving that two phenomena are MI without anything that is neither because the system does not set that off as a separate case.

Answer in debate: The two, p and q, are mutually inclusive.

1. The subjects, p and q, are different because of being phenomena that are diverse.
2. The subjects, p and q, have all eight approaches of pervasion.

The second requirement is that the two principals must have all eight approaches of pervasion. These are:

1. Whatever is a p is necessarily a q.
2. Whatever is a q is necessarily a p.
3. Whatever is not a p is necessarily not a q.
4. Whatever is not a q is necessarily not a p.
5. If there is a p, then there is necessarily a q.
6. If there is a q, then there is necessarily a p.
7. If there is not a p, then there is necessarily not a q.
8. If there is not a q, then there is necessarily not a p.

It seems that if the first two pervasions were true for any p and q, then the remaining six would also have to be true. So, why is the debate done this way? It may be that it is difficult to prove a pervasion, as opposed to proving a lack of pervasion as in the case of MX phenomena, except by substituting other mutually inclusive things in the place of the principals. For instance, why is it true that whatever is an impermanent phenomenon is necessarily a functioning thing? One reason is because they are mutually inclusive.

But, if that is what you're trying to prove, that will not work as your reason. We might say, "Because whatever is an impermanent phenomenon is necessarily momentary and whatever is a functioning thing is also momentary." Those pervasions in that reason and the reason as a whole are accurate, but that reason will not work either. For instance, it is true that whatever is an impermanent phenomenon is necessarily an existent and that whatever is a permanent phenomenon is necessarily an existent, but by no means does that prove that whatever is an impermanent phenomenon is necessarily a permanent phenomenon. This may be the reason that the paradigm requires the Defender to list the eight approaches of pervasion. Another possible reason is so that the speaker learns all the implications of mutual inclusion. The situation is different when proving that two different phenomena are mutually exclusive, for that can be done by stating a couple of pervasions linking the two principals to other mutually exclusive phenomena.

The fifth through eighth approaches of pervasion beginning with the statement "If there is a p, then there is necessarily a q" reflect the "exists" mode of statement, as opposed to the "is" mode of statement for the first four approaches of pervasion. (Recall these two types of modes of statements specified in the definition of the property of the subject in chapter 6, "The Buddhist Syllogism.") The "is" mode of statement says something about the manner of being of p and q in the pervasion. If something is a p, then that thing is a q. The "exists" mode of statement says something about the existence of something. The existence or presence of one thing shows the existence or presence of the other as well because they are just different names for the same thing. If there is a p, then there is necessarily a q. The first two of the eight statements make it clear that if there is a p, then there is a q, and if there is a q, then there is a p. Thus, if there is a p anywhere, that same thing is a q and so we know that a q exists, that there is a q. Also, if there is a q anywhere, that same thing is a p and so we know that a p exists, that there is a p. Such statements may be more literally translated as "If a p exists, then a q exists." Another possible way of saying this is "Wherever there is a p there is a q." This is not meant to say something about the location of a thing or to suggest that everything is physical but that if a p is anywhere, then that proves that there is a q at that same place. Of course, however the statements are expressed, it is clear that the p and the q refer to just the same thing in the world and that thing is being characterized differently as a p and as a q. This is the essence of mutual inclusion—that the two phenomena are just different names for the same things—as every impermanent phenomenon is also a functioning thing and if there is an impermanent phenomenon, then (the existence of that impermanent phenomenon shows that) there is a functioning thing.

EXERCISE 11.1

Working with your debate partner or by yourself, if you are still on your own, answer the following comparisons of phenomena and prove them according to the paradigms. Try to do them verbally and run through them a couple times to put them in mind. You can find the answers to all of these in this book. In forging a good syllogism, you may want to review the advice at the end of chapter 6, "The Buddhist Syllogism."

1. How do the selfless and objects of knowledge compare?
2. How do existents and objects of knowledge compare?
3. How do objects of knowledge and that which is suitable as an object of an awareness compare?
4. How do that which is suitable as an object of an awareness and that which is established by a valid cognizer compare?
5. How do objects of knowledge and functioning things compare?
6. How do established bases and phenomena that are nonthings compare?
7. How do established bases and nonthings compare?
8. How do functioning things and permanent phenomena compare?
9. How do manifest phenomena and hidden phenomena compare?
10. How do functioning things and matter compare?
11. How do matter and form compare?
12. How do external matter and form compare?
13. How do internal matter and visible form compare?
14. How do forms and visible matter compare?
15. How do sounds and sounds arisen from elements conjoined with consciousness compare?
16. How do sounds and phenomena arisen from elements conjoined with consciousness compare?
17. How do forms and tastes compare?
18. How do tastes and the taste of bread compare?
19. How do internal matter and external matter compare?
20. How do functioning things and nonassociated compositional factors compare?

EXERCISE 11.2

Make up your own comparisons using any two existents and prove them according to the paradigms. You can choose from any field but be sure to make up some using terms from the Collected Topics tradition.

12. Consciousnesses in relation to What They Perceive

In a meditative tradition such as Buddhism, the topic of consciousness is of the highest importance. And, in a tradition such as Buddhism that holds that we will be liberated through accurately understanding the nature of what exists, there is considerable reflection on the value of individual consciousnesses in regard to whether or not those consciousnesses are reliable observers of the real world.*

Although everyone will benefit from increasing their skill in analytical thinking, the Buddhist descriptions of what exists—including the descriptions of consciousness—is of little value if one does not reflect on those descriptions. In a way, it is easy to reflect on the nature of mind because it is always with us, we can do it anytime, anywhere. In another way, it is difficult because the mind is always with us and it is hard to pay attention to what is always there. The Buddhists offer detailed descriptions of sense and mental consciousnesses that are geared mainly toward weighing the value of those consciousnesses in accurately engaging their objects. Thus, those descriptions can have real value for all persons who care to measure the reliability of their thoughts and perceptions. This implies that reflection on these Buddhist descriptions of consciousness might be beneficial.

It may be difficult to take the full measure of what is meant by the definition of consciousness as

that which is clear and knowing.

---

*For a full and rich explanation of consciousnesses as understood in Buddhist thought, especially in regard to the role of consciousness in the theory of knowledge, see Lati Rinbochay, *Mind in Tibetan Buddhism*.

However, much of the layout of consciousnesses is easily right at hand, equally within the experience of everyone. Charles Sanders Peirce said, "I think of consciousness as a bottomless lake, whose waters seem transparent, yet into which we can clearly see but a little way."[1] The descriptions of consciousness given in this meditative tradition will assist most anyone in sorting out some measure of what is going on, and would have helped Professor Peirce see clearly a little bit deeper. Thus, I encourage everyone to spend some time reflecting on these descriptions by watching with a mindful sliver of your own thought the flow of consciousness as you go through your day.

Recall from chapter 10, "Basic Buddhist Ontology 2," that in the division of functioning things into matter, consciousness, and nonassociated compositional factors, consciousness is mutually inclusive with awareness and knower.* In fact, a knower and an awareness have the relationship of a definition to a definiendum, for a knower is the definition of an awareness. Also, since the definition of a consciousness is that which is clear and knowing and each definiendum is mutually inclusive with its own definition, these four—awareness, knower, consciousness, and the clear and knowing—are all MI with each other. Recall that the primary division of consciousnesses is into two types:

1. Mental consciousnesses
2. Sense consciousnesses

Thus, the four MI phenomena above beginning with awareness are all 3P with mental consciousness and with sense consciousness as well as with each of the individual sense consciousnesses like the ear consciousness. There is no overlap between mental consciousnesses and sense consciousnesses, for there is no consciousness that is both a mental consciousness and a sense consciousness. Thus, mental consciousnesses and sense consciousnesses are MX, but every individual consciousness is either a mental consciousness or a sense consciousness.

THOUGHT CONSCIOUSNESSES AND DIRECT PERCEIVERS

The most important distinction between consciousnesses to understand is between thought consciousnesses (or conceptual ones) and direct per-

---

*At this point, you may find it helpful to review the material under the heading "Consciousnesses" in chapter 10.

ceivers. Naturally, a person might think that this distinction parallels the one between the mental consciousness and the sense consciousnesses, that thought consciousnesses are equivalent to mental consciousnesses and that direct perceivers are equivalent to sense consciousnesses. However, these parallels do not work. Though of course it is true that only a mental consciousness can be conceptual, Buddhists say that the mental consciousness can be a direct perceiver as well. Also, the sense consciousnesses *may* be direct perceivers, but they are not always.

These two types of consciousnesses are real points of interest in the system because the distinction between them reflects the distinction between ultimate truths and conventional truths as well as other ways of dividing existents. Recall from chapter 9, "Basic Buddhist Ontology 1," that one of the divisions of existents is into ultimate truths, which is MI with impermanent phenomena, and conventional truths, which is MI with permanent phenomena. In the system of the Sūtra School Following Reasoning, impermanent phenomena are raised up as ultimate truths, and permanent phenomena are simply conventional truths. The distinction between the truths is based on the consciousnesses that are able to apprehend them. Every existent is a hidden phenomenon, which means that it *may* be understood by a thought consciousness, but only conventional truths *must* be understood by thought. Ultimate truths are "ultimate" because they *may* be understood by an ultimate consciousness—a direct perceiver—that observes its object exactly as it is.

Thought Consciousnesses

We can take thought consciousness (Skt. *kalpanā,* Tib. *rtog pa*) to mean the same thing as conceptual consciousness or thought or thinking consciousness. A conceptual consciousness is defined as

> a determinative knower that apprehends a sound generality and a meaning generality as suitable to be mixed.[2]

Taking this definition point by point: first, a conceptual consciousness is a "determinative knower." "The meaning of 'determinative' is that such a consciousness thinks, 'This is such and such', That is such and such'."[3] A conceptual consciousness determines that an object is such and such.

A sound-generality, which might also be called a "term-generality," is a generalized conceptual image that you get based on the sound of the name or a description of a thing without actually knowing the real meaning of the thing, like an impression of a person you get from just hearing the name or some comments about that person before you have met.

A meaning-generality is a generalized conceptual image of something that you have previously met with. For example, when someone says "car" or "dog" or "ice cream," something appears to your mind because you know what these terms refer to, you know their meanings. That image appearing to your mind is a meaning-generality. One way to understand these generalized mental images is:

> If someone says the word 'ocean' to you without your knowing its meaning, the image generated at that time is a sound generality, a mere reverberation of the sound 'ocean'. When someone says the word 'ocean' and you know its meaning, the image that appears to your mind is a meaning generality. Although not the actual object, the image appears to be that object.[4]

So, when you know the meaning, the meaning-generality is what appears to your conceptual awareness. For instance, the conceptual consciousness thinking about a table understands its object through the appearance of a meaning-generality of a table. Although there is not a definition of meaning-generality itself, we can construct definitions of specific meaning-generalities. For instance, the meaning-generality of a table is defined as

> that superimposed factor that appears like a table to the thought consciousness apprehending table, although it is not a table.

According to this system, we understand a thing like a table by the appearance of a "superimposed factor," which is the elimination of all that is not exactly identical with a table. Thus, we understand a thing by a negative route, which is accomplished by eliminating all that is other than what is understood by the term or thought. What appears to the thought consciousness apprehending a table is the elimination of nontable. That is, all that is not a table is eliminated, and thought understands what is left.

Through the appearance of a meaning-generality of a table, a thought consciousness understands a table. Thus, thought understands its object in a *general* way, for the internal image represents whatever it is you understand by the term 'table'. It is not a specific table but an image of table in general.

Since what appears to a thought consciousness is a permanent phenomenon, permanent phenomena are called "generally characterized phenomena." Their characters are known only in a general way by an imputing thought consciousness, and since they depend on such imputation by thought, they are not established from their own side. There is no way to realize a permanent or generally characterized phenomenon by way of its own specific entity. The appearance of that internal mental image prevents thought from perceiving the actual impermanent, ultimate truth that is a table. Rather, thought focuses on the static, generalized image of a table in and of itself, understanding the abstract rather than the specific object. Although the image may not last forever, for the time it endures, it is a static, unchanging, permanent phenomenon, as are all appearing objects of conceptuality.

Please appreciate that meaning-generalities are asserted to be permanent. This might seem surprising: it would certainly seem that, since these things come into existence after experiences and are based on those experiences, they are created and are therefore impermanent. For instance, we came to learn the meaning of "dog" in dependence upon seeing a dog and being taught the name. In this way, a meaning-generality of dog came into existence. The internal image may be a mental "snapshot" of a specific dog, frozen in time, and that image now serves as an elimination of all that is not a dog. Also, we can easily note that these internal images are not always the same ones. Once you have a new image of something, it is hard to recall the old one. However, I have caught myself with a new image for a person's name. Suppose that there has never been a big player in your life named "Susan," though you had an image of a Susan you went to school with. Then, a new Susan becomes a big player in your life, and the image of her becomes what appears to you when you think of Susan, not the old one. Have you had an experience like that? If so, it would seem that the image for Susan had changed and therefore was impermanent. However, the thought here is that the image is permanent because it is an elimination of all that is not such and so. Recall the story of the room free of elephants. That room is impermanent; however, the absence of elephants in that room is permanent and static, not created, even if the room had been cleared of elephants. So, the thought in regard to these internal images has to be that the internal image that is a meaning-generality is not like the impermanent room free of elephants but like the permanent absence of elephants. Thus, the image is what appears in order to represent the exclusion of all that is other than what is being understood—Susan, a table, ice cream, and so forth. Also, the image is not a visual object but a mental object, even if it appears like a visible object. Sometimes these internal images appear like sounds or tastes or tangible objects, but they can never be any of those things. This is why we cannot share them. And this is why the definition says, "appears like a table to the thought consciousness apprehending table, *although it is not a table.*"

Finally, the above definition of a conceptual consciousness specifies that a thought "apprehends a sound generality and a meaning generality as suitable to be mixed." A conceptual consciousness takes these generalities as *suitable to be mixed,* meaning that a person associates a sound—especially a term—with a meaning—that which the term refers to. They are merely "suitable to be mixed" because it is clear that a person does not always associate the meaning and the term. For example, sometimes you don't know what to call such a thing, or sometimes you have never seen such a thing before, so in those instances you know the object but not the name. It can also happen the opposite way, so that you are taking cognizance of the meaning-generality without mixing it with the sound-generality. For instance, some scholars say that "there are thought consciousnesses arisen from meditation such as those realizing impermanence or selflessness that are not apprehending a sound generality."[5]

Thus, it is possible to have a thought taking cognizance of a sound-generality without knowing the meaning, like when you ask your friend about so and so, whom you are interested in meeting but now know only that person's name. And, it is possible to know a meaning-generality without knowing the sound-generality. For instance, presumably a cow knows the meaning of a saltlick, those big yellow blocks farmers put in the pasture for the animals, but she would not know the name "saltlick." And, of course, it is suitable to mix the sound-generality and the meaning-generality, when you know both the term and the meaning.

If you look closely, you will see that some of your internal mental images are the words themselves. This does not happen with things like ice cream and dog and cat that you learned very early on, probably before you knew how to read. However, it seems to happen often with more abstract notions such as economic inflation or sexism. It seems to me that with these sorts of internal images, I get a snippet of television-style imagery, like an introduction that includes the words and some visual images that might be associated with inflation or sexism. Just watch, like you are playing a game to see if you can catch them. Anyway, maybe they are not real. You figure it out.

Direct Perceivers

Although conceptual consciousnesses may be completely reliable and correct, it is direct perceivers (Skt. *pratyakṣa,* Tib. *mngon sum*) that are held up as the most reliable and accurate consciousnesses. They are called *"direct perceivers"* because they realize their objects *directly* without depending on the appearance of an internal image. The actual object appears to a direct perceiver, not in a representative way, but nakedly. On the other hand, a thought consciousness might be called an *indirect* consciousness because it gets at its object *indirectly,* in a representative manner, only by means of an appearing internal generality. A direct perceiver is defined as

a non-mistaken knower that is free from conceptuality.[6]

A direct perceiver is a *knower,* meaning it is a sort of consciousness. Such a consciousness is *nonmistaken* in regard to both what appears to it and what it understands. The eye consciousness can see the blue of the sky, and it is the blue of the sky that it understands. Direct perceivers are *free from conceptuality,* meaning that they do not know their objects by way of an internal image but contact them directly.

Do not think that direct perceivers are the same as sense perceptions. First of all, at least according to Buddhists, the mental consciousness too may function as a direct perceiver. Second, direct perceivers are always accurate, true perceptions, but you may easily observe that not all of your sense perceptions are accurate and true. Sometimes we misperceive things. One classic example of a sense misperception in Indian thought is seeing white snow as blue. In certain lighting conditions, the white snow appears to the eye to be blue. We know this is a matter of the way in which the water molecules of the snow reflect the subdued light. In fact, even the camera records the color of the snow in that light as blue. However, if you go look closely, the snow is invariably white. This example does not always sit well with the scientific mind, though it may continue to be the standard. There are many more examples. If you are watchful, you will likely note a sensory misperception within the next hour. If you want to make one now, just manipulate your lower eyelid while looking at a light and notice that it appears that there are two lights. This effect too is due to the play of the light. Though you might wonder if the color of snow is really blue in that setting, you will not wonder whether or not you actually have two of those lamps. Thus, sense perceptions may or may not be right, and only some of them are direct perceivers.

Corresponding to the primary division of consciousnesses into sense and mental consciousnesses, direct perceivers fall into two groups:

1. Sense direct perceivers
2. Mental direct perceivers

There are five types of sense direct perceivers corresponding to the five sense consciousnesses—eye, ear, nose, tongue, and body sense consciousnesses. Consciousnesses of all types are impermanent phenomena, and, in the case of directly perceiving consciousnesses, their explicit objects are also impermanent phenomena, objects that disintegrate moment by moment. Thus, some have raised the qualm that since consciousnesses last for only a moment and their objects too are momentary phenomena, how can a sense consciousness know any object? One Buddhist answer is: "What we experience as sense perception is a continuum of moments of consciousness apprehending a continuum of moments of an object which is also disintegrating moment by moment."[7]

There is some bias on the part of those who seem to suggest that direct perceivers are dumb consciousnesses, like a bias in favor of "the life of the mind." This is not a bias shared by Buddhists, who think it is possible for sense perceptions to have remarkable clarity. "Sense consciousnesses are also capable of comprehending their object's ability to perform a function; thus, an eye consciousness itself can perceive that fire has the ability to cook and burn."[8] Therefore, direct perceivers do not merely register sensory input but are nonmistaken knowers capable of realizing their objects.

Although direct perceivers may induce conceptuality, they themselves are totally free of conceptuality. Such consciousnesses do not name or classify their objects but experience them apart from *conceptually* determining types and so forth. Still, this does not mean that direct perceivers are not aware of their objects' qualities. "Sense consciousnesses can also be trained such that an eye consciousness can know not only that a person being seen is a man but also that that person is one's father."[9]

A sense consciousness would not *conceive* that its object is one's father, but it may induce a conceptual consciousness that affixes names, determines types, remembers associations, and so forth. In this way, people are drawn into conceptuality, quickly abandoning the richness of direct perception in favor of mental imagery and abstraction. Impermanent phenomena appear nakedly to direct perceivers; however, ordinary beings do not perceive them nakedly because (1) generally these objects maintain a continuum of similar type moment by moment and thereby appear to persist and (2) such beings are under the influence of predispositions for naming objects.

The second group of direct perceivers are mental direct perceivers, and again these are of several types.[10] Included among these is mental direct perception in the continuums of ordinary beings. "The Ge-luk-bas assert that at the end of a continuum of sense direct perception of an object there is generated one moment of mental direct perception; this in turn induces conceptual cognition of that object, naming it and so forth."[11] Such mental direct perceivers serve to link the knowledge of raw sense data to conceptual consciousnesses that notice, name, determine types, and so forth. Lasting only an instant, these mental direct perceivers are too ephemeral for an ordinary person to notice; however, they are ascertained by advanced practitioners who have more stable and insightful awarenesses.

The most important type of direct perceivers are yogic direct perceivers, a kind of mental direct perceiver that is a nonconceptual, direct realizer of such profound objects as subtle impermanence and selflessness (or, more specifically, the mind and body qualified as selfless). Such yogic direct perceivers must be cultivated through engaging in meditative practice. The yogi first understands, for instance, subtle impermanence conceptually. Then through continued and sustained familiarization with that conceptual realization, the meditator is able to bring the image appearing to that inferential cognizer—that is, a meaning-generality of subtle impermanence—into exceptionally clear focus. Having cultivated a conceptual understanding to the peak of its capacity, the yogi eventually passes beyond the need for a representative image of what is understood and develops a direct perception of the object. These yogic direct perceivers are the most exalted of all knowers; being able to realize the profound truths in a totally unmistaken manner, they are the actual antidote to ignorance, which Buddhists assert to be the source of all suffering in cyclic existence. Thus, the achievement of yogic direct perceivers is the goal of all Buddhist reasoning.

DRAWING THE DISTINCTION BETWEEN THOUGHT CONSCIOUSNESSES AND DIRECT PERCEIVERS

As you have probably already anticipated, the distinction between conceptual consciousnesses and direct perceivers is easiest understood by noting the difference between what appears to these consciousnesses and what they are getting at, engaging, or understanding. In this regard, the Buddhists speak of two types of objects of consciousnesses:

1. Appearing objects (Skt. *pratibhāsa-viṣaya, Tib. snang yul)
2. Objects of engagement (Skt. *pravṛtti-viṣaya, Tib. 'jug yul)[12]

An appearing object is the object that is actually appearing to the consciousness, though it is not necessarily what the consciousness is understanding. For a direct perceiver, what appears to it is indeed what it understands. However, for a thought consciousness, what appears to it is a generalized image, a sound-generality or a meaning-generality, but what it understands is whatever that generalized image represents. The object of engagement of a consciousness is the object that it is actually getting at or understanding. For example, for both a direct perceiver apprehending blue and a thought consciousness conceiving blue, the object of engagement is blue.

Since all nonconceptual consciousnesses, including direct perceivers, proceed in a nonrepresentative way, what appears to such a consciousness is what it understands. If the appearing object is factually concordant, then what the consciousness is getting at, engaging, or understanding is real, the perception is accurate and faultless, and the consciousness is a direct perception. However, if what appears to a sense consciousness is not factually concordant, like two lamps instead of one, then that perception is not accurate but faulty, and the consciousness is not a direct perception. Rather, such a mistaken sense perception has a "clearly appearing non-existent as its appearing object,"[13] and a knower can never engage a non-existent.

On the other side, a conceptual consciousness always proceeds in a representative way. It may be right or wrong, factually concordant or not, but it always gets at its object by way of apprehending a generalized mental representation of that object. Thus, a conceptual consciousness is indirect. For a thought consciousness conceiving blue, the appearing object is just an internal mental image of blue, but the object of engagement is the actual object the thought is getting at—blue for a thought consciousness apprehending blue.

As described here, the ideal consciousness is one for which what appears to it and what it understands are the same thing. This can occur only in direct perception, and it can never occur in conceptuality. For a nonconceptual consciousness, if what appears to it is wrong, then what it understands is wrong. Such a consciousness perceives what it "sees," and, if it sees something that is not real, it perceives something that is not real. However, a thought consciousness will always "see" wrongly because it perceives a mere representation. Still, it may or may not be correct about what it understands. Thus, a thought consciousness is always a mistaken consciousness (Skt. *bhrānti-jñāna*, Tib. *'khrul shes*), which is defined as

> a knower that is mistaken with regard to its appearing object.

This is because what appears to a thought consciousness is an internal mental image, and what it is trying to understand does not appear to it. That internal image appears to a thought to be what it is getting at, although it is not. Still, even though a thought consciousness is necessarily mistaken with regard to its appearing object, it is not necessarily a wrong consciousness (Skt. *viparyaya-jñāna*, Tib. *log shes*), which is defined as

> a knower that is mistaken with regard to its object of engagement.

This means that a wrong thought consciousness is wrong about what it is trying to get at. If a thought is not wrong about what it is trying to get at, we may call it a "correct," "right," "accurate," "factually concordant," and even a "true" consciousness, for a correct thought consciousness is able to realize validly and incontrovertibly its object of engagement, the actual object it is getting at.* That is, within the context of being mistaken with regard to its appearing object—an internal image—a conceptual consciousness may be correct with regard to its object of engagement—the actual object it is cognizing.† For instance, an inferential cognizer (Skt. *anumāna*, Tib. *rjes dpag*) realizing the impermanence of sound—necessarily a thought

---

*See Lati Rinbochay, *Mind in Tibetan Buddhism*, 109–10.

†It is very jarring to say that an accurate and factually concordant thought is "correct but mistaken," meaning that it is correct with regard to its object of engagement but mistaken with regard to its appearing object. Thus, here I have adopted the convention of always spelling it out using the definition, saying "a consciousness mistaken with regard to its appearing object" rather than just "a mistaken consciousness." Note that a nonmistaken consciousness would have to be nonmistaken with regard to both its appearing object and its object of engagement. This is not just a convention. Rather, for any type of consciousness, if it is not mistaken with regard to its appearing object, it will also not be mistaken with regard to its object of engagement.

consciousness—is mistaken with regard to its appearing object—a meaning-generality of impermanent sound that appears to be sound but is not. However, such a thought consciousness is a *correct* consciousness because it is not mistaken with regard to its object of engagement—the impermanence of sound—that it realizes correctly.

Thus, every thought consciousness is such that what appears to it and what it understands are different. This is not the ideal sort of consciousness, which is one for which what appears to it and what it understands are the same thing. To some extent, from the point of view of a modern, results-oriented society, this seems like such a trivial problem. I mean, you got there, you understood, you made the sale! However, from the point of view of a meditative tradition that says we are liberated by seeing the nature of things, this little problem looms large. It is not that thought always yields wrong results. It is that you are not actually *seeing* the nature of things. It might be helpful to think of it as the difference between getting an accurate report of an event and actually being there. Being there, you had the experience yourself. Another analogy is that thoughts are limited to knowing their objects indirectly by the appearance of a representation of that object, which is like seeing an image reflected in a mirror. How many times have you wheeled around to see something directly after first seeing it in a mirror? You had solid knowledge of it from seeing the reflection.

Another way of describing the shortcoming of conceptuality is to focus on the falsity of the appearing object. Recall that the meaning-generality of a table is defined as:

> that superimposed factor that appears like a table to the thought consciousness apprehending table, although it is not a table.

It is easy to understand that it appears like a table, although it is not a table. We can verify this from experience and common sense. Still, it can be a viable symbol that gets you to the understanding. The problem is that it is stale and vague, as opposed to seeing the fresh, detailed object directly.

One way of describing this staleness is that the generalized, representative image is confused with objects of other times, places, and natures.[*] For

---

[*]The source for the meanings of the mixture of time, place, and nature is Ngak-wang-dra-shi, *sGo mang bsdus grva*, 406–8, 411–12. For a somewhat more detailed explanation, see Perdue, *Debate in Tibetan Buddhism*, 300–304.

instance, since almost all of us met with ice cream when we were very young and we continue to care about it deeply, most of us can catch the internal image of ice cream that we "see." In all likelihood, this image probably came into being when we had an experience with ice cream very early on. For me, it is a cone of strawberry ice cream. This image of ice cream came into being when Eisenhower was the president, and it still serves to represent. To this day, when I hear "ice cream," read "ice cream," or think of ice cream, even with ice cream right before me, what appears to the *thought* conceiving ice cream is an internal image of ice cream that I met with in an earlier time, in a different place, and of a different nature. The confusion of time is that the specific ice cream of an earlier time does not exist with the ice cream of the present. This is like when you introduce someone as your "friend from years ago," whereas the person has changed moment by moment since those days. Since all impermanent phenomena, including persons and ice cream, change moment by moment, the ice cream or friend of years ago cannot exist now just like then. The confusion of place is that the ice cream I met with in that other place is not present in the ice cream here in this place. And, the confusion of nature is that the ice cream long since gone, which is not of the same nature as the present ice cream, appears to conceptuality to be present with this ice cream of a different nature. You can see that strawberry ice cream is not all ice cream, but it stands in the place of all ice cream. This is something like when you say that this is the river that carried away my shoes, though it is completely new water. Recall that being "of the same nature" is such that, in one direction or both, if one of them does not exist, then the other one too cannot exist. If there were never any ice cream at all, there would have been no ice cream years ago or in the bowl before you now; thus, the ice cream in the bowl before you now is related as the same nature to ice cream in general but not to a serving of ice cream years ago. And, if a river no longer exists, that fact alone would not negate the fact that it carried away your shoes years ago.

Even with thought's problems of being representative understanding, this does not necessarily imply that thought is unreliable. Rather, even though it is able to understand its object only in an indirect, representative manner, through the appearance of an internal image, "thought is a reliable way to ascertain objects."[14] As a sign of the reliability of thought, the Dignāga-Dharmakīrti schools of reasoning present inferential cognizers, which are always thought consciousnesses, as one of the two types of valid cognizers (Skt. *pramāṇa,* Tib. *tshad ma*).

Thoughts, Direct Perceivers, and Their Appearing Objects

According to the *Tutor's Collected Topics*, part of which is translated in *Debate in Tibetan Buddhism*, permanent phenomena are mutually inclusive with the appearing objects of thought consciousnesses (*rtog pa'i snang yul*) and functioning things are mutually inclusive with the appearing objects of direct perceivers (*mngon sum gyi snang yul*).[15] This means that the only thing that can appear to a thought consciousness is a permanent phenomenon and the only thing that can appear to a direct perceiver is an impermanent phenomenon. However, appreciate that it is not quite that simple, for a thought can understand any impermanent phenomenon as well, as when you are thinking of ice cream. The point to take away from this alignment is that the only thing that can *appear* to a thought is a permanent phenomenon, and the only way a thought can get at ice cream is by the appearance of a generalized, permanent, static, internal image of ice cream. Thinking about ice cream is not as good as eating ice cream. So, in this way, thought can be seductive but unfulfilling.

It may be helpful at this point to note one clear distinction between Zen Buddhism and the Buddhism of the debate tradition. Both find some fault with conceptuality. Again and again in these Asian religions we see the suggestion that conceptuality prevents us from seeing the nature of things. The content of a fully realized mind is free of conceptuality, and so both of these types of Buddhists agree to move toward awareness free of conceptuality. Appreciate that these people are friends and they are both moving in the same direction. It is just a difference of approach. You may think of Zen's approach as more typically one of zero tolerance—by stopping thinking, clarity free of thought will emerge. And, you may think of the Buddhist debate tradition's approach as more typically one of "the only way out is through"—by stopping wrong thought with right thought, clarity free of thought will emerge. Both of these approaches may be traced to the Buddha. The approach of debate and reasoning in bringing analysis to bear against obstructive thought is reflected in a quote by the Buddha from the *Kāshyapa Chapter Sūtra*. Suppose there is a fire created by rubbing two branches together and then the two branches are burned in the resultant fire:

> Once the fire has arisen, the two branches are burned. Just so, Kashyapa, if you have the correct analytical intellect, a Superior's [Skt. *ārya*, Tib. *'phags pa*] faculty of wisdom is generated. Through its generation, the correct analytical intellect is consumed.[16]

The metaphor is that the branch of right thought rubs against the branch of wrong thought, eventually both are consumed in the fire, and the need for thought is surpassed. Both the Zen approach and the Buddhist debate approach agree that thought, good or bad, must be transcended and that reasoning alone is not sufficient to do that.

The only appearing object of a direct perceiver is an impermanent phenomenon, and the only appearing object of a thought is a permanent phenomenon. What's more, whereas for a thought, its object is "seen" in only a generalized, representative form, for a direct perceiver, its object is "seen" in a specific, authentic form. A thought does not "see" what it is understanding at all (its object of engagement), but a direct perceiver "sees" exactly what it is understanding. Just as the sound "ice cream" does not give you ice cream and an image of ice cream does not give you ice cream, so you cannot fully appreciate ice cream from an internal image of ice cream. However, direct perceivers actually get at ice cream, and that's something you can work with. Direct perceivers always observe their objects just as they are, together with all of their specific characteristics. Thus, impermanent phenomena are also called "specifically characterized phenomena" because of the way that direct perceivers are able to observe them just as they are in their own unique character. Permanent phenomena are also called "generally characterized phenomena" because of the way that thoughts can observe them only in a generalized way. Thus, in the system of the Sūtra School Following Reasoning, impermanent phenomena are raised up as ultimate truths, for they may be observed just as they exist by direct perceivers, and permanent phenomena are simply conventional truths, for they cannot be observed just as they exist. In this system, phenomena are called "ultimate" or "conventional" in dependence on the awarenesses that take them as their appearing objects. Impermanent phenomena are "truths for an ultimate awareness," and permanent phenomena are "truths for a conventional awareness."

A RANGE OF CONSCIOUSNESSES IN RELATION TO WHAT THEY PERCEIVE

Now, with some acquaintance with the Buddhist descriptions of conceptual consciousnesses and direct perceivers, it is easier to understand the range of consciousnesses in relation to what they perceive. This is a graded list of seven consciousnesses that are ordered from the least reliable, which does not engage its object at all, to the most reliable, which engages its object exactly as it is.

Though it is a "graded" range of consciousnesses, do not think that it is necessary to move through the list in order. Clearly, depending on your consciousness and your object, you can jump in anywhere on the list. For instance, just look at a patch of color nearby, and in all likelihood you have a direct perception of that color. As you would imagine, direct perception is the best on the list.

Also, bear in mind that this is not a comprehensive list of all consciousnesses. There are types left over that are not included here, such as an awareness to which the object appears but is not ascertained.* For example, this is like when you are walking along tapping on your magic box, and you do not see the blossoms of spring all around you. The objects appear, but they do not cause you to ascertain them. An awareness to which the object appears but is not ascertained is not always due to a lack of vivid attention but may be a natural disability of the consciousness. For instance, whereas a direct perceiver is always a consciousness to which a specifically characterized phenomenon *appears* together with all of its uncommon characteristics, such a direct perceiver does not necessarily *ascertain* those appearing characteristics. In the case of a directly perceiving eye consciousness apprehending blue, it is a nonmistaken knower correctly ascertaining the color that appears to it. However, it does not ascertain the subtle impermanence of that specifically characterized phenomenon even though that naturally appears along with it as a characteristic of the color. Thus, with respect to its appearing object, blue, it is a direct perceiver; however, with respect to the subtle impermanence of blue, it is an awareness to which an object appears but is not ascertained.† Such an eye consciousness is a nonmistaken, nonconceptual knower of blue, but because subtle impermanence is an object of engagement for a mental consciousness only, the eye does not cognize all that appears to it. Thus, the content of direct perception is influenced by the perceiving consciousness.

This list of consciousnesses focuses on the issue of how we know what we know and suggests how to distinguish between what we know and what we merely believe. Some consciousnesses know their objects clearly and accurately. Others are mere beliefs, whether that which is perceived is real or not. Others are outright wrong. Think of this as a scale of seven consciousnesses

---

*See Lati Rinbochay, *Mind in Tibetan Buddhism,* 99, 102–6.
†See ibid., 99–106.

that a person may have in relation to some particular object or belief. Here they are listed in order from the least reliable to the most reliable.

1. A Wrong Consciousness

Definition: a knower that is mistaken with regard to its object of engagement.[*]

Divisions: There are two types of wrong consciousnesses:

1. Conceptual wrong consciousnesses, like a thought consciousness apprehending the horns of a rabbit or the belief that the Earth is flat
2. Nonconceptual wrong consciousnesses, like a sense consciousness apprehending two moons (where there is only one) or an eye consciousness seeing white snow as blue

Wrong consciousnesses are 3P with consciousnesses and with consciousnesses mistaken with regard to their appearing objects. They are 4P with sense consciousnesses, mental consciousnesses, conceptual consciousnesses, and nonconceptual consciousnesses.

A wrong consciousness is mistaken with regard to both its appearing object and its object of engagement, whether it is a sense consciousness or a mental consciousness and whether it is a conceptual consciousness or a nonconceptual consciousness. Both what appears to it and what it perceives do not accord with the fact. Such a consciousness is wrong, incorrect, inaccurate, and not factually concordant, for it does not get at its object of engagement at all. Wrong consciousnesses of all types are the least reliable of all consciousnesses.

2. An Uncertain Consciousness Leaning toward Believing Something That Is Not Factual

The next three on the list of seven consciousnesses in relation to the objects they perceive are three different kinds of uncertain consciousnesses or doubts.[†] These consciousnesses are mere suspicions tending to believe some-

---

[*] See Lati Rinbochay, *Mind in Tibetan Buddhism*, 109–10.
[†] In both Lati Rinbochay, *Mind in Tibetan Buddhism* and Perdue, *Debate in Tibetan Buddhism*, the Tibetan *the tshom* was translated as "doubt." Here I prefer to translate it

thing but are entirely uncertain about it. All three of these are ahead of a wrong consciousness, which is decisive and settled in its wrong belief or perception.

An uncertain consciousness is compared to a double-headed needle (that is, a needle shaped like the letter "Y"). You cannot sew with a double-headed needle, as it will not pass through the fabric. In the same way, a consciousness that is a mere uncertain suspicion is stuck like the needle. We all know that feeling of getting stuck in uncertainty so that we cannot pierce through to see how things are. It's like having too many variables in a formula. You just can't sort it out. A mere uncertain consciousness always reflects some measure of confusion or at least a failure to settle on a belief right or wrong. According to Lati Rinpoche:

> Doubting consciousnesses are among the worst types of mind. If one is travelling along a road constantly wondering, 'Is this the right road or not', it is difficult to arrive at one's destination. Similarly, if one is on a path of liberation and constantly wonders, 'Is this a path of liberation or not?' 'Will this help or not?' 'Can I attain liberation or not?' it is difficult to make any progress in one's meditation.*

In a dispute, creating doubt effectively beguiles others and keeps them from knowledge. We see this all the time. A friend of mine, who was attending law school at the time, said that they were taught three steps in regard to courtroom procedure. First, if at all possible, prove your case by what they call "black letter law." This refers to the legal code, which is printed in black letters. This is the easiest, for you just point out the relevant part of the law, and it is settled. It is hard to believe that many cases go to trial and get settled by black letter law. Then, my friend said, if you cannot prove your case by the written law, seek to prove it by precedent. This happens frequently. The lawyers will argue that this case before the court today is like that case that

---

as "uncertain consciousness." In English, we tend to use the word "doubt" in the sense of "probably not," as when someone says, "I doubt I will go to that party Saturday." In this system of epistemology, the word here translated as "uncertain consciousness" is meant to indicate a sense of unsettled belief tending to believe one way or the other in regard to an issue or a consciousness that is simply unsure.

*Lati Rinbochay, *Mind in Tibetan Buddhism,* 109. In this quote we see the suggestion of shared ground with what Christians call "struggling with doubts."

was before another court on another occasion, that case was settled in such and so way, and so the case before the court today should also be settled in the same way. Finally, my friend said, if you cannot prove your case by black letter law or by precedent, then muddy the waters. Just as you imagine, this means to stir up the sediment so that you cannot see through the water. Thus, the third step, if you have to do it, is to create doubt and uncertainty. This too happens all the time. Muddying the waters is often the last refuge of scoundrels.

Definition (of an uncertain consciousness in general): a knower that has qualms with regard to its own object.[17]

Divisions: The three types of uncertain consciousnesses, and the next three on the list of seven consciousnesses, are:

1. An uncertain consciousness leaning toward believing something that is not factual,* like "a two-pointed mind thinking, 'Sound is probably permanent'."
2. An equivocating uncertain consciousness wavering between believing something that is not factual and believing something that is factual, like "a hesitating consciousness which wonders whether sound is permanent or impermanent."
3. An uncertain consciousness leaning toward believing something that is factual, like "a two-pointed mind thinking, 'Sound is probably impermanent'."[18]

These three are listed in a graded series from the least reliable, tending to believe something that is not real, to the more reliable, tending to believe something that is real.

Uncertain consciousnesses in general and each of the three types are 3P with consciousnesses, consciousnesses mistaken with regard to their

---

*"Factual" means concordant with the fact, accurate, actual, real, or true. For now, let us set aside the question of what is ultimately real and what is not. Although in the long run this discussion is geared toward settling that profound question, for now let's think of this in a simpler way. For example, consider how this material relates to ordinary issues such as, "Did you see John Doe in the bank that day?" "In your experience, is fire hot or not?" Remember that in this particular system of Buddhist thought, they do assert a truly established external reality. They say the world is real, in some sense.

appearing objects, mental consciousnesses, and conceptual consciousnesses. They are all MX with sense consciousnesses and nonconceptual consciousnesses.

The first of these three is an uncertain consciousness leaning toward believing something that is not factual. Here the belief is not decisive like a wrong consciousness, but in this type of uncertain belief the person is tending to go the wrong way, to believe something that is not accurate. People with such a doubting consciousness think, "Probably such and so is the case," when actually it is not the case.

3. An Equivocating Uncertain Consciousness Wavering between Believing Something That Is Not Factual and Believing Something That Is Factual

This second type of uncertain consciousness, the third on the list of seven, is a two-pointed mind that is wavering equally between yes and no. This sort of consciousness is a slight improvement over the previous one, an uncertain consciousness leaning toward believing something that is not factual, because it has trended away from the wrong decision. None of these types of uncertain consciousnesses is decisive, but this type is not coming close to any decision, neither favoring one side or the other. The improvement is that it is not leaning toward the wrong decision. People with such an equivocating uncertain consciousness think, "Perhaps such and so is the case, and perhaps it is not."

4. An Uncertain Consciousness Leaning toward Believing Something That Is Factual

This third type of uncertain consciousness, the fourth on the list of seven, is a two-pointed mind that is leaning toward believing something that is real. Still, this belief is not at all decisive, and it can be reversed. It is just *leaning* in one direction. In this case, a person tends to believe something that is accurate, but the belief may not be held strongly, and the person still does not really know. This is like the case of a scientific theory that is still unproven but eventually turns out to be right. This sort of consciousness is again a slight improvement over the previous one, an equivocating uncertain consciousness, because it is trending toward the right decision. People with this type of uncertain consciousness think, "Probably such and so is the case," and their belief is concordant with the fact.

5. A Correctly Assuming Consciousness

A correctly assuming consciousness is one that is correct in its assumption, but it is still a belief and not knowledge. This consciousness makes an assumption that is concordant with the fact, and, though a person may have been trained to get to this level of understanding, it is not based on either full experience or reasoning. For instance, when something has been explained to you, as you continue to think about it and try to complete your understanding, that is correct assumption. Much of what we say we know is actually correct assumption.

Definition: a knower that does not get at an object with respect to which superimpositions have been eliminated although it adheres one-pointedly to the phenomenon which is its principal object of engagement.[19]

"Getting at an object" would mean that the consciousness has actually grasped it, understood it, realized it, engaged with it, and knows it as it is. A correctly assuming consciousness is definitely trending in the right direction, but it has not fully grasped its object. Such a consciousness has eliminated superimpositions with respect to its object.

A superimposition, or superimposing consciousness, is one which adds on something with respect to its object of engagement, as, for example, a thought apprehending sound as permanent or apprehending the mental and physical aggregates as a substantially existent self.[20]

These add-ons or superimpositions are not true to the phenomenon. To think that sound has the quality of permanence or that the aggregates are a substantially existent person is to believe in something that has just been added on or superimposed by conceptuality. These superimpositions cannot be understood as true to the phenomenon, so "if a consciousness does not eliminate superimpositions with respect to its object, it could not get at that object and could not realize it."[21] Still, the correctly assuming thought adheres one-pointedly to its ascertainment. It is decisive without the two-pointed wavering that uncertain consciousnesses have. Naturally, since the thought is consistent and additional information continues to support that thought, we often imagine that we *know* the object of the thought.

Alternative Definition: a mind newly and one-pointedly determining its own true object, which is devoid of either of the two ascertainments—that is, does not actually eliminate superimpositions in dependence on either the power of experience or a reason that is its basis.[22]

This definition specifies that a correctly assuming consciousness is a thought that has not eliminated superimpositions *in dependence on* the power of experience or a reason that gave rise to the understanding. Excluding that the thought arose in dependence on experience makes clear that such a consciousness is not a direct perceiver, and excluding that it arose in dependence on a reason that gave rise to the understanding makes clear that it is not an inferential cognition. These specifications serve to set off correctly assuming consciousnesses from the last two on the list of seven. Note that this definition does not say that superimpositions have not been eliminated, which would contradict the earlier definition. Rather, it says that they have not been eliminated by experience or reasoning.

Divisions: There are three types of correctly assuming consciousnesses:[23]

1. A correctly assuming consciousness without a reason, like an awareness that thinks, "Sound is impermanent," without any reason at all
2. A correctly assuming consciousness that has not really ascertained the reason, like an awareness that thinks, "Sound is impermanent," based on the sign of being a product, but without having yet ascertained that sound is a product and that whatever is a product is necessarily impermanent
3. A correctly assuming consciousness depending on a faulty reason, like an awareness that thinks, "Sound is impermanent," from the sign of being an object of comprehension (for which there is no pervasion)

Correctly assuming consciousnesses are 3P with consciousnesses, consciousnesses mistaken with regard to their appearing objects, mental consciousnesses, and conceptual consciousnesses. They are MX with sense consciousnesses and nonconceptual consciousnesses.

For this sort of consciousness, what you believe is true, but the thought is reversible because it does not have the stability of real knowledge, which you would never abandon as long as you remember.

I suppose that, in this day and age, we have to wonder if what we see in media sources counts as experience of something factual or not, in the sense of the specification in the definition that a correctly assuming consciousness has not actually eliminated superimpositions in dependence on the power of experience. Clearly much of what we see in movies and television shows is not real. If you see a man morph into an elephant, that is not real. However, what about the news reports we see? There too, much of what we see and hear should not be taken as we first imagine, and we add on superimpositions in regard to the images and words. However, it seems to me that if we are seeing the same images over and over, and it is not really rational to think that there could be a conspiracy so complete and so broad that the images in news reports are a ruse, perhaps what we are seeing is at least sometimes experience of something factual. This consideration is pressing.

6. An Inferential Cognizer/Inferential Cognition

The last two types of consciousnesses on this list of seven are the only two types of consciousnesses that Buddhists identify as valid cognizers/valid cognition—inferential cognizers (Skt. *anumāna,* Tib. *rjes dpag*) and direct perceivers (Skt. *pratyakṣha,* Tib. *mngon sum*). The other five consciousnesses listed here do not cognize, realize, or know their objects. These last two do. Thus, only these last two are incontrovertible consciousnesses, meaning that a person will not turn away from the knowledge gained with these consciousnesses, at least so long as that person remembers.

Definition: a determinative knower that, depending on its basis, a correct sign, is incontrovertible with regard to its object of comprehension, a hidden phenomenon.[24]

Inference is "determinative," which means that it is always conceptual. Inference is "incontrovertible," which implies that it is "a consciousness [that] has gotten at an object with respect to which superimpositions have been eliminated."[25] Since such a consciousness has actually realized the object, it is incontrovertible, meaning that one will not turn away from the knowledge. You know what you know. It is a consciousness arisen from a correct logical reason. You can understand from this definition that inference has access only to existent phenomena, for the definition refers to "its object of comprehension, a hidden phenomenon."

In this theory of knowledge, inferential cognition is the conceptual branch of knowledge. Since it is conceptual, it is always a consciousness mistaken with regard to its appearing object. Thus, we can say that inference is the means for understanding phenomena that are not observed directly.

An inferential cognizer is the consciousness that a person generates in dependence on a correct sign. Such a consciousness is actual knowledge, and, since it has arisen from correct reasoning, it cannot be wrong. The classic example, which shows vividly the way that inference yields knowledge about phenomena not seen directly, is the syllogism:

> With respect to the subject, on that mountain pass, there is fire because there is strongly billowing smoke.

You understand how to unpack the syllogism. You see strongly billowing smoke on that mountain pass. You know that wherever there is strongly billowing smoke, there is fire. Therefore, you know that on that mountain pass there is fire. You infer the presence of something not seen directly. Even if an object understood through inference is manifestly right in front of you, because it is understood through inference, it is something not seen directly, but seen in a representative manner.

Divisions: There are three types of inferential cognizers:

1. Inference through belief
2. Inference through renown
3. Inference by the power of the fact

Please look into these divisions, in accordance with your wish.[*]

Inferential cognizers are 3P with consciousnesses, consciousnesses mistaken with regard to their appearing objects, mental consciousnesses, conceptual consciousnesses, valid cognizers, incontrovertible consciousnesses, and correct consciousnesses. They are MX with sense consciousnesses, nonconceptual consciousnesses, and wrong consciousnesses.

In this theory of knowledge, inferential cognition is actual knowledge but, in a sense, it is somewhat less preferable than direct perception because such a consciousness does not "see" directly what it understands. Still, though you don't see the fire, you know it is there. It is effective.

---

[*]See Lati Rinbochay, *Mind in Tibetan Buddhism,* 77–82; and Perdue, *Debate in Tibetan Buddhism,* 178–83.

7. A Direct Perceiver/Direct Perception

The seventh and last on the list is a direct perceiver/direct perception (Skt. *pratyakṣa*, Tib. *mngon sum*). Direct perception is the nonconceptual branch of knowledge and, along with inferential cognition, is the only other type of consciousness that the Buddhists identify as a valid cognizer/valid cognition.

Definition: a non-mistaken knower that is free from conceptuality.[26]

Direct perception is the most preferred type of consciousness because it is nonmistaken with regard to both its appearing object and its object of engagement. It perceives its object directly and accurately, both "seeing" and understanding the same thing. It is raised up as the most reliable sort of knowledge possible.

In the example of inferring the presence of fire on that mountain pass from the sign of there being strongly billowing smoke, imagine that after observing the smoke, finally you see fire raging on the mountain. Seeing fire, you understand the presence of fire. What you observe and what you understand are the same.

Direct perception excludes mistaken perceptions such as seeing white snow as blue, mirages, hallucinations, and so forth. Still, distinguishing between valid perceptions and invalid ones may prove challenging at times. Remember the lawyers' last resource of muddying the waters. Some may attempt to assail peoples' perceptions by saying something like "How do you know you saw John Doe rob the bank that day?" This is an attempt to pervert direct perception into doubt. Well, if there were (1) no circumstance that would prevent normal perception (such as darkness, disguise of the suspect, and so on), (2) no fault in the perceiving consciousness (such as blindness, deafness, influence of hallucinogenic drugs, and so on), and (3) no valid perception contradicting the perception of John Doe robbing the bank that day (such as seeing Jane Doe robbing the bank that day or seeing John Doe in another place at that time), then it is difficult to defeat the direct perception. You know what you saw, and you know what you know.

Divisions: There are four types of direct perceivers:

1. Sense direct perceivers
2. Mental direct perceivers

3. Self-knowing direct perceivers
4. Yogic direct perceivers*

There are five sense direct perceivers corresponding to the five sense consciousnesses: sense direct perceivers apprehending visible forms, sense direct perceivers apprehending sounds, sense direct perceivers apprehending odors, sense direct perceivers apprehending tastes, and sense direct perceivers apprehending tangible objects.

Mental direct perceivers include the moment of mental direct perception that is induced by a former moment of a sense direct perception and "mental direct perceivers induced by states arisen from meditation,"[27] such as the clairvoyance of the memory of former lifetimes and the clairvoyance of knowing others' minds. All mental consciousnesses other than conceptual consciousnesses are direct perceivers.

A self-knowing direct perceiver is an accompanying consciousness that experiences an internal consciousness. For instance, the consciousness that experiences an eye consciousness apprehending blue is a self-knower. Most scholars agree that self-knowers are mental direct perceivers.

Yogic direct perceivers, which are also a type of mental direct perceiver, are the fruit of the development of wisdom. These consciousnesses are like mental direct perceivers such as the clairvoyance of knowing others' minds in that they are developed from meditation, but in the case of yogic direct perceivers, the consciousness is focused on objects of insight, such as subtle impermanence and selflessness. A yogic direct perceiver is the result of "a meditative stabilization which is a union of calm-abiding and special insight"[28] in the continuum of a superior.† Such a direct perceiver realizes subtle impermanence directly or realizes selflessness directly, or at least implicitly realizes selflessness by a direct perceiver. Although this sort of direct perceiver is the fruit of effort on the path, the meditator has become so familiar with the object such as selflessness that no further effort is required to make the realization.

> Its basis is stable because the mind cognizing selflessness has as
> its basis clear light. It does not require or depend on renewed
> exertion because once one has become conditioned to it, it arises

---

*See Lati Rinbochay, *Mind in Tibetan Buddhism*, 52–72.
†See chapter 10, "Basic Buddhist Ontology 2," for a discussion of superiors.

automatically; it is unlike, for instance, high-jumping where, no matter how much you practice, each time you jump you must again make effort. . . . The difference is that one does not have to depend on renewed effort for those things to which the mind has become familiarized.[29]

Direct perceivers are 3P with consciousnesses, nonconceptual consciousnesses, valid cognizers, incontrovertible consciousnesses, and correct consciousnesses. They are 4P with mental consciousnesses and sense consciousnesses. They are MX with consciousnesses mistaken with regard to their appearing objects, conceptual consciousnesses, and wrong consciousnesses.

Believing in Something That Is Real

Is it possible to mature a belief to the point of knowledge? Of course. Think of the many things that formerly you merely believed but now you know to be true. It does not have to be profound. This process happens all the time. We often move from a mere belief to actual knowledge. Think of the many instances in the history of science when people moved from believing the opposite of what is true to correct theory and on to knowledge.

In relation to something that is real, a person may have any of these seven consciousnesses. In relation to something that is not real, a person may have only the first four, from wrong consciousness through to an uncertain consciousness leaning toward believing something that is factual. Clearly, we all understand that the question of what is real and what is not real is today, as always, hotly contested. So *for the purposes of these illustrations,* let us assume, in accordance with the pervasive Buddhist assertion, that sound is indeed impermanent. The seven consciousnesses in relation to the impermanence of sound would be:

1. Wrong consciousness: the confident belief* that sound is not impermanent
2. Uncertain consciousness leaning toward believing something that is not factual: an uncertain consciousness tending to believe that sound is probably not impermanent

---

*Belief, right or wrong, must always be a thought consciousness.

3. Equivocating uncertain consciousness: an equivocating uncertain consciousness wavering between believing that probably sound is not impermanent and believing that probably sound is impermanent

4. Uncertain consciousness leaning toward believing something that is factual: an uncertain consciousness tending to believe that sound is probably impermanent

5. Correctly assuming consciousness: a confident belief that sound is impermanent, though that belief has not arisen from inference or experience

6. Inferential cognition: the inferential cognition that sound is impermanent by the sign of being a product

7. Direct perception: a direct perceiver realizing that sound is impermanent

Although it is possible to have had (at different times) all seven of these consciousnesses in relation to something that is real, such as the impermanence of sound, a person would not necessarily have had all seven. It is possible that a person will never progress through to the seventh, or it is possible that a person may never have had any of the erroneous ideas. Also, it is possible that even if a person eventually moves from wrong consciousness to direct perception, he or she would not necessarily go through all seven of these stages. Just look at a light in your room. In all likelihood, you have direct perception of that light. You had no period of doubt and uncertainty, wondering if that was light. You just knew. This points out another important factor to remember here: direct perception is the highest-ranked type of consciousness, but it is not necessarily a big deal. However, if indeed such a thing is possible, a yogic direct perception realizing selflessness would be a big deal. It is especially in regard to such an understanding of selflessness that Buddhists describe the process for maturing a wrong consciousness to a direct perception as one mainly dependent on study, reasoning, and repeated observation.

Believing in Something That Is Not Real

Of course, if you believe in something that is not real, it is impossible to *know* that you are believing in something that is not real. We all believe that what we believe is true. Otherwise, we would not believe it. Even so, as we have all experienced, some of our beliefs have turned out to be unfounded and false. So, in relation to something that is not real, such as the assertion that sound is permanent, a person can have only the first four consciousnesses on this list of seven, as follows:

1. Wrong consciousness: the confident belief that sound is permanent
2. Uncertain consciousness leaning toward believing something that is not factual: an uncertain consciousness tending to believe that sound is probably permanent
3. Equivocating uncertain consciousness: an equivocating uncertain consciousness wavering between believing that probably sound is permanent and believing that probably sound is not permanent
4. Uncertain consciousness leaning toward believing something that is factual: an uncertain consciousness tending to believe that sound is probably not permanent

It is not possible to further mature this consciousness in relation to something that is not real, such as the belief that sound is permanent. That is, one can never come to have a correctly assuming consciousness, an inferential cognition, or a direct perception that sound is permanent.

Comments: Put in mind clearly that this list of seven consciousnesses is not comprehensive. According to the Buddhist layout of consciousness, there are consciousnesses that are not included here in this list of seven. What's more, this list is not even the main division of consciousnesses, which is well and truly laid out in Lati Rinbochay, *Mind in Tibetan Buddhism*. It seems that the main lesson here is the difference between what we know and what we merely believe. The first five in the list of seven are simply beliefs, some right and some wrong, or misperceptions. These descriptions of consciousnesses grow out of the consideration of what are and what are not reliable sources of knowledge. This is the topic of the next chapter.

For now, please take away from this description of consciousnesses these two ideas:

1. There are things I do not know.
2. There are things I believe that are not true.

We are all pretty comfortable with the first of these. Sometimes we work diligently to try to get control of what we do not know. Sometimes we rest easy in not knowing and knowing that we do not know. It is the second one that we more often find disturbing. We believe what we believe, and we believe that we believe correctly. Just to entertain the possibility that there may be things we believe that are not true, and we all do this sometimes, shows a measure of open-minded inquiry. Debate and analytical thinking require this.

Within the traditional Buddhist setting for this description, it is mainly a guide and set of standards for something positive—sorting out what is actual knowledge and what is not. However, in the context of modern Western society, this list also serves as an escape from the all-too-common idea that it is impossible to know anything. In this age of relativism, it is important to recognize that we know many things. Often we are beguiled, and our confidence is attacked; for example, some suggest that we can't even know what we perceive directly. Under the influence of the slumber of relativism, many say such things as, "We can never really *know* whether the earth is flat or not." (I understand that relativism does not generally assert that the earth is flat, only that consciousness is flat.) For such people, no amount of evidence will ever lead a person to knowledge. Even if we could put such thinkers in a spacecraft and shoot them into orbit and, looking out the window, point out to them "See! The earth is largely spherical, not flat," they would still deny that they could know that! They would explain that the appearance is perhaps a misperception; that if you close one eye, it still looks flat; that perhaps the image is created by an evil genius merely trying to beguile us; and so forth. This view may strike some as part of the sophisticated reserve of the intellect, but it strikes others as mere childishness. It is not so much a serious philosophical position as an emotional reaction. Despite the overwhelming evidence of the curvature of the earth both from the ground and the sky, do these people really believe that the assertion of a largely spherical earth is a mere conspiracy? Do they think that all the people who have gone into space have been coached and coerced into continuing a worldwide deception? Do they think we could never really know the truth of it?

EXERCISE 12.1

Working with your debate partner or by yourself, answer the following comparisons of phenomena and prove them according to the paradigms. Try to do them verbally and run through them a couple times to put them in mind and increase your skills. You can find the answers to all of these in this book, mostly in this chapter. If you need to, you may want to review the advice at the end of chapter 6, "The Buddhist Syllogism," and you should review the paradigms in chapter 11. How do each of these pairs of phenomena compare?

1. Sense consciousnesses and mental consciousnesses
2. Mental consciousnesses and conceptual consciousnesses
3. Sense consciousnesses and conceptual consciousnesses
4. Consciousnesses and direct perceivers
5. Sense consciousnesses and direct perceivers
6. Mental consciousnesses and direct perceivers
7. Consciousnesses and valid cognizers
8. Sense consciousnesses and valid cognizers
9. Mental consciousnesses and valid cognizers
10. Direct perceivers and wrong consciousnesses
11. Thought consciousnesses and correct consciousnesses
12. Consciousnesses mistaken with regard to their appearing objects and thoughts
13. Consciousnesses mistaken with regard to their appearing objects and valid cognizers
14. Consciousnesses mistaken with regard to their appearing objects and wrong consciousnesses
15. Consciousnesses mistaken with regard to their appearing objects and correct consciousnesses
16. Direct perceivers and nonmistaken knowers
17. Direct perceivers and incontrovertible consciousnesses
18. Wrong consciousnesses and mental consciousnesses
19. Wrong consciousnesses and sense consciousnesses
20. Wrong consciousnesses and conceptual consciousnesses
21. Wrong consciousnesses and nonconceptual consciousnesses
22. Wrong consciousnesses and nonmistaken knowers
23. Mental consciousnesses and correct consciousnesses
24. Sense consciousnesses and correct consciousnesses

EXERCISE 12.2

Make up at least a dozen of your own comparisons using any two consciousnesses and prove them according to the paradigms. It would be really good to verbalize these with your partner.

EXERCISE 12.3

If you have not already done so, please develop the habit of being reflective about your own perceptions and thoughts. Try to find where they would be on the list of seven above. Notice especially when you are ranking something as knowledge when it is not really knowledge.

THE LOTUS RISES FROM THE MUD

The lotus is a beautiful water plant that is a symbol of the purity of the mind of all beings and a symbol of a buddha, whose mind is thoroughly purified. The symbol is that the lotus is rooted in the mud at the bottom of the pond, and, when it grows up, it reaches above the level of the water and opens up, free of the stains of the mud in which it developed. Similarly, a buddha is from the mud, the mud of the round of rebirth, but not of the mud, for the fundamental nature of the mind is pure. Of course, most flowers have no dirt on them when they open up, but lotuses are especially superhydrophobic. That is, they shed water especially well in what is called the "lotus effect." This provides them with a self-cleaning process and effective protection against dirt particles and pathogens.

13. Valid Cognition

The ancient spiritual siblings of mother India—Jainism, Hinduism, and Buddhism—are all wisdom traditions. This means that they are based on the realizations and insights of great teachers of the past and that they all hold that suffering, as well as death, is related to a failure of wisdom. At least from the time of the Vedas forward, all of these traditions have held that a person may be freed from the constraints of suffering and death by the power of wisdom, by seeing the nature of things. Moreover, it has generally been the opinion of these traditions that achieving this liberating wisdom is within the capacity of each and every one of us. They assert that the problems that afflict us may be cured by the power of wisdom. Thus, in this effort to develop clear, accurate wisdom, one of the approaches that Indians adopted millennia ago is the tradition of philosophical debate. In India, debate was so valued that if a person lost a debate with an opponent, that person would have to convert to the view of the winning opponent. If a guru debated with another guru and lost, not only the guru but also all of his disciples too would have to become disciples of the winning guru. The thought behind this sort of custom is a radical commitment to consistency of explanation and integrity of view. If a debater could not put forth a sensible view and defend it, then that view must be flawed and it should be abandoned. If another puts forth a view that cannot be harmed by debate, then we should accept it.

In this atmosphere of such lively debates, naturally the discussions came to the vital issue of what we can depend upon as valid sources of knowledge. How can we begin to sort out what is real and what is not real if we do not have reliable tools to use? In the long history of Indian spirituality, different groups settled on different answers to this issue, which we can call "valid cognition" or "the sources of valid cognition." As mentioned in the previous chapter, the Buddhists settled on there being only two valid cognizers (Skt. *pramāṇa,* Tib. *tshad ma*)—inferential cognizers and direct perceivers.

In his *Pramāṇavarttikakārikā* (Commentary on [Dignāga's] "Compilation of valid cognition"), Dharmakīrti "proves extensively that there are only two prime [that is, valid] cognizers by way of showing that more than two are unnecessary and less than two would not include them all."[1] In the third chapter of *Commentary on (Dignāga's) "Compilation of Valid Cognition,"* the chapter on direct perceivers, Dharmakīrti says, "Because objects of comprehension are two, valid cognizers are two."[2] Objects of comprehension are divided into specifically characterized phenomena, which are objects suitable to appear explicitly to direct perceivers, and generally characterized phenomena, which are objects that must appear to thought consciousnesses. Since all objects of comprehension, that is, all existents, are the objects of just these two sorts of consciousnesses, Buddhists assert the need for just these two sources of valid cognition, one direct and the other a thought consciousness.

Other Indian groups proposed additional sources of valid cognition. One of these is knowledge gained by context. For instance, if you go into your garage and find that your car is not in there, you can know that your car is outside of the garage.[3] Another proposed source of knowledge is analogy, example, or comparison (Skt. *upamāna*). This is the new knowledge that you gain when you hear the description of something you had not known about and then you understand that thing based on the similarity with something you already know about. The Buddhists deny that these two are separate sources of valid cognition and would probably classify both of them as types of inference. A third proposed source of valid cognition found among Hindu schools is verbal authority (Skt. *śabda*). This is mainly textual authority, though it may extend to spoken authority. When the text is authentic, the Buddhists call such appeal to the word of scripture "a correctly assuming consciousness because it is induced by a mere term and does not realize its object."[4]

As the Buddhists describe it, the only sources of valid cognition are the two types of reliable *consciousnesses.* Only consciousnesses know things. Even so, of course, the Buddhists rely on scripture too. However, even reading a definitive teaching by the Buddha himself is not a valid cognition until readers realize it on their own. Just because the Buddha said something straight, and I can repeat it just as he said it, does not mean that I know it. It means only that I know the words of it. Of course, within Buddhist

THE VALID COGNIZER

The Buddha is called a "Valid Cognizer" and a "Valid Teacher," though technically only consciousnesses are valid cognizers. In fact, one purpose of Buddhist reasoning is to establish the Buddha as a Valid Teacher who has extinguished all faults and gained all good qualities. This is essential so that his sayings may be taken as validly established. Even so, his words are not to be accepted on faith, "Monks and scholars should / well analyse my words, / like gold [to be tested through] melting, cutting and polishing, / And then adopt them, but not for the sake of showing me respect." Quoted in Tenzin Gyatso, *The Buddhism of Tibet and the Key to the Middle Way* (New York: Harper and Row, 1975), 55.

thought, there is nothing the Buddha understood that we too cannot come to understand, since Buddhists believe that the Buddha was formerly an ordinary person wandering the round of rebirth, just like us.

Even so, one of the purposes of Buddhist reasoning and debate is to establish that the Buddha and the Buddhist scriptures are reliable, though the scriptures are sorted into definitive teachings and those requiring interpretation. Thus, along these lines, Buddhists give a division from the point of view of the name "valid cognizers" into three: "persons such as Buddha, scriptures such as the teaching of the four noble truths, and minds—direct perceivers and inferential cognizers."[5] This is called a "division from the point of view of the name" because it is not a true division of valid cognizers. Rather, it is a division of *things that are called by the term "valid cognizer."* The Buddha is called a "valid cognizer" or a "valid person" because Buddhists find that they can rely upon his sayings as validly established. Some scriptures are called "valid cognizers" or "valid scriptures" because they teach validly and definitively the way things are. And some consciousnesses are called "valid cognizers" too. However, from among the three—valid persons, valid scriptures, and valid minds—only the minds are actual valid cognizers; the others are merely called "valid cognizers."

14. The Three Spheres of Agent, Action, and Object

As mentioned in chapter 10, "Basic Buddhist Ontology 2," training in Buddhist reasoning and debate serves in a similar way to training in special insight, known as "Vipassana" in Pāli, a set of meditation practices that have become popular in Europe and America. Just as the practitioner of Vipassana is trained to be mindful of the field of appearances, both internal and external, so the Buddhist debater is trained to be mindful of the field of appearances. The intent of this chapter on the three spheres of agent, action, and object,* as the last chapter in part 1, is to bring together some of the material covered in this part. As I have said before, the descriptions of phenomena and consciousnesses are of little value if you do not reflect on their meaning. Thus, this description of the three spheres is a way of encouraging you to be mindful of what appears externally and internally. With a subtle portion of the mind, pay attention to what you are perceiving and by what means you are perceiving. The advice given to Buddhist meditators is that in watching, you should be like a person who hears a thief in the night. You should get up and quietly try to see who the thief is, rather than getting up and making a lot of noise, thereby scaring the thief off. That way, you stand a chance of observing the culprit. This means that you should not think so forcefully, for example, "Now I am watching my thoughts about such and so," so that no portion of the mind is left over. (This is not the advice given by modern American law enforcement! Modern-day police

*There is an important disambiguation here. Within Buddhist debate, the phrase "three spheres" is used as a warning, sort of like checkmating an opponent in the game of chess. In this sense of a warning, the three spheres are that the opponent in debate has (1) accepted the reason of the argument, (2) accepted the pervasion of the argument, but is (3) seeking to deny the irresistible conclusion of the argument. This is not the sense of the three spheres in this chapter, which describes a way of analyzing the range of sense and mental perceptions.

advise us to stay in bed and pretend to be asleep for fear that a startled thief would harm us.)

So, what are the three spheres of agent, action, and object? It is fine to think of this in terms of grammar: (1) the agent is that which is acting, (2) the action is what the agent is doing, and (3) the object is that upon which the agent is acting. For the event in which a person hits a ball, the person is the hitter—the agent, hitting is the action, and the ball is the object that was hit. Here are some ways of sorting out these three—the agent, the action, and the object:

The Three Spheres

AGENT	ACTION	OBJECT
Doer	Doing	That which is done
		That done
		The done
		The deed
Driver	Driving	That which is driven
Cook	Cooking	That which is cooked
Experiencer	Experiencing	What is experienced
Eye consciousness	Seeing	Blue
Nose consciousness	Smelling	Smoke
Mental consciousness	Perceiving	A mental object
Inferential cognizer	Inferring	The presence of fire

For a sense experience or a mental experience, it is the consciousness that is the agent of a perception, aware of and sometimes realizing an object. Of course, we commonly say such things as, "I see a pot," and in a sense that is true. Whereas Hindus predominantly assert a permanent soul who is a silent observer of the fields of experience and consciousness, all Buddhists deny that such a soul exists. In the system of the Sūtra School Following Reasoning, the person is merely imputed to the aggregates of body and consciousness and does not exist independently of those aggregates. Still, *in a sense,* the person does experience and perceive, but these activities are accomplished through the aggregates. In the case of a sense perception or a mental perception, it is the consciousness that performs the action of knowing. Recall that the definition of a consciousness is *that which is clear and knowing.* The nature of consciousness is clear, and the function of consciousness is to know things. The range of objects of sense and mental perceptions includes any phenomenon, permanent or impermanent, and non-existents may appear as well, though they would be "objects" only in a grammatical sense. Again, we say such things as "I see a pot," but the eye is limited to its own domain of the color and shape of a pot, the visible form. Recall that the Collected Topics debaters draw a distinction between *what the eye consciousness sees* and *an object apprehended by the eye consciousness*. What the eye consciousness sees is whatever we normally say we see—a pot, a flower, a person, and so on. An object apprehended by the eye consciousness must be only the visual forms that the eye consciousness has dominion over—the color and shape of a pot, the color and shape of a person's body, and so on.

As you have learned, the primary division of consciousnesses is into the two, mental and sense consciousnesses, and the sense consciousnesses are further divided into the five. The five subtle internal sense powers and the five sense consciousnesses—eye, ear, nose, tongue, and body consciousnesses—are always cited in this same order. Recall that some scholars say that they are given in this order because that is the order of reliability—the eye consciousness being the least reliable, and the body consciousness being the most reliable. Other scholars say that the forms and consciousnesses are listed in this order because it reflects the range of perception—visible objects being perceptible from the greatest distance and tangible objects being perceptible only when in direct contact with the body. Still others point out that the given order of the sense powers and consciousnesses merely reflects the physical placement of those senses within the body. Roughly, the eye is above the ear, the ear above the nose, and so forth, and the body consciousness is present throughout the body. The seat of the mental consciousness is mainly at the heart, so it is in order as well.

Consciousnesses

Sense
   Eye consciousness   Visible objects
   Ear consciousness   Sounds
   Nose consciousness   Odors
   Tongue consciousness   Tastes
   Body consciousness   Tangible objects

Mental   Hidden phenomena

The best and most reliable sort of visual perception is direct perception, in which both what the eye consciousness sees and what it understands are exactly the same thing:

Visual Direct Perception

PERCEIVER	PERCEPTION	OBJECT PERCEIVED

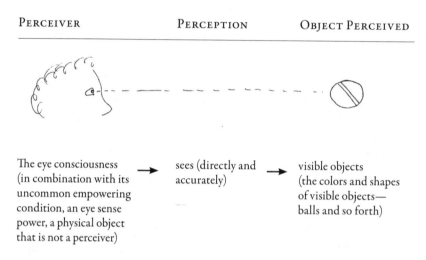

| The eye consciousness (in combination with its uncommon empowering condition, an eye sense power, a physical object that is not a perceiver) | → sees (directly and accurately) → | visible objects (the colors and shapes of visible objects— balls and so forth) |

However, as we all have observed, visual perception is not always accurate and reliable. Sometimes the eye simply does not ascertain a visible object. The object appears, but it is not noticed. Imagine a moment when you are walking along the path, deeply involved in a conversation with a friend walking with you, and someone you know passes going the other way. Though that person tries to catch your eye, you are too engrossed to see. Visible objects, such as the color of that friend's clothes, did appear, but you just did not notice. In such an event, the eye consciousness is unclear.

Sometimes the eye consciousness is outright mistaken. The stock examples of this are seeing white snow as blue or seeing a single moon as two moons. In these cases, the eye consciousness takes a clear appearance of a non-existent as its object. Such a consciousness is mistaken.*

The next table shows the range of visual perceptions:

---

*See Lati Rinbochay, *Mind in Tibetan Buddhism*, 112–13.

Visual Perception

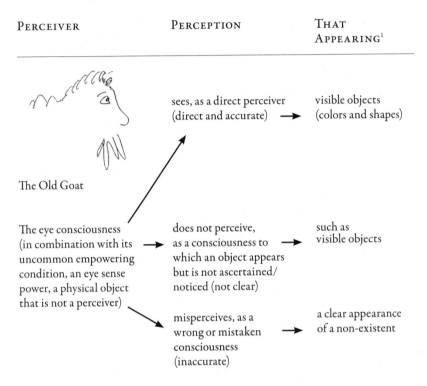

PERCEIVER	PERCEPTION	THAT APPEARING[1]
The Old Goat	sees, as a direct perceiver (direct and accurate) →	visible objects (colors and shapes)
The eye consciousness (in combination with its uncommon empowering condition, an eye sense power, a physical object that is not a perceiver) →	does not perceive, as a consciousness to which an object appears but is not ascertained/ noticed (not clear) →	such as visible objects
	misperceives, as a wrong or mistaken consciousness (inaccurate) →	a clear appearance of a non-existent

1. There is a little problem here in that the third sphere should not be "That Appearing" but should be "That Perceived" in order to fit with the other two spheres of the perceiver and the perception. However, often things appear to us but we do not perceive them, as in the second case above. "Perceive" should indicate clarity, active ascertainment, actively noticing an appearing object.

Clearly, the mental consciousness is the most complex. As described by the Buddhists, the mental consciousness is capable not only of thought but also direct perception. In fact, other than when it proceeds by thoughts, the mental consciousness is always a direct perceiver. As with sense direct perception, mental direct perception is always unmistaken and correct. A thought consciousness always operates indirectly by way of the appearance of a generalized mental image that may represent anything. The third column in the next table is "That Appearing" and the fourth is "That Perceived." This could have been done with the sense consciousnesses too; however, it is only for a thought consciousness that there can be a difference between what appears and what is perceived.

Mental Perception

PERCEIVER	PERCEPTION	THAT APPEARING	THAT PERCEIVED
			Perhaps—any impermanent phenomenon[1]
The mental consciousness	Direct (nonrepresentational)	An actual object	or
			Perhaps—any phenomenon (permanent or impermanent)[2]
	Indirect/ conceptual (always representational)	A meaning-generality (a permanent phenomenon)	Anything (existent or non-existent)
		and/or	
		A sound-generality (a permanent phenomenon representing a sound or term, for which the referent is not known to the hearer)	Sound (as perceived by the mind)

1. It is the assertion of the Theravāda/Hīnayāna schools of philosophy (which provide the point of view for basic Buddhist logic and epistemology) that the mental direct perceiver can perceive explicitly only impermanent objects.
2. It is the assertion of the Mahāyāna or Great Vehicle schools of philosophy that the mental direct perceiver is able to perceive any existent, whether impermanent or permanent.

EXERCISE 14.1

1. Be reflective about appearances, internal and external, in the way that I described at the end of chapter 10, "Basic Buddhist Ontology 2." Put mental labels on appearances as they pass. Just pay attention. Then, to the extent you can, notice the noticer. Ask yourself, "By what sort of consciousness am I noticing this object?" Is this consciousness reliable? If not, can I improve it? How or why not?

FPG/Archive Photos/Getty Images.

A Good Witch

Actress Elizabeth Montgomery (1933–95) played the witch Samantha Stephens in 254 episodes of the ABC situation comedy *Bewitched* between 1964 and 1972.

Reflection: Years after I had been exposed to this material and had reflected on it some, I had a very strange insight, a moment of epiphany, one day. I was watching a rerun of *Bewitched,* and I thought to myself, "You know, Samantha—she 'ay fine, boy!" And then I realized what a strange thought that was. I mean, exactly what was I lusting after? The images captured in the episode had to have been shot between about 1963 and 1972. It might have even been that by the time I was watching that episode, she had passed away. Even if she were still alive at that time, that particular fine form I was viewing would no longer have been, as we all change moment by moment. And, what was the evidence I was basing my desire on? I was seeing a fuzzy reproduction of the color and shape of part of her body and hearing the sounds of her voice, all this being reproduced by electronics. Yet, these sounds and images were enough to prompt a desirous thought in me! I felt deceived, vulnerable, unaware, and confused. It is not at all that Elizabeth Montgomery was not a great-looking woman. Surely, she was. Even so, it was a strange thought I had. Noticing such thoughts, it is not hard to imagine that we live unaware in a world of illusion.

PART TWO

Interactive Debate

15. Choosing Your Debate Partner

THE FIRST LESSON of interactive debate is to choose well your opponents. Most people are not worthy debate partners, for a variety of reasons. First, they must be rational. Second, they must have integrity. Third, they must be willing to admit when they are wrong. If any of these qualities are missing, there is little point in trying to debate with the person.

One time, Denma Lochö Rinpoche told a story from the old days at Lo-sel-ling College of Dre-bung Monastic University in Tibet. The monastery was vast, with as many as fourteen thousand monks, and by no means did all the monks study and debate. In fact, as he told it, there was a group of monks, sometimes known as monk-guards or "fighting monks," called the *dap dop* (*rdab rdob*) who would "choose to carry stones up a mountainside rather than study." Still, sometimes they would end up in a discussion on a question of the dharma. When they would disagree because of not understanding, Lochö Rinpoche reported that they would remind them of the saying, "Don't bang your head against the wall, and don't debate with ge-shays." If an opponent is not competent in rational procedures, then there is little point in trying to engage that person in debate. In my own limited experience on the debating courtyard with Tibetan youngsters,* I saw that there were some young monks whom most would refuse to debate with. This is because they were not able to get on with it. They had not developed their skills in rational discourse. They would just give answers, shots in the dark, without rhyme or reason. Eventually, they would drop out of the program

---

*Probably because the preferred place for debating year round is outside, the debating courtyard is thought of as a place *on* which rather than *in* which debate takes place. In this sense it is more like an athletic field *on* which competition takes place or a stage *on* which there is a performance than an enclosure such as a room or an auditorium *in* which events take place.

of studies and pursue other interests such as cooking or working as a tailor, which are still important.

Second, people worthy of debating with should have integrity. They should be sincere and honest in the undertaking. For instance, if someone is constantly changing the report of what was said earlier, how can you proceed? There is no use trying to build on shifting sands. The ideal is when both opponents are sincere in trying to work together to figure out what is real, to establish what is true and defensible.

Third, worthy opponents must be willing to admit errors. The basic procedure in Buddhist reasoning and debate is to describe a position for which the consequences are compatible and acceptable. If the consequences of your position contradict what you said, there is something wrong with your position. Thus, worthy opponents have to be able to accept that their position is faulty. Thupten Jinpa Langri, a ge-shay of the Shar-dzay College of Gan-den Monastic University, said that when a debater is defeated because of having misunderstood a point but then comes to understand better, a good monk will thank the opponent who defeated him.[1] This is integrity. It is not about winning the debate; it is about being right or wrong in the real world.

In modern-day America, at least, we have an unfortunate tendency to value aggression over rationality. You can see this in television, movies, games, and life. Thus, attempting to actually engage in debate can sometimes be risky. I have seen and experienced many times that one person will express a view, another will question or deny that view, the first will simply repeat what was said earlier, the second will question or deny it again, and then the first will respond with hostility. Many students who have completed this course have reported that when they tried to apply the procedures with friends and roommates, the others would just get angry. How nice it would be if they too had the tools to proceed; then we could get somewhere. But, if they don't, don't waste your time, and be careful.

CARD CARRIERS AND TRUTH SEEKERS

Sometimes, even when people are civil, there is little point in engaging in debate with them. A friend of mine who is a great philosopher and college professor told a story about a student who had come by his office to engage him in a discussion about creationism versus evolution theory. The student was a fundamentalist Christian whose position was settled according to the Biblical narrative. My friend is very interested in the philosophy of science and knows a tremendous amount about biology and evolution theory. Their discussion went on for over two hours, and he made no headway in convincing this young man that there may be some merit in evolution theory. No appeal matured into any fruit. When he told me this story, I said simply, "I don't think you choose your opponents well." Actually, at the time, I think this comment irritated him a little. I went on to praise him for his integrity in seeking the truth that corresponds to the facts in the real world (at least to the extent that we are able to observe what is real) and his willingness to engage in a sincere exchange between truth seekers. Years later, he said that the comment about choosing opponents well was some of the best advice he had ever received, and it had saved him countless hours that would have been wasted.

I think of this story as an encounter between a card carrier and a truth seeker. Usually, when we use the phrase "card carrier" it is about someone who is a confirmed member of some group, like a card-carrying Communist or a card-carrying Republican. This is probably not literally true. There may be card-carrying party members, I'm not sure, but I think this is modeled after people who are card-carrying electricians, plumbers, and so on, that is, people who have earned certification in a trade. That is one sense of a card carrier, but not the sense in which I mean it. What I am thinking of here is suggested by the philosopher Ludwig Wittgenstein in his stratospheric critique of a very common model of the relationship between thinking and language use:

> When I hear the word "red" with understanding, a red image should be before my mind's eye. But why should I not substitute seeing a red bit of paper for imagining a red patch? The visual image will only be the more vivid. Imagine a man always carrying a sheet of paper in his pocket on which the names of colors are co-ordinated with coloured patches. . . . We could perfectly well, for our purposes, replace every process of imagining by a process of looking at an object or by painting, drawing, or modelling.[2]

In the way I am applying this example, a card carrier understands a new thought only by comparing it to the cards that certify what he or she has already settled on. There is no *imagining* what may be true, only a process of modeling after what is "known" to be true. If the new thought is compatible with the cards, then probably that thought is true. If a new thought is not compatible with the cards, it is not true. It is just that simple. In effect, this approach is: "If this new thought agrees with what I already believe, it is true. And, if it disagrees with what I believe, I know that it is false." Unless you yourself are the Lord of All Truth, this is an approach without integrity. It denies the possibility that, at least in this area for which I have cards, there may be things I believe that are not true.

As opposed to card carriers, there are truth seekers who proceed on the assumption that there are things they do not know and there may be things they believe that are not true. The goal of a truth seeker is to find the truth. As Thomas Jefferson once wrote of the University of Virginia, "Here we are not afraid to follow truth wherever it may lead."[3] At its best, this is true open-minded inquiry with integrity. This does not mean that if you are a card carrier in regard to some understanding, then you don't have integrity. However, if omniscience, or knowledge of all things, is possible, as Buddhists believe, and you have not yet achieved it, then there are things left to learn, and the approach of a truth seeker might be conducive to that effort.

Now, one of the problems that arises is that in almost every case, card carriers will claim to be truth seekers. I believe they are not being deceitful. Sometimes they think that they are open-minded, when actually they are not. More typically, they think that they are truth seekers because they have found the truth (which is on a card in their pockets), and they found it because they are truth seekers. In any case, for card carriers, real investigation has stopped. Part of having integrity is trying to understand when you have settled on an established truth about something and no further investigation is needed and when you have settled on something that may not be final. Distinguishing these two circumstances requires a lot of introspection and can be devilishly challenging.

In nearly four decades teaching in college classrooms, I have observed that the number-one obstacle to learning is thinking that you already know. If you already know, what need is there to learn? This is like a cup that is already full, so you cannot pour anything more into it.

One day in his office, Professor James Cargile was talking with me about how there are two kinds of professors of philosophy. Most all of them are able to explain topics of philosophy and the writings of some of the greats gone by, but only a few are true original thinkers who can express new thoughts. The abilities of the second type would hopefully indicate a higher standard of true open-mindedness and creative analytical thought. Professor Cargile's comments are suggestive of what I am trying to say about card carriers and truth seekers.

You see this in the Tibetan monasteries too. Most people are learning the positions as set forth in just their own monastic textbooks. There are a few scholars who actually go out of their way to read and try to understand the thoughts of other monastic groups and other sects of Buddhism as well. In the defense of all professors of philosophy and Buddhist debaters, it is hard enough just to get the topics straight in your own mind. It is another step beyond that to use what you know to create something new. Both in European and American philosophy and in the Tibetan monasteries, the number of authors is far fewer than the number of people studying the topics, and this is as it should be.

To the extent possible, truth seekers should debate with truth seekers. It is fine for people carrying the same cards to discuss topics with each other, especially within the limits of their own cards. It is a great way to deepen your understanding of those topics.

STATEMENTS OF BELIEF AND RATIONAL DISCOURSE

All of us have heard the old saying about how you should not talk about religion and politics. All too many times, discussions of these topics have led to argument and even bloodshed. But, of course, the entire history of Buddhist reasoning and debate is a history of talking about religion, so the warning should not be heeded all the time. One guideline for when it can be safely ignored is when your opponent has the three qualities you should look for in a suitable opponent: rationality, integrity, and the ability to admit errors. As part of integrity, a suitable opponent should be sincere and honest in the debate, actually seeking to develop clarity with an open mind.

Thus, despite the old warning, it is clear that discussions about religion and politics can proceed within an atmosphere of civility and mutual respect as long as the circumstances and individuals are appropriate.

Another guideline for choosing someone to have a rational exchange with is to make sure that you are both engaged in the same activity. In this regard, we should draw a bright line between statements of belief and rational discourse. A statement of belief such as "I believe in rebirth" says something about the person who spoke the statement. Now we know, as you have said, that you believe in rebirth. However, a statement of belief does not establish the truth of the belief. On the other hand, rational discourse may lead us to try to understand the justifications for a person's beliefs. But always bear in mind that not everybody wants to talk about why they believe what they believe, and by no means is everyone qualified to do so. Thus, a statement of belief should not always be taken as an invitation to rational discourse.

So understand clearly the distinction between statements of belief and rational discourse. When a person supports an assertion with analytical thinking and reasoning, that says something about the assertion—that is, the reasoning relates to the truth of the assertion. However, when someone says something like, "I believe in God," or "I believe in rebirth," these are statements of belief that say something about the persons who believe them but not necessarily anything about the truth of the assertions. We cannot legislate reality, even with fervent votes.

A COMMITMENT TO FINDING THE TRUTH

Recall that in ancient India, there was the custom that if a person lost a debate, the loser would have to convert to the view of the winner. Moreover, if a guru debated with another guru and lost, not only the losing guru but also all of his disciples too would have to become disciples of the winning guru. This custom shows a radical commitment to finding the truth, or at least a defensible presentation of truth, over fervent declarations, browbeating, and strong-arm tactics.

In line with this Indian custom, when Buddhism was first becoming established in Tibet, during the reign of King Songtsen Gampo (circa 740–98), the Tibetans arranged a debate that would set the course for the future of Buddhism in Tibet. In this period, there developed some disagreement between Tibetans who felt that they should follow the teachings and practices of Indian Mahāyāna Buddhism and those who felt that Tibet should follow the teachings and practices of Chinese Ch'an, the parent of Japanese Zen. Teachers of both traditions were coming to Tibet to help spread the dharma, but the teachings conflicted on the question of sudden and gradual enlightenment. The legend is that representatives of the two sides of the issue met at Samye, the first monastery built in Tibet, in the year 792. The agreement was that the debate would settle the question for the future of Tibetan Buddhism, that "the system of the winner would become the standard in Tibet, and the losing side would be forbidden to spread its doctrines."[4] The Indian side was represented by the monk Kamalaśhīla, and the Chinese side was represented by the monk Hashang Mahāyāna. The story goes that when Kamalaśhīla, an experienced debater, first saw Hashang Mahāyāna, the Chinese monk made a gesture that let Kamalaśhīla know that he would be a worthy opponent in debate. (I don't know what the gesture was.) Also, according to the legend, after the debate was settled in favor of the Indian approach and the Ch'an teachers were made to leave Tibet, Hashang Mahāyāna and his companions left in a hurry, and he left behind a single shoe. This was interpreted to mean that there would be some remnant of the Ch'an teachings that would remain in Tibet.

CHOOSING YOUR DEBATE PARTNER FOR THIS COURSE

The first priority is to choose someone with whom you will be able to find times when you can talk together. It is best if you can speak face to face. If not, you can converse over the phone. Another guideline is to choose someone to work with who doesn't have too many distractions and who does not cause too many distractions in you. That is, try to find someone you can work with so that you will both stay on task.

CHALLENGERS AND DEFENDERS ON THE DEBATING COURTYARD

The Challenger stands and asks questions, mainly through giving arguments following up on the sitting Defender's positions. The Defender lays out a position by interpreting passages or phrases from texts, giving answers for comparisons of phenomena, giving subjects for debate, justifying stated positions with reasons, and responding to the Challenger's arguments with any of several answers.

Photograph by author.

16. Challengers and Defenders

THE STYLE of reasoning and debate presented here assumes that, at least in theory, a debate takes place between one Challenger and one Defender. This measure of discipline, setting up the two roles and then staying within them for the duration of the debate, is essential to allow debates to proceed. If there were no agreed-upon guidelines, soon we would just decline into arguing and fighting. Then, it would be hard to reach any conclusions. Buddhist debate shares this need for procedure and constraint with every organized system of disputation.

Challengers and Defenders in the Traditional Tibetan Setting

Traditionally in Tibet and in India before, the vast majority of debaters were monks, but in recent years the Tibetans have made tremendous progress in including and supporting nuns too in the practice of debate. Nowadays there is also a movement toward teaching debate outside the communities of monks and nuns to laypersons as well.

Upon first seeing Tibetan monks or nuns debating, what fascinates and intrigues everyone is the performance of the person in the role of Challenger because the Challenger is standing, does most of the talking, sometimes shouts, and every few moments claps loudly. The Challenger is called the "one with the path of reasoning" (*rigs lam pa*), for the Challenger's job is to attack the Defender's stated position, mainly by drawing out the logical consequences of what the Defender is saying and forming arguments that oppose the Defender's position, right or wrong. The Defender is called the "one [defending] a thesis" (*dam bca' ba*), for the Defender's job is to put forth a sensible position, which the Defender believes is correct, and then defend that position by responding to the Challenger's questions and arguments.

People always wonder why the debaters are so animated. What could possibly have stirred them up so much? To an outsider who does not know what they are saying, it seems as if the debaters, especially the Challenger, might even be angry about something. It sort of looks like an argument. Challengers speak loudly, clap their hands in the Defenders' faces, demand responses, and scold and mock the Defenders when they don't reply quickly or when they give a bad answer. Sometimes they even push each other. You can see all this without understanding the language. However, this is just normal behavior in debate. Sometimes they do get angry, of course, but that is not what they are supposed to be doing. What they are supposed to be doing is working toward developing wisdom in order to achieve liberation, and they are supposed to help each other along in this process. If realization and liberation were easy, we would likely see it more frequently; however, supposing it is possible at all, some effort would be required. The goal is clear knowledge, and remember that the two types of valid cognizers are called "incontrovertible," meaning nonreversible, because the insights are final.

So, the debaters are animated in challenging each other and in defending their positions. And, of course, they use every trick in the book, just like every other pair of disputants all over the world. Whether the Defender is giving right answers or wrong ones, the Challenger will not affirm them. In fact, Challengers will deny the Defender's answers and draw on their powers of persuasion and skill in debate to trick, test, and befuddle the Defender. Just like other debaters around the world and lawyers in courtrooms, sometimes they just want to win the debate, but the ideal is to work together to develop a liberating, clear view of reality that is solid and incontrovertible. If a Defender withdraws from a correct position because of qualms posed by a clever Challenger, then that Defender's understanding was not solid. Further, there is a strong tradition in debate of leaving people to figure it out on their own. Teachers do that with confused students, and Challengers do that with confused Defenders. That is, very often a Challenger, and sometimes even teachers, will leave a student with questions. They will point out inconsistencies in their position but will not sit down and explain the answers. Sometimes this is to give the Defenders a chance to reach their own understanding, and sometimes it is because the Challenger too does not know the answer but is able to express the problem. Thus, one reason the debaters are so animated is that they are passionate about the learning. They are good students involved in verbal combat, and it is an article of their faith, for which they have some evidence, that learning will advance them on the spiritual path. They believe that wisdom is liberating and that this life is an opportunity to develop it. Never forget: for the monks and nuns of Tibet, debate is a spiritual practice. Often in Western countries we have a notion that religious practice is separate from intellectual inquiry, but in Tibetan Buddhism this is definitely not the case.

The monks and nuns have joined a community that is wholly designed to nurture members in their spiritual growth. As Thupten Jinpa Langri, who was a monk of the Shar-dzay College of Gan-den Monastic University, said in his recollections of his years of study and debate, "The debating courtyard is the classroom." Of course, the monks and nuns will gather with their teachers and will study on their own, but the main learning takes place on the debating courtyard where they develop a clarity of understanding. Essentially they are learning from each other.[1] As in every classroom, at least in every classroom where the students are passionate about learning, they are watching each other. One of the qualities of a class of debaters is that they all have a sense not only of their own abilities but also the abilities of every other student in the class. In this regard, debate classes are like foreign language classes, for everyone fully displays their strengths and their weaknesses. You cannot hide when you have agreed to be in a community where someone is about to challenge you and clap their hands in your face. This is part of the discipline they share. They are watching each other, and they give support to each other. In the setting of a monastery or nunnery, this always goes on. It is what we call a "fishbowl," a small community in which we all have to live together, like it or not. What's more, these are communities with shared rules and agreements governing behavior, so they watch each other for many reasons. They watch each other in the classroom of debate, encouraging and challenging each other, keeping the bar high, and, when someone is weak and not trying, they will eventually ignore that person and move on. This is another reason why they are so animated in debate. The community supports it. They are not faking it. They are not posing. They are sincere. In the old days in Tibet, every monk learned how to read and write. These days, in exile, the tradition has developed that monks and nuns are all expected to study through the Collected Topics. After that, only the better students continue on.

On first impression, it seems that the role of the Challenger is more difficult because the Challenger has to say so much more than the Defender. However, what the Challenger has to say is guided by the Defender's responses, and, once you learn the basic techniques for the Challenger's role, knowing what to say is pretty straightforward. The Challenger is required only to give fair consequences of what the Defender is saying, and if that is done, the Challenger is not held personally responsible for the content of the statements. Thus, the Challenger's role is in general the easier one because, even without a firm understanding of the topic, it is still possible to proceed and to look for apparent inconsistencies in the Defender's positions.

The truth is that the role of the Defender is more difficult because it is the Defender who has to establish a sensible position and then give quick responses to defend that position. What's more, the Defender is bound to the position personally, charged with giving accurate answers and held accountable for them. As evidence that the Defender's role is harder, students proceed through the program of studies, passing from one class to the next, by taking examinations in the role of Defender before the assembled community. That is how they demonstrate control of the material and readiness to pass to the next level. When a student is being examined before passing to a higher class, any of the classmates may challenge the candidate on topics they have just completed in their class. When a person sits in the role of Defender for the final examination for the Ge-shay (Geshe/Geshay) degree, any debater from the newest to the most accomplished may challenge the examinee on any topic covered in the entire program of studies.

One person who brings a unique insight to the actual practice of debate in the Tibetan monasteries is Georges Dreyfus, who was the first Westerner to earn the Ge-shay degree. He was born in Switzerland, spent fifteen years studying Buddhism through debate in India, and then moved on to receive a PhD from the University of Virginia. He said of debating in the role of the Defender:

> The great thing that one can learn in debate is to be willing to expose one's ideas and to admit that one is wrong. That does not mean wondering and wavering; it means being open to the possibility of being wrong and yet being able to maintain a strong, well-thought-out, well-argued opinion.[2]

The emphasis on learning to hold a position against the assertions of others does not mean that all debaters are learning precisely the same things. Nor does it mean that they are just learning an accepted dogma that is to be defended against all possible objections. Rather, debate is an intense and imaginative critical analysis. The debaters learn to make their own conclusions and to check their own and others' assertions for sense and consistency. Of course, there is guidance for an interpretation of the material. They rely on the great texts and commentaries of India, the works accepted by their own colleges, and oral instruction from their own teachers, but ultimately the understanding is always individual and personal. As Georges Dreyfus said in regard to the balance between learning the system and independent thought,

> In the monastery, the validity of the tradition is presupposed, and although it can be questioned, it cannot really ever be seriously questioned. But there is in the tradition, especially in debate, an element of critical inquiry in which you constantly submit your ideas to the possibility of being undermined. That is what debate is about.[3]

Each debater may be learning the same things that others have learned before, but the valid cognition of those objects of understanding is only to be found in each debater's own consciousness. The new, original thought that is the goal of debate is the dawning of new understanding in your own mind.

If debate were just repetition, then the disputants would not be able to garner a great deal of enthusiasm for the progress of the debate because they would know the outcome beforehand. However, debates follow their own course, guided by the Defender's answers and the Challenger's counterarguments. Because they are not preplanned but are made fresh, the debaters remain passionate about the undertaking. Even long after the studies are completed, the enthusiasm for debate still remains. Often, when discussing a topic of debate, an old Ge-shay's eyes will light up, and he will once again become animated.*

As you can see in many images, it is only in theory that a debate takes place between one Challenger and one Defender. In actual practice on the debating courtyard (*chos ra*), the debaters may start out that way, two by two, but then, as the session wears on, especially in the open-ended evening sessions, the debaters begin to gather into larger groups. When two debaters are engaged in a particularly interesting debate, naturally others gather around to listen in. Then, because they are all active debaters, some

---

*At this point, all the "old Ge-shays" are males.

who agree with the reasoning the Challenger is laying down will join in, clapping and shouting arguments at the Defender, sometimes even pushing the others out of the way because they think they have a better argument to oppose the Defender. More than once, in the intellectual passion of the young, these pushing matches have become more physical and less scholarly. Also, on the other side, sometimes as the debaters clump up at the end of a session, some will join the Defender's side, thinking that is the right position. Very often, these groups are what you see in the video recordings.

Also, you will see images of the examinations. People sit for an examination either to prove their competence so they can move to the next level of study or because they are taking a final examination at the end of the program of studies. The person being examined is in the role of the Defender, wearing the tall hat of a monk, which is yellow in the Ge-luk-ba order. Here again, at least in theory or at least at the beginning, there is one person who sits for the examination, and all the others sit in rows in front of the Defender/examinee. Sometimes, there may be two or more examinees sitting together as Defenders, and they may be challenged individually or together. For the exams, eventually others will join with a Challenger, but in this setting it is less frequent for others to join with the Defender, who is actually taking an exam.

Whether in a regular debate or in an examination, the usual procedure is that the Challenger approaches the Defender with a question. The Defender gives an answer, and the Challenger then presents consequences of the Defender's position that seem to oppose that view. The Challengers cannot lose the debate, mainly because they do not take a stance on the question. Rather, they just draw out the consequences of the Defender's statements. They are responsible for giving fair consequences of the Defender's position, and, if they don't, the debate cannot proceed. On the other hand, the Defender is the one who can lose the debate because the debate begins with the Defender's staking out a position and being held responsible for it. The Defender loses the debate by contradicting his or her earlier statements. The Challenger points out this contradiction to the Defender by clapping, palms up, and shouting "*Tsha!*" This means "Finished!" which indicates that the Defender's earlier thesis is finished. You might hear this several times as the debate goes along as the Defender contradicts several statements in a particular line of reasoning. When the Challenger shouts "*Tsha!*" three times, that means that the Defender has contradicted the basic thesis in the debate, and that is the end of that debate. As Georges Dreyfus reported,

So the whole exercise really rests on one person taking positions and the other person trying to show contradiction. That kind of training obviously involves an enormous ability to take a critical look at any kind of idea just for the sake of debate.[4]

You will know that your opponent is giving up and feels that the debate is lost not only by his or her open admission of contradiction but also by signs shown in body language. The Defender will start smiling, perhaps laughing lightly, looking around, and maybe even bringing up other topics.

As practiced in Tibetan monasteries and nunneries, the preferred setting for debates is outside, summer and winter. Kensur Yeshi Thupten said he found some advantages for the clapping even in extreme weather. He said that in the summer, especially in the exile communities in India, because it's so warm, you get a really loud clap. And, in the winter, because it's so dry and your skin cracks, you get blood when you clap.[5] Of course, as we all imagine, Tibet can be very cold in the winter. Lati Rinpoche recalled from his days as a boy in the monastery back in Tibet that the place where they debated at Shar-dzay College of Gan-den Monastery was a riverbed, and it was covered with little pebbles. He said that, as they were debating hour after hour, they would put those little pebbles in their mouths to make them wet and then stack them up row by row to let the saliva freeze in the cold air to make little pillars and pyramids.[6] Boys will be boys.

Reflecting the Buddhist affirmation of there being just two types of *consciousnesses* as the sources of valid cognition, the debaters are not allowed to read books on the debating courtyard or even to bring them there. You know what you know, not what you can access, search, and find. There is a joke among debaters that if a person has studied a topic and knows where to find the information in a text or in their notes but is not able to explain it from their own understanding, then that person "has their learning in a box" (where the books are stored). Nowadays, it seems that most everybody in the world "has their learning in a box," that is, in these magic boxes (phones and computers) we carry around. Of course, since stable knowledge does not just arise spontaneously, the debaters begin with memorization of the definitions, divisions, illustrations, and even whole texts. They create their own internal databases over which they have instant control. Beyond that, they also get instruction from senior scholars, study on their own, and then take it to the classroom of the debating courtyard. The daily schedule of the monasteries that have been reestablished in India includes two hours of debate in the morning and two hours in the evening after dinner, although advanced classes may extend these sessions.

The monks and nuns in Tibetan orders practicing debate begin with learning a few basic, solidly established forms of reasoning and then use those basics to study within a well-developed program working up to the great texts of India, both the sūtras and commentaries but mostly the commentaries. At the end of the program of studies, in the case of monks the successful candidate is awarded the title of "Geshe/Ge-shay" (Skt. *kalyāna-mitra,* Tib. *dge bshes*), which means "virtuous friend" or "spiritual guide," and in the case of nuns the successful candidate is awarded the title of "Geshema/Ge-shay-ma," which means "virtuous female friend."* The program consists of fifteen or sixteen classes, some lasting for two years each. Listed in order, these classes are arranged according to five quintessential topics:

1. Collected Topics of Valid Cognition (*bsdus grva*) [three classes—the Introductory, Middling, and Greater Paths of Reasoning]
2. Perfection of Wisdom (Skt. *prajñā-pāramitā,* Tib. *shes rab kyi pha rol tu phyin pa*) [five classes]
3. Middle Way (Skt. *madhyamaka,* Tib. *dbu ma*) [two classes]
4. Discipline (Skt. *vinaya,* Tib. *'dul ba*) [two classes]
5. *Treasury of Knowledge* (Skt. *abhidharmakosha,* Tib. *chos mngon pa'i mdzod*) [two classes]

In addition to these classes devoted to particular topics, senior students join one or both of the retainer classes, ka-ram and hla-ram, in which they engage in lengthy review prior to examinations for the Ge-shay degree.

Buddhist debate "is not a marginal phenomenon in Tibetan culture, but part of the cultural focus."[7] The basic reasoning techniques used in these studies may be applied to anything a person is interested in, but for the monks and nuns practicing debate in the Tibetan orders, it is a spiritual practice. Every debate session begins with praise of Mañjuśrī, who is

---

*In 2011, Venerable Kelsang Wangmo, a nun born in Germany, became the first woman to be given the title of Geshema, when she was awarded the Rime Geshe degree from the Institute for Buddhist Dialectical Studies in Dharamsala, H.P., India. Currently, more than two dozen Tibetan nuns have completed the first year of a four-year testing process leading to the Geshema degree. Debaters who are not monks or nuns are blocked from completing the program because nonclerics are not able to fulfill the requirement of the two classes in the area of monastic discipline.

respected as the manifestation of the wisdom of all the buddhas. As such, Mañjuśhrī is the special deity of debate. The goal of the debate tradition is to both broaden and deepen participants' understanding, increasing their capacities so they are better able to make progress toward liberation. The defilements that stain the mind have been accumulated over countless eons, and if it is possible to remove them at all, it will take effort, sharpness, and insight. The environment of the monastery and the technique of debate, complete with its trappings of verbal combat, are aimed at the development of an intense and definite knowledge, which they believe will destroy the enemy of ignorance.

CHALLENGERS AND DEFENDERS IN OUR COURSE AND BEYOND

It usually seems to those first learning about Buddhist reasoning and debate that the hard parts are learning the reasoning procedures and learning the material. This makes a lot of sense. However, one essential factor that slips in almost unnoticed is that the participants must adopt the roles of Challengers and Defenders and stick to them. This is not so remarkable in a way; however, this single bit of discipline is one thing that (1) makes the whole process possible and (2) very much sets off this practice of debate from ordinary discourse and even ordinary debate. What usually happens in ordinary disputes, as you may observe at every level, from your own personal life to the opinion television shows, is that the roles continually slip back and forth. In Buddhist reasoning and debate, the Challenger asks questions of the Defender, asks for information from the Defender, and poses argument-responses to the Defender's statements. The Defender gives answers, supplies information, and justifies the information and answers with reasons. In ordinary disputes, one person will challenge another with an argument, get an answer from the other, and then come back again with a counter. What usually happens at that point is that the one who was first questioned will then challenge back with an analogy, a criticism, or a counterargument against the first person. Thus, in just a few moves the Challenger has been pressed into the role of Defender because the Defender assumed the role of Challenger. There's no discipline there, and so it is hard to reach a conclusion. This happens among Tibetan debaters too, of course. Sometimes a Defender will fling back a consequence to the Challenger, or both of them will lapse into conversation. One time Lati Rinpoche sort of poked fun at me, saying I was "truly like a Mongolian Ge-shay." He was pointing out that if someone stated something to me in debate format, I would give a response, but if they said it to me in ordinary colloquial Tibetan, I wouldn't get it. He went on to say that this was sometimes an advantage for the Mongolians studying in Tibet, because the Tibetans would more frequently lapse into conversation, but the Mongolians had to stay on task because the debate terminology was in Tibetan, and they could not easily discuss it in Mongolian. Even though there is some role slippage and lapsing into conversation, the Tibetan debaters always know what they are supposed to be doing, and they maintain a high level of discipline.

Every organized system of dispute requires some sort of discipline and constraint, or it can never proceed. In our culture, we observe debate and dispute in two main settings. The classic debate forum is Oxford-style debate. In that style, two opposing teams of three or so speak one by one within the constraints of time limits and reserved quiet on the part of everyone else. There is also the discipline of the way the topic is set forth. Usually there is an issue posed in the form: Resolved: Such and So, and the teams on one side are pro, that is, in support of, and on the other side are con, that is, opposed to the resolution. After listening to the statements by team members on both sides, usually in a round or two, the audience votes and that determines the winners. Classically, at the Oxford Union, there are two doors leading out of the hall, one pro and one con, and the audience members vote by going out one door or the other.

The other main setting in which we see argument and dispute in our society is the legal setting, mainly in the courtroom rather than the legislature. In the legislature, what passes for debate can be called "speechifying," in which the members speak their pieces to support their views. You do not see members questioning each other and responding back and forth in the American legislature, though there seems to be more of this in the British House of Parliament. Legislature style is more like Oxford-style debate, except that the members cast the final votes.

Many of my acquaintances working within the American legal system complain that the television courtroom dramas are not at all like the actual practice of law. Even so, we know these things about the system: It is an advocacy system with two opposing sides. Both sides put forth arguments. There is sometimes a jury of peers who weigh the arguments with an eye to the relevant law, and there is always a judge. When the jury reaches a verdict in a case, in a sense, they are like the audience members in the Oxford

Union. If a judge renders a verdict in a case, then the judge is like an audience member with the only vote that counts. At no time in the American courtroom is either lawyer-advocate allowed to question the other advocate.

Beyond these two settings, sometimes there are genuine discussions with people reasoning together in academic settings. In these settings, there can be real give and take between discussants. However, these are not typical experiences for the public as are Oxford-style debates and courtroom trials. Georges Dreyfus, with his unique perspective as the first Westerner to earn a Ge-shay degree and who then went on to earn a PhD and work as a professor, says of the contrast between debate in the monastery and life in the Western academy,

> One of my biggest disappointments is that in a Western academic environment I did not find the same possibility of debate that I used to have in the monastery. I found that the monastery has, in a way, a much freer atmosphere than a [Western] university because there are fewer constraints which limit the intellectual exchange. That was a big surprise for me.[8]

His comments clearly imply that spiritual practice does not require foregoing intellectual activity. Also, since debate in Western academia, whether in the sciences or the humanities, usually takes place in written exchanges, even in our space age of communication, those exchanges are slow by comparison to the quick cadence of Buddhist debate.

Thus, one thing that sets Buddhist debate apart is the quick back-and-forth response of argument and answer. Another thing that separates it out is that the participants do a good job of maintaining the discipline of staying in the roles of Challenger and Defender for the duration of the debate. Another distinctive feature of Buddhist debate is that only the Defender can lose the debate; the Challenger cannot lose. The Challenger might do a poor job by giving arguments that are not a fair reply to the Defender's answer or by posing weak arguments, but there are plenty of other debaters standing around ready to push that person aside and do a better job. Also, in Buddhist debate, the Defender loses by contradicting his or her earlier claims, either losing out on the present line of reasoning or losing the whole debate. In Oxford-style debate and in the courtroom, it is up to the audience to notice whether or not the advocates are contradicting themselves. The lawyers listen carefully for the witnesses to contradict themselves, and

PRAYER BEFORE DEBATE

The monks or nuns sit together in rows and pray to Mañjuśhrī, the special deity of debate. This prayer ends with everyone clapping three times while saying, "*Chir! Chir! Chir!*" which means literally, "Because! Because! Because!" or perhaps, "Because of what?" Lati Rinpoche explained this as seeking an answer to the question "Why is the world as it is?" or "What is the reason that the world is as it is?" The young monk walking down the aisle is about to take an examination.

Photograph by author.

it seems that brings their whole testimony into question, though it is not necessarily dispositive for the case. Also, the legislators seem to listen very carefully for contradictory statements, but there too that alone would not mean the member would lose the argument in the final vote.

So, how will your practice of Buddhist debate play out in life? You cannot limit dispute to just those individuals who have some experience with this style of discourse. Thus, you will often have to proceed in a stealth mode. Follow the discipline to the extent you can and let your opponents cast about, as they will. In the moment, you will not be able to stop them, or train them, or insist they follow some protocol. You may be able to say things like, "Well, wait! I will answer your question, but first please give an answer to mine." If they claim that a counterargument is their answer, then say, "No, I'm sorry. That's a counterargument, not an answer." You will develop your own techniques. Please note that I am saying things here such as "please" and "I'm sorry." There are several reasons to be polite. As Josh Billings said, "One of the greatest victories you can gain over someone is to beat him at politeness."[9] Also, always remember that in America nowadays there are over one hundred million handguns and just about as many fools who are ready to use them. At the very least, there is no strategic disadvantage for you to be polite.

Do what you can to stay on task, so that the discussion may proceed rationally. The more you practice within this style of debate with your chosen partners, the more you will be able to adapt the style to real-world settings.

17. THE CLAP!

LATI RINPOCHE reported that in ancient India the debaters would sit across from each other and the Challenger would punctuate questions and arguments to the Defender by snapping the fingers. Then, when the tradition of debate came to Tibet, the Tibetans created the more active and dramatic style of moving around and clapping because Tibet is so much colder than India.[1]

Of course, in our modern era of the predominant scientific/physicalist view, we tend to believe that there must be a physical reason for these movements, and that may be so. It could be that they really are just trying to stay warm. But that does not seem to explain the facts very well. First of all, debaters in the exile community in India, where it's plenty warm, still move around and clap. Also, even back in snowy Tibet, the Defenders sat on the ground, with little activity, so that would not warm them at all. Some might believe that there are physiological effects of the movement, especially the clapping, and that the movements were designed to bring these about. For example, they may say that it assists the debater in developing new neural connections as they learn, or perhaps that the clapping assists the debater in coordinating left brain and right brain for a better whole brain activity. It is possible that these effects are real.

In any case, the Tibetan debaters think of the stylistic trappings and movements in debate as potent symbols that support their spiritual practice, their learning, and their efforts on behalf of the welfare of all suffering beings.

AUSPICIOUS BEGINNING

The Challenger is standing, and the Defender is sitting. At the beginning of a session of debate, when someone is in the role of Challenger for the first time in that session and before making any statement, he or she claps the hands together lightly and holds them apart just a bit, palm to palm. With this movement, the Challenger audibly recites *dhīḥ!* in a high-pitched voice. This is the seed syllable of Mañjushrī, the buddha of wisdom. The Challenger's attitude is that a debater must have a good motivation, the best of which is to conceive the special motivation of the Great Vehicle, the thought to establish all sentient beings in liberation. "But to fulfill this wish is not easy. You must have great knowledge and wisdom; and for this you recite '*dhīḥ*', asking Mañjushrī to pour down a torrent of wisdom upon you. . . . The seed syllable '*dhīḥ*' has a very special effect upon Mañjushrī."[2] The full statement the Challenger begins with is not just the seed syllable of Mañjushrī but "[*oṁ a ra ba dza na*] *dhīḥ!* The subject, in just the way [Mañjushrī debated] (*dhīḥ ji ltar chos can*)." The Challenger recites the first six syllables of the seven-syllable mantra of Mañjushrī under the breath, and all you can hear is *dhīḥ ji ltar chos can* with the *dhīḥ* spoken louder, in a high tone, and drawn out. According to Denma Lochö Rinpoche, the meaning of this statement is: "Just as Mañjushrī stated subjects in order to overcome the wrong views and doubts of opponents, so I with a good mind will do also."[3] Other scholars say that the syllables *ji ltar*, literally "what-like," in the phrase "the subject, what-like" (*ji ltar chos can*) refer to the mode of being or ultimate nature of phenomena, indicating that the subject of debate is the mode of being of phenomena. This is a compelling interpretation because realization of the mode of being of phenomena is the liberating wisdom.

QUESTIONING

Photograph by author.

QUESTIONING

The attitude is as if the Challenger is respectfully approaching the Defender with a question in hopes of getting a good answer. The Challenger asks the Defender about passages in texts, the meaning of a quotation, definitions, divisions, how two things compare, information proving the claims, subjects that exemplify the qualities being discussed, and reasons proving the claims. Every bit of this is fodder for further debate.

THE APOGEE
Photograph by author.

SIMULTANEOUS CLAP AND STOMP

The Challenger brings together the hands to clap at just the same moment as he stomps his left foot. Note that the left hand is turned palm up, and the right hand is turned palm down. The Challenger times the clap so that it coincides with the end of the question or argument to the Defender. As explained by Lati Rinpoche, the left side is associated with wisdom, which alone is able to overcome the process of being powerlessly reborn again and again into cyclic existence, for the wisdom cognizing selflessness is the actual antidote to cyclic existence. The right side is associated with method, which for the Great Vehicle is the altruistic intention to become enlightened, called the "mind of enlightenment" (Skt. *bodhi-chitta,* Tib. *byang chub*

SIMULTANEOUS CLAP AND STOMP
Photograph by author.

DRAWING BACK FROM THE CLAP
Photograph by author.

kyi sems), motivated by great love and compassion for all sentient beings. The clap is a practice of the union of wisdom and method. Tantric practitioners of the Great Vehicle cultivate these in a single practice, for they believe that it is only in dependence on the union of wisdom and method that a person is able to achieve the final freedom of a buddha. The union of wisdom and method represented by pressing together the palms has to do with subtle wind channels of wisdom in the wrists, which meet when the debater claps the hands together.[4] Stomping the left foot down is interpreted as slamming shut the door to rebirth in the lower migrations as a hell being, hungry ghost, or animal, as if there were a door in the floor through which we could all fall.

DRAWING BACK FROM THE CLAP

After clapping and stomping simultaneously, the Challenger then immediately draws back the right hand and at the same time holds out the left hand as if in a gesture of stopping. Holding out the left hand of wisdom after clapping symbolizes holding shut the door to all rebirth in any form, not just rebirth in the lower migrations. At the same time, the Challenger uses the right hand of method to raise up the prayer beads around the left arm. The beads represent all suffering beings, and the gesture symbolizes raising them up out of helpless rebirth, a gesture born of love and compas-

FINISHED!

Photograph by author.

sion that is the essence of Great Vehicle practice. There are 108 prayer beads, an auspicious number in Indian-based religion, which are counted as one hundred for recitations of mantra. On the debating courtyard, the debaters may use only "sūtra-style" prayer beads without counters, as opposed to "tantra-style" beads with counters, which are often little bells and vajras.

FINISHED!

The Challenger shouts "*Oh-ah Tsha!*" and claps one hand onto the other with both palms up. At this point the Challenger shouts, "Finished (*tshar*)!" According to Lati Rinpoche, what is finished is the Defender's earlier claims or the Defender's earlier misconception. When the Defender contradicts the original assertion he or she made at the beginning of the debate, the Challenger shouts "*Oh-ah Tsha!*" three times and claps three times, palms up. Some scholars say that what the Challenger shouts at this point is "Amazing (*mtshar*)!" That a person would first say one thing and then later contradict his or her own assertion is amazing![5] One piece of evidence for the understanding of this syllable as "finished" is that often at this point the debaters will laugh, "[Your] basic thesis is finished (*rtsa ba'i dam bca' tshar*)!"

MAÑJUŚHRĪ

Mañjuśhrī is regarded as the physical manifestation of the wisdom of all the buddhas; thus, he is the special deity of debate. The large representation of Mañjuśhrī in the center is his outer form; to his lower right, on our left, is the inner form of Mañjuśhrī, shown in union with his consort Sarasvatī; and, to his lower left, on our right, is the secret form of Mañjuśhrī, also shown in union with his consort Sarasvatī.

The image was painted by the Venerable Sangye Yeshi, a famous thangka painter who lived in Dharamsala. Photograph by Ann Swanson.

18. Mañjuśrī

The Special Deity of Debate

MAÑJUŚRĪ IS REGARDED as the physical manifestation of the wisdom of all of the buddhas. As such, he is a protector and a fully realized buddha, though he is often included as a "celestial bodhisattva." This is suitable because a buddha is a bodhisattva superior, having completed the path of a bodhisattva. As the manifestation of the omniscient wisdom of the buddhas, of course it is Mañjuśrī who is the special deity of debate, all logic and epistemology studies, and, more broadly, all topics of philosophy.*
In fact, all Buddhist texts, sūtras as well as commentaries, on topics included in the basket of knowledge (Skt. *abhidharma*, Tib. *chos mngon pa*) begin by paying homage to Mañjuśrī.

In this image (see facing page), Mañjuśrī is shown in the form of a sixteen-year-old boy, the age that is regarded as the height of a person's brightness, luminosity, and vigor. He is adorned with jewelry and sits with his legs crossed in the style of the vajra posture, often called the "lotus posture," and he is tilted somewhat to his left.

His left hand is in the gesture (Skt. *mudrā*) of teaching, and he holds the stem of a lotus, with the flower rising up on his left side (the right side of the image). Resting on top of the lotus is a scripture of the Perfection of Wisdom (Skt. *prajñā-pāramitā*, Tib. *shes rab kyi pha rol tu phyin*).† The text is in the shape of a long rectangular solid. Unlike an ordinary, modern book, it is in the style of ancient Indian or Tibetan texts, which is a stack of unbound pages wrapped together. That Mañjuśrī holds a text of the Perfection of

---

*A buddha is often called a "deity" (Skt. *deva*, Tib. *hla*), especially in Great Vehicle Buddhism. Of course this is not meant to imply an equivalence with a creator deity.
†The Perfection of Wisdom is a genre of texts, not a specific text; therefore, the title is not italicized.

Wisdom indicates that "he sees all objects just as they are with his pure and clear intelligence."* The Perfection of Wisdom Sūtras "express the superior of all of Buddha's teachings and are the main of the eighty-four thousand masses of doctrine."[1] Mañjushrī holds the scripture on his left side, the side associated with wisdom, indicating that his wisdom is in accordance with the Buddha's highest teachings of the most profound emptiness (Skt. *shūnyatā*, Tib. *stong pa nyid*).

In his right hand, Mañjushrī holds a flaming sword above his head, as if he is prepared to swing it. This sword "clears away the darkness of ignorance and cuts every sprout of suffering."[2] Mañjushrī holds the sword in his right hand, the side associated with method, indicating his method (Skt. *upāya*, Tib. *thabs*). As a buddha, that method includes the motivation of the Great Vehicle, the wish to establish all sentient beings in a state free of suffering. The sword is in flames, for it illuminates. Just as the light of a flame is able to clear away darkness in a room, so the light of wisdom is able to *clear away the darkness of ignorance* and thereby free beings from suffering. Also, this flaming sword *cuts every sprout of suffering,* for wisdom is the actual antidote to ignorance, the root cause of all suffering. Wisdom destroys the root causes of suffering, making it impossible for suffering to arise again. In another way of understanding the flaming sword, the flames around it indicate that *it is unobstructed* with regard to any phenomenon and is able to cut through false appearances.

Behind Mañjushrī's head there is a halo, and there is a larger one behind his body. These indicate his luminosity and potency. He sits on a moon disk, another symbol of compassion. It is as if the moon were made flat and used as a cushion. The moon disk is on top of a sun disk, which is a symbol of wisdom. You can see that there are two disks. The sun and moon disks rest on a lotus, which is a symbol of the fundamental purity of the mind, for if the mind were not pure in its nature, it would be impossible to purify the stains of ignorance and become liberated. Mañjushrī and the entire seat rest on a plateau in the mountains. On the upper right, over the left shoulder of Mañjushrī, is the sun, and on the upper left, over his right shoulder, is the moon. At the bottom of the image, in the foreground, are offerings such as

---

*This line is from a popular prayer to Mañjushrī. For the Tibetan of this prayer, see *Daily Recitations of Preliminaries* (Dharamsala: Library of Tibetan Works and Archives, 1975), 4. According to Kensur Yeshi Thupten, this prayer was composed by a group of Indian Buddhist pandits who planned that the next day each would bring a prayer to Mañjushrī. When they gathered the next day, they found that all of them had composed the same prayer.

would be offered to a peaceful deity. In addition to the many round figures, which are bags of jewels, there are pleasant offerings for the five senses. In the middle is a mirror for the eyes. Below the mirror are two cymbals as an offering to the ears. On the bottom right is a conch shell of incense for the nose. On the bottom left, among the collection of bags of jewels, is fruit to please the tongue. And, laced between the two cymbals, there is a flowing silk scarf to please the sense of touch.

Mañjuśhrī ('Jam dpal) is also called Mañjughoṣha ('Jam dbyang), and even Mañjushrīghoṣha ('Jam dpal dbyang):

> He is called *mañju*—gentle, agreeable, soft—because he is free from the harshness of afflictive and non-afflictive obstructions. He is called *ghoṣha*—speech, sound, melody—because he is the lord of speech and his speech possesses the sixty qualities of vocalization. He is called *shrī*—glorious—because he has the glory of the completion of the two collections, merit and wisdom.[3]

Although many of us might like to think that it is not so, every variety of Buddhism is devotional, especially Tantric Buddhism. It is a mistake to label Tibetan Buddhism as only Vajrayāna Buddhism or Tantric Buddhism, but the perspective of tantra is always in the background of things in Tibet. Thus, Mañjuśhrī is always greeted with praise and offerings. The attitude is that we need all the help we can get. "In order to penetrate the subtle meaning of Buddha's teaching, it is necessary to have the wisdom discriminating phenomena, and Mañjuśhrī along with [his consort] Sarasvatī [dbYang can ma] are the two deities that bestow wisdom to others."[4]

Mañjuśhrī is called a protector (*mgon po*), a buddha who protects sentient beings from suffering and establishes them in happiness.

> The Protector Mañjuśhrī, who has great love and compassion for sentient beings suffering in cyclic existence, dispels the darkness of ignorance in their minds through the rays of light of his wisdom as sunlight dispels darkness. Mañjuśhrī will clear away the darkness of mind of all those who pray to him.[5]

When Tsong-kha-pa, the founder of the Ge-luk-ba order of Tibetan Buddhism, heard that Mañjuśhrī is able to bestow wisdom upon trainees, he resolved not to turn away from him.

> When a trainee pleases him, Manjushri can, with merely a glance, bestow the wisdom discriminating the truth in the sense of quickly increasing realisation, like lighting a flame. Tsong-ka-pa says that having heard such a marvellous account, he has relied on Manjushri as his special deity over a long time and will not forsake him in the future.[6]

The story goes that Tsong-kha-pa made great effort and actually achieved a meeting with the Protector Mañjuśrī.

> There was a painting of Manjushri on the wall of Tsong-ka-pa's Ga-wa-dong retreat, and upon improvement of his meditation a great light emitted from Manjushri's heart. That was the first time Tsong-ka-pa saw Manjushri, and thereafter at his wish he met with Manjushri, who taught him the difficult points of the stages of the path.[7]

The belief is that Mañjuśrī is able to bestow wisdom on disciples in the way that a spark is able to ignite a fire.[8] In a self-powered tradition* such as Buddhism, and especially within the context of the debate tradition, where trainees work so hard to develop their own realizations, what could it mean that Mañjuśrī "bestows wisdom"? There are stories in Buddhism of disciples receiving a transmission of wisdom, but that is not what is indicated here. Rather, the comments given here refer to "lighting a flame" or a spark that "ignites a fire." The imagery suggests that a person might be able to get a start on wisdom from Mañjuśrī, but ultimately the flame must burn in your own mind, and that would require effort to sustain and further the flame.

THE MANTRA OF MAÑJUŚRĪ

In the traditional context of debate in Tibetan monasteries and nunneries, each session of debate begins with a communal prayer in praise of Mañjuśrī.

---

*Buddhism is a self-powered religious tradition, as opposed to an other-powered religious tradition such as Christianity, because it holds that the capacity for freedom (liberation or salvation) lies within oneself. In Buddhism, this capacity is specifically in one's own ability to overcome all ignorance—the root cause of suffering and death—within one's own continuum and to replace it with wisdom—the cause of peace and happiness.

Also, as an auspicious seed, at the beginning of every session of debate, each Challenger declares, "*dhīḥ ji ltar chos can,*" which means literally, "The subject, like *dhīḥ*." *Dhīḥ* is the seed syllable of Mañjushrī, like his name, and it is the last syllable in the full seven-syllable mantra of Mañjushrī. Here is the mantra as carved in stone in Tibetan script by a Tibetan craftsman in Dharamsala, Himachal Pradesh in northern India:

MAÑJUSHRĪ MANTRA CARVED IN STONE
Photograph by Jeremy T. Williams.

As represented in loose phonetics, the mantra above is:

Oṁ a ra ba dza na dhīḥ

Like almost all mantras of Tibet, this mantra is Sanskrit, not Tibetan, and the image above shows the way the Sanskrit is represented with Tibetan letters. The Tibetans have a time-honored way of pronouncing Sanskrit that mostly reflects the way those letters are pronounced in parts of northern India even today, though it is not the universal style throughout India. Therefore, there are some variances in styles of pronouncing the Sanskrit syllables. This is not a case of proper Sanskrit pronunciation versus the Tibetan style of pronunciation but two ways of pronouncing Sanskrit within India. For instance, the fourth syllable of the mantra above, "ba," is more popularly pronounced in Sanskrit as "pa," and the fifth syllable of the mantra, "dza," is more popularly pronounced in Sanskrit as "ja." Thus, the more prevalent way of pronouncing the Sanskrit would be:

Oṁ arapajana dhīḥ

"*Arapajana*" is represented as *arapacana* in standard Sanskrit transliteration. The fourth syllable, represented as "ja" here, is spoken as a high, sharp, and short syllable. It could be written as "cha" so long as one understands that it is sounded without much breath. The way the Tibetans say these syllables, the mantra is pronounced as:

Oṁ a ra ba dza na dhīḥ

and both the "ba" and the "dza" are sounded as high, sharp, and short syllables.

In either case, the mantra begins with the sacred syllable *oṁ*, which is untranslatable, for the potency of it is in the sound itself. Even so, we may speak of the meaning of this syllable. "*Oṁ* is composed of three letters, A, U, and M. These symbolize the practitioner's impure body, speech, and mind; they also symbolize the pure exalted body, speech, and mind of a Buddha."[9] You can easily understand that *oṁ* is "composed of *A*, *U*, and *M*, by voicing these three letters, though not as you would usually say "a" and "u" if you were reciting the alphabet but pronouncing "a" like the vowel in "cup" and "u" like the vowel in "boot." *Oṁ* is usually the first syllable of a mantra because it commences with the sound "a," and so it is very easy for the person reciting the mantra to loop it back around, beginning each round again with the "a" sound, which comes out of the throat without any involvement of the tongue or lips.

Arapajana is a name of Mañjushrī, "a mystical collective name of the five Buddhas (each being represented by a letter [that is, a syllable])."[10] The "five buddhas" referred to are the five heads of the five buddha lineages or the five buddha families—Vairochana, Amoghasiddhi, Ratnasambhava, Akṣhobhya, and Amitābha. Almost all of the many buddhas are associated with one or another of the five buddha families. Since Mañjushrī is regarded as the manifestation of the wisdom of all the buddhas, it makes sense that one of his names is drawn from all of the buddha families.

It is suitable to recite this mantra in either the style the Tibetans follow or in the more prevalent style. Since English and Sanskrit are both Indo-European languages but Tibetan is not, it may be easier for those reading this book to pronounce the Sanskrit in the more popular style than it is for Tibetans. However, the intent and devotion are the heart of it. One time, the great Ka-gyu lama Kalu Rinpoche told me a story, I think, because he knew I had studied Sanskrit. The story goes that there was a *yogī* living outside the gates of a monastery, and one day a visiting student dared to say that the way the *yogī* was reciting his mantra was not the proper way to pronounce the Sanskrit. The *yogī* was smoking a pipe, and upon hearing this comment, he set his pipe down in mid-air and said to the young man, "If you can do this with your pipe, it is okay to say the mantra as I do."[11]

This mantra is intended to help increase intelligence and the power of speech. First, settle on one of the two ways to say the mantra, either following the Tibetan style based on a less prevalent Indian style or following the more prevalent Indian style. (The "English version" is no different from the more prevalent Indian style.) Note that there are only two main variances between the two styles of pronouncing the mantra and both of these variances come in the mystical name of Mañjuśhrī. The more prevalent pronunciation of the Sanskrit name is *Arapajana,* which the Tibetans pronounce as *Arabadzana.* The variances are in the third and fourth syllables of the name only; those who follow the more prevalent style pronounce the Sanskrit as "pa ja," and the Tibetans pronounce the Sanskrit as "ba dza." Experiment with both ways of saying the mantra, pick the one you like, and stick to it. In practice, the Tibetans typically voice the third and fourth syllables of the name, *pa ja* or *ba dza,* in a high, sharp, short tone BUT NO LOUDER than the other syllables. This voicing makes the mantra more percussive, perhaps rendering it more effective for the increase of intelligence and the power of speech.

Note once again that the Sanskrit name of Mañjuśhrī is represented here as *Arapajana* rather than the standard *Arapacana,* the only variance being that it is spelled with "ja" rather than "ca." There is a time-honored way of representing Sanskrit in English transliteration that is often confusing for nonspecialists. Almost invariably, those who speak American English will pronounce *Arapacana* as if it were *Arapakana,* giving a "ka" sound for the "ca" rather than the "cha" or "ja" it is supposed to be. I suppose it would be fine to pronounce it as "ka" if you can set your pipe down in mid-air, but it has nothing to do with the Sanskrit pronunciation in either style.

The uniqueness in the way the mantra is recited shows not in the pronunciation but in the way it is recited, and the way of reciting this Mañjuśhrī mantra is different from any other I know. In all other cases of reciting mantras that I know of, you say the whole mantra over and over again. However, for this seven-syllable mantra of Mañjuśhrī, you recite the whole mantra in the standard way one time, three times, seven times, twenty-one times, or one hundred times, and then you repeat the seed syllable *dhīḥ* as many times as you can. With practice, you can build up your breath control, and you can time your recitation so that you start the repetition of the seed syllable with a full breath. Then it will be possible for you to keep the repetition going quite a while.

According to Denma Lochö Rinpoche, the visualization that goes with the recitation of this mantra is that you imagine a small Mañjuśrī in your throat and his consort Sarasvatī in the back of your mouth on the right side. Imagine that it is actually his voice reciting the mantra and not your own.[12]

SARASVATĪ

Photograph © Dr. Benjamín Preciado/Wikimedia Commons/CC-BY-SA-3.0.

19. The Three Purposes of Debate

The three purposes of Buddhist debate, or the three approaches in Buddhist debate, are to defeat misconceptions, to establish your own correct view, and to clear away objections to your view. It is like the approach of a physician—to remove what does not belong and to strengthen what does. Thus, for Buddhists, reasoning and debate are not ends in themselves or idle intellectual speculation. Rather, they are part of the path to spiritual wellness, for the purposes of Buddhist debate are to move a person closer to the health of liberation through these efforts to remove mistaken views that do not belong and to strengthen correct ones that do.

These three purposes are reflected in the layout of chapters in the commentarial tradition, such as in the Collected Topics texts. Each chapter is subdivided into three separate sections that together present and clarify the author's position on a topic. Representing three methods of approach to the central topic, the sections are refuting of mistaken views (*'khrul ba dgag pa*), presenting of our own system (*rang lugs bzhag pa*), and dispelling objections (*rtsod pa spong ba*) to our own system. These three approaches fulfill the purposes of debate. All systems of reasoning and debate, extending to philosophical discourse in general and other intellectual activities as well, have these three purposes. Within Buddhism, not only are the debate manuals laid out in these three sections, but an important portion of the Tibetan commentaries are also laid out in the same way.

The first purpose of reasoning and debate is to refute wrong ideas and faulty reasoning. "It is the nature of things that mistaken conceptions are prevalent; so, the first purpose for debate is to dispel wrong views. This is the predominant usage of debate, for usually the reasoning is used to overcome fallacies and misunderstandings."[1] The standard way of refuting others' mistaken positions is through the use of consequences (Skt. *prasaṅga*, Tib. *thal 'gyur*) of that mistaken position. If an idea is wrong, testing it and challenging it through considering the consequences of that idea will reveal the unwanted results that flow from that position, proving that the basic assertion is flawed. There are logical consequences of every assertion. So, if an assertion is factually concordant, then reasoned analysis can confirm that too, and the consequences that flow from that idea will not conflict with the basic assertion.

One of the things that discourage so many people about debate is that it can seem like just a game, rhetorical trickery used to embarrass people. Indeed, according to Lati Rinpoche, even when someone says something that is correct, a skillful debater can use consequences to draw out issues that seem to involve that person in contradictions. If an opponent says that something *is* such and such, then a skillful debater can push that opponent into accepting that it *is not* such and such. And, if an opponent says that it *is not* such and such, a skillful debater can push that opponent the other way, into accepting that it *is* such and such.[2] Of course, this does not mean that there is no correct position in debate but that a skillful debater is able to raise many qualms to any position. As one Tibetan scholar, Geshé Rabten of the Jay College of Se-ra Monastery, said,

> Logic is studied to train the mind in subtle reasoning, enabling later appreciation of the great scriptures. After developing his intelligence and discriminatory powers in this way, the monk is able to apply as many as twenty logical arguments to just one point of teaching. Like monkeys that can run freely in and out through a dense forest, our minds must be very supple before we can comprehend the depth of the concepts presented in the texts. If our minds are rigid like the antlers of a deer . . . we will never be able to reach to this depth.[3]

Debate serves to increase the agility and clarity of a person's mind, supplying a critical attitude for investigating assertions. Of course, skill in debate can be used to embarrass others with rhetorical trickery, but "the purpose for debate is not to defeat and embarrass a mistaken opponent, thereby gaining some victory for oneself; rather, the purpose is to help the opponent overcome his [or her] wrong views."[4] This true purpose of debate plays out in the three approaches that work together to enable a person to set aside wrong ideas and figure out correct ones.

Since Buddhist debate in its natural setting has always been a spiritual practice rather than just an intellectual one, its core purpose is actually its practical application on the path. As the Dalai Lama said about this:

> If we are forced to choose between a sense of practical application and learnedness, a sense of practical application would be more important, for one who has this will receive the full benefit of whatever he knows. The mere learnedness of one whose mind is not tamed can produce and increase bad states of consciousness, which cause unpleasantness for himself and others instead of the happiness and peace of mind that were intended. One could become jealous of those higher than oneself, competitive with equals, and proud and contemptuous towards those lower and so forth. It is as if medicine had become poison. Because such danger is great, it is very important to have a composite of learnedness, a sense of practical application and goodness, without having learnedness destroy the sense of practical application or having the sense of practical application destroy learnedness.[5]

For those who think themselves clever, these words are worthy of reflection. Which is really more clever—to win the battle or to win the war? You see the "mere learnedness of one whose mind is not tamed" plenty in the academic

ONE WHOSE MIND IS NOT TAMED COMING AT YOU, BABY!

setting. That is why so many professors have the reputations they do. On the other side, for those who think that all they need is a sense of practical application and goodness, these words encourage learnedness.

The second purpose of reasoning and debate is the presentation of "our own" system. Here "our own" means the author's system. Although there is a great deal of agreement on basic topics, there is a lot of difference on many topics school to school and even monastery to monastery. Thus, "our own system" does not mean some universally accepted Buddhist position. Even on the most basic topics, such as the presentation of forms, there are differences. This second section, at least in the Collected Topics texts, often just lays out the definitions, divisions, mutually inclusive phenomena, and illustrations for each point of the topic. However, sometimes the author explains "our own system" through debates between two opponents, with the definitions and so forth being presented as a part of the debaters' discussion.

This side of debate is the effort to establish something irrefutable. It calls on a person's skills in the role of a Defender more than as a Challenger. Any good Challenger may be able to raise qualms against any position, but if the position is well founded, a skillful Defender will be able to resolve those apparent qualms. It is more difficult to establish a defensible position. In introductory debate, a person learns how to ask the questions to draw out the implications of an assertion. However, this procedure is not complete. Rather, asking questions, raising qualms, and drawing out the implications of a view are merely investigative tools, so they do not always lead a person to an irrefutable conclusion. Thus, the more important position is that of the Defender, who asserts and holds a view. If debate is for the sake of establishing the truth, it is in the role of the Defender that a person learns to really test a thought. Of course, as we normally experience it ourselves when we reflect on something, part of the tradition is to anticipate possible objections to what we believe to be true, to think about it from multiple angles. We challenge ourselves. A competent Defender cannot just wait for a good Challenger to come along and raise qualms about the stated position.

Given that the Tibetans describe multiple, conflicting, Buddhist tenet systems and non-Buddhist (mainly Hindu) ones as well, why should anyone believe that any position is final and "irrefutable"? Indeed, the word translated here as "tenets" (Skt. *siddhānta,* Tib. *grub mtha'*) means "established conclusions." However, if you look into it, especially on a vital topic like the ultimate reality of emptiness, there are many different and conflicting Buddhist "established conclusions." How could this be? I mean, science does not hold on to older theories long after newer ones seem to have been confirmed and have supplanted the older ones. The older theories are abandoned and relegated to the museum of the history of science.

So, why don't Buddhists settle on a final view and just explain that one? Why are so many different tenet systems preserved? There are at least three possible answers. First, there is real life in the different views. There are real Buddhists who believe different things. Thus, the explanation of a philosophical position as an "established conclusion" is not that it is final for all but that it is the view some people have settled on as final. It is not your tenet if you think that it may be transcended. This points at one aspect of religious systems, which is that they supply a worldview for their followers. We see the world in accordance with our beliefs. That is why it is called our "view." The second possible reason so many different tenet systems are preserved is that they might think that each is needed as part of a program of gradual development, where first you understand this view, only then can you understand this next view, and so on, until you can understand a final "established conclusion." For example, within the Ge-luk-ba order, which is one of the sects of Tibetan Buddhism and the one in which we predominantly find Buddhist debate in modern days, there are disagreements, but there is also broad agreement on countless assertions. Even so, within the Ge-luk-ba tradition of debate, they preserve the many Buddhist tenet systems. They must see them as somehow essential for developing a final view. A third possible reason so many conflicting tenet systems are preserved, which is likely a refinement of the second reason, is not that a student would have to adopt the different views as final in a story of philosophical and spiritual development but that the student would have to have a clear and "established" understanding of how that system can be internally consistent and sensible. In any case, however it may be understood, the second purpose of debate is to put forth a position that you can defend. It may be that either (1) you settle on that position as final, or (2) you just settle on a final understanding of that position from the point of view of that tenet system, even if it is not your own view.

The third purpose of reasoning and debate is to dispel any possible objections to "our" system, to clear up any uncertainties about our position. Of course, people snipe at whatever you put forth; sometimes they just pick at it in hopes of finding a fault, and sometimes they simply don't understand. Sometimes further explanation is needed to resolve an apparent inconsistency. This third purpose of debate is basically accomplished in the same style as is the first purpose, refuting mistaken views—through pointing out the opponent's failure of reasoning that shows in the misinterpretation of our system. However, here the roles have switched. When accomplishing the first purpose, refuting mistaken views, the author of a text speaks in the role of the Challenger. When accomplishing the third purpose, dispelling objections to the system that has been presented, the author speaks in the role of the Defender.

These three purposes of debate work together to move a student toward a refined understanding of any topic. It is easy for most of us to see this in the progress of science. For instance, think of the story of dinosaurs, which were unknown to us until the last couple hundred years. Every year we develop a clearer understanding of the dinosaurs through defeating wrong ideas about them, developing more and more of a factual narrative backed up with evidence, and refining that factual narrative further through ongoing, rational discourse.

20. Definitions, Divisions, and Illustrations

In Tibet the study of philosophy is known as the study of definitions (*mtshan nyid*). Think of this approach as looking for the essential characteristics of things along with identifying the range of phenomena that have those characteristics. More broadly, the main ways of explaining any topic are through a survey of the definition of that thing, the divisions of that thing, and the illustrations of that thing. This is a very natural way of explaining a topic. It identifies exactly what we are talking about, the different types of that thing, and real examples of that thing. If you are able to do this clearly for any topic of human concern such as arachnids, cancer in humans, firearms, human twins, and so on, you have at least begun to have control of that topic.

Definitions

A definition exists in relation to its definiendum. Normally we think of a definition as a string of words that captures and expresses very clearly exactly what is meant by a term. That term is the definiendum, the thing defined. In this way of thinking of definitions and definienda (the plural of "definiendum"), both the definition and the definiendum are words, and we use these words to refer to things in the world. In the Buddhist way of thinking, the definienda are still words, handy labels for things, but the definitions are the real things themselves. For instance, there is a definition of a pot:

> a bulbous, flat-based phenomenon able to perform the function of holding water.*

---

*I use this definition in part because it's so silly. Still, it really is used in beginning debate, though it is hardly core to the system.

According to this definition, the nature of a pot is to be a bulbous, flat-based phenomenon, and the function of a pot is to be able to hold water. So, in the Buddhist way of thinking of definitions and definienda, a bulbous, flat-based phenomenon able to perform the function of holding water is a real thing, like the kind of thing found in your kitchen, not just a string of words that describes a pot. "A pot" is an expression that we use as a handy convention to refer to all of these bulbous, flat-based phenomena able to perform the function of holding water.

Because a definition is a real thing and this Buddhist system asserts a truly existent external reality, a definition such as a bulbous, flat-based phenomenon able to perform the function of holding water is called a "substantial existent" (Skt. *dravya-sat,* Tib. *rdzas yod*). It exists substantially as a real thing. On the other hand, a definiendum such as a pot is called an "imputed existent" (Skt. *prajñapti-sat,* Tib. *btags yod*). A definiendum is an imputed existent because it is just the name imputed to its own particular definition, the things with those characteristics. However, because of the way pervasion works, do not take this to mean that whatever may be referred to by any particular definiendum like a pot, a functioning thing, an existent, and so on is necessarily a name. For instance, a pot is not a name—a mere sound—but a tangible object. However, the word "pot" is a name or conventionality commonly accepted as meaning something along the lines of a bulbous, flat-based phenomenon able to perform the function of holding water.

The Collected Topics logicians present naming as an essentially arbitrary process and names as mere conventionalities. Whatever exists is suitable to be designated by any name, and we just agree to call something by a particular name, to follow the established pattern. The name for anything is merely *imputed* to that thing, just added on to it or ascribed to it. If the name were a part of the thing in and of itself, we would all call it the same thing. However, since there are many languages, we can see that this is not the case. For some things that are unique like particular places, we all call it the same thing. However, here too we can see that the name is not built into the thing, for if it were, no one would have to ask what it is.

The first part of understanding a definition (Skt. *lakṣhana,* Tib. *mtshan nyid*), which might also be called a characterizer, and its definiendum (Skt. *lakṣhya,* Tib. *mtshon bya*), or that which is characterized, is to identify the essential characteristics of that defining phenomenon, the characteristics we refer to by that handy name. The second part is to identify the measure, range, or extent of that definition and to assure ourselves that the range of that particular definition coordinates exactly with the range of the things referred to by that particular definiendum. This means that any particular definition and its definiendum must be MI, or mutually inclusive, that is, they must be different and mutually pervasive. Recall that any two phenomena that are different are existents that are not *exactly* the same in both name and meaning. Any appropriate definition and its definiendum are certainly different in name, but their meaning—all the phenomena that they include or all those things to which their names may properly refer—must be just the same. (This does not back off the idea of a definition as a substantial existent, not just a name. Think of it in terms of pervasion: whatever is a bulbous, flat-based . . . is necessarily a pot, and vice versa. Or, perhaps: everything we refer to as a bulbous, flat-based . . . is necessarily a pot, and vice versa.) Beyond being different, as MI phenomena, a definition and its definiendum must be mutually pervasive; whatever is the one is necessarily the other, both ways. Thus, a proper definition must include each and every thing that is referred to by its own definiendum, not more and not less, and there must be at least one thing that illustrates that definition.

So, any particular definition and its definiendum are mutually inclusive, but they must relate in a very particular way. Lati Rinpoche laid out the following method for establishing the relationship between a particular definition and its definiendum.[1] Here it is better to use the example of color and its definition, that which is suitable as a hue, rather than a pot and its definition because it is easier for us to intuit the meaning. In the form of a syllogism, the method for establishing something as the definition of its own particular definiendum is:

> The subject, that which is suitable as a hue, is the definition of color because (1) it and color are ascertained as having the eight approaches of pervasion [that exist between] a definition and definiendum and also (2) it and color are established in the relationship of a definition and definiendum.

The first main component of the reason of this syllogism is "that which is suitable as a hue and color are ascertained as having the eight approaches of pervasion [that exist between] a definition and definiendum." The eight approaches of pervasion that exist between color and that which is suitable as a hue are:

1. Whatever is a color is necessarily suitable as a hue.
2. Whatever is suitable as a hue is necessarily a color.
3. Whatever is not a color is necessarily not suitable as a hue.
4. Whatever is not suitable as a hue is necessarily not a color.
5. If there is a color, then there is necessarily something that is suitable as a hue.
6. If there is something that is suitable as a hue, then there is necessarily a color.
7. If there is not a color, then there is necessarily not something that is suitable as a hue.
8. If there is not something that is suitable as a hue, then there is necessarily not a color.

The eight approaches of pervasion play on the facts that if something is the one then it is necessarily the other and that the presence of the one necessitates the presence of the other. Any particular definition and its definiendum are necessarily coextensive in terms of pervasions of being (*yin khyab*) and pervasions of existence (*yod khyab*).

These eight pervasions exist between any two mutually inclusive phenomena whether or not they are a definition and its definiendum. For instance, products and impermanent phenomena, though not a definition and its definiendum, are mutually inclusive, so whatever is a product is necessarily an impermanent phenomenon and vice versa, and if there is a product, then there is necessarily an impermanent phenomenon, and so on for all eight. Since the eight approaches of pervasion exist not only between a definition and its definiendum but also between any two mutually inclusive phenomena, the reason given to justify that suitable as a hue is the definition of color specifies that the two "are ascertained as having the eight approaches of pervasion that exist between *a definition and definiendum.*" In this way, the reason excludes other mutually inclusive phenomena such as products and impermanent phenomena that, although they have the eight approaches of pervasion, are not a definition and its definiendum.

The second part of the reason above makes another distinction between a definition and its definiendum, on the one hand, and other types of mutually inclusive phenomena. The reason specifies that "suitable as a hue and color are established in the relationship of a definition and definiendum." According to Lati Rinpoche, this specification means that in order to ascertain color with valid cognition a person must first ascertain that which is suitable as a hue with valid cognition. The claim is that a person must first have a correct understanding of the definition, the actual object, before that person can have a correct understanding of the definiendum, the conventionality or name that designates that object. In order to understand with valid cognition the meaning of the term "color," a person must first be acquainted with the existents that are suitable to be demonstrated to an eye consciousness as a hue—blue, yellow, white, red, and so forth. This implies that there are persons who have ascertained that which is suitable as a hue with valid cognition but have not ascertained the definiendum "color" with valid cognition. For instance, a child untrained in language or a cow might have a correct understanding of that which is suitable as a hue but not have a correct understanding of the name "color." On the other hand, a person who correctly knows the meaning of "color" yet does not know that which is suitable as a hue is not possible.[2]

Since definitions are the actual objects, as a bulbous, flat-based . . . is a real pot, the characterizer itself, specific definitions cannot be, in turn, defined again. For instance, there is no definition of a bulbous, flat-based . . . However, even though specific definitions cannot be defined, there is a definition of definition itself:

> that which is a triply qualified substantial existent.

A definition is called a "substantial existent" because it is the actual object, the meaning or referent of its definiendum. So, if a definition is "triply qualified," what are the three qualities of every definition? In the *Tutor's Collected Topics,* the author Pur-bu-jok Jam-ba-gya-tso lays out the three qualities of a definition, in the form of a syllogism:

> There is a way to adduce the three qualities of a substantial existent because it is reasonable to adduce the three: (1) in general, it is a definition, (2) it is established with its illustrations [*mtshan gzhi*], and (3) it does not define anything other than that which is its own definiendum.[3]

For example, *a bulbous, flat-based phenomenon able to perform the function of holding water* is the triply qualified substantial existent of a pot because

(1) in general, it is a definition, (2) it is established with its illustrations, and (3) it does not define anything other than a pot. First, in general, a bulbous, flat-based phenomenon able to perform the function of holding water (often abbreviated as "the bulbous" [*lto ldir pa*]) is renowned as a definition, not a definiendum. Second, the bulbous is established with its illustrations such as a bulbous, flat-based copper phenomenon able to perform the function of holding water, a bulbous, flat-based stainless steel phenomenon able to perform the function of holding water, and so on. We know the bulbous in dependence upon knowing its illustrations. Third, the bulbous is not the definition of anything other than a pot. A definition cannot have more than one definiendum.

Just as there is a definition of definition, in general, so there is a definition of definiendum, in general. A definiendum is defined as

> that which is a triply qualified imputed existent.

A definiendum is called an "imputed existent" because it is the name imputed to or ascribed to those things that have the quality of its definition. The name of a thing is just laid onto that thing by common convention. We agree to call it that, but the name is not part of its character in the way that being a functioning thing is part of the character of a pot. The Tutor Pur-bu-jok Jam-ba-gya-tso also gives a description of the three qualities of a definiendum:

> There is a way to adduce the three qualities of an imputed exis-
> tent because it is reasonable to adduce the three: (1) in general,
> it is a definiendum, (2) it is established with its illustrations, and
> (3) it is not the definiendum of anything other than just its own
> definition.[4]

For example, *a pot* is the triply qualified imputed existent of a bulbous, flat-based phenomenon able to perform the function of holding water because (1) in general, it is a definiendum, (2) it is established with its illustrations such as gold pots, copper pots, and so on, and (3) it is not the definiendum of anything other than a bulbous, flat-based phenomenon able to perform the function of holding water.

Since there is a definition of definition, this means that definition itself, understood as a collective entity—definition in and of itself in isolation from all else, including its own instances*—is a definiendum and a triply qualified imputed existent. Definiendum itself, as a collective entity, is a definiendum and a triply qualified imputed existent. This means that definition is not an exemplifier of itself, though each and every thing that is a definition is both a definition and a triply qualified substantial existent. Definiendum is an exemplifier of itself. As for the definitions of these two, the triply qualified substantial existent is itself a triply qualified substantial existent, but the triply qualified imputed existent is not a triply qualified imputed existent. Please read the following correct syllogisms carefully and understand each of them. If you need to, remember to use the checking procedure—first the property of the subject, then the pervasion, and then the irresistible conclusion.

1. The subject, definition,† is not a definition because of being a definiendum.
2. With respect to the subject, definition, it is a definiendum because there is a definition of it.‡
3. With respect to the subject, definition, there is a definition of it because the triply qualified substantial existent is the definition of it.
4. The subject, definiendum, is a definiendum because of being the definiendum of the triply qualified imputed existent.
5. The subject, the triply qualified substantial existent, is a definition because of being the definition of definition.
6. The subject, the triply qualified imputed existent, is a definition because of being the definition of definiendum.

---

*See Perdue, *Debate in Tibetan Buddhism,* 617ff. on instances.
†Not "a definition" but the collective entity "definition" in and of itself.
‡This syllogism is not composed in the usual way but with a grammatical subject and predicate in both the second and third parts of the syllogism. Because of this, it has to begin "with respect to the subject." It is set up this way because there would be a verbal fault, if it just said, "The subject, definition, is a definiendum because there is a definition of it." Then somebody will ask you, "What is the definition of it?" See? *It* is no longer tied to definition, and there is no definition of *it.* To avoid this unusual phrasing, you could say, "The subject, definition, is a definiendum because of being a triply qualified imputed existent."

The way you do the checking procedure for a syllogism phrased like this is to fill in the *its* with the subject, so: (1) Is it the case that there is a definition of definition? (2) Is it the case that if there is a definition of definition, then definition is a definiendum? (Or, more generally, is it the case that if there is a definition of something, then that thing is a definiendum?) (3) If these are both true, then doesn't it have to be the case that definition is a definiendum?

7. The subject, the triply qualified imputed existent, is not a definiendum because of being a definition.
8. The subject, the triply qualified imputed existent, is not a triply qualified imputed existent because of being a triply qualified substantial existent.*
9. The subject, the triply qualified imputed existent, is a triply qualified substantial existent because of being the triply qualified substantial existent of definiendum.

It is unusual to have something that does not exemplify itself in the normal way as color (or a color) is a color or as functioning thing—the collective entity—(or a functioning thing) is a functioning thing. However, in beginning Buddhist reasoning and debate, they come up with several of these. They are curious, but that is not the point. Rather, they are stressing the difference between the two types of statements—statements of qualities and statements of pervasion. (See chapter 5, "Two Kinds of Statements.") First, definition is not a definition, but every definition is a definition. Definition is not a triply qualified substantial existent, but every definition is a triply qualified substantial existent. That which is a triply qualified imputed existent is not a triply qualified imputed existent, but every triply qualified imputed existent is a triply qualified imputed existent. That which is a triply qualified imputed existent is not a definiendum, but every triply qualified imputed existent is a definiendum. These statements may not be particularly profound, really, but it is very important to note clearly how they stress the differences between statements of qualities and statements of pervasion.

Thus, definition is a definiendum but not a definition; definiendum is a definiendum but not a definition; the triply qualified substantial existent is a definition but not a definiendum; and the triply qualified imputed existent is a definition but not a definiendum. It should be clear from these facts that definition and definiendum, understood as abstract singulars, are mutually exclusive. There is nothing that is both. Each and every particular definition is mutually inclusive with its own definiendum. However, even though they exist only in relation to each other, definition and definiendum in general,

---

*Please note here that, when the defining characteristic is in the predicate position, it is better to say "a triply qualified imputed existent" rather than "that which is a triply qualified imputed existent." It is just more normal English.

do not have the relationship of a definition and its definiendum and are not mutually inclusive. There is no common locus of the two. Whatever is the one is necessarily not the other because there is no one thing that is both a definition and a definiendum. Definitions are not themselves definienda, for they are not in turn defined—they may be described or explained but are not defined by their own definitions.

One of the most important points of emphasis in Buddhist reasoning and debate is the effort to identify the essential characteristics of phenomena and to measure the extent of those phenomena. The debaters report the definitions as given in the texts and then analyze each component to ascertain its purpose, identifying what a particular component includes and what it excludes. Also, the debaters consider alternative definitions to determine whether or not they stand up. This helps them understand something of the differences between their own and other systems and prompts further reflection on the topics.

DIVISIONS

The second main way of exploring any topic in Buddhist reasoning and debate is through a survey of the divisions of phenomena. This goes to the consideration of the range of a phenomenon and to the understanding of the varieties of that phenomenon.

In Buddhist philosophy, there are several different ways that things are divided, and some of these ways are quite surprising. We normally think of a division as a process of segmenting something into its component types so that everything is included in one or another of those types, nothing is found in more than one of the types, and nothing is left over. This is like the division of integers into even numbers and odd numbers. Every integer is either even or odd but not both. Although that sort of clean division is found here, there are at least four ways that phenomena are divided in the Buddhist sources:

1. **A True Partition with Nothing Left Over:** This is the standard model of a division. An example in Buddhist thought would be a division of existents into impermanent phenomena and permanent phenomena. Each and every existent is either an impermanent phenomenon or a permanent phenomenon and nothing is both. Also, existent itself is included as a permanent phenomenon, impermanent phenomenon is

impermanent, and permanent phenomenon is permanent. Nothing is left over. All dichotomies, like dividing existents into cows and non-cows, would be true partitions with nothing left over.

2. **A Noncomprehensive Division with Some Left Over:** In this case, there is a division of a phenomenon into types, but something is left over. An example of this kind is the division of colors into primary colors and secondary colors. That part of the division is clean. Nothing is both a primary color and a secondary color; however, color itself, the collective singularity in and of itself, is neither a primary color nor a secondary color. This kind of division might also be called a non-exhaustive division, for it does not exhaust all the possibilities.

3. **A Division in Name Only:** In this case, there is a nominal division, but everything is included into one of the "divisions." An example of this kind would be the division of objects of comprehension into manifest phenomena and hidden phenomena. Recall that manifest phenomena are MI with impermanent phenomena, and hidden phenomena are MI with existents. Everything that exists—including all the manifest phenomena—are hidden phenomena. Thus, it is a division in name only. The division is informative, but it is not a real partition.

4. **A Division from the Point of View of the Name:** In this case, there is a division of things that are called by the same name, even though some of those things that are called by that name are not real examples of that. For instance, there is a division of things that are called "valid cognizers" into the three—persons, scriptures, and consciousnesses. Of these three, only consciousnesses can be valid cognizers. Some persons such as the Buddha and some reliable scriptures are called "valid cognizers," but they are not actual valid cognizers, just called by that name. Such a division is sometimes called a terminological division. When there is a division of this kind in the Buddhist literature, it is always identified as a division from the point of view of the name because the Buddhists recognize that it is not a real division like the first case above.

ILLUSTRATIONS

All phenomena are shown by their illustrations (*mtshan gzhi*). Typically, when someone uses a word you don't know and you ask what it means, the person will give examples or illustrations of what the word refers to rather than trying to define the word. Both definitions and definienda are established with their illustrations, which are essentially observable existents that exemplify or illustrate what is being named or what is being defined. We understand definitions and definienda in dependence upon understanding their illustrations.

What does it mean to say, as it does in their definitions, that definitions and definienda are established with their illustrations? An illustration of a color is, for instance, red. An illustration of an impermanent phenomenon is, for instance, a pot. An illustration is defined as

> that which serves as a basis for illustrating the appropriate definiendum by way of [its] definition.[5]

The definition includes the qualification that it must illustrate the *appropriate* definiendum. This specification is added because the definition is being stated in general. In order to avoid the possible problem of indicating that an illustration might suitably illustrate just any definiendum, it is specified that it must illustrate the *appropriate* definiendum.

This qualification need not be stated in the definition of an illustration for which the definiendum is specified. For instance, the definition of an illustration of color is

> that which serves as a basis for illustrating color by way of [being] suitable as a hue.

For instance, red serves as a basis for illustrating color by way of being suitable as a hue.

Recall that, as explained in this system, a person must ascertain a definition—the actual object—before that person would be able to ascertain the proper meaning of its definiendum. In the same way, a proper illustration must be something that a person might have ascertained without necessarily having ascertained what it illustrates; otherwise, there would be no need for an illustration. For instance, it is conceivable that a being might know red without knowing the definiendum color or a person might know a pot without knowing the definiendum impermanent phenomenon. An illustration serves as a basis for *illustrating* something. If it embodied all of the particular qualities of what it illustrates or if by merely knowing that thing, a person would know what it purports to illustrate, then it would not be a proper illustration. An illustration must serve as a basis that is able to cause one to know something. For instance, a gold pot is not an illustration of a pot because if a person has ascertained a gold pot correctly, then that person would necessarily have ascertained a pot correctly. You see, you would have to understand "pot" in order to understand "gold pot." However, a bulbous, flat-based gold phenomenon able to perform the function of holding water is a suitable basis for illustrating what a pot is.

A proposed definition may fail because it includes more than it should, because it includes less than it should, or because there is nothing to illustrate it. If there is no illustration for something, then that thing cannot be either a definition or a definiendum. For instance, what would illustrate a prime number that is not an integer? When there is no illustration, a definition has the third possible fault of definitions—the fallacy of nonoccurrence. According to Denma Lochö Rinpoche, this fallacy comes into play for the proposed definition of a non-existent (Skt. *asat,* Tib. *med pa*) as

that which is *not* observed by valid cognition.

A non-existent is not an existent, so it is not experienced as an existent, and it does not occur.[6] Thus, something such as a non-existent, which has no illustrations, is neither a definition nor a definiendum, for all definitions and definienda must be established together with their existent illustrations.

Exercise 20.1

In order to increase your facility of tongue, working with your debate partner and speaking out loud, prove a dozen definitions as the definitions of their own particular definienda according to the pattern laid out by Lati Rinpoche above in the "Definitions" section. Of course, this exercise will also help you with memorizing definitions. Take turns assuming the roles of Challenger and Defender and follow this dialogue pattern:

C: What is the definition of a color?
D: The subject, that which is suitable as a hue.
C: It follows that the subject, that which is suitable as a hue, is the definition of a color.
D: Yes, that's right.
C: Why do you say that the subject, that which is suitable as a hue, is the definition of a color?

D: Because (1) it and color are ascertained as having the eight approaches of pervasion [that exist between] a definition and definiendum and also (2) it and color are established in the relationship of a definition and definiendum.

C: It follows that that which is suitable as a hue and color are ascertained as having the eight approaches of pervasion that exist between a definition and definiendum.

D: Yes, that's right.

C: Really? What are those eight?

D: Yes, there are all eight because (1) whatever is a color is necessarily suitable as a hue, ..., and (8) if there is not something that is suitable as a hue, then there is necessarily not a color. [Recite all eight of the pervasions.]

C: It follows that, if those eight pervasions exist between that which is suitable as a hue and color, then that which is suitable as a hue and color are ascertained as having the eight approaches of pervasion that exist between a definition and definiendum.

D: Yes, that's right.

C: Now, it follows that that which is suitable as a hue and color are established in the relationship of a definition and definiendum.

D: Yes, that's right.

C: Why do you say that that which is suitable as a hue and color are established in the relationship of a definition and definiendum?

D: Because (1) they are mutually different phenomena and (2) in order to ascertain a color with valid cognition, a person must first ascertain that which is suitable as a hue with valid cognition.

C: It follows that if (1) they are mutually different phenomena and (2) in order to ascertain a color with valid cognition, a person must first ascertain that which is suitable as a hue with valid cognition, then that which is suitable as a hue and color are established in the relationship of a definition and definiendum.

D: Yes, that's right.

EXERCISE 20.2

Review the nine syllogisms in the "Definitions" section above that use the four players—definition, definiendum, the triply qualified substantial existent, and the triply qualified imputed existent. Then, in order to make sure you understand each of them clearly, work with your debate partner to verbalize the checking procedure for each syllogism part by part. Beyond that, at this point, you should also be able to create your own new syllogisms using these four players and check them too with your partner. Using as an example the first syllogism above,

> The subject, definition, is not a definition because of being a definiendum,

take turns with your partner in the roles of Challenger and Defender and follow this dialogue:

C: Is it the case that [that subject]* definition is [that reason] a definiendum?

D: Yes.

C: Why do you say that definition is a definiendum?

D: [Then you make up a reason that will justify the property of the subject—that definition is a definiendum—in the original syllogism, a reason such as:] Because of being a triply qualified imputed existent.†

C: [Return to the original syllogism to continue the checking procedure:] Is it the case that whatever is [that reason] a definiendum is necessarily [that predicate to be proven] not a definition?

D: Yes, that's right.

C: Why do you say that whatever is a definiendum is necessarily not a definition?

D: [Then give a reason justifying the pervasion in the original syllogism. The best way to justify a pervasion is with another pervasion, such as:] Because whatever is a definiendum is necessarily not a triply qualified substantial existent, [or] because the two, definiendum and definition, are mutually exclusive.

---

*You do not need to speak the parts inside the brackets.

†Do you see that at this point you and your partner could go on to explore issues that derive from the syllogism just composed? You could explore whether or not definition is a triply qualified imputed existent if the Challenger were to say, "It follows that the subject, definition, is a triply qualified imputed existent," and then goes on to ask for another reason. Or you might explore whether or not it is the case that whatever is a triply qualified imputed existent is necessarily a definiendum if the Challenger were to say, "It follows that whatever is a triply qualified imputed existent is necessarily a definiendum," and then you go on from there. From each of these issues, you then move on to more.

C: It follows that if whatever is a definiendum is necessarily not a triply qualified substantial existent, then whatever is a definiendum is necessarily not a definition.

D: Yes, that's right.

C: [Return to the original syllogism to finish the checking procedure by weighing the value of the conclusion:] Then it must be the case that [that subject] definition is [that predicate to be proven] not a definition.

D: Yes, that's right. [Now, abiding in bliss, dissolve into rainbow light.]

EXERCISE 20.3

Practice the following dialogue with your debate partner, taking turns back and forth in the roles of Challenger and Defender. Make up your own questions too, of course, to test your partner. This exercise will help with increasing facility of tongue and will help you in memorizing divisions.

C: If colors are divided, how many are there?

D: There are two.

C: It follows that there are not two. What are the two?

D: There are two. The subjects, the two—primary color and secondary color.

C: It follows that the subjects, the two (primary color and secondary color) are the same two, when colors are divided into two.

D: Yes, that's right.

EXERCISE 20.4

For each of the following, identify what would be the problem with defining that definiendum in that way. You will find that the problem is that the proposed definition does not include all that it should, the proposed definition includes more than it should, or there is the fault of nonoccurrence.

1. What would be the problem with defining color as that which is suitable as a red hue?

2. What would be the problem with defining color as that which is visible?

3. What would be the problem with defining a permanent phenomenon as the nonmomentary?

4. What would be the problem with defining a sound as that arisen from the elements?

5. What would be the problem with defining a consciousness as a non-mistaken knower?

6. What would be the problem with defining an uncertain consciousness (that is, a doubting consciousness or a consciousness of suspicion) as a knower that thoroughly engages its object?

7. What would be the problem with defining a correctly assuming consciousness as a knower without a reason that does not get at an object with respect to which superimpositions have been eliminated although it adheres one-pointedly to the phenomenon that is its principal object of engagement?

8. What would be the problem with defining a valid cognition as a non-mistaken knower free from conceptuality?

EXERCISE 20.5

As an exercise to better appreciate the value of divisions in understanding a category of phenomena, take something you are familiar with and try to list all the divisions of that type of thing. Always go for a true partition with nothing left over, which is what we typically think a division should be. It is better to use something for which there are not already clearly identified divisions as there are in mathematics and biology. However, if you are not familiar with the divisions of a thing, then try to project the divisions and then look them up to see how you did.

Here are some possible ideas: sports, boats, ships, cars, trucks, airplanes, firearms, chairs, houses, and on and on and on as you please. You will soon see that you can easily divide any of these into two, such as boats equal to or greater than twenty feet in length and those less than twenty feet in length. That is not very interesting. Try to imagine dividing firearms by different metrics, like loading mechanisms, barrel length, types of projectiles that can be used, and so on. Imagine dividing chairs by materials, by structure, and so on.

21. One and Different

THERE IS AN important division of established bases into the two, [phenomena that are] one (Skt. *ekatva,* Tib. *gcig*) and [phenomena that are] different (Skt. *nānātva,* Tib. *tha dad*). This division is a true partition with nothing left over. Every existent and every group of existents we may speak of are included in one or the other but not both, depending on what we refer to. This also includes established base itself.

One may also be described as a singular phenomenon. The one, or a singular phenomenon, is defined as

   a phenomenon that is not diverse.

If a phenomenon is "not diverse," it must be singular. Diversity requires duality or multiplicity. An example of one or a singular phenomenon is a pot. Different, or different phenomena, are defined as

   phenomena that are diverse.

If phenomena are diverse, there must be at least two of them. Thus, the definition specifies the plural "phenomena." An example is the two—a gold pot and a copper pot—which are separate and distinct phenomena.

Both of these definitions limit one and different to phenomena. This is a division of established bases, and in this tradition of thought they are saying that a non-existent is neither one nor different. "The horn of a rabbit" is grammatically singular, but it is not a phenomenon that is not diverse because of not being a *phenomenon.* Also, the horn of a rabbit is not different from, for instance, a pot because of not being a *phenomenon* that is diverse from a pot. Normally, we would say something like, "The horn of a rabbit is different from a handsaw," and that is true enough, but the horn of a rabbit does not have the *quality* of being different from a handsaw, and it is not a *phenomenon* that is diverse from a handsaw. What does not exist is neither one nor different.

The definitions for one and different in general may be applied to any particular phenomenon to generate definitions of what is one with that phenomenon and what is different from that phenomenon, so these can be extended endlessly. For instance, the definition of something which is one-with-sound is

a phenomenon that is not diverse from sound.

The only illustration is sound itself, for sound alone is a phenomenon that is not diverse from sound. In the same way, the definition of something that is different-from-sound is

a phenomenon that is diverse from sound.

An illustration is the sound of a drum, a pot, or a consciousness. Each of these is a phenomenon that is diverse from sound.

Both one and different are permanent phenomena. Of course, this does not mean that whatever is one is permanent or that whatever phenomena are different are permanent, but that, in and of themselves, one is permanent, and different is permanent. One way to understand this is that, as categories that include both permanent and impermanent phenomena, the categories of one and different are permanent. Another way to understand this is that one and different are considered permanent because they are abstractions. Probably an impermanent phenomenon's quality of being single is itself impermanent, something that appears explicitly to a direct perceiver. It should be as simple as what is appearing to any sense field, a *single* table appears or whatever. This should be true as well for a diverse group of impermanent phenomena. On the other hand, a permanent phenomenon's quality of being single or the quality of being different that exists among the members of a group of permanent phenomena must be permanent.

The division of established bases into [phenomena that are] one and [phenomena that are] different is completely exhaustive, a true partition with no existent left over. Thus, the two, (1) established bases and (2) either of the two (one or different), are mutually inclusive. Unlike the division of colors into primary colors and secondary colors such that color itself is a color but neither a primary color nor a secondary color, established base is included within this division as something that is one. *All* established bases are one or different. One is itself—it is one—because it is a phenomenon that is not diverse. Also, different is one because it too is a phenomenon that is not diverse. Different phenomena must be pairs or groups of phenomena, and since different itself is a singular existent, it is one. Any different phenomena are necessarily not one, but different itself is one.

ONE-WITH-*x* AND DIFFERENT-FROM-*x* AS PREDICATES

It is simple enough to sort out whether or not an existent is singular or different. If it is just one existent, then it is one, and, if there are multiple existents—two or more—then they are different. More interesting is the use of one and different in a comparative sense—is one thing the same as or different from another. These are the phrases "one-with-*x*" and "different-from-*x*." For instance, a table is one-with-a-table. The gloss, or explanation, of the phrase "one-with-*x*" is

a phenomenon that is exactly the same in name and meaning as *x*.

This means that only a table is one-with-a-table because only a table is a phenomenon that is exactly the same in name and meaning as a table. So, this is not about being singular or plural. This is about being self-identical. A table is identical with a table, and all other existents are different-from-a-table. Even an oak table is different-from-a-table because an oak table is not a phenomenon that is exactly the same in name and meaning as a table. Indeed, an oak table is a table, but a table and an oak table appear differently to a thought consciousness. Even if the meaning-generality for a table, which is the appearing object for a conceptual consciousness, is an oak table, that meaning-generality represents a table, not an oak table. And, even if it is essentially the same image that appears to your mind when you think of an oak table, in that case the image represents an oak table, not a table. They appear differently to thought.

Whatever is one with something must be one with that thing in both name and meaning; thus, what is one with something must be *exactly the same as* that phenomenon. This means that they are identical, not just the same in some way. Even two mutually inclusive phenomena such as product and impermanent phenomenon are not one, for, although they have the same meaning or referent, they do not have the same name; thus, they are different but mutually inclusive. Remember that what is translated here as "mutually inclusive" is literally "one meaning" (Skt. *ekārtha,* Tib. *don gcig*). Thus, different terms for the same thing, like "pot" and its Tibetan language equivalent *pum-ba (bum pa)*, are not one but are mutually inclusive because, although their meaning may be the same, the terms expressing that meaning are different. In the same way, although it is true that $2 + 2 = 4$, since "$2 + 2$" is not exactly the same expression as "4," "$2 + 2$" is not one with "4." So, "$=$" may mean "is one with" or "is identical to" as in $a = a$, but it may also mean "is mutually inclusive with."

Whatever exists is necessarily one with itself and different from all else. A pot is one-with-a-pot but only with a pot. Being one with something is a completely self-reflexive relation. Even a group of objects of knowledge are one with themselves. For instance, the two—a pillar and a pot—are one-with-(the two—a pillar and a pot). In this Collected Topics system, there is nothing that is the two—a pillar and a pot—but they are still one with themselves. The two—a pillar and a pot—comprise the classic example of objects of knowledge of which being them is not possible.* This means that there is nothing that exemplifies them. Still, the fact that there is nothing that exemplifies them does not imply that they are not one with themselves. All existents—no matter what we name it or them—are self-identical and not different from themselves. This is in line with what the definition of a phenomenon suggests, that whatever exists bears its own entity. Phenomena may or may not be themselves in the sense of being exemplifiers of themselves, but without exception they bear their own entity, they are one with themselves and are not different from themselves.

Difference too may be used in the comparative sense, as in the phrase "different-from-*x*." For instance, a table is different-from-a-chair. The gloss, or explanation, of the words "different-from-*x*" is

a phenomenon that is not exactly the same in name and meaning as *x*.

---

*For more on objects of knowledge of which being them is not possible and objects of knowledge of which being them is possible, see Perdue, *Debate in Tibetan Buddhism,* especially 327–31.

This means that every existent other than a table, expressed as "a table," is different-from-a-table. However, every non-existent is still excluded from the consideration of whether or not it is different-from-a-table because non-existents are not one or different in any way. That is why the gloss specifies a *phenomenon* that is not exactly the same in name and meaning. Corresponding to the use of the phrase "one-with-*x*" as specifying self-identity, the phrase "different-from-*x*" specifies the lack of identity with something.

Different phenomena may be different in terms of name, meaning, or both name and meaning. Thus, different phenomena may compare in any of the four possible ways—three possibilities, four possibilities, mutually inclusive, or mutually exclusive. As you know, the analytical comparison of phenomena presumes that the two phenomena being compared are different. As mentioned above, things that are mutually inclusive are different phenomena having the same meaning but different names. Mutually exclusive phenomena, phenomena having three possibilities, and phenomena having four possibilities are all different phenomena having different names *and* meanings. It is immediately apparent that two mutually exclusive phenomena, such as functioning things and permanent phenomena, are different because there is no common locus of both of them—no one thing that has both the quality of being a functioning thing and also the quality of being a permanent phenomenon; thus, they are different in both name and meaning. Also, two phenomena such as functioning things and pots, which compare as three possibilities, are different phenomena *even though* there is something such as a gold pot that is a common locus. A pot is a functioning thing, but it is also different-from-(functioning thing). Being something does not mean being exactly the same as that thing. Also, if something is different from a particular phenomenon, that does not necessarily imply that it is not an example of that phenomenon, as we see that a pot is different-from-(functioning thing), but it is still a functioning thing.

The glosses offered above are not definitions, but they will work to justify something as being either one-with-*x* or different-from-*x,* in the same way that the definitions do. For instance, suppose you are trying to prove that sound is one-with-sound. It is suitable to justify it in a syllogism using the definition as the reason:

The subject, sound, is one-with-sound because of being a phenomenon that is not diverse from sound.

And, it is also suitable to use the gloss as the reason, as in the syllogism:

> The subject, sound, is one-with-sound because of being a phenomenon that is exactly the same in name and meaning as sound.

In the same way, it is suitable to justify something as different-from-sound by either the definition or the gloss. For instance:

> The subject, a table, is different-from-sound because of being a phenomenon that is diverse from sound.

And, it is just as effective to say:

> The subject, a table, is different-from-sound because of being a phenomenon that is not exactly the same in name and meaning as sound.

The description of oneness and difference laid out here hardly seems to cover the normal notions of sameness and difference. For instance, we normally think of two duplicate things produced in the same way, like two apples from the same tree or two bottles of the same kind of soda, as being the same. Of course, Buddhists are not blind to this, and they offer an extensive description of several different types of sameness and difference.* Here, the layout of one and different is in its starkest form, strict identity or lack of identity within the world of existents. So, from this point of view, the Buddhists agree that two apples from the same tree are the same in some sense, but whatever is the one is necessarily not the other. Though each is self-identical, as are all other existents, the two are not identical in this strictest sense. Rather, they are different and diverse. If I eat one apple, the other will remain.

Even though the oneness of an impermanent phenomenon probably is something that appears explicitly to a direct perceiver, the quality of an impermanent phenomenon's being one with itself, such as a pot's being one with itself, is permanent. The factor of a phenomenon's being self-identical is not something that appears explicitly to a direct perceiver. That something

---

*For more information on the various types of sameness and difference, like two bottles of soda or two apples from the same branch, see Perdue, *Debate in Tibetan Buddhism*, 568–96.

is one with itself is an object of intellectual abstraction. The same is true for the factor of a pot's being different-from-a-table. That is something that can be understood only conceptually.

ONE-WITH-*x* AND DIFFERENT-FROM-*x* AS SUBJECTS

Since it is merely a matter of self-identity or not, reckoning whether something is one-with-*x* or different-from-*x* is pretty straightforward. The most interesting use of this division of established bases comes in looking at the natures of one-with-*x* and different-from-*x* standing on their own as subjects. Please note that here one-with-*x* and different-from-*x* are always connected with hyphens. When used in the *subject* position, this is done to show that the words stand together as a description of a single entity in and of itself. When used in the *predicate* position, as in "sound is one-with-sound," "one-with-sound" is still connected with hyphens. This is because, in that context, the words mark a quality of sound in the way that a red car is red. It is an adjectival use, and the hyphens hold the phrase together as a single quality of the subject.*

Because of the way oneness is understood as self-identity and difference is understood as the lack of identity, it turns out that one-with-*x* and different-from-*x* have surprising qualities, reminiscent of the way that definition is not a definition. Thus, once again in this Collected Topics tradition, the layout of topics puts stress on the difference between statements of qualities and statements of pervasion. For instance, as you already understand that sound is the only thing that is one-with-sound, you can easily see that one-with-sound is not one-with-sound. (Rather, one-with-sound is one-with-[one-with-sound].) However, since sound is the only existent that is not different-from-sound, different-from-sound is different-from-sound.

When we first hear of something such as different-from-(functioning thing), most people naturally think that this refers to anything that is not a functioning thing. However, think of the world of phenomena that are included in different-from-(functioning thing). It includes every existent other than functioning thing itself, expressed as "functioning thing." Thus,

---

*The use of hyphens to mark "one-with-*x*" and "different-from-*x*" in the predicate position is a change from what I did in *Debate in Tibetan Buddhism,* where the hyphens were used when the words formed a subject but not when they formed a predicate. I have found that that style was sometimes confusing for people and that they simply get it better when the words are held together with hyphens in both the subject and predicate positions.

it includes every permanent phenomenon and all impermanent phenomena not called by the name of "functioning thing" in and of itself, but no non-existents. So, on first impression, it may seem that functioning thing and different-from-(functioning thing) would be mutually exclusive, but actually they compare as four possibilities:

1. Something that is both is a pot, a pillar, an ultimate truth, or any functioning thing other than functioning thing itself.
2. Something that is different-from-(functioning thing) but is not a functioning thing is uncomposed space, object of knowledge, or any permanent phenomenon.
3. Only functioning thing itself is a functioning thing but not different-from-(functioning thing).
4. Something that is neither a functioning thing nor different-from-(functioning thing) is the horn of a rabbit.

It is easy to see that if functioning thing is simply negated to non-(functioning thing), then different-from-(functioning thing) and non-(functioning thing) too compare as four possibilities. All you have to do is to move the examples around:

1. Uncomposed space or any permanent phenomenon is both different-from-(functioning thing) and a non-(functioning thing).
2. Something that is different-from-(functioning thing) but not a non-(functioning thing)—that is, is a thing—is an eye consciousness.
3. Something that is a non-(functioning thing) but is not different-from-(functioning thing) is any non-existent.
4. For something that is neither, the only thing that can be put is functioning thing itself, as functioning thing alone is not a non-(functioning thing) and is also not different-from-(functioning thing).

Since there are four possibilities between these two, it is apparent that something's being different-from-(functioning thing) does not mean that it is not a functioning thing.

For any existent x, both one-with-x and different-from-x are permanent phenomena. Bearing in mind the difference between statements of qualities and statements of pervasion, note clearly that this does not say that whatever is one-with-an-existent-x is necessarily permanent. For instance, a pot is one-with-a-pot, but it is not permanent. Also, it is not the case that whatever is different-from-x is necessarily permanent because, for instance, a table is different-from-a-chair, but it is not permanent. However, one-with-a-table and different-from-a-table, understood on their own as subjects, are considered to be permanent. One way to understand different-from-a-table as permanent is that the category as a whole includes both permanent phenomena and impermanent phenomena; thus, the category as a whole is permanent. However, this way of thinking does not cover one-with-a-table because the only thing that is one-with-a-table is an impermanent table. The way to understand this assertion is that both one and different on their own are intellectual abstractions. One-with-a-table and different-from-a-table are permanent phenomena, appearing objects of thought consciousnesses "because of being merely imputed by a nominal expression or a thought consciousness and not being established from the side of the object itself."[1]

For any non-existent x, one-with-x is non-existent and different-from-x is existent. For any non-existent x, one-with-x is a non-existent because a phenomenon that is not diverse from a non-existent would have to be a non-existent; therefore, it could not be "a *phenomenon* that is . . . ." For instance, one-with-(the horn of a rabbit) is non-existent because there is no *phenomenon* that is not diverse from the horn of a rabbit. If it is easier, there is no *phenomenon* that is exactly the same in name and meaning as the horn of a rabbit. However, for any non-existent x, different-from-x is an existent because, for instance, different-from-(the horn of a rabbit) includes all existents. For instance, a table is different-from-(the horn of a rabbit) because of being a phenomenon that is not exactly the same in name and meaning as the horn of a rabbit. Since different-from-(a non-existent) includes all phenomena, it is existent and permanent. Also, whatever is different-from-(a non-existent) is necessarily existent, but it is not necessarily permanent.

SUMMARY

The division of phenomena into one and different has to do only with what are described as singular existents and what are described as groups of existents. This characterization includes "what are described as" because everything is one on its own, and existents in any size group are different. It just depends on how the existent or existents are described. (This is not intended to allow for a possibility that if someone describes the horn of a rabbit as existent, then it is a singular existent. Rather, the provision in regard to description is meant only to certify the importance of descriptions and words in reasoning and debate. If someone speaks of a tool with a handle made from the horn of a rabbit, what the person is talking about does not exist.)

The comparative predicates "one-with-*x*" and "different-from-*x*" have to do, not with singular and plural, but with identity. Each and every existent is identical with itself and different from all other things, existent and non-existent. Again, this has to be "as described" because the name of the existent is part of the consideration. What you said, that is what we are talking about. For instance, suppose there is a vase on your table, a vase from China that you bought at a sale a couple years ago. The vase is one-with-the-vase but different-from-(the vase on your table) and different-from-(the Chinese vase on your table). Even though there is just the one thing, the descriptions or names are not the same, so what we are talking about are different things, at least in name.

The consideration of how things are expressed is essential to understanding one-with-*x* and different-from-*x* and is critical to understanding the whole enterprise of reasoning and debate. Note that, when one-with-*x* and different-from-*x* are used as subjects, the qualities of these categories on their own may differ radically from their qualities when they are understood as predicates. When expressed as subjects in statements of qualities, "one-with-*x*" and "different-from-*x*" must be understood as abstract singulars. When expressed as predicates either in statements of qualities or in statements of pervasion, like "whatever is one-with-*x* . . ." and "whatever is different-from-*x* . . .," they must be understood not as abstract singulars but as qualities of other phenomena. Thus, reading these correctly puts stress on understanding the differences between these two types of statements.

Exercise 21.1

Give reasons justifying the following incomplete syllogisms. None of these are phony or trick questions. They can all be justified according to the assertions of this system. By now, the checking procedure—first the property of the subject, then the pervasion, and then the irresistible conclusion—should be fairly automatic. Even so, it would be good practice for you and your partner to check the syllogisms below, complete with your reasons, by using the dialogue in exercise 20.2.

Double up on each reason: give one reason, check it, and then give another reason and check it. Think of different reasons for each.

Try to think of the consequences of the reasons you are giving. Especially when thinking of whether or not the pervasion works, consider the range of things that satisfy the antecedent, "Whatever is/is not..." What is included? What is excluded? Will that reason work for the pervasion in the syllogism? In preparation for a future exercise, **write down your answers to this exercise on a separate sheet of paper, and save that sheet for later.**

1. The subject, established base, is one because of being/not being

   _____.

2. The subject, established base, is not different because of _____.

3. The subject, one, is one because of _____.

4. The subject, different, is one because of _____.

5. The subject, different, is not different because of _____.

6. The subject, one, is a permanent phenomenon because of _____.

7. The subject, one, is not impermanent because of _____.

8. The subject, a pot, is one-with-a-pot because of _____.

9. The subject, a pot, is different-from-a-table because of _____.

10. The subject, the horn of a rabbit, is not one-with-(the horn of a rabbit) because of _____.

11. The subject, the horn of a rabbit, is not different-from-(the horn of a rabbit) because of _____.

12. The subject, a table, is not one-with-(the horn of a rabbit) because of _____.

13. The subject, a table, is different-from-(the horn of a rabbit) because of _____.

14. The subject, uncomposed space, is not a functioning thing because of _____.

15. The subject, uncomposed space, is different-from-(functioning thing) because of _____.

16. The subject, one-with-sound, is not one-with-sound because of _____.

17. The subject, one-with-sound, is different-from-sound because of _____.

18. The subject, one-with-sound, is a permanent phenomenon because of _____.

19. The subject, one-with-(the horn of a rabbit), is a non-existent because of _____.

20. The subject, different-from-(the horn of a rabbit), is an existent because of _____.

EXERCISE 21.2

Working with your debate partner and speaking out loud, create your own questions in the form of an incomplete syllogism, as in the previous exercise. Take turns assuming the roles of Challenger and Defender and, as Challenger, ask the person in the role of Defender to give a reason justifying why "The subject, _____ , is/is not _____." Once again, think about the consequences of the reasons you are giving.

22. Consequences

ONE OF THE most natural ways we have to check an idea is by looking at the consequences (Skt. *prasaṅga,* Tib. *thal 'gyur*) of that position. If the consequences and implications of an idea are acceptable and consistent with that basic position, we gain evidence in support of the original idea. If the consequences and implications that flow from that idea are inconsistent with that idea, then we have to conclude that the original position must be flawed. Contradiction implies error.

It is not likely that looking into the consequences of something develops by nature alone, though we do seem to have a natural tendency to look for patterns and, therefore, for breaks in patterns. Probably looking for consequences develops as a function of learning language. However it comes to be, practically everyone over a certain age just automatically does it, whether they have training in reasoning or not. So, for those of us with basic language skills, looking at consequences seems to come quite easily. In this system of Buddhist reasoning and debate, looking at consequences is the most important tool in the box. I believe that reliance on consequences is part of what Professor Cargile was referring to when he compared Buddhist reasoning and debate to learning to climb a mountain on your own, rather than building a railroad to carry you up the mountain.

Consequences draw out the implications of ideas, and if that idea is not sensible, they can very effectively help a person overcome a mistaken notion in a very natural way. We simply cannot hold contradictory ideas in mind at the same time. The use of consequences to defeat wrong ideas fits perfectly with the goal of clarifying consciousness to allow liberation to unfold. Even so, the use of consequences is only as good as the one doing the thinking because we are limited by the measure of our understandings. For instance, how much serious weight can the ordinary person bring to bear on the issue of whether or not Pluto is a proper planet or in regard to whether or not there will be a Big Crunch that collapses all the matter in the universe into a single point? Some people have sophisticated understandings of these issues and have settled their conclusions, but not many of us. By the same token, how useful would a theoretical physicist be to your grandmother when she is trying to remember where she left her crochet basket? For all of us, we know what we know, and that much we can use. (As always, I encourage you to be observant and to build up your own internal database.)

The consequence may be used to check both types of basic statements—statements of qualities and statements of pervasion. For instance, if someone makes a simple statement of a quality like,

Lassie is a dog,

we can look at the consequences of this position and check to see whether or not it is accurate. For instance, we may reason that, if Lassie is a dog, as you say, then:

Lassie is a mammal.
Lassie is not a human.
Lassie is either a male dog or a female dog.

And on and on. Really there are countless consequences and implications of every position, but just a few will normally indicate whether or not the assertion is sensible.

In checking the implications of a statement of a quality, the procedure is that you look to see what the predicate of the statement implies about the subject. For instance, you can see that, if indeed Lassie is a dog, then she would have to have the qualities of a dog: she would be a mammal—vertebrate and so on, she would not be human, and she should be either a male dog or a female dog, and so on. If all of these predicates fit the subject at hand, then it looks as if the statement will stand.

In this system of debate, it is much more typical that consequences are used to question a statement of pervasion in order to verify it or refute it. We use this sort of reasoning all the time. That is, we check up on an idea by applying it to cases, and if it appears that the idea is wrong, we give a counterexample to the person. Whether a person's statement of pervasion is right or wrong, the template for flinging a consequence is as follows. Suppose someone says,

Every arachnid is a spider.

However, you understand that is not accurate because arachnids also include, among others, scorpions and ticks, which are not spiders. We would normally just say something in response like,

No, scorpions and ticks are arachnids too.

That usually takes care of it. They may doubt you, but they can look it up. In this system of debate, the formal statement of an unwanted consequence lays out the full import of the response:

Then it would follow that the subject, a scorpion, is a spider because of being an arachnid.

In both normal speech and in the formal statement of a consequence, we are doing the same things. That is, in order to check the idea, you need to come up with examples of things that have the quality of the antecedent of the pervasion—the first part, every arachnid—which is the part that ends up being in the third position of the consequence, as the reason. And then you look to see how the things with that quality compare to the phenomenon spoken of in the second part of the pervasion—in this case, spiders. If the statement of pervasion is accurate, then every example you come up with will just give further evidence to support it. However, if the statement of pervasion is not accurate, perhaps you can come up with a counterexample, something that has the quality of the universal—an arachnid—but does not have the quality of being a spider. In that case, the person's statement of pervasion is not accurate. Since all spiders are arachnids, but not all arachnids are spiders, here you can give the counterexample of a tick or a scorpion. This is always the pattern to follow.

When you respond simply, "No, scorpions and ticks are arachnids too," that means, "No, scorpions and ticks are arachnids, *but they are not spiders*." The import is the same. However, it is helpful to lay out the entire consequence in order to make clear what you are saying in response to the statement of pervasion, right or wrong. The formal consequence also helps the Defender, who is putting forth the statement of pervasion, by giving a compelling proof that something is wrong with the original statement or by giving clear targets to shoot at. The next chapter spells out the Defender's answers to the Challenger's arguments.

Here is a parallel example from the Collected Topics tradition. If someone says,

Whatever is not impermanent is necessarily permanent,

that seems right, on first impression. However, "whatever is not impermanent" applies not only to all permanent phenomena but also to non-existents as well. Thus, to this statement, you can fling the consequence:[*]

Then, according to what you say,[†] it would follow that the subject, the horn of a rabbit, would be permanent because of not being impermanent.

In the original claim here, "whatever is not impermanent" is too broad in the same way that the class of arachnids is broader than the class of spiders. It is too broad because it takes in possible subjects that should not be included. For example, some of the things referred to in the universal part of the statement of pervasion—the first part, what is not impermanent—are also not permanent, such as the horn of a rabbit.

Please appreciate that a correct consequence is an accurate conclusion drawn from a person's stated position. That is one reason they can be so effective. The one who draws out the consequence supplies the subject for debate, but the predicate of the consequence and the reason are drawn from the person's statement. In the usual way of expressing a pervasion, the first phenomenon mentioned is the one that is governed universally—that is, the statement says something about each and every p-phenomenon—so that becomes the reason of the consequence, the one that is pervaded. Since the person has said that every p is a q, then this thing that is a p should also

---

[*] That's right, kids—*fling* the consequences!

[†] In ordinary conversation, it is usually helpful to frame the consequence with something like, "Then, according to what you say, . . ." or "Well, if that is right, then . . . " or "Wouldn't that mean that . . . ," so that the Defender is alerted to what's going on.

be a *q*, at least according to what you said. Thus, the second phenomenon mentioned in the pervasion—the *q*-phenomenon—becomes the predicate or point of clarification of the consequence, the one that is the pervader. So, a proper application of a consequence to a statement of pervasion may be illustrated like this:

Whatever is a *p* is necessarily a *q*.

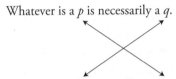

Then it follows that the subject is a *q* because of being a *p*.

This is the correct way of applying a pervasion to a consequence, whether the pervasion is accurate or not. If the pervasion is accurate, you will not find any consequences that are discordant. If the pervasion is not accurate, you will be able to find a discordant example for the subject.

In order to create an effective consequence for any sort of statement of pervasion, you have to find an example of something that definitely has the quality of the universal part of the statement of pervasion. Otherwise, it does not work. For instance, let's use the same example:

Whatever is not impermanent is necessarily permanent.

Suppose that in response, you choose an example of something that does not satisfy the universal part of the statement of pervasion, "whatever is not impermanent," and give this consequence:

Wouldn't that mean, from what you say, that the subject, a chair, would be permanent?

To this, the person defending the original claim might say:

What? What do you mean? Why would a chair be permanent?

To which you would have to respond:

Because of not being impermanent.

But that is just wrong. Of course chairs are impermanent, or they wouldn't sell so many every year. So, the first essential, whether you are trying to verify, test, confirm, or defeat a statement of pervasion, is to find examples that definitely have the quality of the universal part of the statement. Otherwise, your examples will simply not be effective.

Remember that in a *valid* syllogism—and consequences do not abide by all the same rules as syllogisms—the range or extent of the quality of the reason (in the third position of the syllogism) must be either less than or equal to the range of the quality of the predicate to be proven (in the second position of the syllogism). In turn, the reason that it must be so for a *valid* syllogism is because a true statement of pervasion—one that is accurate, concordant with nature, and factual—is such that the extent of the universal stated in the first part of the pervasion (which would become the reason) must be equal to, or smaller than, the extent of the quality mentioned in the second part (which would become the predicate to be proven). For instance, the two qualities are equal in the following pervasion:

Whatever is a product is necessarily impermanent.

All products are impermanent, and all impermanent phenomena are products. They are equal in extent. Productness and impermanence are concomitant.

The only other pattern for a true statement of pervasion is when the range of the universal stated in the first part of the pervasion is smaller than the range of the second quality, as in the pervasion:

Whatever is a product is necessarily an existent.

All products are existents, but there are existents that are not products, such as uncomposed space; thus, the range of products is smaller than the range of existent phenomena. When such a true pervasion in either of these two patterns is used in a syllogism and all the other requirements are met, the sign is called a correct sign.

A statement of pervasion can work in either of these two ways. However, there are three ways left over in which the two phenomena in a statement of pervasion can align, and in all three of these cases, the statements will be false: (1) if the range of the quality in the first part of the statement (which would be applied as the reason in a syllogism or consequence) is greater than the range of the quality in the second part (which would be applied as the predicate to be proven in a syllogism or as the point of clarification in a consequence), (2) if the ranges of the two qualities do not overlap at all, and (3) if the ranges of the two qualities overlap but neither is wholly included in the other.* An example of the first is:

Whatever is a product is necessarily a material phenomenon.

This statement of pervasion is inaccurate and does not work because the range of products is broader than the range of material phenomena; yet, this statement wrongly says that every product is a material phenomenon. That is not true because there are some products that are not material phenomena, like consciousnesses and persons. Productness is a quality not only of all material phenomena but also of other things that are not material. This statement is parallel to the claim above that all arachnids are spiders. When such a failing pervasion is used in a syllogism, the reason is called an "indefinite reason."

The second type of false statement of pervasion is one in which the two qualities don't overlap at all. For instance, one might say,

Whatever is a product is necessarily permanent.

Products and permanent phenomena are mutually exclusive (MX), so the pervasion will not work either way. It is easy to give a counterexample to such a false statement of pervasion. For instance, in response to the statement above, one could say:

Then it would follow that the subject, a chair, is permanent because of being a product.

In fact, we do not find anything produced by causes and conditions that is permanent. Another way to attack this backward statement of pervasion is

---

* Of course the importance of these five types of statements of pervasion is not just as stand-alone statements but also as they are used in argument forms. For a full description of "quasi-reasons" for which the sign is the property of the subject but the pervasions are not established, see Rogers, *Tibetan Logic,* 327–50.

to link the two qualities to other things that are clearly contradictory. For instance, you might say,

> No, that can't be right. All products are momentary, and no permanent phenomena are momentary (that is to say, whatever is a product is necessarily momentary, but whatever is a permanent phenomenon is necessarily not momentary).

When such a false pervasion is used in a syllogism, the sign is called a "contradictory reason" and the failed pervasions are called "perverse."

The third and final alignment of a false pervasion is when the range of the quality in the first part of the statement (which would be applied as the reason in a syllogism or consequence) and the range of the quality in the second part (which would be applied as the predicate to be proven in a syllogism or as the point of clarification in a consequence) overlap but neither is wholly included in the other. This is the alignment in the following statement,

> Whatever is a wrong consciousness is necessarily a mental consciousness.

Of course, some wrong consciousnesses are mental consciousnesses and some are not, and some mental consciousnesses are wrong and some are not; so this statement is false. When such a false pervasion is used in a syllogism, the sign is called an "indefinite reason."

As you must perceive, an important way of tracking how a person seems to understand two different things is by using the tool of the comparisons of phenomena to analyze the way they are talking about them. This is always in play in a discussion that includes claims of pervasion, and it can quickly be brought into play for a discussion of the qualities of a thing. For instance, for a statement of pervasion to be true, the two qualities must compare as 3P, with the phenomenon lesser in extent mentioned in the first part of the pervasion—the universal part that goes to the reason—or the two qualities must be MI. For a false statement of pervasion in which the first quality—the p-phenomenon—is greater in extent, the two will compare as 3P, but the phenomena are stated in the wrong order. If the two phenomena compare as MX, the pervasion will always fail. If the two phenomena compare as 4P, then neither phenomenon wholly includes the other, and so there can be no accurate pervasion either way. For instance, think of blue and the color of cloth or conceptual consciousnesses and valid cognizers. Please review the examples given above and understand them in terms of how the phenomena compare. Chapter 24, "Strategies in Debate," focuses on this way of reasoning.

Of course, you can use this technique of analyzing the consequences of ideas for your own thoughts and words as well as for the written and spoken words of others. If you are thinking about the implications of your own thoughts or words, then you own them, for they flow from your own positions. However, if you are thinking about the consequences of others' words, then you do not own them. You are simply weighing the value of what was said. This simple fact points toward the substantial difference between the two types of arguments in Buddhist reasoning and debate—syllogisms and consequences.

Syllogisms are the basic argument form, and the type of consequence stated in Buddhist debate is modeled after syllogisms. The two argument forms are structurally similar; however, there is also a wide gap between them. Valid syllogisms express the natural states of phenomena, and the person who states a syllogism is personally responsible for the argument, right or wrong. On the other hand, when consequences are used as arguments that reflect the positions put forth by others, the person giving voice to a consequence is not held personally responsible for the truth or falsity of the argument, only that it has to be a fair implication of what the person said. For instance, perhaps someone confuses consciousnesses with valid cognizers, and says,

All consciousnesses are valid cognizers.

A fair response to this is:

Then it would follow that the subject, a wrong consciousness, is a valid cognizer because of being a consciousness. You asserted the pervasion.*

---

*The one stating the consequence, in the role of the Challenger, reminds the Defender, "You asserted the pervasion." This is like "Check" in chess, I suppose. It is a warning that if the Defender now denies the pervasion of the consequence, that would be an immediate reversal of the stated position. This would contradict what he or she said earlier and would signal the failure of the Defender's position.

This response is an accurate implication of the person's stated view. The subject has the quality of the universal part of the statement of pervasion, for it is a consciousness. However, a wrong consciousness is not a valid cognizer, so the consequence is not compatible with the person's view. It is a fair response, and it should be effective in defeating the wrong idea. The argument put forth in a consequence is in accordance with and *follows* from the views already expressed. However, the person who states the consequence is not bound to accept the establishment of the reason, the pervasion, or the "thesis," and we should not think that this is what the person believes, only that it is a fair implication of what was first said. However, this protection against being responsible for arguments addressing others' words does not apply when analyzing your own thoughts and words. Then, of course you are responsible for every bit of it, and consequences will be a tremendous aid in your personal reflection.

Since syllogisms and consequences are structurally similar, the parts are thought of in largely the same ways, and the parts are related in the same ways to form the premises. However, in a syllogism, the quality in the second position is *the predicate to be proven* as a quality of the subject. That is the point of the argument. But, in the case of a consequence, the quality in the second position is known as a *clarification* or *point of clarification* (*gsal ba*). That is the purpose of a consequence, to clarify whether or not the quality in the second position is a quality of the subject. In the case above, the one stating the consequence is trying to make clear that being a valid cognizer is not a quality of a wrong consciousness.

The main reason for the predominant reliance on consequences in Buddhist debate is that they are much more effective in bringing a person to a new understanding. If a person asserts a faulty position, a consequence that is a fair reflection of those views is able to force the person to see the unwanted implications and to overcome misconceptions. You are meeting the person on his or her own grounds. Rather than trying to school a person with the logic of syllogisms, it can be more effective to use the terminology and assertions that the person already accepts. In trying to do this, it is essential to make sure you are accurately representing the person's ideas, and, if that is not the case, you yourself will understand something new. Also, at the very least, this effort can make opponents look more closely at their own positions, express them with more care, and clarify their positions. These three reflect the three purposes of debate. According to Denma Lochö Rinpoche, syllogisms are especially effective for overcoming doubts or uncertainties, and consequences are especially effective for overcoming wrong views.[1] Reasoning with syllogisms can help a person get it straight. Facing consequences, based on your own views, can dislodge you from a mistaken notion.

According to the *Tutor's Collected Topics,* a correct consequence must be such that there is a person for whom it is a correct consequence and this person must not be able to give a factually concordant response to the argument.[*] Thus, it is more than just a fair consequence of the person's views; it is a fair and effective response. Arguments do not exist in a void but are related to persons and their ideas. Consequences are designed to address actual views held to be true. The first requirement is that there must be a person who holds the position that is drawn out in the consequence. Second, the consequence must be such that the person to whom it is stated cannot give a factually concordant answer that would defeat the argument. Thus, the person is forced to understand an implied correct thesis relating the subject and the point of clarification. A consequence to which an opponent is able to give an effective answer or one that does not address views held by the opponent is not a valid argument. As in the description of the requirements for a valid syllogism, here again the value of this type of argument is determined by its epistemological efficacy, its ability to cause a person to generate a new understanding. A consequence is correct or not in dependence on the opponent's level of understanding of the implied thesis.

EXERCISE 22.1

Formulate a three-part consequence—one with a subject, a point of clarification, and a reason—in response to each of the following statements of pervasion:

1. Whatever is a color is necessarily red.
2. Whatever is a color is necessarily white.
3. Whatever is a color is necessarily a primary color.
4. Whatever is a visible form is necessarily a shape.
5. Every established base is a permanent phenomenon.
6. All hidden phenomena are manifest phenomena.

---

[*]For more information on consequences see Pur-bu-jok Jam-ba-gya-tso, *Rigs lam che ba* [The greater path of reasoning] in *Tshad ma'i gzhung don 'byed pa'i bsdus grva'i rnam bzhag rigs lam 'phrul gyi lde mig,* 1b.3–23a.6. See also Hopkins, *Meditation on Emptiness,* 443–51.

7. If something is not a functioning thing, then it is necessarily a permanent phenomenon.
8. Every specifically characterized phenomenon is a consciousness.
9. All products are necessarily clear and knowing.
10. If it is a manifest phenomenon, it cannot be a hidden phenomenon.
11. All valid cognizers are necessarily not conceptual consciousnesses.
12. All wrong consciousnesses are conceptual.
13. A direct perceiver is always a sense consciousness.
14. Every functioning thing is a definiendum.
15. Whatever is an established base is necessarily a definition.
16. Whatever is a permanent phenomenon is necessarily not one.
17. Anything that is a non-(non-[functioning thing]) is necessarily one-with-(functioning thing).
18. All objects of comprehension are different.
19. Everything that is selfless is different-from-(the horn of a rabbit).
20. Whatever is one-with-(functioning thing) is necessarily permanent.
21. Everything different-from-(functioning thing) is permanent.
22. Whatever is not different-from-(functioning thing) is necessarily a functioning thing.
23. Whatever is not one-with-(functioning thing) is necessarily different-from-(functioning thing).
24. Whatever is a non-cow is necessarily a non-(functioning thing).

EXERCISE 22.2

Working with your debate partner, take turns in the roles of Challenger and Defender to voice false statements of pervasion and then formulate consequences in response. Use examples from anything you know, but be sure to include some from the Collected Topics tradition including some from the explanation of one and different and some from the explanation of consciousnesses.

EXERCISE 22.3

Now that you have more exposure to consequences, go back and find that sheet of paper on which you wrote your reasons for exercise 21.1, and check carefully to see how you did.

KAMALAŚHĪLA

At least according to legend, Kamalaśhīla, an eighth-century Indian Buddhist monk, won what was doubtless the most influential debate ever in Tibetan history. It was early in the transmission of Buddhism to Tibet, and the Tibetans were receiving teachers from both India and China, as Buddhism was flourishing in both places. However, their teachings were not harmonious. So, King Songtsen Gampo convened a debate at Samye between Kamalaśhīla, representing the Indian side, and the monk Hashang Mahāyāna, representing the Chinese side. It was settled that Kamalaśhīla's side won the debate. Since then, Tibetans have almost exclusively followed the Indian model of Buddhism and Chinese teachings have not been allowed. Painting by Buchung Nubgya.

23. Procedures in Debate

ONE SUMMER, I was teaching at the American Institute of Buddhist Studies camp held at Hampshire College in Massachusetts. The college rented its space out during the summer months for additional income, and that summer there was a strange mix of groups—the Buddhists, the folks doing movement therapy, and a group of karate black belts. One day, some of us Buddhists were talking with some of the black belts, and they explained that, though they knew many karate forms, they did not know any that did not begin with a defensive move. That is, karate was intended as a response to aggression.

The normal flow of Buddhist debate is something like that too because the debate almost always begins with the standing Challenger approaching the sitting Defender with a question typically framed as a consequence. The question may be about any of a number of things, including a comparison of phenomena, the interpretation of a word or phrase in a definition or a passage in a text, or the intent of the passage as a whole. Just knowing that alone helps you to understand much of the narrative in traditional Buddhist lectures because so much of the narrative is about the interpretation of a word or passage and the distinctions between differing views. However, unlike beginning with aggression, the Challenger's attitude should be respectful, as if really seeking an answer to a troubling qualm. Then, as in the karate forms, the Defender has a set of possible answers to the opening debate question.

So, within these constraints, how does a debater in the role of Defender, the one putting forth a view, manage to explain his or her position? Georges Dreyfus (aka Geshe Sangye Samdrup), the first Westerner to earn the geshay degree, has a very rare measure of insight into the actual practice of debate in the Tibetan style. In addition to the usual technique in which the

Defender lays out a position only by answering the arguments and questions presented by the Challenger, he reported, "Ideally—and it is sometimes done like this, though it is fairly rare—the responder can just state his position. It can be done in a formal way. I know of one case in which someone sat in debate and announced publicly, 'This is my position. Please come and debate with me'."[1]

Beginning this way or by the more usual way of the Challenger's approaching with a question, the debate proceeds by following these six protocols:

1. The Challenger initiates a debate by approaching the Defender with a question of some sort, which is framed as an argument.
2. The Defender gives answers to the Challenger's statements. Since they are all framed as arguments, they may be accepted or denied.
3. After the Defender has answered the Challenger's initial statement, the Challenger presents arguments, one by one, in reply to the Defender's answers. In these replies, the Challenger is seeking to find fault in the Defender's answers and to support his or her own line of reasoning.
4. If the Challenger's line of reasoning does not play out and becomes senseless (because the Defender gives effective answers or because the Challenger did not think through the arguments and possible answers adequately), then the Defender does not ultimately contradict earlier statements and would not lose the debate.
5. If the Defender gives up on a line of defense and contradicts earlier statements, the Challenger leads the Defender back through all the earlier wrong answers, shouting "*Tsha!*" ("Finished!") to each contradiction along the way.
6. Finally, the Challenger poses the original question again, and the Defender, who has been shown that the earlier answer is indefensible, now gives another answer contradicting the first one. To this, the Challenger shouts "*Tsha! Tsha! Tsha!*" signaling that the original answer has been contradicted.

With the sixth step, that particular debate is over. The Defender has abandoned the original position. However, there are lots of ways to go on from there, such as checking the comparison of the principal phenomena in the debate.

It will be easier to understand the variety of ways that a debate may begin and what comes after, if we cover the Defender's answers first. That way, you will be able to get the first part of the debate, not just the opening question, but a snippet of the opening volleys.

THE DEFENDER'S ANSWERS

We are now familiar with the arguments, both syllogisms and consequences, that the Challenger can pose. So, what are the Defender's possible answers to these arguments? There are two sets of answers, depending on the argument that the Challenger has stated. It is not a matter of whether or not the Challenger states something in the form of a syllogism or in the form of a consequence that prompts the different sets of answers. The only thing that determines which set of answers to draw from is the structure of the Challenger's argument—whether or not it is a complete argument with a reason. If the Challenger states a stem of an argument—a subject and a point of clarification of a consequence without a reason—the Defender goes to a set of just two possible answers. If the Challenger states a full, three-part consequence—one complete with a subject, a point of clarification, and a reason—the Defender goes to a set of four possible answers. Understand that very often the opening volley from the Challenger is not the stem of an argument so much as a question framed in the terminology of a consequence. In addition to these two sets of answers, there is always an optional response that denies that a reliable answer can be given.

To a Two-Part Consequence with a Subject and a Point of Clarification

As you recall, a point of clarification is the predicate portion of a consequence. For instance, a Challenger might give the stem of a consequence without a reason:

It follows that the subject, a pot, is a permanent phenomenon.

The Defender has just two possible answers. These have the force of disagreement/denial and agreement/acceptance:

1. Why?

   Formulated in general: Why does that subject have the quality of*
   that predicate of the consequence?†

   Formulated with numbers: Why does that ① have the quality of
   that ②?

2. I accept it.

   Formulated in general: I accept that that subject has the quality of
   that predicate of the consequence.

   Formulated with numbers: I accept that that ① has the quality of
   that ②.

Of course, to the above stem, the correct answer, according to the Collected
Topics tradition, is disagreement/denial, so the Defender says, "Why?"
which means, "Why is a pot a permanent phenomenon?" Scholars in the
tradition always explain the "Why?" answer as meaning "No." Still, it seems
that the answer could simply be seeking more information, as is usual for
"Why?" in normal conversation. However, the reason they consistently gloss
this as "No" may be because the Defender already knows the reason that
can be given.

An easy example of a consequence stem to which the correct response
would be "I accept it" is the following:

---

*These formulas are different from those offered in Perdue, *Debate in Tibetan Buddhism*,
which were, for instance, "Why is that subject that predicate?" Rather than saying "is," the
formulas offered here say "has/have the quality of." The reason for the change is, first, to be
truer to the intent of the sentences and second, to avoid the ridiculous statement that "that
subject is that predicate." Do you see what I mean? It can happen that that subject is that
predicate, such as in the statement, "It follows that the subject, a functioning thing, is a
functioning thing," but that is not typical. It is also not the point, for the sentence says that
that subject has that quality, even that a functioning thing has the quality of a functioning
thing. Also, in the same way, if you think about it, a ① never has the quality of a ②, but all
of these formulas are only for purposes of illustration.

†If the mode of statement for an argument is one of existence rather than one of being, such
as in the consequence:

It follows with respect to the subject, on that mountain pass, there is fire,

then the formulas for the answers need to reflect that existence mode of statement. So,
for the Defender's response of "Why?" the formula would be: "Why is it that where that
subject is there is that predicate of the consequence?" For the sample stem of a consequence,
this would be, "Why is it that on that mountain pass there is fire?" Apply this to the other
answers in the same way.

It follows that the subject, a pot, is a functioning thing,

and the answer of agreement/acceptance here means "I accept that a pot is a functioning thing."

The formulas for the answers using the numbers ①, ②, and ③ as appropriate rather than "that subject," "that predicate," and "that reason" are much more helpful for newcomers learning the Defender's answers because they allow us to skip a step in our thinking. Although it may seem automatic for old hands to know the position of the subject, the predicate, and the reason, it is not automatic for newcomers. So, when given the information that the answer "I accept it" means "I accept that that subject has the quality of that predicate of the consequence," a newcomer has to pause a moment to reflect on the positions of the two players. It must have been true as well for us in the distant past that we had to think a moment to line up the numbers—① before ②, ② before ③, and so on, but it is no longer true for anyone reading this book. Thus, it is just easier initially, and we quickly transcend the need for the numbers.

Note Well: The comments above and the two possible answers are in regard to the case when a Challenger has stated a point of clarification, which is part of a consequence. If the Challenger states a syllogism thesis—the first two parts of a syllogism—to a Defender, the expectation is not that the Defender will give one of the two answers above but that the Defender will supply a reason justifying the thesis. Remember that in this system, a valid syllogism is an expression of a natural state of phenomena, not just words or even words in the right order. Thus, when the Challenger states the first two parts of the syllogism, the Defender is called upon to give a correct reason. This happens only when the Challenger is following up on something the Defender has already said. It is a way of getting the Defender to justify claims.

To a Three-Part Consequence Complete with a Reason

When a Challenger states a full consequence with a subject, a point of clarification, and a reason, such as

It follows that the subject, a pot, is a functioning thing because of being a product, the Defender goes to the other set of answers. These are the four answers, together with their formulas:

1. The reason is not established.

    Formulated in general: The reason, that that subject has the quality of that reason, is not established.

    Formulated with numbers: The reason, that that ① has the quality of that ③, is not established.

2. There is no pervasion.

    Formulated in general: It is not the case that whatever is that reason necessarily has the quality of that predicate of the consequence.*

    Formulated with numbers: It is not the case that whatever is that ③ necessarily has the quality of that ②.

3. The pervasion is opposite.

    Alternatively: It is a contradictory pervasion.

    Formulated in general: Whatever is that reason necessarily does not have the quality of that predicate of the consequence.

    Formulated with numbers: Whatever is that ③ necessarily does not have the quality of that ②.

4. I accept it.

    Formulated in general: I accept that that subject has the quality of that predicate of the consequence.

    Formulated with numbers: I accept that that ① has the quality of that ②.

The first of the four possible answers to a full argument is "The reason is not established," which is the appropriate answer to a consequence such as the following:

> It follows that the subject, a pot, is a functioning thing because of being a permanent phenomenon.

The Defender answers, "The reason is not established," meaning "The reason, that a pot is a permanent phenomenon, is not established." It is clearly true, as the Defender's answer claims, that a pot is not permanent. Still, one might think that it would be okay to accept this consequence because it is

---

*Of course, there are many ways of stating a pervasion, positive or negative, as laid out in chapter 5, "Two Kinds of Statements."

true that a pot is a functioning thing—that that subject is that predicate of the consequence. However, even though it is true that a pot is a functioning thing, here that is not justified because of the bad reason. Remember that a correct consequence must be one to which a Defender cannot give an effective answer.

The second of the four possible answers to a full argument is "There is no pervasion," formulated in general as "Whatever is that reason is not necessarily that predicate of the consequence" or "It is not the case that whatever is that reason is necessarily that predicate of the consequence." This is the appropriate answer to a consequence such as the following:

> It follows that the subject, a pot, is a functioning thing because of being an established base.

The Defender answers, "There is no pervasion," meaning "It is not the case that whatever is an established base is necessarily a functioning thing." It is true that a pot is an established base; however, there is no pervasion here because there are also permanent phenomena, which are established bases but not functioning things. Once again, and this is not always the case, one might think that it would be okay to accept this consequence because it is true that a pot is a functioning thing. However, even though that is true, here it is not justified because of the bad reason. A Defender could give an effective answer.

The third of the four possible answers to a full argument is "The pervasion is opposite," or, "It is a contradictory pervasion," formulated in general as "Whatever is that reason is necessarily not that predicate of the consequence." This is the appropriate answer to the consequence:

> It follows that the subject, a pot, is a permanent phenomenon because of being a functioning thing.

The Defender answers, "The pervasion is opposite," meaning "Whatever is a functioning thing is necessarily not a permanent phenomenon." Recall from chapter 5, "Two Kinds of Statements," that a pervasion of the form "Whatever is a p is necessarily not a q" implies the equivalent "No p is a q" as well as the equivalent "No q is a p." Thus, in this example, the pervasion that is opposite may be understood as "No functioning thing is a permanent phenomenon" and "No permanent phenomenon is a functioning thing." It is true that a pot is a functioning thing; however, there is no pervasion here because no functioning thing is a permanent phenomenon. This reason is not justified in any way, and any Defender could give an effective answer.

The force of this answer is technically included within the third answer, "There is no pervasion," because in every case in which the pervasion is opposite, the response that there is no pervasion is also appropriate, though weaker. That is, if it is the case that whatever is that reason is necessarily not that predicate, then it naturally follows that it is also the case that whatever is that reason is not necessarily that predicate. Using the same example, if a Challenger states the consequence:

> It follows that the subject, a pot, is a permanent phenomenon because of being a functioning thing,

then the appropriate response is "The pervasion is opposite," meaning that whatever is a functioning thing is necessarily not a permanent phenomenon. Since it is the case that whatever is a functioning thing is necessarily not a permanent phenomenon, it naturally follows that it is also the case that whatever is a functioning thing is not necessarily a permanent phenomenon. To say it another way, pointing out that the pervasion is opposite has the force of asserting "No functioning things are permanent phenomena," whereas pointing out that there is no pervasion has the force of asserting "Some functioning things are not permanent phenomena." Naturally, if no functioning things are permanent phenomena, then some (in fact, all) functioning things are not permanent phenomena. If a Defender is faced with a consequence to which the answer that the pervasion is opposite is appropriate, this is a stronger and more specific answer than merely pointing out that there is no pervasion. However, this does not go the other way. The lack of pervasion does not imply that the pervasion is opposite. Thus, (1) statements of pervasion for which "not necessarily" is appropriate and (2) statements of pervasion for which "necessarily not" is appropriate compare as 3P. You may like to remember this point as: "'Necessarily not' implies 'not necessarily', but 'not necessarily' does not necessarily imply 'necessarily not'."*

The fourth and final of the four possible answers to a full argument is "I accept it." This is the one answer that is in both sets of answers. This would be the appropriate response to this argument:

---

*I know many of us like remembering it that way.

It follows that the subject, a pot, is a functioning thing because of being a product.

Here, "I accept it" means, "I accept that a pot is a functioning thing." According to Denma Lochö Rinpoche, it is a point of etiquette in debate that, when the Challenger has stated a full argument with a reason and the Defender wants to accept it, the Defender does not simply say, "I accept it," but spells out the answer in full saying, "I accept that that subject is that predicate."[2]

Note Well: These four answers in response to a full argument with a reason could be used equally to answer a syllogism or a consequence.

Note Well: The Defender should always try to give the right answer. Many times I have seen American students accepting unwanted consequences of their original bad assertions, often smiling and looking around, knowing full well that they were in the wrong. Perhaps the American students hang on even after things are going badly because we are so resistant to admitting when we are wrong. But this is not the way of Buddhist debate. If you are speaking as a Defender, in a formal debate setting or not, and you realize your mistake, the thing you should do is admit it and accept the punishment, which is nothing more than a big, fat "*Tsha!*" in your face. It is better to be embarrassed and learn, to have a willingness to change your position on things, than not to learn at all. It is a good way to be in education, politics, and life in general.

Note Well: You may have perceived it already, but there is a rule of the system that it is appropriate to give the answers "There is no pervasion" and "The pervasion is opposite" if and only if the reason is established. If the reason is not established, that is where the Defender has to go first. This also means that, for an argument in which both the reason is not established and there is no pervasion, such as:

It follows that the subject, a pot, is a valid cognizer because of being a consciousness,

the Defender first has to deny the establishment of the reason, in this case by saying, "The reason, that a pot is a consciousness, is not established." The backing for this procedure in Buddhist reasoning and debate has to do with the three modes of a correct sign and the order for understanding them—first, the property of the subject; second, the forward pervasion; and third, the counterpervasion.

Thus, in order for the second and third modes of the sign to be established, the first mode—the property of the subject—must first be established. That entails that a fully qualified opponent must ascertain by valid cognition the property of the subject in the syllogism at hand. Using the syllogism that is the standard for explaining Buddhist rules of logic, *for certain persons,* product is a correct sign in the syllogism:

> The subject, sound, is an impermanent phenomenon because of being a product.

Recall from chapter 6, "The Buddhist Syllogism," that each of the three modes of a correct sign has epistemological requirements for the person to whom the argument is stated. Thus, even if the sign is a property of the subject in the real world and the forward pervasion and counterpervasions are true to the way things are in the world, they do not hold as components of a correct sign unless they are ascertained as such by the person to whom the argument is stated. For instance, it may be that the pervasion in the sample syllogism above—that all products are impermanent phenomena—is *true* in the sense of being the way things are in the world; however, even if that is the case, if the reason is not established, that pervasion is not *valid* with respect to asserting a correct sign. It simply does not apply. What is important, and what we should keep in mind, is whether or not the syllogism is valid. The validity of the syllogism taken as a whole is what determines the truth and correctness of its components. So, if one component holds but the other two fail, the syllogism is not valid and thus its components are not "true" or "correct." Even if the pervasion holds in all cases in the real world, it cannot be considered to be true for a person who does not understand, such as a person who does not understand speech, nor for a person who is not seeking to know the truth of the pervasion, such as a person who has already understood it; thus, the pervasion cannot be true for such persons and the syllogism would not be a valid argument.

That the reason must be established in order for a pervasion to be true seems to imply that the Buddhist truth table for a conditional sentence would be at odds with the one found in most Western logic texts. I do not mean to equate pervasions in the Buddhist syllogism with the conditional statements as referenced in the standard truth table. Both pervasions and conditional sentences are of various types. What I am saying is that in reference to statements of the kind that can be used in the truth table, Western logic and Buddhist logic would construct differing truth tables. In understanding why Western thinkers would rule one way, while Buddhist thinkers would rule another way in that circumstance, we can start to see why even pervasions that are in accordance with the way things are in the world are deemed to be false in relation to certain persons to whom the argument may be stated and, for such persons, the failed syllogism is not valid. Moreover, the nuanced differences between the systems is instructive with regard to both.

By way of explanation, one of the ways that the Buddhist pervasion may be expressed is as a conditional sentence, one of the form "If p, then q." The first part of a conditional sentence is known as the antecedent, and the second part is known as the consequent. The truth of a conditional can be illustrated with a truth table; however, it seems that the truth value of certain cases would be assigned differently in Western logic and Buddhist logic. The usual way of understanding such a sentence is that it is false only when its antecedent is true and its consequent is false. Otherwise, in the other three possible cases, the sentence is true. The usual truth table for a conditional sentence is:

p	q	If p, then q.
T	T	T
T	F	F
F	T	T
F	F	T

If we look at this from the point of view of the Buddhist system—bearing in mind that, when the reason is not established, the pervasion cannot be valid—the Buddhist truth table for the conditional sentence would be F – T – F for the third line, rather than F – T – T, and the truth value of the fourth line would be F – F – Indeterminate, rather than F – F – T. For instance, using the standard for explaining syllogisms:

> The subject, sound, is an impermanent phenomenon because of
> being a product,

the forward pervasion of this argument is formulated in the style of a standard conditional sentence as "If something is a product, then it is necessarily an impermanent phenomenon."

On the first line, this table says that if p is true and q is true, then the statement "If p, then q" is true. For instance, in reference to the pervasion of the sample syllogism "If something is a product, then it is necessarily an impermanent phenomenon," if it is true that something is a product and it is true that that same thing is an impermanent phenomenon, then the pervasion conditional is true. For the Buddhists, for certain qualified persons who have already understood that the subject of the syllogism is a product, the pervasion conditional would be true. Thus, in relation to such a fully qualified opponent to whom the argument is stated, the syllogism would be valid.

The second line says that if p is true and q is false, then the statement "If p, then q" is false. For the sample syllogism, this line would be that if something is a product but that thing is not an impermanent phenomenon, then the claim that if something is a product, then it is necessarily an impermanent phenomenon would be false. Both systems agree on this line. For the Buddhists, the pervasion conditional would be false, and the argument would not be valid.

The most interesting issue is with the third line. The third line of the typical Western truth table says that if p is false and q is true, then the statement "If p, then q" is true. As applied to the standard Buddhist syllogism above, if I have it right, this would mean that if something is not a product but it is an impermanent phenomenon, then the pervasion conditional is still true.[*] However, the Buddhist guideline is that if the reason is not established, then the pervasion (that is, the conditional sentence) cannot be known to be true, and so it cannot be a component of a valid argument. Again, this

---

[*] Since products and impermanent phenomena are equal in extent, we will not ever be able to find an example of something that is an impermanent phenomenon but not a product. However, in the form of pervasion in which the p-phenomenon is smaller in extent than the q-phenomenon, such as "All cats are mammals," we can easily find an example of a mammal that is not a cat. Clearly, this does not disprove the pervasion that "If something is a cat, then it is a mammal." What is relevant here is that such an example also does not prove that if something is a cat, then it is a mammal. Knowing that there are some things that are mammals but not cats does not lead us to know whether or not all cats are mammals.

is related to the order of understanding. If we think of validity as derived solely from considerations of the form of the argument, it may seem to us that whether or not all products are impermanent (the second mode) does not depend on whether or not we have established that sound is a product (the first mode). Indeed, these two "facts" are independent on paper, but in Buddhist reasoning and debate as understood in this system, for both the syllogism and the consequence, there are epistemological concerns—they are arguments in relation to persons. If someone has not understood that sound is a product, the information that all products are impermanent will not impact that person's understanding of sound. Thus, even if it is "true" that all products are impermanent, in relation to certain persons, an argument that includes that pervasion is not *valid* in the sense that it does not further the knowledge of the listener with respect to the subject because the reason is not established—such persons have not ascertained that sound is a product. For the epistemologists in this system, an argument is valid only when it is able to bring forth new understanding.

Thus, in this system of thought, whether or not a pervasion holds is not relevant until the first mode of the sign, the property of the subject, holds because it is the syllogism as a whole that is important. In a valid syllogism, the sign is called a *correct* sign. The understanding in the Buddhist epistemology is holistic in the sense that the validity of the syllogism as a whole determines the correctness of all the components of that syllogism. In this system of thought, they would not say "Well, the pervasion is correct but the sign is incorrect, and these two things can be taken separately." If one is not correct, all are not correct. Thus, even if all the components are true on paper, the argument may not be valid. While Western systems of reasoning would say that line three of the truth table would read F – T – T, perhaps because the lack of correlation between the antecedent and the consequent means that we cannot definitively know that statement to be a false conditional, this Buddhist system would say that line three would read F – T – F because the lack of sufficient correlation between the antecedent and the consequent does not allow us enough evidence to believe with certainty that the conditional statement is true. To think of this issue in another way, the standard Western truth table for a conditional indicates that unless a conditional has been demonstrated to be false, it is considered to hold true, whereas for the Buddhist thinkers in this system, unless something has been shown to be true, it should be in doubt.

Finally, the fourth line of the standard truth table says that if *p* is false and

q is false, then the statement "If p, then q" is true. For the sample Buddhist syllogism, this line would be that in reference to something that is not a product and that same thing also is not an impermanent phenomenon, then the claim that if something is a product, then it is necessarily an impermanent phenomenon would be true. In terms of the truth or correctness of this pervasion in the real world, I believe the Buddhists would have to rule this case to be indefinite for the person to whom such an argument is stated. For instance, suppose we have the following syllogism:

> The subject, uncomposed space, is an impermanent phenomenon because of being a product.

No part of this is accurate. Uncomposed space, as a permanent phenomenon, is not a product; thus, the reason is not established and the first mode of the sign cannot obtain for anyone. Since there cannot be a person who understands the first mode of the sign, that uncomposed space is a product, there cannot be either forward pervasion or counterpervasion, the last two modes of a correct sign. Thus, for the Buddhists, the truth value of the conditional pervasion in this fourth line would be indefinite for a person to whom the above syllogism would be stated. A person just could not get to the point of understanding the pervasion and so would not know whether or not it is true. As I understand the system, for the Buddhists, the fourth line of their truth table for the pervasion conditional would be F – F – Indeterminate. Thus, such a pervasion could never be valid in a Buddhist syllogism.

These distinctions between the Western and Buddhist renderings of the truth table might initially seem trivial. However, understanding these distinctions makes clear why so many Buddhists have adopted the method of reasoning and debate as necessary spiritual practice. They are making the effort to empower themselves to actually be able to grapple up the side of the mountain under their own power. It is not the form of the argument that matters. It is the understanding of the argument.

In any case, in this system of Buddhist reasoning and debate, the truth or falsity of the pervasion is rendered completely irrelevant *unless and until* the reason has been established. If the pervasion is "correct" but the reason is not established, the whole argument fails. If the pervasion is incorrect and the reason is not established, the whole argument fails. Therefore, no time should be spent even considering whether or not the pervasion is correct until the reason is established. The reason must always be established first, because it would be useless to consider pervasions, whether they hold or fail, if the reason is not established. Thus, if the reason is not established, that is the Defender's first answer. Also, if an argument is such that both the reason is not established and there is no pervasion, the Defender first has to deny the establishment of the reason.

The Order of the Answers

It is devilishly difficult to catch yourself in the process of thought, even if it is something you do over and over again. I have never heard any debater lay out the procedure for deciding which answer to give to an argument. Perhaps they don't lay it out because people do it differently. Perhaps it is one of those things that is so obvious, debate teachers don't feel that they need to explain it, but I know American students—and American students need some explanation of the procedure to sort out the answers. Here are some guidelines provided by the system that lead us to consider what answer we should give to an argument and what the checking procedure is. You know how it goes: if you do this by rote repetition for a while, then you will come to the point where you won't need to think about it any longer. Think, for example, of driving to a place for a job interview, your first trip there, and how now, years later, having gotten the job, you drive there effortlessly. This is like that, so it is good to develop the habit of following the procedures in the right order, so that you will come up with right answers.

When you are weighing the value of a full three-part argument stated to you, whether a syllogism or a consequence:

1. First, check to see if the reason is established.
   Wonder: Does that ① (that subject) have the quality of that ③ (that reason)? Or, another way: Is that reason a quality of that subject?
   If the reason is itself a pervasion, for example, "because whatever is a functioning thing is necessarily an established base," you weigh the value of the reason without reference to any subject. If the reason has both a subject and predicate inside, like "because it is an established base," you decide the value of the reason by replacing the "it" with the stated subject.

2. If the reason is not established, that is your top-priority answer. At this point, you do not need to look any further.

Note Well: Even if the point of clarification is true of the subject, if the reason is not established, you cannot accept it. For instance, in the consequence

> It follows that the subject, sound, is a functioning thing because of being permanent,

even though it is true that sound is a functioning thing, you cannot accept it because the Challenger did not prove it.

3. If the reason is established, check to see if there is pervasion.
Wonder: Is it the case that whatever is that ③ (that reason) is necessarily that ② (that predicate)?

Note Well: As in the case above for an argument in which the reason is not established but the point of clarification is true of the subject, here too, though the point of clarification may be true of the subject, if there is no pervasion, you cannot accept it. For instance, for the consequence

> It follows that the subject, sound, is a functioning thing because of being an established base,

even though it is true that sound is a functioning thing, you cannot accept it because the Challenger did not prove it.

4. If there is no pervasion, with a quick glance, check to see if the pervasion is opposite.
Wonder: Is it the case that whatever is that ③ (that reason) is necessarily not that ② (that predicate)?

Note Well: It is not *required* to give the answer "The pervasion is opposite," even when you can. It is just a stronger answer if it is appropriate.

5. If the pervasion is opposite, that is your answer.
6. If the pervasion is not opposite, since you checked that only because there is no pervasion, then answer, "There is no pervasion."
7. If the reason is established and there is pervasion, accept the argument.

It is helpful to see this process in a graphic form:

The Defender's Answers Decision Tree

This graphic was created by Kyle Gigliotti in the author's fall 2011 Buddhist Reasoning and Debate course.

Learning to Spell Out Your Answers

The tradition is that new debaters are required to spell out their answers in full. For instance, they will initially answer simply, "I accept it," and then the Challenger will say, "Spell out your answer, 'I accept it'." Then the new debater will fill it in saying, for instance, "I accept that sound is an impermanent phenomenon."

There would seem to be two main reasons for this custom. First, it is to make sure that the new debaters are not just answering randomly, like shooting in the dark, to make sure they know what they are saying. The second is so that they come to think automatically what the answer means. It seems that, young or old, you don't need to do this for long, but it is an important step. For sure, you need to do it until the understanding is automatic.

The guideline for spelling out the answers is the way the answer is formulated in general. Using snippets of exchanges between the Challenger (C) and the Defender (D), here is how it goes:

1. Why?
   Formulated: Why does that ① have the quality of that ②?

   C: It follows that the subject, a pot, is permanent.
   D: Why?

C: Spell out your answer, "Why?"
D: Why is a pot permanent?

Note Well: Since a consequence without a reason may also present a pervasion, the "Why?" may be applied to that too:

C: It follows that whatever is a color is necessarily red.
D: Why?
C: Spell out your answer, "Why?"*
D: Why is whatever is a color necessarily red?

2. The reason is not established.
   Formulated: The reason, that that ① has the quality of that ③, is not established.

C: It follows that the subject, one-with-(functioning thing), is a permanent phenomenon because of being one-with-(functioning thing).
D: The reason is not established.
C: Spell out your answer, "The reason is not established."
D: The reason, that one-with-(functioning thing) is one-with-(functioning thing), is not established.

Note Well: Sometimes the reason contains both a subject and a predicate inside. The subject is usually a pronoun that refers to the logical subject of the argument. In this situation, the Defender simply fills in the referent of the pronoun when spelling out the answer. For instance:

C: It follows with respect to the subject, the horn of a rabbit, that it is an established base because it is a functioning thing.
D: The reason is not established.
C: Spell out your answer, "The reason is not established."
D: The reason, that the horn of a rabbit is a functioning thing, is not established.

Note Well: Normally the answer of "The reason is not established" takes issue with a statement of a quality; however, a consequence may also present a pervasion wholly included within the reason. The procedure is the same. For instance:

---

*Or, "What do you mean when you say, 'Why?'"

C: It follows with respect to the subject, a pot, that it is different-from-(functioning thing) because whatever is an established base is necessarily different-from-(functioning thing).

D: The reason is not established.

C: Spell out your answer, "The reason is not established."

D: The reason, that whatever is an established base is necessarily different-from-(functioning thing), is not established.

3. There is no pervasion.

Formulated: It is not the case that whatever is that ③ necessarily has the quality of that ②.

C: It follows that the subject, sound, is a functioning thing because of being an established base.

D: There is no pervasion.

C: Spell out your answer, "There is no pervasion."

D: It is not the case that whatever is an established base is necessarily a functioning thing.

4. The pervasion is opposite.

Formulated: Whatever is that ③ necessarily does not have the quality of that ②.

C: It follows that the subject, sound, is permanent because of being a product.

D: The pervasion is opposite.

C: Spell out your answer, "The pervasion is opposite."

D: Whatever is a product is necessarily not permanent.

5. I accept it.

Formulated: I accept that that ① has the quality of that ②.

C: It follows that the subject, a pot, is a functioning thing.

D: I accept it.

C: Spell out your answer, "I accept it."

D: I accept that a pot is a functioning thing.

Note Well: A normal two-part consequence, the subject and point of clarification, presents a statement of a quality; however, a consequence without a reason may also present a pervasion. The procedure for answering "I accept it" to such a consequence is the same. For instance:

C: It follows that whatever is red is necessarily a color.
D: I accept it.
C: Spell out your answer, "I accept it."
D: I accept that whatever is red is necessarily a color.

Incorporate the procedure of spelling out the answers for a while, until it is really second nature. Please practice them as they are written above. Do not adopt the habit of automatically spelling out the answers before you have been asked. Wait for the Challenger to ask, and then do it.

One Special Answer

Beyond the five answers that clearly respond to the Challenger's arguments, there is one more answer that can be used. It is not so much an answer to the logic of the Challenger's argument as it is like stepping back from the mark to halt your play. There are some things we simply cannot answer. For instance, suppose a Challenger says,

> It follows with respect to the subject, this place in front of us, that a flesh-eater is present there.

A "flesh-eater" is a kind of spirit that Buddhists say may be around us at any time. However, such a spirit is not apprehensible to a normal person, though the Buddhists say such a creature might be apprehensible to a developed meditator. Thus, for most people, even if such creatures do indeed exist, we would not apprehend them. Also, even if a debater were a developed meditator who could apprehend flesh-eaters, what would be the point of claiming it? Thus, the answer for such a question is, in Tibetan, "*the tshom*," meaning "doubt," not in the sense of "I doubt it," but in the sense of uncertainty. For this use, the best way to translate this answer is, "That is not something I know now."[3] In *Tibetan Logic,* Katherine Manchester Rogers reports:

> Someone who has had no experience of flesh-eaters has no way of knowing if one is present in a particular place. Such persons

could not know of its presence by direct valid cognition, because even if it were present it would be invisible to them; and they could not know of its presence by inferential valid cognition, because even if it were present, its presence could not be proved by reasoning. According to Ge-shay Pel-den-drak-pa, ". . . There is no way for that person to say one way or the other."

Similarly, ordinary beings have no way of knowing if another person has spiritual qualities, such as omniscience, because these are supersensory objects for them. Pur-bu-jok writes,

> Sutra says: "A person cannot estimate the measure of [another] person. [If one does so,] one will degenerate." By the mere fact of their not appearing to oneself, it is not reasonable to say that another does not have such-and-such good qualities.[4]

Rogers then quotes Lati Rinpoche, who says that this passage indicates that it is unreasonable to hold that what one does not see does not exist.[5] So, the commentarial tradition associates this answer of "That is not something I know now" with at least these two impossible speculations: (1) whether or not there is a flesh-eater in this place in front of us and (2) whether or not another person has spiritual qualities such as omniscience. In both cases these are impossible speculations because "it is unreasonable to hold that what one does not see does not exist."

More Than Just These Answers

The Defender is not limited to just these answers lined up above. Being a Defender is not just limited to a passive position of defending against what is coming your way. If that were the way of Buddhist debate, it would often be very hard for the Challenger to understand what the Defender believes, and it would make it hard for the Defender to express a belief. Thus, the Defender does not just passively respond but may also be called upon to posit definitions, divisions, and illustrations; to make a claim about how two phenomena compare; to posit subjects for debate and give reasons in support of claims; to explain the meaning of a word or phrase in a definition or a textual passage; and to explain the meaning of a whole passage.

As the experienced debater Georges Dreyfus said, "In practice, the challenger draws out of the defender a certain number of positions by asking him questions."[6]

Some think that the Challenger controls where the debate goes, but it seems the Challenger and the Defender have rather equal control. The Challenger raises the debate topic initially, but after that, all the Challenger can do is follow up on what the Defender is saying, though there is room for creativity and cleverness in the way the Challenger does this. The Defender can only respond to the arguments and questions the Challenger is stating, but the answers the Defender gives determines the way the debate has to go. It seems that neither has full control, but both have some control.

If the Defender were limited to trying to explain a position just by giving answers to the Challenger's arguments, that constraint would be too confining. It would be like an emotional encounter with someone who keeps saying something along the lines of "Is this what you mean?" or "When you say that, aren't you saying such and so?" In this sort of emotional narrative, the person may not really have any idea what you are saying or why you are saying it. This is why the Defender is frequently called upon to give more information than just one of the answers. In addition, a Defender can speak up to explain a position. Georges Dreyfus said, "It can be done slightly less formally; during a debate, a person will say, 'OK, wait a second. I have something to say. This is really my position. Please try to show me that I am wrong', and then the debate can start from that."[7]

THE CHALLENGER RESPONDS TO THE DEFENDER

In the same way that the Defender has a choice of answers at every turn, so, in response to any of the Defender's answers, the Challenger has a choice of ways to go. Like normal conversation, there is some freedom of movement and space for creativity. There are constraints on both parties, otherwise it would not be formal debate; however, it is not an assembly line such that you know what is going to happen every time. The Challenger's possible responses are basically of two sorts: (1) the Challenger may go against the answer given by the Defender and give further reasoning in support of what he or she said earlier or (2) the Challenger may seek to find out why the Defender is giving that answer, to understand what the Defender is thinking. Taking the Defender's possible answers one by one, here are at least some of the ways the discussion can go. Please bear in mind that in all of these examples, the Defender's answers are mistaken.

After the Defender Says, "Why?"

In the Collected Topics literature, the predominant way that debates are represented involves having a Defender asserting a false pervasion. It might go like this:

D: I accept that whatever is a valid cognizer is necessarily a direct perceiver.

C: Then it follows that the subject, an inferential cognizer realizing sound as an impermanent phenomenon by the sign of being a product, is a direct perceiver.

D: Why [is an inferential cognizer realizing sound as an impermanent phenomenon by the sign of being a product a direct perceiver]?

C: Because of being a valid cognizer. You asserted the pervasion.

Here, in this snippet of debate, the lines are generated automatically. There is only one way for the Challenger to go—supply the full consequence with a reason that is in accordance with what the Defender has just accepted. This is a standard unwanted consequence. So, the Challenger reminds the Defender that he or she has already asserted the pervasion and that to deny it now would contradict the earlier assertion.

Remember that "Why?" is understood as having the force of an answer of "No." So, when the Defenders question something, it is fair to assume that they hold the opposite view. For instance, it might go like this:

C: It follows that the subject, a pot, is different-from-(functioning thing).

D: Why [is a pot different-from-(functioning thing)]?

C: Then it follows that the subject, a pot, is not different-from-(functioning thing).

D: I accept [that a pot is not different-from-(functioning thing)].

C: [Give a reason justifying that] the subject, a pot, is not different-from-(functioning thing).

Alternatively, at this point the Challenger could have said:

C: It follows that the subject, a pot, is different-from-(functioning thing) because of being a phenomenon that is diverse from functioning thing.

Note Well: At the end of the first version above, before the Challenger's alternative answer, the Challenger asks the Defender to "[Give a reason justifying that]. . . ." In the Tibetan, what the Challenger is saying is a setup for the first two parts of a syllogism, more literally translated as: "The subject, a pot, is not different-from-(functioning thing)—" as was done in *Debate in Tibetan Buddhism*. Just like countless other things in the process of debate, both the Challenger and the Defender know what this means in this context: the Challenger is prompting the Defender to give a reason justifying the thesis just accepted. And, since the statement is a syllogism, they both understand that the Defender is called upon to give a straight answer that will indeed form a valid argument. This is one of the ways that the Challenger draws out what the Defender's positions are. Experience has made it clear that English speakers understand the straightforward direction to give a reason better than they understand a rising inflection at the end to mark the expectation. However, since it is not actually there in the Tibetan, the direction is given in brackets, though the direction should be spoken out in the English version.

After the Defender Says, "The Reason Is Not Established."

When the Defender questions the establishment of the reason, the predominant response from the Challenger is to give another reason justifying the earlier one. It might go like this:[8]

D: I accept [that whatever is a color is necessarily red].
C: It follows that whatever is a color is necessarily red.
D: I accept it.
C: Then it would follow that the subject, the color of a white religious conch shell,* is red.
D: Why [is the color of a white religious conch shell red]?

---

*A religious conch shell is a conch shell converted into a horn by cutting the curled end and inserting a mouthpiece. It is an auspicious subject here because, from the time of the Indian monasteries, such a conch shell horn was used for calling monks and nuns to prayer.

C: Because of being a color. You asserted the pervasion [that whatever is a color is necessarily red].

D: The reason [that the color of a white religious conch shell is a color] is not established.

C: It follows that the subject, the color of a white religious conch shell, is a color because of being white.

Note that the Challenger dropped out the old point of clarification, [whether or not the color of a white religious conch shell is] red, and drops in a new one, [whether or not the color of a white religious conch shell is] a color, in response to the Defender's answer. The Challenger has moved on to address the new point of clarification, the current issue.

Here is the maneuver. It is simple, and it is essential to know this. The reason from the earlier consequence becomes the predicate of the next consequence, the old predicate drops out, and a new reason is given in support of the new predicate. It's easy.

As applied to the above snippet of debate, the reason of the earlier consequence has become the predicate of the next consequence. The earlier consequence was:

It follows that the subject, the color of a white religious conch shell, is red because of being a color.

In that argument the Challenger was trying to show that, in accordance with the Defender's view that whatever is a color is necessarily red, being red would be a property of the color of a white religious conch shell. Once the Defender denies the establishment of the reason, that the color of a white religious conch shell is a color, the Challenger then moves to address that concern and prove that the subject is a color. The issue of whether or not the subject is red is set aside for the moment while the Challenger addresses the Defender's present doubt, whether or not the subject is a color.

It follows that the subject, the color of a white religious conch shell, is a color because of being white.

Thus, the new consequence, given in response to the Defender's answer, takes color as the new point of clarification—whether or not being a color is a quality of the subject. The former reason has become the new predicate, the old predicate drops out, and a new reason is given in support of the new consequence. This flow may be illustrated:

It follows that the subject is *red* because of being *a color.*

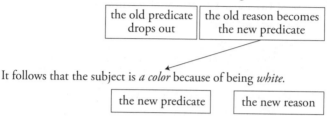

It follows that the subject is *a color* because of being *white.*

This is like normal discussion in that people tend to address the issue at hand, to seek to justify their claims that are being denied, before they can proceed. Of course, the debate may grow into a long stream of new consequences justifying the former ones.

When the Defender gives the answer that the reason is not established, the other way the Challenger can go is to try to get the Defender to justify the answer. This is like the approach above of holding the Defender to the opposite, when he or she answers "Why?" to a point of clarification. This is a fair approach because—since the Defender has gone on record as saying that the reason is not established—the Defender is asserting the position that the opposite of the reason is established as a quality of the subject. For instance:

C: It follows that the subject, uncomposed space, is a hidden phenomenon because of being a conventional truth.
D: The reason [that uncomposed space is a conventional truth] is not established.
C: It follows that the subject, uncomposed space, is not a conventional truth.
D: I accept [that uncomposed space is not a conventional truth].
C: [Give a reason justifying that] the subject, uncomposed space, is not a conventional truth.

Of course, there is no real justification for that.

After the Defender Says, "There Is No Pervasion."

When the Defender answers that there is no pervasion, as in the other cases, the Challenger may go on to justify why that pervasion was put forth or the Challenger may ask the Defender to justify why he or she gave that answer. The first approach might go like this:

C: It follows that the subject, uncomposed space, is not a product because of being a conventional truth.

D: There is no pervasion [that is, it is not the case that whatever is a conventional truth is necessarily not a product].

C: It follows that whatever is a conventional truth is necessarily not a product* because a common locus of the two, product and conventional truth, does not exist.

When the Defender gives the answer that there is no pervasion, the other way the Challenger can go is to try to get the Defender to justify the answer. For instance:

C: It follows that the subject, uncomposed space, is not a product because of being a conventional truth.

D: There is no pervasion [that is, it is not the case that whatever is a conventional truth is necessarily not a product].

C: It follows that it is not the case that whatever is a conventional truth is necessarily not a product.

D: I accept [that it is not the case that whatever is a conventional truth is necessarily not a product].

C: It follows that [that lack of pervasion] does not exist. If it exists, posit [something that is a conventional truth and is also something other than not a product].

Again, there is no real justification for that. What the Defender is being asked to posit would have to be a common locus of a conventional truth and a non-non-product. Such cannot exist.

---

*Notice that the pervasion has become the point of clarification.

Note Well: Even though the answers "There is no pervasion" and "The pervasion is opposite" may be given only for an argument in which the reason is established, the Challenger would not normally attack that implicit assumption by the Defender that the reason is established. Thus, that implicit assumption is not treated in the same way as taking the opposite stance when the Defender answers "Why?" or "The reason is not established" because in those cases the Defender's position is explicitly stated. In the case of the implicit assumption, the issue of the establishment of the reason would have to come up in later discourse, if it is an issue.

After the Defender Says, "The Pervasion Is Opposite."

When the Defender answers that the pervasion is opposite—meaning that whatever is that ③ is necessarily not that ②—here too, the Challenger may go on to justify why that pervasion was put forth or the Challenger may ask the Defender to justify why he or she gave that answer. The first approach might go like this:

C: It follows that the subject, uncomposed space, is a hidden phenomenon because of being a conventional truth.
D: The pervasion is opposite [that is, whatever is a conventional truth is necessarily not a hidden phenomenon].
C: It follows that it is not the case that whatever is a conventional truth is necessarily not a hidden phenomenon because there is a common locus of the two, conventional truth and hidden phenomenon; because *nirvāṇa* is that and definition is that.

Here too, the other way the Challenger can go is to try to get the Defender to justify the answer. For instance:

C: It follows that the subject, uncomposed space, is a hidden phenomenon because of being a conventional truth.
D: The pervasion is opposite.
C: It follows that whatever is a conventional truth is necessarily not a hidden phenomenon.
D: I accept it.
C: [Give a reason justifying that] whatever is a conventional truth is necessarily not a hidden phenomenon.

D: Because whatever is a conventional truth is necessarily a non-existent and whatever is a hidden phenomenon is necessarily an existent.

Of course the Defender's attempted justification makes no sense, but it serves to demonstrate another possible way to try to justify a pervasion.

After the Defender Says, "I Accept It."

The main thing that determines the way this will go is whether the Defender is accepting something that has just come up or something that was earlier denied. Starting with what the Challenger says *if the Defender is accepting something that has just come up*, it may go like this:

C: It follows that the subject, sound, is a permanent phenomenon because of being a product.
D: I accept [that sound is a permanent phenomenon].
C: It follows that the subject, sound, is not a permanent phenomenon because of being a momentary phenomenon.

Here, the Challenger simply contradicts the Defender's acceptance, denies the wrong thing that the Defender has agreed to, and offers a reason that the answer was wrong. However, bear in mind that the Challenger is not bound to lay it all out for the Defender. That is, what the Challenger says may or may not be reliable. It might be a ruse. It is up to the Defender to see what is going on. At this point, after the Challenger's full argument in response to the acceptance, the Defender has the usual choice of four answers to give to this consequence, and it will go from there.

If the Defender accepts something earlier denied, it may go like this:

C: It follows that the subject, sound, is not a permanent phenomenon because of being a product.
D: I accept [that sound is not a permanent phenomenon].
C: *Tsha!* It follows that the subject, sound, is not a permanent phenomenon.*

---

*The Challenger says "*Tsha!*" here because the Defender has now accepted something that he or she earlier denied, which is the setup for this pattern. The two-part consequence here is mere repetition to make sure the Defender means what was said.

D: I accept it.*

C: [Give a reason justifying that] the subject, sound, is not a permanent phenomenon.

D: Because of being a functioning thing.

Note Well: Please bear in mind that Buddhist debate is not like an assembly line. The direction the debate will go is certainly not predetermined, and there are choices at every turn. Basically, the Challenger has two directions in which he or she can go, either presenting an argument against the Defender's last answer or asking the Defender to give some proof justifying that last answer.

The Opening Volleys

Just as ordinary conversations can start in many ways, so too debates may start in many ways. In expressing a position, a Defender is not limited to just giving the five answers addressing the Challenger's arguments, for Defenders are frequently called upon to give information explaining their thought, including giving subjects for debate, reasons, and more. Thus, in this section there are some samples of ways that a debate may be started.

Note Well: It would be a good exercise for you and your debate partner to read these exercises out loud, as if you were reading the lines of a play. Then, you can substitute many things for the phenomena mentioned in these debates in order to create your own debates. As you go through these:

1. Notice how extremely incremental the movements are from one step to the next.

2. Notice how the reasons are categorical, not descriptive. They are not necessarily meant to elucidate every point as we go along, just to justify the point.

3. Notice as you say the lines, things go better when you go quickly. You are forced to pay attention, and it is easier to remember what was just said and where you are in the flow of the debate.

4. Notice that, at every stage, there could be more debate. The Defender might give a wrong answer. The Challenger might have to fling a con-

---

*You would not ask the person to spell it out again, immediately.

sequence for a bad reason. The Challenger might have to follow up to ask more questions about a suspect line of reasons.

Recall that with the first debate of a session, the Challenger begins by reciting the seed syllable of Mañjuśrī. So, here, treating the first sample as beginning a new session of debate, the Challenger begins with the homage to Mañjuśrī. Supporting comments are in brackets after the lines. The first sample begins with a question about a statement of pervasion:

C: *Dhīḥ!* The subject, in just the way [Mañjuśrī debated]. Is whatever is a color necessarily red?
   [In some styles of debate, this first question has to be stated within a reason, for example, "Because whatever is a color is necessarily red." You may think of the sense of this—the unstated point of clarification—as "It follows that the world is as it is because . . ." Then, if the Defender does not agree, in this style of debate the answer is that the reason is not established.]
D: I accept [that whatever is a color is necessarily red].
C: It follows that whatever is a color is necessarily red.
D: I accept it.
C: Then it follows that the subject, the color of a white religious conch shell, is red.
D: Why [is the color of a white religious conch shell red]?
C: Because of being a color. You asserted the pervasion.

The Challenger might start a debate by asking the Defender to posit a definition. Note that the volleys back and forth are typically contentious:

C: It follows that there is no definition of a functioning thing.
   [Alternatively, "Because there is no definition of a functioning thing."]
D: Why [is there no definition of a functioning thing]?
C: It follows that there is a definition of a functioning thing.
D: I accept [that there is a definition of a functioning thing].
C: It follows that there is not. Posit it.
D: There is. The subject, that which is able to perform a function.
C: It follows that the subject, that which is able to perform a function, is the definition of a functioning thing.

D: I accept [that that which is able to perform a function is the definition of a functioning thing.]

C: [Give a reason justifying that] the subject, that which is able to perform a function, is the definition of a functioning thing.

C: Because (1) it and functioning thing are ascertained as having the eight approaches of pervasion [that exist between] a definition and definiendum and also (2) it and functioning thing are established in the relationship of a definition and definiendum.

D: I accept it.

Then the debaters would go on to establish each part of this, reciting the eight approaches of pervasion and so on and proving the relationship. (See chapter 20, "Definitions, Divisions, and Illustrations," for specifics.)

The Challenger might start a debate by asking the Defender to posit a **division**:

C: It follows that there is no division of colors into two.

D: Why [is there no division of colors into two]?

C: It follows that there is a division of colors into two.

D: I accept [that there is a division of colors into two].

C: It follows that there is not. Posit the division of colors into two.

D: There is [such a division]. The subjects, the two—primary colors and secondary colors.

C: It follows that, when colors are divided into two, these are the two that are to be posited.

D: I accept it.

C: Now, it follows that it is not because there is no division of primary colors.

D: The reason [that there is no division of primary colors] is not established.

C: It follows that there is a division of primary colors.

D: I accept it.

C: It follows that there is not. If primary colors are divided, how many are there?

D: If primary colors are divided, there are four.

C: It follows that there are not four. Posit the four.

D: There are four. The subjects, the four—blue, yellow, white, and red.

You see, this can go on and on. It is a good way to practice the definitions and divisions and the debate format at the same time.

The Challenger might start a debate by asking the Defender to posit an **illustration**:

C: It follows that there is no illustration of a sense direct perceiver apprehending a visible form.

D: Why [is there no illustration of a sense direct perceiver apprehending a visible form]?

C: It follows that there is an illustration of a sense direct perceiver apprehending a visible form.

D: I accept [that there is an illustration of a sense direct perceiver apprehending a visible form].

C: It follows that there is not. Posit an illustration of a sense direct perceiver apprehending a visible form.

D: There is something. The subject, a visual direct perceiver apprehending blue.

C: It follows that the subject, a visual direct perceiver apprehending blue, is an illustration of a sense direct perceiver apprehending a visible form.

D: I accept [that a visual direct perceiver apprehending blue is an illustration of a sense direct perceiver apprehending a visible form].

C: [Give a reason justifying that] the subject, a visual direct perceiver apprehending blue, is an illustration of a sense direct perceiver apprehending a visible form.

D: Because of being something that serves as a basis for illustrating a sense direct perceiver apprehending a visible form by way of being a nonmistaken, nonconceptual knower that is produced in dependence on its own uncommon empowering condition, the eye sense power, and an observed object condition, a visible form.[9]

Then the debaters can analyze each part of this. Recall from chapter 20 that an illustration is described as illustrating a definiendum by way of manifesting the qualities of the defining characteristics. For instance, red serves as a basis for illustrating color by way of being suitable as a hue.

The Challenger also might start a debate by asking the Defender to answer a **comparison of phenomena**. The procedure for that important framework for debate is laid out in chapter 25.

REVIEWING THE DEFENDER'S ANSWERS

The last point here on the procedures in debate is how to review the Defender's answers. Sometimes the Defender will give a bad answer and, after that, the debate has to follow out a line of reasoning that flows from the bad answer. Eventually, if the skills and knowledge of the Challenger are adequate, and the Defender is alert and open-minded, the Defender will be brought to the moment of realizing that the whole line of reasoning that he or she had been defending is just wrong. At that point, the Defender contradicts an earlier answer, and that brings that particular line of reasoning to an end.

Then the Challenger leads the Defender back through the line of reasoning in reverse order and makes sure that the Defender now gives the correct answer to all the consequences that were denied on the way out. This is the review, and it goes back to the point where the Defender gave the first bad answer that sent them off on that line of reasoning. In the reviewing process, the Defender must accept all of the Challenger's statements or, upon objection, receive further justification for those reasons until they can be accepted. You can see that because of this scrutiny and repetition, the debate can follow any number of routes, one consequence leading the discussion to an ancillary topic, then eventually returning to proceed ahead on the route of the primary topic.

Here is a snippet of a debate in the implied form that demonstrates this process in brief. Explanatory comments are in brackets after the debaters' lines:

C: It follows that whatever is a color is necessarily red.
D: I accept [that whatever is a color is necessarily red].
   [This is the Defender's fundamental bad answer.]
C: Then it follows that the subject, the color of a white religious conch shell, is red.
   [The Challenger states the point of clarification of an unwanted consequence.]
D: Why [is the color of a white religious conch shell red]?
C: Because of being a color. You asserted the pervasion [that whatever is a color is necessarily red].
   [This reason flows from what the Defender has already accepted, so the Challenger reminds the Defender of what he or she just said.]

D: The reason [that the color of a white religious conch shell is a color] is not established.
[The Defender is trying to defend a bad position with another bad answer.]

C: It follows that the subject, the color of a white religious conch shell, is a color because of being white.
[The reason in the earlier consequence—color—becomes the new point of clarification in this consequence, and the Challenger gives a new reason in support of the new point of clarification.]

D: The reason [that the color of a white religious conch shell is white] is not established.
[Another bad answer.]

C: It follows that the subject, the color of a white religious conch shell, is white because of being one-with-(the color of a white religious conch shell).
[Just as before, the reason in the earlier consequence—white—becomes the new point of clarification in this consequence, and the Challenger gives a new reason in support of it.]

D: I accept that the color of a white religious conch shell is white.
[Here the Defender has seen the error and with this answer is reversing the line of reasoning resulting from trying to deny that the color of a white religious conch shell is a color.]

C: Tsha! It follows that the subject, the color of a white religious conch shell, is a color.
[Here the Challenger says, "Tsha!" meaning "Finished!" because the Defender has contradicted an earlier answer. In the immediately preceding line, the Defender accepted that the subject is white. That the subject is white was given as the reason to prove that it is a color. Thus, the Challenger has gone back to make sure that the Defender now accepts that the subject is a color.]

D: I accept [that the color of a white religious conch shell is a color].

C: Tsha! It follows that the subject, the color of a white religious conch shell, is red because of being a color.
[The Challenger is restating the unwanted consequence that resulted from the Defender's accepting that all colors are red. Earlier the Defender tried to deny the reason, and that did not work. There is no effective answer to this consequence, but the Challenger offers it again.]

D: I accept that the color of a white religious conch shell is red.
[This is the second bad answer to the unwanted consequence.]

C: It follows that the subject, the color of a white religious conch shell, is not red because of being white.
[The Challenger moves to the option of trying to prove to the Defender that the color of a white thing is not red.]

D: There is no pervasion [that is, it is not the case that whatever is white is necessarily not red].
[The Defender continues to try to maintain this bad line of reasoning and gives another bad answer.]

C: It follows that whatever is white is necessarily not red because a common locus of the two, white and red, does not exist.
[Now the pervasion has become the point of clarification.]

D: The reason [that a common locus of the two, white and red, does not exist] is not established.
[Continuing down a line of bad answers.]

C: It follows that a common locus of the two, white and red, does not exist because those two are mutually exclusive.

D: I accept that a common locus of the two, white and red, does not exist.
[Here, the Defender gets it. Now, by accepting the Challenger's good reason, that is the end of the line of reasoning resulting from the Defender's accepting that the color of a white religious conch shell is red.]

C: *Tsha!* It follows that whatever is white is necessarily not red.
[You see, here the Defender has accepted that there is no common locus of white and red. That reason—that there is no common locus—was given to prove that whatever is white is necessarily not red. That is why the Challenger went back to that issue here.]

D: I accept [that whatever is white is necessarily not red].

C: *Tsha!* It follows that the subject, the color of a white religious conch shell, is not red.
[This was the preceding issue, so the Challenger now returns to it.]

D: I accept [that the color of a white religious conch shell is not red].

C: *Tsha!* It follows that the subject, the color of a white religious conch shell, is red because of being a color. You asserted the reason and the pervasion.

[Even though the Defender was correct in accepting that the subject is not red, the Challenger immediately contradicts the answer to state the fundamental unwanted consequence again. Also, the Challenger gives the warning that the Defender has already accepted both the reason and the pervasion, so there is no answer left.]

D: There is no pervasion [that is, it is not the case that whatever is a color is necessarily red].

[Now the Defender has given up on the original bad answer that precipitated the fundamental unwanted consequence and both lines of reasoning—the one in which the Defender tried to deny the reason of the fundamental consequence and the one in which the Defender tried to accept the fundamental consequence. Thus, this snippet of debate has come full circle.]

C: It follows that whatever is a color is not necessarily red.

[The Challenger just repeats this line for clarity.]

D: I accept it.

C: *Oh-ah! Tsha! Oh-ah! Tsha! Oh-ah! Tsha!*

[The Challenger says, "*Oh-ah! Tsha!*" three times to indicate that the Defender has contradicted the fundamental bad position.]

This sample of debate is quite short, but sometimes the debaters can go on and on. So, you can imagine that sometimes the process of reviewing the Defender's answers requires good memory, but debating helps a person increase the power of memory.

Once you have developed this skill of reviewing the Defender's answers, it will be wise to be sparing in your use of it, except with your debate partners who understand that this is part of Buddhist debate. Ordinary people will just get aggravated by this checking of the old answers. It seems like nagging. You can probably recall some argument in your personal life, when the other person was saying, "Oh! And that means you were wrong when you said such and so. And that means you were wrong when you said that other thing too." So, be sparing in using this skill with the untrained. In modern day America, this might result in gunplay. However, for trained people like you and your debate partner, it is an important part of debating in the Buddhist style.

EXERCISE 23.1

The exercises for this chapter are obvious. Practice the snippets of debates that are laid out here. Work with your debate partner, taking turns back and forth as Challenger and Defender. Once again, notice the following as you practice:

1. The movements are extremely incremental, but you still go somewhere.
2. It is easier but still elucidating to use reasons that are categorical, not descriptive.
3. It all works better when you go quickly.
4. At every stage, there could be more debate than what is laid out in the text.

Now, do the following exercises:

1. As Challenger, make up points of clarification and full consequences and state them to the Defender. Be creative to set up circumstances for all the answers. As Defender, try to give the correct answer. Then, together go through the procedure to spell out the answers.
2. Continue the same exercise as above, but add on the Challenger's responses after the Defender has given an answer. Practice every option.
3. Practice the opening volleys using lots of different pervasions, definitions, divisions, and illustrations.
4. Practice reviewing the Defender's answers. For this, the Defender may need to be a little slow to answer correctly, so that you will have a string of points to review.

24. Strategies in Debate

Normally, we think of a strategy for debate as some sort of offensive or defensive move that will put you at an advantage. We do not normally think of avoiding the fight as a strategy. However, as mentioned in chapter 15, "Choosing Your Debate Partner," the first advice for anyone interested in rational discourse is to choose well your opponents. There is no use wasting your time, and most people are not suitable opponents. This is not meant to be cruel or disrespectful of others. We can all benefit by rational discourse, but most people are simply not prepared or not willing to participate in good faith. Basically, there is no reason to start down that road with somebody if you are not going to go anywhere.

Related to this decision, there is a Buddhist example of how people should be when listening to the dharma, the Buddha's teaching. The example suggests that people are ready to hear the teachings when they are like a cup turned right side up, with room to pour something in, clean, and not leaky. You know, if you want to pour your tea into a cup, you need a cup like that—a proper vessel. This advice is given within the context of religious practice, but it is good advice for listening and paying attention to someone speaking on any topic. The example recommends that a person should be like a cup turned right side up. You can't pour tea into an upside-down cup, and you cannot convince people if they are not receptive and will not or cannot listen. This example of the cup also recommends that people should avoid the fault of being like a cup that is turned right side up but does not have any room left to pour anything in. Sometimes, out of commitment to a view, an opponent simply cannot take in what you are saying. Such an opponent is not participating in good faith. This is like the "card carrier" I referred to in chapter 15, "Choosing Your Debate Partner." If a person is not committed in an open-minded way, don't waste your time. The example also recommends that a person should avoid the fault of being like a cup with filth in it. Clearly, you don't want to pour your tea in a cup with poop in it! This would be like people who are so much under the influence of the mental poisons that they cannot listen, like an opponent who is very angry, someone who is too prideful to listen, or someone who talks with you only because of desire, like a salesman pretending to care what your concerns are. Finally, the example of the cup recommends that a person should avoid the fault of being like a leaky cup. As applied to judging an opponent for debate, this is essentially the advice that a worthy opponent should have adequate memory to stay in the game. So, in trying to decide whether or not someone is suitable to debate with, watch to see if the person is suitable according to the guidelines of the cup. If not, you may be able to engage with them only in other ways. Bear in mind that the example also applies to you, so it might be appropriate to stop yourself before you waste another person's time.

If it looks suitable to actually engage in debate with a person, what forms the framework for Buddhist reasoning and debate are the three purposes of debate, as laid out in chapter 19. Again, these are:

1. To reveal and defeat mistaken ideas
2. To establish a correct position
3. To overcome objections to the position that has been established

The first purpose of Buddhist reasoning, to reveal and defeat mistaken ideas, is more offensive than defensive. In this function, a debater is called upon to attack and reject others' positions by pointing out the problems and shortcomings in their thought. The second purpose of Buddhist reasoning, to establish a correct position, and the third, to overcome objections to the position that has been established, are more defensive in nature than offensive. You put something out there, and now you need to defend it. When you set forth a solid position, you have to outline a defensible understanding carefully and clearly.

Together, the three purposes function to raise our consciousnesses. In sorting through the oceans of information in life, the first purpose is to consider carefully what you are hearing or reading as well as what is coming out of your own mouth or rumbling around in your noggin, perhaps to discover faulty understandings or to see that a criticism is inappropriate. Second, the reasoning process calls upon us to think about a problem and settle on a conclusion. The third tool of reasoning and debate is to refine and clarify, to defend and shore up your conclusion. With all of these together, you should have a more developed awareness and much greater clarity in regard to whatever you consider. So, if you find a suitable opponent and decide to engage in debate, these three purposes form the framework for the undertaking, the overall strategies.

Once you are in a debate of any sort, whether within yourself or with a suitable opponent, rely on the tools you already have in your toolbox as well as the tools you have learned to work with in this course. These include your abilities to distinguish between things in terms of 3P, 4P, MX, or MI, to formulate a valid argument in the Buddhist style, to evaluate the known definitions, divisions, and illustrations of things and to hypothesize with regard to those you do not know, to consider the implications of positions, to formulate fair consequences that support those positions or call them into question, and to give appropriate answers to arguments that are presented to you.

All of these tools can be brought to bear in the main strategic approach laid out in this chapter, which is to try to understand what people are saying in terms of how the things they are talking about compare as 3P, 4P, and so on, and then to reason together to confirm that assessment or to address any issues with what they are saying through using your tools.

Implications about the comparisons of phenomena are always in play in a discussion of pervasions because you have to be speaking of two things in order to form a statement of pervasion. Also, this framework for making comparisons can quickly be brought into play for a discussion of the qualities of things. Of course, analysis of the comparisons of phenomena is not the whole of Buddhist reasoning and debate by a long shot, but it is probably the main procedural framework, and it provides a format in which you can use all of your skills.

With practice, when listening to a discussion, you can come to see the "bubbles" just floating by. (This is in reference to the Euler diagrams used to demonstrate the different comparisons of phenomena.) I am reminded of the story I once heard of a mathematician who saw the two sides of an equation in colors, and, if I remember correctly, if the colors weren't the same, then he knew there was a problem with the equation. Listen to natural discourse, pay attention to what you are reading, track the arguments that you are hearing, and you will begin to notice the rampant abundance of bad thinking out there.

In terms of the layout of these strategies, there are four main categories—3P, 4P, MX, and MI. Within each of these are four cases for each, also corresponding to 3P, 4P, MX, and MI. The first cases are those in which you tend to agree with the person, and the strategy concerns how you may reason together to sort out whether or not you are right. The next three cases in each category are the cases in which the person seems to be speaking of two things as if they compared in some way other than what you think is the case. The prevailing strategy for these cases of apparent disagreement is to go directly to the problem.

Sometimes, for the life of you, you just can't make out what a person intends to say and how it might relate to the different comparisons of phenomena. At those times, just ask questions to try to understand and clarify. Sometimes that alone will shake a person off of a wrong understanding. Then, once you have been able to ferret out what the person is suggesting in terms of the comparisons, the following guidelines and strategies are intended to help you sort it out and get it straight. So, going through these comparisons and cases one by one, what are helpful strategies for analyzing the person's position?

Note Well: In the illustrations for these strategies, ① is used to represent a *real example* in the comparison. However, sometimes a person seems to imagine that something exists, when you believe that there is no such thing. Such an *imaginary example* is represented by ②.

These two symbols, ① for something that you believe exists and ② for something that you believe does not exist, indicate the two main scenarios that emerge from analyzing what someone is thinking in terms of the comparisons of phenomena. The first scenario is that the person is not aware that there is something that qualifies but was excluded, like perhaps that there is an arachnid that is not a spider. For this scenario, the ① is placed appropriately in the illustration, and the prevailing strategy is to try to make the person aware that there is such a thing. The other main scenario is that the person imagines that there is at least one example of a thing that qualifies in a way that does not seem to accord with reality, like believing that there could be a spider that is not an arachnid. For this scenario, the ② is placed inside the diagram where the person seems to believe it would exist. In this case, the prevailing strategy is to ask the person to give an example of such a thing.

Note Well: In all the sections of this book in which I have discussed the comparisons of phenomena, I have followed the predominant Tibetan way of ordering these—3P, 4P, MX, and MI. Here, I continue that, but the order may seem confused because in each section a different one is taken to the top. It might be helpful to have the outline of the arrangement of cases first:

1. As if 3P, and you agree.
   As if 3P, but they are actually 4P.
   As if 3P, but they are actually MX.
   As if 3P, but they are actually MI.
2. As if 4P, and you think that is right.
   As if 4P, but they are actually 3P.
   As if 4P, but they are actually MX.
   As if 4P, and you think they are MI.
3. As if MX, and you think that is right.
   As if MX, but you understand them to be 3P.
   As if MX, but you understand them to be 4P.
   As if MX, but they are actually MI.
4. As if MI, and you agree.
   As if MI, but you say they are 3P.
   As if MI, but you say they are 4P.
   As if MI, but you perceive that they are actually MX.

WHEN A PERSON SEEMS TO BE SPEAKING OF TWO PHENOMENA AS IF THEY WERE THREE POSSIBILITIES

As if 3P, and You Agree

If you agree that those two things seem to be three possibilities, make sure that you are on the same wavelength. It is usually clear enough whether he or she is thinking that every p is a q or that every q is a p, though you may need to clarify this first. For instance, ask,

Well, you seem to be saying that every p is a q. Is that right?

If the person *disagrees* with that, then the discussion may go in any of many directions, so consult the appropriate section for these strategies.

More typically, you have understood correctly what the person was saying, and he or she will confirm it. The next step is to check to see if the person thinks that the pervasion between p and q runs both ways, so ask,

Well then, do you also think that every q is a p as well?

If the person agrees with this too, then he or she has the idea that p and q are actually mutually inclusive. Since you believe that they are three possibilities, refer to the strategy below for the case when someone seems to be saying that two things are MI, but you think that they are 3P.

If you both think that p and q compare as 3P, then you can confirm that belief by following the paradigm for establishing 3P:

Answer in debate: There are three possibilities between p and q.

1. Something that is both a p and a q is the subject, x.

   The subject, x, is a p because of [supply a valid reason].
   The subject, x, is a q because of [supply a valid reason].

2. Whatever is a p is necessarily a q, but whatever is a q is not necessarily a p. For example, the subject, x, is a q but not a p.

   The subject, x, is a q because of [supply a valid reason].
   The subject, x, is not a p because of [supply a valid reason].

3. Something that is neither a p nor a q is the subject, x.

   The subject, x, is not a p because of [supply a valid reason].
   The subject, x, is not a q because of [supply a valid reason].

Remember that the paradigm is only a skeleton and can be filled out with the flesh of the debates. The implied complete form of debate for this answer is provided in chapter 25, "Bringing It All Together: Debating a Comparison of Phenomena."

As if 3P, but They Are Actually 4P

It frequently occurs that people seem to be speaking of two things as if they were three possibilities, but they are actually four possibilities. The problem here is that they are thinking that either every p is a q or that every q is a p,

but in fact, in both directions, the truth is that "some are and some are not."
A visual representation is helpful here.

This person seems to believe
that every p is a q.

What this person does not realize
is that there is at least one p (①)
that is not a q.

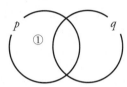

First, try to tack down exactly which way the person seems to think the
pervasion is running. Again, this is usually clear from earlier statements.
In fact, usually, it was the earlier faulty idea of a pervasion between the two
things that tipped you off that there was a problem. Still, sometimes it may
be helpful to get it straight, even if this just means pointing out the implied
or clearly stated pervasion to the person. So, you might say,

> Excuse me, do I understand you correctly? Are you saying that every
> p is a q?

Usually you have understood correctly, and your opponent will confirm
that that is what he or she is saying. So, then, because you understand that
these two things are actually 4P, you may politely point out that "some are
and some are not":

> Well, no, actually there are p's that are not q's. For instance, there are
> p's, such as an x or a y. These are p's that are not q's.

Of course, another tack is to fling a consequence of the person's view, saying,

> Then it would follow that the subject, x, is a q because of being a p.

However, it often happens that for most people a consequence is not very
effective here. It just depends. Gentle prodding might be better.

To tie this to an example, suppose someone thinks that a consciousness
that is mistaken with regard to its appearing object (p) must be a mental

consciousness (q). It is asserted in this system that every conceptual consciousness is mistaken with regard to its appearing object, but such mistaken consciousnesses may also be nonconceptual ones, such as a visual perception of white snow as blue or misperceiving the odor of fresh-cut grass as the odor of watermelon. These are consciousnesses mistaken with regard to their appearing objects (p's) that are not mental consciousnesses (q's). So, this factor of being mistaken with regard to what is appearing happens with both mental and sense consciousnesses.

Other possible examples for this point:

1. Legal and moral: In a legalist society, often the powers that be will insist that the legal is always moral, but this is not always so. For instance, consider the institution of slavery that formerly existed legally in the United States.
2. Politicians and either Democrats or Republicans: Some politicians in the United States survive outside the two-party system, and most Republicans and Democrats are not politicians.
3. Functioning things and different-from-(functioning thing): A person might easily imagine that everything that is different-from-(functioning thing) is not a functioning thing, but the phrase "different-from-(functioning thing)" does not mean non-(functioning thing). Rather, it refers to any existent that is not exactly the same in both name and meaning as functioning thing. For instance, a chair is a functioning thing but is nonetheless different-from-(functioning thing).

As if 3P, but They Are Actually MX

This person seems to believe that every p is a q.

What this person does not realize is that there is no p that is also a q.

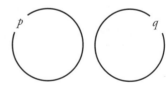

When a person seems to be speaking of two things as if they were 3P, but they are actually MX, the problem is that they are thinking that there is at least one thing that is both a p and a q, but there is not. This imagined thing is represented by ⑦, a question mark inside an imagined sphere of existence, which is inside the p circle, which in turn is wholly included inside the q circle. For instance, someone might say,

> Well, we know each other by our appearance; we are defined and identified by our appearance, so every individual is nothing more than his or her body. Persons are material things.

This is a popular physicalist position, that the person is merely a physical thing, made up of atoms. From the point of view of the Collected Topics logicians, and all Buddhists in general, the person—whether human, animal, Buddha, or whoever—is not physical, not material, an impermanent phenomenon designated to mind and body but not "a material thing." There is little to do here but give an opposing explanation to the person who speaks of a human as a material thing, perhaps drawing out some unsavory implications of the position, if you can. For instance, one of the debates in the first chapter in the Collected Topics literature makes it clear that a white horse is not white because the horse is not physical and not visible. The color of a horse may be white, but the horse is the nonphysical person merely designated to the mind and body of a horse.

Another compelling example for this point:

1. Knowledge and correct suspicion: Herein lie many stories, treasures of drama. We have all heard people claim—prior to knowing something such as the infidelity of a partner—"I just know such and so. I don't have proof yet, but I know that's what's going on." And we have all heard the claims after the facts are in that, "I just knew it." From the point of view of the epistemology of the Collected Topics system, these are wrong claims. Suspicion is not knowledge, even when it turns out that it was correct.

As if 3P, but They Are Actually MI

This person seems to believe that there could be something that is a q but not a p.

Though this person *may* understand correctly that every p is a q, what this person does not understand is that it is also true that every q is a p.

If a person seems to be speaking of two things as if they were 3P, but you think that they are actually MI, then the problem here is that the person is thinking that there is at least one thing that is one but not the other, here represented as ②, something that is a q but not a p. The first strategy is to ask the person to give an example of something that is one but not the other. Or speak more clearly to guide the discussion. For instance, if it sounds like the person is suggesting that there are three possibilities between impermanent phenomena (p) and products (q), such that every impermanent phenomenon is a product, but it is not the case that every product is an impermanent phenomenon, then say, for example,

> Well, I agree that every impermanent phenomenon is a product, but I also think that every product is an impermanent phenomenon. So, can you give me an example of a product that is not an impermanent phenomenon?

Of course, people who hold such a position to be true won't be able to come up with a counterexample to what you know to be true, though they may try. If they try, you have to shoot their examples down one by one. You can affirm that they are products by pointing out the causes and conditions that give rise to such an impermanent phenomenon, and then you can show that every product has coarse impermanence. If even great galaxies arise, abide, and dissolve, what could there be that arises from causes and does not dissolve away? Ultimately, when they cannot give a successful example, then that would seem to give support to your position that the two things are actually mutually inclusive.

Other possible examples for this point:

1. Objects of knowledge and existents: It is a fundamental assertion of Buddhism that each and every existent is "suitable as an object of an awareness" and "observed by a valid cognizer." However, a person might easily think that there are some existent things in the fullness of space that are simply not known by anyone.

2. Awarenesses and knowers: In the epistemology of the Collected Topics system, these two are taken as mutually inclusive. It is hard to imagine that there could be a knower that is not an awareness, but one might imagine an awareness that is not a knower, like an undirected consciousness or a consciousness to which an object appears but is not noticed, for example, when you pass someone on the street but fail to notice the person.

WHEN A PERSON SEEMS TO BE SPEAKING OF TWO PHENOMENA AS IF THEY WERE FOUR POSSIBILITIES

As if 4P, and You Think That Is Right

If you agree that the two principals are 4P, then initially all you have to do is check to make sure by thinking of examples of each of the four. Remember that 4P is most easily understood as "some are and some are not," so long as there is at least one thing that is both a p and a q. This means that there is at least one thing that is a p but not a q and that there is also at least one thing that is a q but not a p. For instance, if you are talking about women and college students, you can settle this by thinking of suitable subjects for each of the four possibilities: (1) an example of a woman who is a college student, (2) an example of a woman who is not a college student, (3) an example of a college student who is not a woman, and (4) an example of someone or something that is neither a woman nor a college student.

The more complete way of establishing that two phenomena are 4P including something that is neither is to follow the paradigm:

Answer in debate: There are four possibilities between p and q.

1. Something that is both a p and a q is the subject, x.

    The subject, x, is a p because of [supply a valid reason].
    The subject, x, is a q because of [supply a valid reason].

2. Something that is a p but not a q is the subject, x.

    The subject, x, is a p because of [supply a valid reason].
    The subject, x, is not a q because of [supply a valid reason].

3. Something that is a q but not a p is the subject, x.

    The subject, x, is a q because of [supply a valid reason].
    The subject, x, is not a p because of [supply a valid reason].

4. Something that is neither a p nor a q is the subject, x.

    The subject, x, is not a p because of [supply a valid reason].
    The subject, x, is not a q because of [supply a valid reason].

This paradigm is the skeleton of the debate. The full implied form of debate for this answer is in the next chapter.

As if 4P, but They Are Actually 3P

It frequently happens that someone will speak of two things as if they were 4P, but they are actually 3P.

This person seems to believe that there is at least one *p* (⑦) that is not a *q*.

What this person does not realize is that every *p* is a *q*.

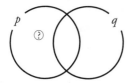

This person believes that there could be something that is a *p* but not a *q*. This imagined thing is represented by ⑦ inside the *p* circle and outside the *q* circle. The problem here is that the person does not realize that it is not just that some *p*'s are *q*'s but that each and every *p* is also inside the circle of *q*, as, for example, each and every sound is included among impermanent phenomena.

Thus, the strategy is to ask the person to give you an example of something that is a member of the group (*p*), which you understand is wholly included in the other (*q*), but is not a member of the larger group (*q*), for example, as you might ask for an example of a sound that is not impermanent.

There are many interesting examples of this type of mistake from every field of human endeavor. A good one from the Collected Topics tradition is if someone were to say,

> Some conceptual consciousnesses are not mistaken.

Perhaps the person is thinking that a conceptual consciousness such as an inferential cognizer is not mistaken because it is a valid cognizer, a correct and incontrovertible awareness of a real object. This seems reasonable, but in the Collected Topics epistemology, an inferential cognizer is indeed correct in understanding the object it is trying to get at, but nonetheless it is considered a mistaken consciousness. This is because it is mistaken with regard to the object appearing to it, a mental object that is a mere representation of what it is understanding. Thus, a conceptual consciousness can be correct (or not wrong) and still be mistaken, in the sense of being mistaken with regard to its appearing object, as are all conceptual consciousnesses. To say that an inferential cognizer is correct but that it is mistaken in some way is irritating, but I think it is irritating in Tibetan and Sanskrit too. The Tibetan translated as "mistaken consciousness" is 'khrul shes, which means a "roundabout consciousness," and this follows along with the Sanskrit bhrānti-jñāna. The name is especially in reference to the way a conceptual consciousness understands its object, not directly but through the appearance of an internal, mental image that represents that object. Thus, it is best to always provide the gloss that it is "a consciousness mistaken with respect to its appearing object." Still, it is a mistaken consciousness.

Also, for mistaken consciousnesses and conceptual consciousnesses, there is no pervasion running the other way either, for a mistaken consciousness is not necessarily conceptual. A wrong sense consciousness is doubly mistaken, for it is mistaken with regard to both what appears to it and what it perceives or engages. A wrong conceptual consciousness is mistaken in both ways as well. Thus, all wrong consciousnesses are mistaken with regard to both their appearing objects and their objects of engagement, but not all mistaken consciousnesses (that is, those mistaken with regard to their appearing objects) are wrong (that is, mistaken with regard to their objects of engagement).

As if 4P, but They Are Actually MX

This person seems to believe that there is at least one thing (?) that is both a p and a q.

What this person does not realize is that there is no overlap at all between p and q.

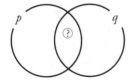

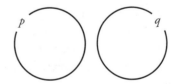

If a person seems to be speaking of two phenomena as if they were 4P, but they are actually MX, the problem is that he or she is thinking that there is at least one thing that is both a p and a q. So, the strategy is to ask the person what it could be that is both.

The most compelling example of two phenomena that are mutually inclusive from the point of view of this system of reasoning and debate is the case of permanent phenomenon and functioning thing. These are asserted to be mutually exclusive. Remember that in the Collected Topics system, permanent phenomena are affirmed as actual existents. They are objects of intellectual understanding only, not perceivable by any of the senses or a mental direct perceiver, but still existent. (In other Buddhist systems of thought, permanent phenomena are said to be objects of direct perceivers.) Also, permanent phenomena are of two types, those that are stable in time and those that exist for an occasion, but neither ever performs a function. Stable permanent phenomena last forever, like selflessness itself or existent itself. They are stable, abiding, and eternal. Permanent phenomena that exist for an occasion do not change moment by moment, but they do not last forever either. Examples of such permanent phenomena are the selflessness of the text source in your hands or a book's lack of being an elephant. Permanent phenomena do not perform functions because if they were to perform a function in one moment but not in the next or if they performed a different function in the next moment, then they would have changed. In this system, if something is permanent, that does not necessarily imply that it is eternal, only that it does not change so long as it survives. Moreover, there are impermanent phenomena or functioning things, such as the mind, which continue on forever, according to Buddhist thought. Indeed the mind does not last even a second moment, but the Buddhists assert that the continuum of the mind will go on forever.

One reason this issue of whether or not permanent phenomena can perform functions is so prominent for Buddhists is the assertion in many religions of a permanent God who functions to create the world. The Buddhists do not take this to be possible. If a creator God acts to create the world in one moment and then rests, such a creator has changed and therefore cannot be permanent and unchanging. If one imagines that the creator God creates the world anew every moment, then, because the world changes, the creator is creating one world in one moment and another in another moment, thus changing moment by moment along with the world.

In this case, where a person seems to be speaking of two phenomena as if they were 4P, but they are actually MX, you need to get the person to understand that if something is a p, then it cannot be a q, and that if it is a q, it cannot be a p. Then it is often helpful to explain why or to link those two things you are talking about to two other things that are clearly mutually exclusive.

Another compelling example for this point:

1. Definition and one-with-definition: Someone might easily think that there could be a definition that is one-with-definition. This would be based upon a confused idea that every definition is one-with-definition because it is a definition and that definition exemplifies itself. However, remember that definition is not itself a definition but a definiendum, so it does not exemplify itself. Still, as an existent, definition is self-identical, it is one-with-definition, for definition is exactly the same in name and meaning as definition. Thus, whatever is a definition is necessarily not one-with-definition and whatever is one-with-definition is necessarily not a definition because the only thing that is one-with-definition is definition itself and definition itself is a definiendum.

As if 4P, and You Think They Are MI

This person seems to believe that there is at least one thing (②) that is a *p* but not a *q* and another (②) that is a *q* but not a *p*.

What this person does not understand is that every *p* is also a *q* and that every *q* is also a *p*.

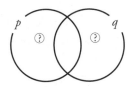

For the final case in this group, if a person seems to be speaking of two things as if they were 4P, but you know that they are actually MI, then the problem is that that person is thinking that there is at least one thing that is a *p* but not a *q* and that there is at least one thing that is a *q* but not a *p*. So, this case is somewhat easy because you can go either way. Ask the person to give an example of something that is one but not the other, either way—either a *p* that is not a *q* or a *q* that is not a *p*. Or clarify the discussion by saying something like,

Well, no, actually they are basically the same thing,

or

No, really, they are just different names for the same thing.

For instance, someone might be talking about manifest phenomena and impermanent phenomena as if they were 4P, though they are MI. Perhaps the person is thinking that a manifest phenomenon might be anything at hand—like a tangible object or even the absence of an elephant in a room. This person might say, "It is manifestly obvious that there is no elephant in this room." That is true enough in almost all cases; however, the way the Collected Topics logicians think of this, the absence of an elephant is a permanent phenomenon because it is a mere absence. A room free of elephants is an impermanent phenomenon, but the quality of being free of elephants is a permanent phenomenon. Remember that "permanent" here does not mean everlasting, just that it is unchanging moment by moment. So, a person might think that some manifest phenomena are impermanent, and some are not. Also, this person might think that some manifest phenomena are manifest, right at hand, and others such as distant galaxies are impermanent but not manifest. Finally, about all you can do is point out to them that p and q are just different names for the same things and that in fact every p is a q and every q is a p.

Another compelling example for this point:

1. Existents and objects of knowledge: A person might easily think that some existents are known and others are not and that some objects of knowledge are existent and others are not, perhaps recalling a time when they "knew" something that turned out not to be real. In this system of thought, however, all existents are taken to be objects of knowledge, and all objects of knowledge are taken to be existent. This system of Buddhist thought asserts that there is nothing that exists that is not known and that it is not possible to know something that does not exist. This is not to say that you cannot imagine that you know something that is not real, but imagining something does not make it real.

When a Person Seems to Be Speaking of Two Phenomena as if They Were Mutually Exclusive

As if MX, and You Think That Is Right

If you tend to agree that indeed the two things are MX, check up on the issue by trying to think if there might be any p that is also a q or any q that is also a *p*. If you find an example of either, the two things you are talking about are not MX. Also, it may be helpful to relate *p* and *q* to two other phenomena that are acknowledged to be MX, noting that *p* is the same as such and so and *q* is the same as something else. Then, since everyone knows that those two (the things you compared *p* and *q* to) clearly don't overlap, then *p* and *q* must not overlap either. Right?

The paradigm for proving that the two phenomena are MX is:

Answer in debate: The two, *p* and *q*, are mutually exclusive.

1. The subjects, *p* and *q*, are different because of being phenomena that are diverse.
2. Whatever is a *p* is necessarily not a *q* because of [supply a valid reason].*
3. Whatever is a *q* is necessarily not a *p* because of [supply a valid reason].

As if MX, but You Understand Them to Be 3P

This person seems to believe that there is nothing that is both a *p* and a *q*.

What this person does not realize is that there is at least one *p* (①) that is also a *q*.

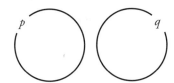

If someone thinks two things are MX, but they are 3P, then the problem here is that the person does not realize that there is at least one thing that is both a *p* and a *q*. In fact, in this case, you believe that every *p* is a *q*.

In the Collected Topics tradition, a good example of this is manifest phenomena and hidden phenomena. On the face of it, a person would surely think that these two, as a division of objects of comprehension, must be

---

*One sort of reason you can give to justify a pervasion is another pervasion. For instance, using the example of permanent phenomena and functioning things, "Whatever is a permanent phenomenon is necessarily not a functioning thing because whatever is a permanent phenomenon is necessarily not a momentary phenomenon, but whatever is a functioning thing is necessarily a momentary phenomenon."

MX. However, manifest phenomenon is one of the many phenomena mutually inclusive with functioning thing and hidden phenomenon is mutually inclusive with established base, so these two are 3P.

Another compelling example for this point:

1. Humans and enemies: At one point in my life, I was spending time with a fellow who was a master gunnery sergeant retired from the US Marine Corps. I asked him how they were able to get those young Marines to go into battle and kill people who had not offended them, people they did not even know. He said it was basically two things. First, they dehumanize the enemy; they convince the fighters that they are not killing actual humans. They do this in part by using dehumanizing names for the enemy, names that I need not report here but are familiar to us. Second, he said that they convince the young Marines that if they don't kill the enemy, the enemy will kill them. Neither of these points is universally true, though the second is certainly more pressing.

As if MX, but You Understand Them to Be 4P

This person seems to believe that nothing is both a p and a q.

What this person does not realize is that there is at least one thing (①) that is both a p and a q.

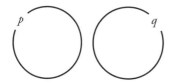
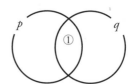

Sometimes people will speak of two things as if they were MX, but they are actually 4P. Again, the best strategy is to try to show the person that there is at least one thing that is both a p and a q.

A good example in the Collected Topics tradition of two phenomena that are 4P but might seem to be MX is internal matter and external matter. Internal matter is matter included within the continuum of a person, such as your skin or the follicles of your hair. External matter is matter not included within the continuum of a person, such as your hair beyond a certain point, your clothes, the sun, the moon, and so on. A person might naturally think that, as a division of matter, whatever is the one is necessarily *not* the other. However, something that is both is the orb of the eye, a material phenomenon that is included within the continuum of one person but is also external to another person. Internal matter that is not external is, for instance, the parts hidden under the skin or subtle matter like the eye sense power.

Another compelling example for this point:

1. Terrorists and freedom fighters: Those in positions of power will almost always say something to the effect that, at least on the other side, no terrorist is a freedom fighter. They will go on to try to characterize terrorists as madmen bent on murder for no other reason than to promote mayhem. Though almost no one who is attacked will ever agree, actually terrorists and freedom fighters compare as four possibilities. Some terrorists are freedom fighters, and some are not. Some freedom fighters are terrorists, and some are not.

   What can you do with such a mistake? Usually there is very little, and often there is danger in trying. It is sometimes helpful to point out that their own former freedom fighters used terrorist tactics in their liberation efforts. Usually, your debate opponent will just claim their own were freedom fighters and not terrorists at all. At least they are being consistent, if not rational.

As if MX, but They Are Actually MI

This person seems to believe that there is nothing that is both a *p* and a *q*.

What this person does not understand is that every *p* is a *q* and every *q* is a *p*.

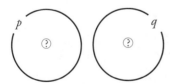

And finally for this group, it can even happen that a person will be speaking of two things as if they were MX, but you understand them to be just the opposite, MI. They imagine that every *p* is not a *q* (that is, no *p* is a *q*) and every *q* is not a *p* (that is, no *q* is a *p*). These imaginary things—a *p* that is not a q and a q that is not a p—are represented by ⊘ inside the p circle alone and inside the q circle alone. However, there are no such things. For instance, someone might say:

> I really enjoy looking at the stars. I just wish I could see the Morning Star and the Evening Star together, so I could finally see which one is brighter.

Actually, the Morning Star and the Evening Star are both the same, and they are not even stars at all. They are just the same planet—Venus. For centuries, stargazers did not understand that they were the same. Naturally one could not see them together, for they are the same thing appearing at different times. Thus, the strategy here is just to explain it as best you can and hope it goes through. These two things appear to be different, but they are actually just the same.

Other possible examples for this point:

1. Existents and objects of knowledge: Of course, you know that in the Collected Topics tradition these two are mutually inclusive. However, from the point of view of epistemological nihilism—the idea that one can never really know anything—whatever exists, if indeed anything exists at all, is not really an object of knowledge. Or, am I wrong about that?

2. One-with-(functioning thing) and non-non-(one-with-[functioning thing]): This plays off of the difference between statements of qualities and statements of pervasion, as does the example of definition and one-with-definition above. Indeed, for every existent thing x, x and non-non-x must be equivalent in the sense of being MI. This means that the mutual pervasion is there; however, this does not say that the one necessarily exemplifies the quality of the other. Whatever is non-non-(one-with-[functioning thing]) is necessarily one-with-(functioning thing); however, non-non-(one-with-[functioning thing]) is not one-with-(functioning thing), for only functioning thing is one-with-(functioning thing) because only functioning thing is exactly the same in both name and meaning as functioning thing. From the other side, one-with-(functioning thing) is not non-non-(one-with-[functioning thing]) because one-with-(functioning thing) is not one-with-(functioning thing). Thus, it may appear at first that they are MX, but they are actually MI.

WHEN A PERSON SEEMS TO BE SPEAKING OF TWO PHENOMENA AS IF THEY WERE MUTUALLY INCLUSIVE

As if MI, and You Agree

If you agree that the two things the person is talking about are actually MI, like products and impermanent phenomena, then look at cases. This would then imply that sounds, for instance, would be impermanent phenomena because they are all produced from causes and conditions, and pots and pans would be impermanent phenomena, and houses, and peoples' bodies, and so on. All this looks good, so it seems to be an accurate understanding.

The paradigm for proving two phenomena as MI follows:

Answer in debate: The two, p and q, are mutually inclusive.

1. The subjects, p and q, are different because of being phenomena that are diverse.
2. The subjects, p and q, have all eight approaches of pervasion.

That they are different is a requirement for all the comparisons. The second requirement is that the two principals must have all eight approaches of pervasion. These are:

1. Whatever is a p is necessarily a q.
2. Whatever is a q is necessarily a p.
3. Whatever is not a p is necessarily not a q.
4. Whatever is not a q is necessarily not a p.
5. If there is a p, then there is necessarily a q.
6. If there is a q, then there is necessarily a p.
7. If there is not a p, then there is necessarily not a q.
8. If there is not a q, then there is necessarily not a p.

As if MI, but You Say They Are 3P

This person seems to understand that every p is a q but also believes that every q is a p.

What this person does not realize is that there is at least one q (①) that is not a p.

If a person seems to be speaking of two things as if they were MI, but you perceive them to be 3P, the problem is that the person doesn't realize that there is something that is one but not the other.

For instance, a person might speak of two things as if they were MI, saying, for example,

> The mental consciousness and the conceptual consciousness are the same thing.

This is probably the predominant view outside the meditative traditions—that the mind is the thinking organ and that it is not capable of nonconceptual perception. However, according to the Buddhist system, mental consciousnesses and conceptual consciousnesses compare as 3P. In their way of thinking, and this is probably universally accepted throughout Buddhism, every conceptual consciousness is a mental consciousness, but not every mental consciousness is a conceptual consciousness. The best strategy is to give the person an example of something that is a mental consciousness but not a conceptual consciousness, such as a nonconceptual, mental direct perceiver. This may seem like an article of the Buddhist faith to some. Still, the Buddhists assert that there are mental consciousnesses that are not conceptual. Thus, if a person seems to be speaking of these two as if they were MI, a Buddhist might give the consequence, gently delivered:

> Well, you know, some people such as the Buddhist meditators, say that not every mental consciousness is a conceptual consciousness. If it were so, then, for instance, a mental direct perceiver observing subtle impermanence would be a conceptual consciousness because of being a mental consciousness. But, you see, it couldn't be because of being a direct perceiver.

Sometimes it is helpful to link the two phenomena to other things that are easier to understand, things that are quite clearly 3P and not MI. For instance,

> Well, you know a conceptual consciousness is a thought consciousness, and a direct perceiver is like a sense consciousness, like the nose sensing the odor of paint, but a sense consciousness does not think at all. So, if indeed there are mental direct perceivers, they would not be thinking consciousnesses.

Other possible examples for this point:

1. Artists and visual artists: If someone qualifies as a visual artist, then that person must qualify as an artist. It seems that for some people only visual artists qualify as real artists; however, there are certainly some fully qualified artists who are not visual artists, such as the majority of musicians.
2. Reasons and valid reasons: Not every reason is valid, though people may often want to convince you of this.
3. Valid consciousnesses and direct perceivers: Every direct perceiver is a valid consciousness, but some valid consciousnesses, such as inferential cognizers, are not direct perceivers.

As if MI, but You Say They Are 4P

This person seems to believe that every *p* is a *q* and every *q* is a *p*.

What this person does not understand is that there is at least one *p* (①) that is not a *q* and that there is at least one *q* (②) that is not a *p*.

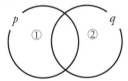

If a person seems to be speaking of two things as if they were MI, but you know that they are actually 4P, the problem is that they do not realize that there is something that is one but not the other. Indeed, if they are 4P, as you believe, there would be something that is a *p* but not a *q*, and there would also be something that is a *q* but not a *p*.

For instance, a person might be speaking of two things as if they were MI, saying something like,

Direct perceivers and sense consciousnesses are the same thing.

However, they are actually 4P because some direct perceivers are sense consciousnesses—such as a visual direct perception of a patch of blue as blue, and some are not—such as a mental direct perceiver. Moreover, not all sense consciousnesses are direct perceivers. Again, some are—such as a visual direct perceiver, and some are not—such as a visual perception of white snow as blue. In a case like this, you need to give the person an example of something that is one but not the other, pointing out, for instance:

> Well, actually there are direct perceivers that are not sense consciousnesses, such as a mental direct perceiver of subtle impermanence,

or

> Well, there are sense consciousnesses that are not direct perceivers, such as a visual perception seeing white snow as blue or misperceiving your own reflection in a mirror as the color and shape of another person in the room.

Other possible examples for this point:

1. Money and value: It is generally true that you get what you pay for, but some expensive things are not very good, and some cheap things are excellent.
2. Artists and creative persons: Some are and some are not. Is it that all artists are creative persons or is it that some are just doing art but not really creating?
3. Pit bulls and mean dogs: Some pit bulls are mean, and some are not. Some mean dogs are pit bulls, and some are not.

As if MI, but You Perceive That They Are Actually MX

This person seems to believe that every p is a q and also every q is a p.

What this person does not understand is that no p is a q and no q is a p.

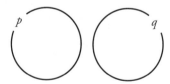

If a person seems to be speaking of two things as if they were MI, but you understand them to be MX, the problem is that the person seems to believe that there is at least one thing, here represented by ⑦ inside the wholly overlapping p and q circles, that is both a p and a q. It is easy to imagine that a person might speak of the two, definition and definiendum,

as though they were MI. However, according to the thought of the Collected Topics logicians, they are MX. No definition is also a definiendum, and no definiendum is also a definition; thus, there is nothing that is both. Remember that in the Buddhist system, the definition is the actual thing, like all these things that are momentary, and the definiendum, like impermanent phenomenon, is the convenient term we use to refer to these things. Thus, the definition is a "substantial existent," and the definiendum is an "imputed existent." You cannot make an impermanent phenomenon that is not momentary, but you could impute a different name to it, other than "impermanent phenomenon," as we do in the many human languages. If the person has some acquaintance with this system of debate, that person would understand that *for every particular definition and its definiendum*, like momentary phenomenon and impermanent phenomenon, whatever is the one is also necessarily the other. Whatever is a momentary phenomenon is also impermanent, and whatever is impermanent is also a momentary phenomenon. *However*, for definition and definiendum themselves, whatever is the one is necessarily not the other.

So, at this point, the only strategy is to ask the person to give an example of something that is both and perhaps point out forthrightly that it seems to you just the opposite.

MISFIRES IN DEBATE

It is important to watch out for misfires in a debate and to watch to make sure you don't make them yourself. This is when a person says something that is inappropriate or off target. The list of misfires offered here is not intended to be complete. Here are a number of things that seem to happen very frequently and prevent helpful, rational discourse. In fact, some of these are not so much failures in debate as they are emotional encounters, but there are some strategies to counter them.

Remember from chapter 1, "Introduction," that three things are essential for a sensible and productive debate even to be possible: competence in rational procedure, composure, and memory. If any of these are missing, the debate will not proceed well. All of these increase with training and practice. Misfires often happen because a person is not adequately trained, has a lack of integrity, or has inadequate short-term memory. Here are some misfires I notice very frequently.

Firebase Alpha

When any of the three essentials are missing, sometimes a person will just be shooting wildly into the dark—in no particular direction and at no real target. When it goes this way, this is what I call "Firebase Alpha," in recognition of a scene from the movie *Apocalypse Now,* a Vietnam War version of the book *Heart of Darkness.* You may recall that Martin Sheen's character, Captain Willard, is going upriver to find Colonel Kurtz (played by Marlon Brando) and "terminate the Colonel's command" with "extreme prejudice." He arrives at night in the middle of a tremendous firefight at the base farthest upriver, the base closest to enemy lines, Firebase Alpha. We are alerted to the disarray of the base when Captain Willard, just off the boat, asks a passing GI who the commanding officer is at the base, and the GI, seeing Willard's officer's insignia, says, "I thought you were." The men at the base have been fired upon night after night by an enemy sniper, and in turn they are firing wildly into the night around them. Debates too can go this way for lack of rational skills, composure, or memory. The only strategy that can lead to any success is to slow everything down and cause the person to take every step very carefully and very deliberately.

Rhetoric and Bullying

Another frequent misfire in discussions is when one participant relies on rhetoric and bullying rather than rationality. Rhetoric is the bastard child of debate. It does not have the valid heritage of rationality. The goals of rational discourse are the three purposes stated at the beginning of this chapter—to reveal and defeat mistaken ideas, to establish a correct position, and to overcome objections to the position that has been established. The goal of rhetoric is to win the discussion and get your way. In this age of relativism, very often people feel that there is no truth, there is only appearance, so there is no point in trying to sort out the truth of the matter. Thus, they do not participate in good faith. All they know is that they want to get their way, and, if rhetoric helps them to do that, then they will use rhetoric. Bullying is just a more dramatic version of rhetoric and usually means that the person has some sense that he or she is in the wrong and could not win on a level playing field.

Sometimes people do have a position they wish to defend, and they rely on rhetoric to do so, even when they know better. They are not participating with an attitude of equal respect and open-mindedness, so they intentionally seek to derail the discussion. Either they are not interested in the truth of the matter or they know the truth and wish to suppress it. This is all too often the stock in trade in family disputes, business dealings, and political discourse.

What do you do with slick rhetoricians? Usually they are proceeding in bad faith, and they are not interested in rational discourse. However, many have been trained in rhetorical techniques and have adopted them as effective without knowing any better. Sometimes, it is helpful to appeal to the value of fair discussion or to your value as a person. One good technique is to point out that they are not applying the same principles to both sides of the question. Their efforts to justify the unfairness will quickly become ridiculous, and you *should* ridicule them because they have refused to participate with integrity.

One advantage you have over bullies and rhetoricians is your training. Whether the person believes in rationality or not, it is still today fairly impossible to deny the rational and expect to continue as an equal. Also, your training gives you a measure of coolness under fire because you have spent some time there. Just wait, you will see your chance to strike back. Often, it is effective to let such bullies and rhetoricians run their mouths for a while and then deny their opening statement *on the basis of reason*. It seems to undermine everything they just said, so it is deflating for them.

Simple Incompetence

One common misplay happens when one person makes a statement of a quality and the other person responds as if it were a statement of a pervasion. For instance, you might hear something like this:

My golden retriever is so loving!

and the other person responds,

Well, I don't think all golden retrievers are loving!

Who cares? The first person didn't say that. And who would think that anyway? If a person does this sort of thing too often, just speak to him or her with soothing words and avoid trying to discuss things with them very much. The basic strategy here is just to appeal to common sense.

Another frequent misfire in discussions is when a person reverses the parts of a pervasion and thinks it is an implication of the original statement. For instance, suppose someone says,

Spiders are arachnids.

Another person reverses the parts of this and says,

Oh! So that's what arachnids are! They're spiders.

This may strike you as a mistake that only a child would make, but listen for a while, and I'll bet you'll hear an adult make it too.

On these occasions when someone reverses the parts of a pervasion, remember the rule of the contrapositive from the categorical logic of Aristotle:

All p's are q's

does not imply that all q's are p's, by a simple reversal of the categories. Rather, the proper application of the contrapositive—the actual implication—is:

All non-q's are non-p's.

This means that all nonarachnids are nonspiders. If you look among everything that is not an arachnid, you will not find any spiders. Spiders are found wholly *outside* of the class of nonarachnids. Just give examples, and they will get it.

All too often, a discussion will end up with both persons simply restating their positions and with no conclusion to the discussion. This may or may not be a sign that your opponent is not worthy of debate. It is unclear. Perhaps you are both talking about something that neither of you really knows enough about. Sometimes rhetoricians will simply refuse to yield to valid reasoning and just stupidly hold on to whatever they are trying to promote. And it is even worse if they try to beat their "truth" into you. They may even be right, but the delivery is not very effective in convincing people. They may get you to submit, but this does not mean you have come to agree with them. Be aware that only a fool will debate with everyone. Most people are not adequately trained to listen, are not willing to discuss their position, or are not able to change upon hearing your valid explanations. Still, when it is appropriate, rational discourse is our last, best hope.

Alethic Bipolarism

One very annoying misfire is what I call "alethic bipolarism." "Alethic" means having to do with truth, and alethic bipolarism is when someone alters another person's statement so radically in an unjustified way that the truth of what was said swings from one end to the other, like a person cycling through manic and depressive episodes. This is not simple incompetence but grand incompetence, and it has elements of rhetoric and bullying too. For instance, imagine that two folks—Casey and Alex—have been going out for a while, and one day Alex says,

> You know, I think it would be a good idea for us to try living together.

And Casey responds:

> I do too! I think that would be great! But what would you do with your cat? You know I'm allergic to cats.

And Alex comes back with:

> Oh! Well, what would you have me do? Put her down?

Whoa! That was not the suggestion. Alex went way too far and completely corrupted what Casey was saying, also ruining the moment. (Frowny face here.) At this point, Casey is on the defensive and might say something like:

> Whoa! Where in my words do you hear *any suggestion* that we should kill the damn cat?

The only point of this ploy is to try to get the other person to stop talking.

Now, this would always be funny if it did not happen so much and if it did not matter. However, it is very typical in political discourse. Some politicians spend their entire campaigns describing what their opponents believe and never give that person's beliefs and actions a fair review. In doing this, they also tend to never tell us what they believe except broad platitudes.

This sort of statement is usually more of an emotional reaction than anything, although it can be the verbal equivalent of brutality. This may work for young children, but it should not work for anyone over about five or six years of age. Usually, all that you need to do to respond to this is to refuse to shut up and sort of mock what the person is saying. For instance, you might respond in a respectful way, "Oh! Excuse me, that is not what I am saying. I am agreeing with you that we should try living together. I think that would be great! I just cannot live with the cat. I am not saying that the cat should not live. There may be some other solution." There is no need for a brutal response; a polite one will do.

In sum, again, it is important to watch out for people who misfire in a debate and to watch to make sure that you don't make these misfires yourself.

Exercise 24.1

The exercises for this chapter are obvious. Practice the strategies for debate that follow the comparison of phenomena. There are sixteen models offered here. Four of them are when you tend to agree with the person that the two phenomena compare as 3P, 4P, or whatever. The other twelve are when you think the person has it wrong. Work with your debate partner, taking turns back and forth as Challenger and Defender. Verbalize the strategies together. Think of simple examples and then build your way up to more challenging ones. Let the Defender make a statement along the lines of, "You know, isn't it true that every p is a q?" Then you, as Challenger, have to do some thinking on your own to try to understand what is wrong with that statement and then decide how to attack it.

Use all the skills you have built up to formulate consequences when needed, to give answers to those consequences, and spell out your answers. Then review the answers. Just forge ahead bravely. The practice will help. Don't get frustrated with what you cannot do. Take joy in what you can do.

25. Bringing It All Together

Debating a Comparison of Phenomena

DEBATING A COMPARISON of phenomena is not the be-all and end-all of Tibetan debate, but, from the beginning to the end of studies, it is always a ready framework for debate in the Tibetan style. Even in a debate centering around the subtleties of a passage on the final mode of existence of phenomena, the debaters may quickly gravitate to the use of comparisons of phenomena. In trying to understand differing phrases in a definition or passage, a comparison of those phrases helps students to sort out the meaning of the passage—what is included, what is excluded, what is the meaning of every word and the meaning of the phrase all together, why this point is taken up (often in response to scholars of other opinions), and so on. The comparison of phenomena is a ready tool for the debaters that provides the framework for using all of the other tools gained in this course—positing subjects for debate, providing arguments and valid reasons, and investigating the consequences that flow from the points of consideration. Thus, it is probably the single most important and useful framework for Buddhist reasoning and debate, and so it is the culmination of this course.

Recall from chapter 4, "The Comparison of Phenomena," that, in this tradition of debate, the debaters refer to a total of six different ways that two phenomena may compare. There are the four major ways of comparison—3P, 4P, MX, and MI. Also, two more are reckoned for the cases of 3P and 4P for which there is nothing to posit as an example of something that is neither. Conceivably, there could also be cases for MX and MI in which there is nothing that could be posited as something that is neither; however, those two are not marked as separate cases. Thus, there are six answers.

This chapter provides sample debate patterns for each of the six answers. For each of the answers, the paradigm for that debate is also provided. Recall that the paradigm is the skeleton that can be filled out with the flesh of the debates. The patterns for the debates, in turn, are simply more fleshed out but not fully vibrant.

As I advised in chapter 4, do not think that the paradigms must be followed exactly, like a recipe for a cake in which you must beat an egg before you add the flour. The same advice is true for the debate patterns. They are still not living, organic debates, which can only be made fresh by suitable participants. These implied patterns are like specimens, like butterflies pinned to a board. And, like a butterfly pinned to a board, they are lifeless. You have to provide the life to the debates. Still, the specimens do serve to instruct. Within the considerable constraints of the rational procedure in debate, a little flourish can be helpful. Just be sure to hit all the points, in order to verify your analysis or to understand that you need to keep thinking.

THREE POSSIBILITIES

3P

The comparison of three possibilities (*mu gsum*) is so called because there are usually three things to point to in the discussion of the comparison. However, this is one of the two comparisons for which the debaters mark a difference between two cases. The first does indeed have three points of discussion, including something outside the two circles that is neither a *p* nor a *q*. This case is by far more typical. However, for the rare second case, since there is nothing outside the two circles that is neither a *p* nor a *q*, there are not three but only two points of discussion. For both of these cases, an essential point is establishing which way the pervasion goes, that is, establishing which phenomenon is wholly included inside the other.

In the interest of trying to suggest some of the life that may course through a living, organic debate, the first of the six implied debates—the debate for three possibilities including something that is neither—is spelled out extensively.

Three Possibilities including Something That Is Neither

The paradigm for proving that two phenomena compare as three possibilities including something that is neither is:

Answer in debate: There are three possibilities between p and q.[*]

1. Something that is both a p and a q is the subject, x.

   The subject, x, is a p because of [supply a valid reason].
   The subject, x, is a q because of [supply a valid reason].

2. Whatever is a p is necessarily a q, but whatever is a q is not necessarily a p. For example, the subject, x, is a q but not a p.

   The subject, x, is a q because of [supply a valid reason].
   The subject, x, is not a p because of [supply a valid reason].

3. Something that is neither a p nor a q is the subject, x.

   The subject, x, is not a p because of [supply a valid reason].
   The subject, x, is not a q because of [supply a valid reason].

For the debate pattern for two phenomena that compare as three possibilities including something that is neither, direct perceivers and valid cognizers are compared. Of course, the correct answer is that they are 3P, but the debate plays out rather extensively, as the Defender gives first one wrong answer then another, before finally answering correctly.

The debate is supplemented with commentary in brackets after the lines in order to help you track what is going on and why the debaters are saying what they are saying. As you read this, remember that the debates always move in very small, deliberate increments. Also, please bear in mind that, even though it is plodding to read the debate, it would be spoken at a very fast clip.

C: How do these two compare—direct perceivers and valid cognizers? [Recall that the Buddhists assert two types of valid cognizers—inferential cognizers and direct perceivers. Thus, every direct perceiver is

---

[*]There is no need to specify further because this is the standard type of three possibilities.

a valid cognizer, but it is not the case that every valid cognizer is a direct perceiver.]

D: They are mutually inclusive.

[Of course, the correct answer is that they are 3P. However, initially the hypothetical Defender answers wrongly that they are MI. Perhaps the Defender is thinking that they are MI because direct perceivers are raised up as the most reliable consciousnesses and so any valid cognizer would have to be a direct perceiver.]

C: It follows that they are not mutually inclusive. [Give a reason justifying that] they are mutually inclusive.

[The Challenger always denies the Defender's initial answers. So, when the Challenger says, "It follows that they are not MI," that does not necessarily tip off the Defender that the answer is wrong.]

D: Because (1) they are different, (2) whatever is a direct perceiver is necessarily a valid cognizer, and (3) whatever is a valid cognizer is necessarily a direct perceiver.

[In chapter 11, "The Paradigms for Proving a Comparison of Phenomena," the paradigm for proving that two things are MI calls for the Defender to note that the two have all eight approaches of pervasion. However, for any two things, if they have the two pervasions as stated above, they will have all eight approaches.]

C: It follows that whatever is a valid cognizer is necessarily a direct perceiver.

[The Challenger is going directly to the problem. Of the three things the Defender said to justify that the two principals are MI, two of them are correct. Direct perceivers and valid cognizers are different, and whatever is a direct perceiver is necessarily a valid cognizer. The only one of the three that is false is the Defender's idea that whatever is a valid cognizer is necessarily a direct perceiver. So, that is where the Challenger goes first.

Also, this is appropriate and to the point because, when the Defender says that the two are MI, though they are actually 3P, the problem is not whether or not there is something that is both or whether or not one is wholly included in the other. For any two things that are 3P, these will both be true. And, since the Defender thinks these two are MI, the Defender too will think that both of these are true. The problem is that they do not overlap completely as they would have to if they were actually MI. One of the phenomena—valid cognizers—is not wholly included in the other—direct perceivers. So, the Defender does not realize that there is something that is one but not the other—in this case, a valid cognizer that is not a direct perceiver. Thus, the sensible strategy is to go to that point first, and that is what the Challenger does.]

D: I accept [that whatever is a valid cognizer is necessarily a direct perceiver].

C: Then it follows that the subject, an inferential cognizer realizing that sound is impermanent, is a direct perceiver.
[The Challenger initially states just the stem of the consequence.]

D: Why [is an inferential cognizer realizing that sound is impermanent a direct perceiver]?

C: Because of being a valid cognizer. You asserted the pervasion.
[This reason flows from the incorrect pervasion the Defender accepted above.]

D: The reason [that an inferential cognizer realizing that sound is impermanent is a valid cognizer] is not established.
[If the Defender is indeed thinking that every valid cognizer must be a direct perceiver, then it would seem right to deny that an inferential cognizer could be a valid cognizer.]

C: It follows that the subject, an inferential cognizer realizing that sound is impermanent, is a valid cognizer because of being a knower that is incontrovertible with regard to its main object.
[This reason proving that the subject is a valid cognizer is jury-rigged to give a sensible, understandable explanation of what a valid cognizer is. This reason avoids the requirement of newness for a valid cognizer.* Such a consciousness is one that fully engages its object of understanding and is incontrovertible with regard to its main object. That a valid cognizer is "incontrovertible" means that it is irreversible and that it needs no further insight into its object. It has reached the stage of knowledge.]

D: I accept [that an inferential cognizer realizing that sound is impermanent is a valid cognizer].
[The Defender has reversed an earlier denial. Bear in mind that if the Defender had not reversed the earlier answer, the debate could have spun off here on a long consideration of whether or not the subject

---

*For a full explanation of the factors, see Lati Rinbochay, *Mind in Tibetan Buddhism*, 116ff.

is a knower, whether or not it is incontrovertible, exactly what is the "main object" for the subject, and so on, with each of those parts leading into other issues.

The Defender's acceptance brings this line of reasoning to an end. Now, reviewing the Defender's answers, the Challenger returns to the first and most fundamental consequence of the Defender's assertion that all valid cognizers are direct perceivers.]

C: *Tsha!* It follows that the subject, an inferential cognizer realizing that sound is impermanent, is a direct perceiver because of being a valid cognizer. You asserted the reason and the pervasion.

[The Challenger says "*Tsha!*" (meaning "Finished!") because the Defender has reversed an earlier position. Here it is said just once, rather than three times, as it will be done when the Defender reverses the *fundamental* assertion that direct perceivers and valid cognizers are MI.

The Challenger gives the warning "You asserted the reason and the pervasion" so that the Defender will not try to deny them now. The Challenger is forcing the issue to try to get the Defender to see that the consequence is unwanted and that there is no effective answer.]

D: I accept [that an inferential cognizer realizing that sound is impermanent is a direct perceiver].

[Now the Defender tries the only possible defense left, accepting the consequence.]

C: It follows that the subject, an inferential cognizer realizing that sound is impermanent, is not a direct perceiver because of being a conceptual consciousness.

[Here the Challenger chooses to present an argument to the Defender that the subject is not a direct perceiver and why. The other possible way the Challenger could go would be to ask the Defender why he or she gave the answer that an inferential cognizer realizing that sound is impermanent is a direct perceiver. The Challenger has given a good reason here, for it attempts to draw the Defender's attention to the bright line between direct perceivers and conceptual consciousnesses.]

D: The reason [that an inferential cognizer realizing that sound is impermanent is a conceptual consciousness] is not established.

C: It follows that the subject, an inferential cognizer realizing that sound is an impermanent phenomenon, is a conceptual consciousness because of being a determinative knower.

["All thought consciousnesses are determinative knowers. . . . The meaning of 'determinative' is that such a consciousness thinks, 'This is such and such', 'That is such and such'."[1] Such consciousnesses determine, conceptualize, and identify their objects.

Note that the Challenger changed the subject slightly, from "an inferential cognizer realizing that sound is impermanent" to "an inferential cognizer realizing that sound is an impermanent phenomenon." Such alterations are okay. Indeed, these debates seem like assembly lines, and it feels like we need to keep the same component parts coming, but some parts are interchangeable. However, if you do make a change like this, make sure it is interchangeable.]

D: The reason [that an inferential cognizer realizing that sound is an impermanent phenomenon is a determinative knower] is not established.

C: It follows that the subject, an inferential cognizer realizing that sound is an impermanent phenomenon, is a determinative knower because of being an inferential cognizer.
[Of course, all inferential cognizers are determinative knowers, conceptual consciousnesses, but this is precisely what the Defender now denies.]

D: [Whatever is an inferential cognizer is] not necessarily [a determinative knower].

C: It follows that whatever is an inferential cognizer is necessarily a determinative knower because the definition of an inferential cognizer is *a determinative knower* that, depending on its basis, a correct sign, is incontrovertible with regard to its object of comprehension, a hidden phenomenon.*

D: I accept [that whatever is an inferential cognizer is necessarily a determinative knower].
[Here the Defender accepts the point of clarification, which in this case is a pervasion. With this acceptance, that brings this line of reasoning to an end. Now begins the review of the Defender's earlier answers.]

C: *Tsha!* It follows that the subject, an inferential cognizer realizing that sound is impermanent, is a determinative knower.
[The Challenger goes to the immediately preceding point, that the subject is a determinative knower, that the Challenger proved with

---

*See Lati Rinbochay, *Mind in Tibetan Buddhism*, 75ff.

the reason that the subject is an inferential cognizer. There is no need
to go to the point that the subject is an inferential cognizer because,
in accepting the pervasion, the Defender has by implication accepted
the establishment of the reason, that the subject is an inferential
cognizer.]

D: I accept [that an inferential cognizer realizing that sound is impermanent is a determinative knower].

C: *Tsha!* It follows that the subject, an inferential cognizer realizing that
sound is impermanent, is a conceptual consciousness.
[Again, this is the immediately preceding point, that the subject is
a conceptual consciousness, to which the Challenger now returns,
now that the Defender has accepted that the subject is a determinative knower.]

D: I accept [that an inferential cognizer realizing that sound is impermanent is a conceptual consciousness].

C: *Tsha!* It follows that the subject, an inferential cognizer realizing that
sound is impermanent, is not a direct perceiver.

D: I accept [that an inferential cognizer realizing that sound is an impermanent phenomenon is not a direct perceiver].
[It seems to me that this line does not necessarily show the dawning
of new insight. The Challenger just keeps saying that the subject cannot be a direct perceiver because it is conceptual. Even if the Defender
understands now that the subject is a conceptual consciousness, that
does not necessarily mean the Defender really gets what a direct perceiver is.]

C: *Tsha!* It follows that the subject, an inferential cognizer realizing that
sound is impermanent, is a direct perceiver because of being a valid
cognizer. You asserted the reason and the pervasion.
[This brings us back to the first and fundamental consequence of
the Defender's assertion that all valid cognizers are direct perceivers.
Now the Challenger is stating the consequence again, for a second
time, along with the warning that the Defender has asserted both
the reason and the pervasion, but now the Defender has been shown
that the avenue of accepting the fundamental consequence does not
work. It is a moment of truth.]

D: There is no pervasion [that is, whatever is a valid cognizer is not necessarily a direct perceiver].
[The Defender gets it—that the pervasion is wrong. Now the Chal-

lenger will explore what that implies for the Defender's idea that direct perceivers and valid cognizers are MI, the mistaken idea that set into motion all of the dispute till now.]

C: *Tsha!* It follows that whatever is a valid cognizer is not necessarily a direct perceiver.

D: I accept [that whatever is a valid cognizer is not necessarily a direct perceiver].

C: *Tsha!* Then it follows that the two, direct perceivers and valid cognizers, are not mutually inclusive.

[If a valid cognizer is not necessarily a direct perceiver, then those two cannot be MI.]

D: I accept [that the two, direct perceivers and valid cognizers, are not mutually inclusive].

C: *Tsha! Tsha! Tsha!* (Finished! Finished! Finished!) [Your fundamental assertion—that valid cognizers and direct perceivers are MI—is finished!] So, how do the two, direct perceivers and valid cognizers, compare?

D: They are mutually exclusive.

[The Defender has chosen wrongly again. In the foregoing debate, the Challenger showed the Defender that there is at least one thing that is a valid cognizer but not a direct perceiver. So, now the Defender swings too far the other way and thinks that perhaps there is nothing that is both a valid cognizer and a direct perceiver. And, if that were the case, maybe they would have to be MX.]

C: It follows that the two, valid cognizers and direct perceivers, are not mutually exclusive. [Give a reason justifying that] they are mutually exclusive.

D: Because (1) they are different, (2) whatever is a direct perceiver is necessarily not a valid cognizer, and (3) whatever is a valid cognizer is necessarily not a direct perceiver.

C: It follows that whatever is a direct perceiver is necessarily not a valid cognizer.

[Once again, following normal strategy, here the Challenger is going directly to the problem. However, here there are two problems. Both the second and third points that the Defender makes to justify the claim that valid cognizers and direct perceivers are MX are mistaken. That is, it is not true that whatever is a direct perceiver is necessarily not a valid cognizer because, in fact, every direct perceiver is a valid cognizer. Also, it is not true that whatever is a valid cognizer is necessarily not a direct perceiver because some valid cognizers are direct perceivers. Thus, the Challenger could attack either one of these mistaken positions. But it does not matter strategically because defeating either one will shake the Defender off this wrong assertion that the two are MX.]

D: I accept [that whatever is a direct perceiver is necessarily not a valid cognizer].

C: Then it follows that the subject, a visual direct perceiver seeing white snow as white, is not a valid cognizer.
[This is the stem of an unwanted consequence. A visual direct perceiver seeing white snow as white has to be fully correct in engaging its main object, the color of white snow. Such a direct perceiver is in contrast to a visual perception seeing white snow as blue.]

D: Why [do you say that a visual direct perceiver seeing white snow as white is not a valid cognizer]?

C: Because of being a direct perceiver. You asserted the pervasion.
[The reason is supplied from the Defender's earlier incorrect pervasion.]

D: The reason [that a visual direct perceiver seeing white snow as white is a direct perceiver] is not established.
[This answer seems rather weak on the face of it. It is like when a person just stubbornly holds on.]

C: It follows that the subject, a visual direct perceiver seeing white snow as white, is a direct perceiver because of being a visual direct perceiver.

D: I accept [that the subject is a direct perceiver].
[With this acceptance, that brings this short line of reasoning to an end. Now the Challenger simply returns to the fundamental consequence—that the subject is not a valid cognizer—that resulted from the Defender's incorrect pervasion.]

C: *Tsha!* It follows that the subject, a visual direct perceiver seeing white snow as white, is not a valid cognizer because of being a direct perceiver. You asserted the pervasion.

D: I accept [that a visual direct perceiver seeing white snow as white is not a valid cognizer].
[If indeed the Defender believes that whatever is a direct perceiver is necessarily not a valid cognizer (that is, that no direct perceiver is a valid cognizer), then a visual direct perceiver would not be a valid cognizer.]

C: It follows that the subject, a visual direct perceiver seeing white snow as white, is a valid cognizer because of being a knower that is incontrovertible with regard to its main object, the color of white snow.

[Again, the reason used here to justify the subject as a valid cognizer avoids the requirement that a valid cognizer has to be the first moment of new understanding.]

D: I accept [that the subject is a valid cognizer].

C: *Tsha!* It follows that the subject, a visual direct perceiver seeing white snow as white, is not a valid cognizer because of being a direct perceiver. You asserted the reason and the pervasion.

[The Challenger states for a second time the fundamental consequence resulting from the Defender's false statement that no direct perceiver is a valid cognizer, this time with the double warning that the Defender has already accepted both the reason and the pervasion. However, at this point the Defender cannot accept the consequence, that the subject is not a valid cognizer, because that is in direct opposition to the immediately preceding acceptance that the subject is a valid cognizer. It is time to break through!]

D: There is no pervasion [that is, it is not the case that whatever is a direct perceiver is necessarily not a valid cognizer].

[Right! The Defender gets it—the pervasion is incorrect.]

C: Then it follows that there is something that is both a valid cognizer and a direct perceiver.

[The Challenger goes to the main point to show that direct perceivers and valid cognizers are not MX—because there is something that is both. This flows logically from the Defender's acceptance of the lack of pervasion—that it is not the case that whatever is a direct perceiver is necessarily not a valid cognizer. Just to unpack this bit by bit: the pervasion put forth earlier by the Defender—the pervasion, not the lack of pervasion—was that whatever is a direct perceiver is necessarily not a valid cognizer. Recall from chapter 5, "Two Kinds of Statements," that a pervasion of this model implies the more recognizable statement, "No direct perceiver is a valid cognizer." If that statement is not true, and just now the Defender denied it, then that means that it is not the case that no direct perceiver is a valid cognizer; thus, there must be at least one direct perceiver that is a valid cognizer. Get it? So, there would have to be something that is both.]

D: I accept [that there is something that is both a valid cognizer and a direct perceiver].

[Recall that, when the Defender first sought to justify that valid cognizers and direct perceivers are MX, two of the three parts of the reason were wrong: that whatever is a direct perceiver is necessarily not a valid cognizer and also that whatever is a valid cognizer is necessarily not a direct perceiver. The Challenger defeated only the first one of these, but that alone is adequate to disprove the Defender's false statement that direct perceivers and valid cognizers are MX.]

C: *Tsha!* Then it follows that the two, valid cognizers and direct perceivers, are not mutually exclusive.

D: I accept [that the two, valid cognizers and direct perceivers, are not mutually exclusive].

C: *Tsha! Tsha! Tsha!* (Finished! Finished! Finished!) [Your fundamental assertion—that valid cognizers and direct perceivers are MX—is finished!] So, how do the two, direct perceivers and valid cognizers, compare?

D: There are four possibilities.

[Of the two remaining answers not already attempted—3P and 4P—the Defender has once again chosen the wrong one. In the first branch of the debate, when the Defender said that valid cognizers and direct perceivers are MI, the Challenger showed the Defender that there is at least one thing that is a valid cognizer but not a direct perceiver. In the second branch of the debate, the Defender went too far the other way, thinking that there is nothing that is both a valid cognizer and a direct perceiver, but the Challenger showed that there is at least one thing that is both. So, at this point the Defender knows for sure that there is something that is both and that there is at least one thing that is a valid cognizer but not a direct perceiver. In order to sort out exactly how these two compare, the only question left is whether or not there could be a direct perceiver that is not a valid cognizer. If there could be, the correct answer would be 4P. If there cannot be a direct perceiver that is not a valid cognizer (that is, if all direct perceivers are valid cognizers), then the correct answer would be 3P.]

C: It follows that there are not four possibilities. Posit something that is a direct perceiver but not a valid cognizer.

[Again, the Challenger goes straight to the problem.]

D: [Hesitates. Pauses. Says nothing.]

C: *Ya! Chir! Chir! Chir!*
[Literally, "*Ya!* Because! Because! Because!" This is the nudge the debaters shout when the Defender is slow to answer.]

D: There is nothing [that is a direct perceiver but not a valid cognizer].
[Indeed, there is not, at least not according to how these are understood by Buddhists.]

C: Then it follows that the two, direct perceivers and valid cognizers, are not four possibilities.
[If the two principals were 4P, there would have to be at least one thing that is a direct perceiver but not a valid cognizer. Since the Defender cannot posit such a thing, the answer that the two are 4P is untenable.]

D: I accept it.

C: *Tsha! Tsha! Tsha!* [Your fundamental assertion—that valid cognizers and direct perceivers are 4P—is finished!] So, how do the two, direct perceivers and valid cognizers, compare?

D: There are three possibilities.
[Right! Right at last. The rest of the debate that follows is the pattern for the debate implied by the paradigm without any of the frills. The Defender just answers correctly, so there is no need for much back and forth.]

C: It follows that there are not three possibilities. Posit something that is both [a direct perceiver and a valid cognizer].

D: There is something. The subject, a visual direct perceiver seeing white snow as white.

C: It follows that the subject, a visual direct perceiver seeing white snow as white, is a direct perceiver.

D: I accept [that a visual direct perceiver seeing white snow as white is a direct perceiver].

C: [Give a reason justifying that] the subject, a visual direct perceiver seeing white snow as white, is a direct perceiver.
[Note clearly that here the Challenger is using the form of a syllogism rather than a consequence. Indeed, that a visual direct perceiver seeing white snow as white is a direct perceiver flows as a consequence from what the Defender says. However, in this part of the debate, the Challenger is setting up the stem of a syllogism for the Defender to complete. Remember that the one who states a syllogism is held

to the truth of that argument. Thus, there is the expectation on both parts that the Defender will have to give a valid reason proving the assertions.

It often happens that the Defender gives a wrong subject or a wrong reason, so please imagine that the Challenger will then follow up on these points too through relying on the tools you are familiar with—mainly, consequences. Thus, though this part of the debate is laid out in specimen form here, when you actually debate, do not go to sleep during this part. Listen carefully to what the Defender is saying because it might be wrong—fertile ground for more debate.]

D: Because of being a visual direct perceiver.

C: It follows that whatever is a visual direct perceiver is necessarily a direct perceiver.

[In the specimen implied debates, the Challenger always moves to check the pervasion of the Defender's reason. This is the way that Lati Rinpoche usually taught us to go; however, and Rinpoche would certainly have confirmed this, sometimes it is more appropriate to check the establishment of the reason—either because it is wrong or just because it is more interesting.]

D: I accept [that whatever is a visual direct perceiver is necessarily a direct perceiver].

C: It follows that the subject, a visual direct perceiver seeing white snow as white, is a valid cognizer.

[The Challenger is now moving to check the remaining part (that a visual direct perceiver seeing white snow as white is a valid cognizer) of the first foot of the three feet of the paradigm for debating a comparison of 3P including something that is neither (in this case, that a visual direct perceiver seeing white snow as white is something that is both a direct perceiver and a valid cognizer).]

D: I accept [that the subject is a valid cognizer].

C: [Give a reason justifying that] the subject, a visual direct perceiver seeing white snow as white, is a valid cognizer.

D: Because of being a consciousness that is incontrovertible with regard to its main object.

C: It follows that whatever is a consciousness that is incontrovertible with regard to its main object is necessarily a valid cognizer.
[Checking the pervasion.]

D: I accept [that whatever is a consciousness that is incontrovertible with regard to its main object is necessarily a valid cognizer].

C: Now, which is necessarily the other? Which is not necessarily the other? Posit something that is one but not the other.

[Since the Defender has said that the two principals, direct perceivers and valid cognizers, are 3P, the Challenger asks the Defender to lay out exactly which way the pervasion goes. Is it that every direct perceiver is a valid cognizer? Or, is it that every valid cognizer is a direct perceiver? It is sometimes best to go first to this portion of the proof of two things as 3P. For one, this part shows quite clearly the measure of the Defender's understanding of the two principals. If the Defender has this part wrong, the understanding is off and further debate is called for.]

D: Whatever is a direct perceiver is necessarily a valid cognizer, but whatever is a valid cognizer is not necessarily a direct perceiver. For example, the subject, an inferential cognizer realizing that sound is an impermanent phenomenon.

[The procedure here is that the Defender gives the pervasion first, in response to the Challenger's direction, "Which is necessarily the other?" Then the Defender gives the lack of pervasion second, in response to the Challenger's direction, "Which is not necessarily the other?" Third, supporting the statement of a lack of pervasion in one direction, the Defender gives a subject that is one but not the other.]

C: It follows that the subject, an inferential cognizer realizing that sound is an impermanent phenomenon, is a valid cognizer.

[As a rule, I check the positive first. This is just because it is helpful to follow the same procedure every time, in order to remember where we are in the debate.]

D: I accept [that the subject is a valid cognizer].

C: [Give a reason justifying that] the subject, an inferential cognizer realizing that sound is an impermanent phenomenon, is a valid cognizer.

D: Because of being an inferential cognizer.

C: It follows that whatever is an inferential cognizer is necessarily a valid cognizer.

D: I accept it.

C: It follows that the subject, an inferential cognizer realizing that sound is an impermanent phenomenon, is not a direct perceiver.
[This is the second part of the second foot of the debate, the subject that is one of the two principals but not the other.]

D: I accept it.

C: [Give a reason justifying that] the subject, an inferential cognizer realizing that sound is an impermanent phenomenon, is not a direct perceiver.

D: Because of being a conceptual consciousness.

C: It follows that whatever is a conceptual consciousness is necessarily not a direct perceiver.

D: I accept it.

C: Now posit something that is neither.
[This is the third foot—the final part of the 3P debate. They have identified a subject that is both a direct perceiver and a valid cognizer and verified that it has the two qualities the Defender asserted it has. They have agreed on the way the pervasion runs and identified a subject that has one of the qualities but not the other and verified those qualities for that subject. All that is left is to identify a subject that is neither and verify that it is not a valid cognizer and not a direct perceiver.

When positing a subject that is neither, it is a point of etiquette, or perhaps it is a kind of flourish, for the Defender to give an example of something that is an existent, if possible, and to give an example that is clever, even close to wrong, if possible. Frequently, it is easy to use the horn of a rabbit as the subject, but that is often just trivial. In giving a clever example, the Defender shows control of the topic. Also, the more interesting or more difficult cases provide the debaters with more fertile ground for continued debate and deepening understanding.]

D: There is something. The subject, a wrong eye consciousness.
[This subject is not especially clever, but it is a consciousness and shows that the Defender understands that not all consciousnesses are either direct perceivers or valid cognizers.]

C: It follows that the subject, a wrong eye consciousness, is not a valid cognizer.

D: I accept it.

C: [Give a reason justifying that] the subject, a wrong eye consciousness, is not a valid cognizer.

D: Because of being a wrong consciousness.

C: It follows that whatever is a wrong consciousness is necessarily not a valid cognizer.

D: I accept it.

C: It follows that the subject, a wrong eye consciousness, is not a direct perceiver.

D: I accept it.

C: [Give a reason justifying that] the subject, a wrong eye consciousness, is not a direct perceiver.

D: Because of not being a valid cognizer.

C: It follows that whatever is not a valid cognizer is necessarily not a direct perceiver.

D: I accept it.

[This is a strong finish for the Defender, who reflects in this last reason that anything that is not a valid cognizer cannot be a direct perceiver.]

Both Challenger and Defender: *hla gyel lo!*

[American debaters seem to want to have something to say to mark the end of the debate, so over the years in the course, we have developed the custom of saying, "*hla gyel lo!*" ("the gods are victorious!"). The Tibetan debaters do not say anything at this point. I'm sure the Tibetans would find this custom to be hilarious. This is the phrase you hear the Tibetans say in their celebration of Losar, the Tibetan New Year. They throw a pinch of *tsampa* (barley flour) up in the air and shout, "*hla gyel lo!*" In this new year, may the gods—the buddhas—be victorious in their wish for peace and happiness!]

Advice: Please read over this debate carefully, probably repeatedly. This may be the most important passage in the entire book; thus, it is the most important to understand. Do not read it so much for the content, but read it to understand the procedure, which is the main point of this course. When reading it, you may have to force yourself to pay attention. I know very well that phenomenon of running my eyes over the words, seeming to read them, but all the while it is like there is a totally separate narrative going on in my noggin. It is similar to a person sitting, leafing through a magazine, while waiting for someone to show up. One of the obstacles to concentration meditation is subtle excitement, in which one stays on the task, like reading the words, but the mind is distracted. This is compared to seeing fish moving around under the frozen surface of the water. It is stable on top but not underneath.

It will certainly help to read the lines of the debate (without the commentary) with your debate partner, as if you were reading two characters in a play. Read first one part and then the other.

Another exercise that will help you to understand fully the procedure is to read the debate line by line while using a sheet of paper to cover up what comes next. Then imagine what the next line will be. Not every line here had to go the way it went. There is room for creativity and flexibility in debate, though it is driven by strategy and reason.

Again, it is not so much about the content as about the procedure in debate. That is the point of it. If you understand the procedure in this debate, you have gone a long way toward understanding the procedure in any debate. You cannot understand without some background—from this book, other books, or your experiences. However, the good news is that you can understand. And, with effort, you do.

Three Possibilities without Anything That Is Neither

In this rare case of three possibilities, (1) there is something that is both a p and a q, (2) it is the case that there is a pervasion in one direction but not the other—whatever is a p is necessarily a q, but whatever is a q is not necessarily a p—so there is something that is a q but not a p, and (3) there is nothing you can point to that is neither a p nor a q. This would be the comparison, for instance, between the selfless (p) and existents (q). As you recall from chapter 9, "Basic Buddhist Ontology 1," the broadest possible category in the Buddhist theory of what exists is called "the selfless." It refers to all that is free of a permanent, unitary, partless self. Buddhists say that everything that exists is free of, lacks, or is empty of such a self. This is so, they say, because such a self simply does not exist. Thus, they point out that non-existents too are free of such a self. Of course this would have to be so, for non-existents have no self of any sort. You may find it helpful to think of this category as "everything that exists as well as everything that does not exist" or "that which may be referred to." Since everything you may refer to—either existent or non-existent—is inside of the selfless, there is nothing outside of the selfless. Thus, there is nothing that one may posit as something that is neither selfless nor existent. For this sort of comparison, the two existent principals would have to be inclusive of all that exists and all that does not exist. The selfless, or anything that is MI with the selfless, such as its definition or non-(non-selfless), covers all on its own. The paradigm for this case is:

Answer in debate: There are three possibilities between p and q, without anything that is neither.

1. Something that is both a p and a q is the subject, x.

> The subject, x, is a p because of [supply a valid reason].
> The subject, x, is a q because of [supply a valid reason].

2. Whatever is a p is necessarily a q, but whatever is a q is not necessarily a p. For example, the subject, x, is a q but not a p.

> The subject, x, is a q because of [supply a valid reason].
> The subject, x, is not a p because of [supply a valid reason].

The pattern of debate for this answer is the following:

C: What is the difference between the two, the selfless and existents?
D: There are three possibilities without anything that is neither.
C: It follows that there are not three possibilities without anything that is neither. Posit something that is both.
D: There is something. The subject, a chair.
C: It follows that the subject, a chair, is selfless.
D: I accept [that a chair is selfless].
C: [Give a reason justifying that] the subject, a chair, is selfless.
D: Because of being free of a permanent, unitary, partless self.
C: It follows that whatever is free of a permanent, unitary, partless self is necessarily selfless.
D: I accept it.
C: It follows that the subject, a chair, is an existent.
D: I accept [that a chair is an existent].
C: [Give a reason justifying that] the subject, a chair, is an existent.
D: Because of being observed by a valid cognizer.
C: It follows that whatever is observed by a valid cognizer is necessarily an existent.

D: I accept it.

C: Now which is necessarily the other? Which is not necessarily the other? Posit something that is one but not the other.

D: Whatever is an existent is necessarily selfless, but whatever is selfless is not necessarily an existent. For instance, the subject, the horn of a rabbit.

C: It follows that the subject, the horn of a rabbit, is selfless.

D: I accept [that the horn of a rabbit is selfless].

C: [Give a reason justifying that] the subject, the horn of a rabbit, is selfless.

D: Because of being free of a permanent, unitary, partless self.

C: It follows that whatever is free of a permanent, unitary, partless self is necessarily selfless.

D: I accept it.

C: It follows that the subject, the horn of a rabbit, is not an existent.

D: I accept [that the horn of a rabbit is not an existent].

C: [Give a reason justifying that] the subject, the horn of a rabbit, is not an existent.

D: Because of being a non-existent.

C: It follows that whatever is a non-existent is necessarily not an existent.

D: I accept it.

C: Now posit something that is neither selfless nor existent.

D: There is nothing that is neither selfless nor existent.

FOUR POSSIBILITIES

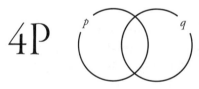

The comparison of four possibilities (*mu bzhi*) is so called because there are usually four things to point to in the discussion of the comparison. However, as with "three possibilities," this is one of the two comparisons for which the debaters mark a difference between two cases: (1) the case of four possibilities for which there is something outside the two circles that is neither a *p* nor a *q* and (2) the case of four possibilities for which there is nothing outside the two circles that is neither a *p* nor a *q*. The first does indeed have four points of discussion, and this case is, by far, more typical. However, for the rarer second case, since there is nothing outside the two circles that is neither a *p* nor a *q*, there are not really four points of discussion but only three. For both of these types of four possibilities, there is no pervasion between the two principals, not in either direction. Remember, this is the comparison in which it's true that "some are and some are not," like happy people and smart people—some happy people are smart people and some are not, and some smart people are happy people and some are not.

Four Possibilities including Something That Is Neither

The paradigm for proving that the two phenomena compare as four possibilities including something that is neither is as follows:

Answer in debate: There are four possibilities between *p* and *q*.[*]

1. Something that is both a *p* and a *q* is the subject, *x*.

 The subject, *x*, is a *p* because of [supply a valid reason].
 The subject, *x*, is a *q* because of [supply a valid reason].

2. Something that is a *p* but not a *q* is the subject, *x*.

 The subject, *x*, is a *p* because of [supply a valid reason].
 The subject, *x*, is not a *q* because of [supply a valid reason].

3. Something that is a *q* but not a *p* is the subject, *x*.

 The subject, *x*, is a *q* because of [supply a valid reason].
 The subject, *x*, is not a *p* because of [supply a valid reason].

4. Something that is neither a *p* nor a *q* is the subject, *x*.

 The subject, *x*, is not a *p* because of [supply a valid reason].
 The subject, *x*, is not a *q* because of [supply a valid reason].

The example here is the comparison of functioning things and different-from-(functioning thing). One might naturally think that whatever is different-from-(functioning thing) would have to be something other than a functioning thing, so the two would probably be MX; however, as this

---

[*]There is no need to specify further because this is the standard type of four possibilities.

is the sample debate here, you know they are 4P. Since this sample is just a sterile specimen, all the answers are correct. The debate pattern for this answer is the following:

C: How do the two, functioning things and different-from-(functioning thing), compare?

D: There are four possibilities.

C: It follows that there are not four possibilities. Posit something that is both.

D: There is something. The subject, a chair.

C: It follows that the subject, a chair, is a functioning thing.

D: I accept [that a chair is a functioning thing].

C: [Give a reason justifying that] the subject, a chair, is a functioning thing.

D: Because of being matter.

C: It follows that whatever is matter is necessarily a functioning thing.

D: I accept it.

C: It follows that the subject, a chair, is different-from-(functioning thing).

D: I accept [that a chair is different-from-(functioning thing)].

C: [Give a reason justifying that] the subject, a chair, is different-from-(functioning thing).

D: Because of being an instance of functioning thing.

C: It follows that whatever is an instance of functioning thing is necessarily different-from-(functioning thing).

D: I accept it.

C: Now, posit something that is a functioning thing but is not different-from-(functioning thing).

D: There is something. The subject, functioning thing.*

C: It follows that the subject, functioning thing, is a functioning thing.

D: I accept [that functioning thing is a functioning thing].

C: [Give a reason justifying that] the subject, functioning thing, is a functioning thing.

D: Because of being a nonassociated compositional factor.

---

*Note that here the subject is stated without an indefinite article "a" in order to mark it more clearly as the singular entity functioning thing in and of itself.

C: It follows that whatever is a nonassociated compositional factor is necessarily a functioning thing.

D: I accept it.

C: It follows that the subject, functioning thing, is not different-from-(functioning thing).

D: I accept [that functioning thing is not different-from-(functioning thing)].

C: [Give a reason justifying that] the subject, functioning thing, is not different-from-(functioning thing).

D: Because of being one-with-(functioning thing).

C: It follows that whatever is one-with-(functioning thing) is necessarily not different-from-(functioning thing).

D: I accept it.

C: Now posit something that is different-from-(functioning thing) but is not a functioning thing.

D: There is something. The subject, non-cow.

C: It follows that the subject, non-cow, is different-from-(functioning thing).

D: I accept [that non-cow is different-from-(functioning thing)].

C: [Give a reason justifying that] the subject, non-cow, is different-from-(functioning thing).

D: Because of being a permanent phenomenon.

C: It follows that whatever is a permanent phenomenon is necessarily different-from-(functioning thing).

D: I accept it.

C: It follows that the subject, non-cow, is not a functioning thing.

D: I accept [that non-cow is not a functioning thing].

C: [Give a reason justifying that] the subject, non-cow, is not a functioning thing.

D: Because of not being a product.

C: It follows that whatever is not a product is necessarily not a functioning thing.

D: I accept it.

C: Now posit something that is neither a functioning thing nor different-from-(functioning thing).

D: There is something. The subject, the horn of a rabbit.

C: It follows that the subject, the horn of a rabbit, is not a functioning thing.

D: I accept [that the horn of a rabbit is not a functioning thing].

C: [Give a reason justifying that] the subject, the horn of a rabbit, is not a functioning thing.

D: Because of being non-existent.

C: It follows that whatever is non-existent is necessarily not a functioning thing.

D: I accept it.

C: It follows that the subject, the horn of a rabbit, is not different-from-(functioning thing).

D: I accept it.

C: [Give a reason justifying that] the subject, the horn of a rabbit, is not different-from-(functioning thing).

D: Because of not being a phenomenon that is diverse from functioning thing.

C: It follows that whatever is not a phenomenon that is diverse from functioning thing is necessarily not different-from-(functioning thing).

D: I accept it.

Four Possibilities without Anything That Is Neither

As opposed to the classic case of four possibilities, for which there are all four points of comparison to touch on, in this case there is nothing to posit that lacks the qualities of both of the principals. Thus, there are only three points to touch on:

1. There is something that is both a *p* and a *q*.
2. There is something that is a *p* but not a *q*.
3. There is something that is a *q* but not a *p*.

This could perhaps be called a variety of three possibilities, and so it is in the system of Lati Rinpoche, which I followed in *Debate in Tibetan Buddhism*. However, here I am following the system of Kensur Yeshi Thupten, labeling this as a variety of four possibilities. His way of thinking of the comparisons seems to suggest that the heart of three possibilities is that there must be something that is both and there must be a pervasion running one way.*

---

*For more details, see Perdue, *Debate in Tibetan Buddhism*, 162–63.

In this case, there is nothing that can be posited that is neither a *p* nor a *q*. However, like the normal case of four possibilities, we can still say "some are and some are not" in both directions. This sort of comparison always involves two phenomena that together include all existents and non-existents as well. The two principals are generally—perhaps always—a comparison of: (1) one phenomenon that is greater in extent and has at least two diverse varieties and (2) the negation of a phenomenon that is a variety of the other principal phenomenon, the one that is greater in extent. An example is functioning things and nonmatter. Functioning things, of course, include all impermanent phenomena, and nonmatter includes everything other than matter—consciousnesses, nonassociated compositional factors, permanent phenomena, and non-existents. Thus, together they take in everything.

The paradigm for proving that two phenomena compare as four possibilities without anything that is neither is as follows:

Answer in debate: There are four possibilities between *p* and *q* without anything that is neither.

1. Something that is both a *p* and a *q* is the subject, *x*.

   The subject, *x*, is a *p* because of [supply a valid reason].
   The subject, *x*, is a *q* because of [supply a valid reason].

2. Something that is a *p* but not a *q* is the subject, *x*.

   The subject, *x*, is a *p* because of [supply a valid reason].
   The subject, *x*, is not a *q* because of [supply a valid reason].

3. Something that is a *q* but not a *p* is the subject, *x*.

   The subject, *x*, is a *q* because of [supply a valid reason].
   The subject, *x*, is not a *p* because of [supply a valid reason].

The pattern for debating this answer is the following:

C: How do these two compare—functioning things and nonmatter?
D: There are four possibilities without anything that is neither.
C: It follows that there are not four possibilities without anything that is neither. Posit something that is both.
D: There is something. The subject, an eye consciousness.

C: It follows that the subject, an eye consciousness, is a functioning thing.

D: I accept [that an eye consciousness is a functioning thing].

C: [Give a reason justifying that] the subject, an eye consciousness, is a functioning thing.

D: Because of being produced from causes and conditions.

C: It follows that whatever is produced from causes and conditions is necessarily a functioning thing.

D: I accept it.

C: It follows that the subject, an eye consciousness, is nonmatter.

D: I accept [that an eye consciousness is nonmatter].

C: [Give a reason justifying that] the subject, an eye consciousness, is nonmatter.

D: Because of not being a form.

C: It follows that whatever is not a form is necessarily nonmatter.

D: I accept it.

C: Now posit something that is a functioning thing but is not nonmatter.

D: There is something. The subject, a pot.

C: It follows that the subject, a pot, is a functioning thing.

D: I accept [that a pot is a functioning thing].

C: [Give a reason justifying that] the subject, a pot, is a functioning thing.

D: Because of being an impermanent phenomenon.

C: It follows that whatever is an impermanent phenomenon is necessarily a functioning thing.

D: I accept it.

C: It follows that the subject, a pot, is not nonmatter.

D: I accept [that a pot is not nonmatter].

C: [Give a reason justifying that] the subject, a pot, is not nonmatter.

D: Because of being matter.

C: It follows that whatever is matter is necessarily not nonmatter.

D: I accept it.

C: Now posit something that is nonmatter but is not a functioning thing.

D: There is something. The subject, uncomposed space.

C: It follows that the subject, uncomposed space, is nonmatter.

D: I accept [that uncomposed space is nonmatter].

C: [Give a reason justifying that] the subject, uncomposed space, is nonmatter.

D: Because of being a permanent phenomenon.

C: It follows that whatever is a permanent phenomenon is necessarily nonmatter.

D: I accept it.

C: It follows that the subject, uncomposed space, is not a functioning thing.

D: I accept it.

C: [Give a reason justifying that] the subject, uncomposed space, is not a functioning thing.

D: Because of not being a product.

C: It follows that whatever is not a product is necessarily not a functioning thing.

D: I accept it.

C: Now posit something that is neither a functioning thing nor nonmatter.

D: There is nothing that is neither a functioning thing nor nonmatter.

A fourth possibility, something that is neither, is inconceivable. Something that is, on the one hand, not a functioning thing and, on the other hand, is also not nonmatter—that is to say, is matter, cannot be posited.

Mutually Exclusive

The debaters could have reckoned two cases of mutually exclusive phenomena (*'gal ba*): one case in which something remains that is neither and one case in which nothing remains that is neither (a true dichotomy). However, in Buddhist reasoning and debate, they do not mark this distinction with separate answers as they do for 3P and 4P. This is probably because whether or not anything is left over does not matter for proving whether or not two phenomena are MX. Thus, there is only one answer for this comparison.

The paradigm for proving that two phenomena are mutually exclusive is as follows:

Answer in debate: The two, p and q, are mutually exclusive.

1. The subjects, p and q, are different because of being phenomena that are diverse.
2. Whatever is a p is necessarily not a q because of [supply a valid reason].*
3. Whatever is a q is necessarily not a p because of [supply a valid reason].

The first requirement in the paradigm is that the two phenomena must be different. This is the first requirement for all of the comparisons, and it means that they must be mutually different, as a permanent phenomenon is different-from-(a functioning thing) *and* a functioning thing is different-from-(a permanent phenomenon). An established base and the horn of a rabbit are not *mutually* different. Indeed, an established base is different-from-(the horn of a rabbit), for it is a phenomenon that is diverse from the horn of a rabbit. However, the horn of a rabbit is not different-from-(an established base) because it is not a phenomenon that is diverse from established base, for it is not a phenomenon of any sort. Thus, the requirement of difference ensures that the two principals are both existents.

The latter two parts of the paradigm ensure that, for mutually exclusive phenomena, their boundaries of pervasion do not meet at all. The two range over completely different groups of phenomena. There is neither any pervasion between the two nor any overlapping at all. Thus, there is no common locus (*gzhi mthun pa*) between them. A "common locus" is a locus, meaning a basis or an existent, that demonstrates two qualities. Although every existent is a common locus of some sort, for mutually exclusive phenomena, no locus demonstrates the two qualities together. The pattern for debating mutually exclusive phenomena is shown by the example of the two, permanent phenomena and functioning things:

C: How do the two, permanent phenomena and functioning things, compare?

---

*To justify a pervasion, it is often best to give a reason that is another pervasion. For instance, using the example of permanent phenomena and functioning things, "Whatever is a permanent phenomenon is necessarily not a functioning thing because whatever is a permanent phenomenon is necessarily not a momentary phenomenon, but whatever is a functioning thing is necessarily a momentary phenomenon."

D: They are mutually exclusive.

C: It follows that the subjects, the two—permanent phenomena and functioning things—are mutually exclusive.

D: I accept [that permanent phenomena and functioning things are mutually exclusive].

C: [Give a reason justifying that] the subjects, the two—permanent phenomena and functioning things—are mutually exclusive.

D: Because (1) they are different and (2) a common locus of the two is not possible.

C: It follows that the subjects, the two—permanent phenomena and functioning things—are different.

D: I accept it.

C: [Give a reason justifying that] the subjects, the two—permanent phenomena and functioning things—are different.

D: Because of being phenomena that are diverse.

C: It follows that for all phenomena that are diverse, they are necessarily different.

D: I accept it.

C: It follows that a common locus of the two, permanent phenomena and functioning things, is not possible.

D: I accept [that a common locus of the two, permanent phenomena and functioning things, is not possible].

C: [Give a reason justifying that] a common locus of the two, permanent phenomena and functioning things, is not possible.

D: Because (1) whatever is a permanent phenomenon is necessarily not a functioning thing and (2) whatever is a functioning thing is necessarily not a permanent phenomenon.

C: It follows that if (1) whatever is a permanent phenomenon is necessarily not a functioning thing and (2) whatever is a functioning thing is necessarily not a permanent phenomenon, then a common locus of the two, permanent phenomena and functioning things, is not possible.

D: I accept it.

Please bear in mind that, for those learning to debate, it will better train the tongue and the mind to say the whole thing, even if it is not explicitly written out here. For instance, in the last line above, the Defender says just, "I accept it." However, it will help you more to say: "I accept that if (1) whatever is a permanent phenomenon is necessarily not a functioning thing and (2) whatever is a functioning thing is necessarily not a permanent phenomenon, then a common locus of the two, permanent phenomena and functioning things, is not possible."

MUTUALLY INCLUSIVE

MI

As in the case of the comparison of two phenomena that are mutually exclusive, the debaters could have reckoned two cases of mutually inclusive phenomena (*don gcig*): one case in which something remains that is neither and one case in which nothing remains that is neither. However, in Buddhist reasoning and debate, they do not mark this distinction with separate answers because whether or not anything is left over does not matter for proving one way or the other that two phenomena are MI. Thus, here too for MI, there is only one answer.

For any two phenomena that are mutually inclusive, their relative boundaries of pervasion completely overlap. The extension of p is precisely equivalent to the extension of q. Whatever is a p is necessarily a q, and whatever is a q is necessarily a p. They pervade exactly the same things.

In this comparison, the two are just different names for the same thing. However, it would be a mistake to think of these as synonyms. Just as noting that two phenomena are mutually exclusive is not the same as saying that they are contradictory terms, so noting that two phenomena are mutually inclusive is not the same as saying that they are synonyms. It is about the phenomena rather than the terms. For instance, impermanent phenomena and products are different existents that are mutually inclusive. Thus, of course, the term "impermanent phenomena" and the term "products" are synonyms, but in this process of comparing phenomena, those two terms are mutually exclusive, for the terms are different existents and there is nothing that is both the term "impermanent phenomena" and the term "products." There is the term for something, the sound representing that thing, and the referent or meaning of that term. The point is that each and every thing that has the quality of being an impermanent phenomenon is also a product and that each and every product is also an impermanent phenomenon. Mutually inclusive phenomena are different only in the sense of not having exactly the same name, for their meanings—the objects that are included within the extension of each—are exactly the same. The paradigm for proving that two phenomena are mutually inclusive is as follows:

Answer in debate: The two, p and q, are mutually inclusive.

1. The subjects, p and q, are different because of being phenomena that are diverse.
2. The subjects, p and q, have all eight approaches of pervasion.

The second requirement is that the two principals must have all eight approaches of pervasion. These are:

1. Whatever is a p is necessarily a q.
2. Whatever is a q is necessarily a p.
3. Whatever is not a p is necessarily not a q.
4. Whatever is not a q is necessarily not a p.
5. If there is a p, then there is necessarily a q.
6. If there is a q, then there is necessarily a p.
7. If there is not a p, then there is necessarily not a q.
8. If there is not a q, then there is necessarily not a p.

Following the lead of the standard syllogism for explaining the Buddhist argument, an example of two mutually inclusive phenomena are impermanent phenomena and products. Thus, the pattern for debating mutually inclusive phenomena is shown by this comparison:

C: How do the two, impermanent phenomena and products, compare?
D: They are mutually inclusive.
C: It follows that the subjects, the two—impermanent phenomena and products—are mutually inclusive.
D: I accept it.
C: [Give a reason justifying that] the subjects, the two—impermanent phenomena and products—are mutually inclusive.
D: Because of (1) being different and (2) having all eight approaches of pervasion.
C: It follows that the subjects, the two—impermanent phenomena and products—are different.

D: I accept it.

C: [Give a reason justifying that] the subjects, the two—impermanent phenomena and products—are different.

D: Because of (1) being existents and (2) not being one.

C: It follows that if the two (1) are existents and (2) are not one, then they are necessarily different.

D: I accept it.

C: It follows that the subjects, the two—impermanent phenomena and products—have all eight approaches of pervasion.

D: I accept it.

C: [Give a reason justifying that] the subjects, the two—impermanent phenomena and products—have all eight approaches of pervasion.

D: Because (1) whatever is an impermanent phenomenon is necessarily a product, (2) whatever is a product is necessarily an impermanent phenomenon, (3) whatever is not an impermanent phenomenon is necessarily not a product, (4) whatever is not a product is necessarily not an impermanent phenomenon, (5) if there is an impermanent phenomenon, then there is necessarily a product, (6) if there is a product, then there is necessarily an impermanent phenomenon, (7) if there is not an impermanent phenomenon, then there is necessarily not a product, and (8) if there is not a product, then there is necessarily not an impermanent phenomenon.

C: It follows that if those eight are established, then impermanent phenomena and products necessarily have all eight approaches of pervasion.

D: I accept it.

Note: At this point, you can understand clearly why the principals in a comparison are referred to in the plural, as opposed to the system in *Debate in Tibetan Buddhism,* where they were referred to in the singular. When comparing two phenomena like products and impermanent phenomena, what is being compared are the *members in the class that includes each and every thing that has the quality of being* a product and the *members in the class that includes each and every thing that has the quality of being* an impermanent phenomenon. It is not a comparison of the abstract singular product and the abstract singular impermanent phenomenon. The focus is not on the classes in and of themselves but on the members of those classes. If it were a comparison of the abstract singulars, we would run into problems.

For instance, if we pose the two principals in a comparison as definition(s) and one-with-definition, and we conceive of definition as the abstract singular definition in and of itself, then these two would not compare as MX, as the comparison is interpreted, but as MI. Since the principal in the comparison, definitions, is understood properly as the class of each and every thing that is a definition, the singular definition is not found in the class. This is because definition itself is a definiendum, not a definition. So, there is nothing that is both a definition and one-with-definition. But, if we mistake this principal as definition in and of itself, definition and one-with-definition would be MI, for only definition in and of itself is one-with-definition.

Another example that shows that the principals should not be understood as the abstract singular is the comparison of functioning things and different-from-(functioning thing), which is used as the pattern for 4P above. If the principals were understood as the abstract singulars, then there would be nothing that is both functioning thing in and of itself and different-from-(functioning thing). This is because functioning thing in and of itself is one-with-(functioning thing), so it could never be different-from-(functioning thing). However, if we understand the principals properly as plurals, as each and every thing that is a functioning thing and each and every thing that is different-from-(functioning thing), then the comparison is 4P, as it is understood in the tradition. Thus, this way of reckoning this comparison too indicates that the principal being compared is the class of *each and every thing that has that quality of* the principal, and this is easiest understood in English using plurals.

However, using the plurals certainly cannot be understood as implying that *each and every* functioning thing compares as 4P with different-from-(functioning thing), because functioning thing itself would not work for that. From the other side too, it is not the case that *each and every thing* that is different-from-(functioning thing) is a functioning thing because a permanent phenomenon would not work for that. So, when the principals are stated in the plurals, like "functioning things," understand that as referring to the class of everything that is a functioning thing. Within the class, all the members share the quality of the principal, but when there are multiple members, they have diverse qualities too.

Still, for many things stated as principals, such as different-from-matter, that which is able to perform a function, or red, it is better to leave them in the singular. It would be awkward to force them into plurals, such as "phenomena that are different-from-matter," "those things that are able to perform functions," and "colors that are red." It would be senseless to try to state something such as one-with-product as a plural because there is only one thing that is one-with-product. For negatives, such as nonmatter, it is even more awkward to say something like "existents and non-existents that are nonmatter," and "nonmatters" is just curious.

As we see, the process of comparison focuses not on the class in and of itself but on the qualities of the members in that class. To establish the various points of comparison, we look for (1) something that has the qualities of both of the principals, (2) whether or not one of the principals is wholly included inside the other, (3) whether there is something that has the quality of one but not the other, and (4) whether there is anything that has neither quality. We look for things that have these two principals as *qualities* (or things—existent or non-existent—that may be properly said to take p and q as predicates in a statement); that is, *something that is* both a p and a q, *something that is* one but not the other, and *something that is* neither a p nor a q. Thus, the point of comparison between two principals is between those two as *qualities* (or as *predicates* properly applied to terms expressing those two). What is being asked is, "Is there anything that has both p and q as qualities (or is it possible for both p and q to be appropriately applied as predicates of some subject), is there anything that has either p or q as a quality but does not have the other (or is it possible to apply one but not the other as a predicate of some subject), and so on?" The process of comparing phenomena involves finding those subjects and thereby delineating the difference between the principals as qualities of real phenomena in the world and as predicates that may be applied to those subjects, whether real or non-existent.

Advice: Unless you are already very practiced and natural at this process, now you are ready to firm up your skills. At this point, you should have all the basic tools. All that is left is practice. To ensure that you develop and maintain good habits:

1. Please review the advice at the end of chapter 4, "The Comparison of Phenomena."
2. Please review the advice at the end of chapter 6, "The Buddhist Syllogism."
3. Remember to continue to speak grammatically correct English. For whatever reason, many American debaters gravitate toward saying things such as:

The subject, chair, is established base because of being functioning thing.

They end up dropping all the articles, "a," "an," and "the," speaking a sort of debate patois. It is very strange, and they all know it is not normal English. This can be corrected easily. So, please speak grammatically correct English whenever possible. Sometimes you cannot avoid saying something that sounds grammatically incorrect. For instance, you have to say:

The subject, definition, is a definiendum because of being a triply qualified imputed existent.

This syllogism is accurate only with the abstract singular "definition" as the subject. It is inaccurate if said of each and every definition, so you cannot say "a definition." There is enough of this sort of weirdness around, so please speak normally, when you can.

4. Most importantly, appreciate that all the patterns provided here are just specimens, like butterflies on a board. So, use them as you would use a butterfly specimen; use these patterns to learn the characteristics and patterns. Then, you have to breathe life into them.

Do not think that you have to follow the patterns word for word. Still, be careful in the ways you alter them, for you may end up making them incomplete. Probably at first it is best to follow the patterns by rote, then in time they will become second nature. That's the hope, that you will use these to gain another tool for rational discourse.

Also, appreciate that there are many different styles for debating the comparisons of phenomena. The approach varies even among monasteries within the Ge-luk-ba order. Apart from differences in style, every debate is as individual as is every butterfly. This is because the development of the debate depends on the answers that the Defender gives and upon the knowledge, skill, and cleverness of the Challenger.

Thus, these patterns are mere sketches and do not accurately reflect the vibrant and versatile nature of actual debate. For instance, in all the sample debates given above except for the debate for 3P, the Defender's answers are always correct according to the assertions of this system, but in actual debate Defenders do make errors, and subsequent debate arises from those errors. Still, these patterns contain all the essential points to demonstrate the procedure in the most straightforward way possible. You can understand that in an actual debate, many opportunities arise for detailed discussion of the individual points of these arguments, and you should be able to use your skills and your mindfulness in the moments of debate to pursue any avenue, either as Challenger or as Defender.

EXERCISE 25.1

Following the patterns for debate laid out in this chapter, debate the following comparisons of phenomena with your partner. Try to always be alert. Try to always be present in the debate. It is okay for both partners to look at the two principals written out, though Tibetan debaters would never do that on the debating courtyard. It is best not to sketch out the subjects and reasons, unless you are working by yourself. How do these compare?

1. Different-from-(functioning thing) and manifest phenomena*
2. Different-from-form and functioning things
3. Definitions and one-with-definition
4. Mental consciousnesses and valid cognizers
5. Direct perceivers and valid cognizers
6. Noncause and different-from-effect
7. Nondefinition and nondefiniendum
8. Different-from-(functioning thing) and persons
9. One-with-(that which is able to perform a function) and products
10. Non-cow and nonassociated compositional factors
11. Consciousnesses that are mistaken with regard to their appearing objects and consciousnesses that are mistaken with regard to their objects of engagement
12. Permanent phenomena and different-from-definiendum
13. Non-(conventional truth) and different-from-(hidden phenomenon)
14. One-with-(object of knowledge) and different-from-(non-existent)
15. One-with-(functioning thing) and different-from-(permanent phenomenon)
16. Nonassociated compositional factors that are nonpersons and different
17. Non-(direct perceiver) and different-from-(direct perceiver)

*Most of these comparisons were drawn from the final exam oral debates of many students over the years in my Buddhist Reasoning and Debate courses.

18. Nonproduct and different-from-(non-[permanent phenomenon])
19. Consciousnesses mistaken with regard to their appearing objects and valid cognizers
20. Consciousnesses mistaken with regard to their appearing objects and correct consciousnesses
21. Different-from-(permanent phenomenon) and non-(functioning thing)
22. Permanent phenomena and the phenomena MI with permanent phenomenon
23. Direct perceivers and mental consciousnesses
24. Different-from-(the selfless) and the selfless
25. Nondefinition and different-from-(nondefinition)
26. One-with-pot and different-from-pillar
27. Definitions and permanent phenomena
28. One-with-definition and different-from-definiendum
29. Functioning things and one-with-(functioning thing)
30. Non-(impermanent phenomenon) and conventional truths
31. Different-from-(direct perceiver) and valid cognizers
32. One-with-(one-with-[non-cow]) and different-from-(different-from-[non-cow])
33. Different-from-(mental direct perceiver) and direct perceivers
34. One-with-(one-with-[functioning thing]) and different-from-(different-from-[functioning thing])
35. One-with-one and different-from-different
36. One-with-different and different-from-one
37. Definienda and the triply qualified imputed existent of that which is able to perform a function
38. Different-from-(one-with-different) and one-with-(different-from-one)
39. Different-from-different and one
40. The definition of functioning thing and one-with-(functioning thing)
41. Different-from-different and different-from-(functioning thing)
42. One-with-definiendum and permanent phenomena
43. One and one-with-one
44. One-with-(functioning thing) and definienda
45. That which is established by valid cognition and the definition of established base

46. Objects of knowledge and golden pots
47. Different-from-form and one-with-product
48. One-with-(conventional truth) and hidden phenomena
49. Different-from-(different-from-[functioning thing]) and one-with-(conceptual consciousness)
50. One-with-(one-with-[impermanent phenomenon]) and permanent phenomena
51. Different and different-from-different
52. That which is able to perform a function and the triply qualified substantial existent of functioning thing
53. One-with-(functioning thing) and that which is able to perform a function
54. One-with-(one-with-pillar) and different-from-(different-from-pillar)
55. That which is able to perform a function and the definition of functioning thing
56. One-with-(different-from-[functioning thing]) and different-from-(one-with-[functioning thing])
57. Different-from-(functioning thing) and non-(functioning thing)
58. The selfless and different-from-existent
59. One-with-(functioning thing) and different-from-(functioning thing)
60. One-with-you and different-from-me

Exercise 25.2

Go back to chapter 12, "Consciousnesses in relation to What They Perceive," and debate the comparisons in exercise 12.1 at the end of the chapter.

Exercise 25.3

Make up your own comparisons using any two existents and debate them according to the patterns. You can choose from any field, but be sure to include some topics from the Collected Topics tradition

26. EFFORTS AND PRACTICES

NOW THE ONLY thing left to do in order to master these skills is to make continued effort. You have all the basic tools and procedures, and with effort, they all become second nature.

Within the traditional context of the monasteries, the debaters were motivated by their belief that through effort in reasoning and debate, they could in time cultivate an awareness that would liberate them from all suffering and death. Lati Rinpoche told of monks who were so determined in their efforts that they would always be reading, even when they were on kitchen duty, holding a book in one hand and stirring the pot with the other. He said that in the monasteries back in Tibet, they did not have electricity, and monks who could not afford candles but wanted to stay up after dark to read would read by the light of burning incense. In America, we tell the story of young Abe Lincoln reading by the light of a fire, but even that is a much better situation than reading by incense light. Whatever your motivation for improving your skills in reasoning and debate may be, almost all of us agree that it is beneficial to do so; thus, we have to agree that it is worth some effort.

In a documentary I once saw on the life of Sir Winston Churchill (1874–1965), there was a story of an intriguing moment of prescience on the part of a British Navy officer. During the period between the First and Second World Wars, just after Britain declared war on Germany in 1939, Churchill was appointed for the second time in his life to be the first lord of the admiralty. That is a civilian post comparable to the secretary of the navy in the United States. As part of his official responsibilities, Churchill was visiting a British naval vessel. During that visit, an officer serving on the vessel said to Churchill, "I expect that the next time we meet, I shall address you as prime minister because you have the combination of wit and plod." By this comment, the naval officer was pointing at Churchill's combination

Popperfoto/Getty Images

ENDINGS AND BEGINNINGS

Sir Winston Churchill (1874–1965), on the occasion of the victory over the German Afrika Korps at the Second Battle of El Alamein in Egypt, November 10, 1942, summed it up this way: "Now this is not the end. It is not even the beginning of the end. It is, perhaps, the end of the beginning."

of good intelligence and consistent efforts. (It does not seem that the comment referred to Churchill's famous wit for the comedic turn of phrase.) Indeed, the officer was right, for within a few months, Mr. Churchill was prime minister.

Now, this is it: wit and plod. Sometimes people ask me who will succeed better in Buddhist reasoning and debate, those who are especially sharp or those who work harder. I respond that I really cannot say, though I have seen that both can end up in the same place; however, the very best are those who have the combination of wit and plod, intelligence and effort. They always succeed best. In this regard, over the years, I have to give respect especially to the young women. For whatever reason, they are just more likely to try harder and give more effort. Perhaps it is a lack of confidence, perhaps it is a clear awareness of the benefits of effort, I just don't know. One time, I was leading a study session in my office before the next test for another course, a big lecture course on world religions. Perhaps twenty students came to ask questions during the two or three hours. Most of the visitors that day were women, and, at one point, I noticed that all the students in my office were young women, six or eight of them filling all the chairs and sitting around on the floor. In a class that was composed of approximately equal numbers of males and females, it was statistically unlikely. So, I pointed this out to the young women and wondered out loud why it would be. One young woman said, "The boys probably all think they know it already." We all laughed at that. Unfortunately, there is an element of truth to what she said. Although confidence is important, it should be based in evidence, not simply cultivated. Churchill was intelligent, quick, and witty, but he was also famous for his long hours of determined efforts. Over the years teaching Buddhist Reasoning and Debate, I have seen teams of young women, showing the same sort of wit and plod, who succeed grandly because of their natural abilities and consistent efforts. Of course, the same is true for some teams of young men. So, the very best are those with the combination of wit and plod, like Churchill. I think Lati Rinpoche's comments were pointing at the same thing.

There is a combination of mental and physical factors that combine in the successful. Of course, we tend to think that it is better to be bright, and that is generally so. However, we also tend to think that our wit is what it is, and that is just the measure we will have to work with, but I believe that is not so. Reasoning does not just require intelligence; it also makes you smarter. Even if some would dispute that, there is widespread agreement that we maintain our intelligence better by using our intellectual faculties. In the beginning, quite often this material and the procedures in debate seem obscure to newcomers. Things such as the comparisons of phenomena seem to come into mental focus and go out of focus. The syllogism seems to be backward or something. It feels difficult to get it. It seems to be opposite to the way we normally reason. But, in time and only with effort, everything clicks into place. And, when it does, it all seems so natural, and it is easy to gain facility with it. I have seen it hundreds of times.

That "click" is one fruit of effort. You cannot get it otherwise. If I understand correctly, there is a physical process going on; the electrical impulses start firing on new pathways, and in time we just get used to that new avenue of thought. It has become something we can use, a new skill.

Practicing debate helps us to develop the new skills and connections, but it also helps us to build up our endurance to stay in the game. You have seen the images of monks and nuns on the debating courtyard, out there passionately engaged in debates for hours on end. You can just imagine the measure of endurance that they have had to develop in order to do that. Recall a time when you tried to stay engaged in an intellectual conversation for a sustained period, but at some point you just had to give up. (We vary a lot on this, person to person and even day to day.) But the vast majority of university professors and lawyers could not stay engaged in an intellectually taxing discussion anywhere near as long as the Buddhist debaters typically do. Why is this? It is not a difference in wit or a difference in motivation. It is because, by their consistent efforts, the Buddhist debaters have developed their endurance.

Think of it as like a program of jogging that you might put yourself on. The first day, you feel pretty good about just getting around the block. But, day by day, week by week, month by month, you can run a little farther, and in time you can run ten miles. It is like that with debate. The more you practice, the more you can stay with it. There must be physical processes at play here. You just get used to it.

The example of a program of jogging is a good one too because if you drop out for a while, you have to build your endurance back up. It might be that you could lose everything, but it seems that there is a basis of development that you can always count on. Debate is like that too. Those trained neural pathways don't go away, though you may have to refamiliarize yourself if you have been away for a while.

Here are two more exercises; one is especially helpful for building up your endurance, and one is especially helpful for building up your wit.

CHRISTMAS TREE DEBATES

What I call "Christmas tree debates" are terrific for helping build up your endurance because, even though they are generally rather simple, it takes several minutes just to run through the debate.* So, you have to stay with it

---

*These kinds of debates, the Christmas tree debates, were first introduced to me by Denma Lochö Rinpoche.

and get more used to debating. That helps to wear in those neural pathways, so you last longer, and these debates also help to improve your short-term memory.

Of course, in Tibet, these are not called "Christmas tree debates," but they are like Christmas trees in the way that there are ornaments hanging down on each side. The ornaments are complete debates that, in a Christmas tree debate, serve to prove only one side of one foot. Thus, these are debates that are ornamented with debates.

For instance, how do the two, phenomena that are 4P with functioning things and phenomena that are 4P with permanent phenomena, compare? You can see that in order to prove that something is 4P with functioning things, you have to go through the debate. So, what are some of the things that are 4P with functioning things? One, different, definitions, definienda. Notice that all of these are also 4P with permanent phenomena. Thus, there are things that are 4P with both functioning things and permanent phenomena, so the two principals here are not MX.

Next, are there things that are 4P with functioning things but not 4P with permanent phenomena? Yes, for instance, different-from-(functioning thing) is 4P with functioning things but 3P with permanent phenomena. Others here include different-from-matter, different-from-consciousness, different-from-color, and so on.

Examples of things that are 4P with permanent phenomena but not 4P with functioning things include different-from-(permanent phenomenon), different-from-(uncomposed space), different-from-(established base), and so on.

Some things that are neither 4P with functioning things nor 4P with permanent phenomena are established bases, impermanent phenomena, chairs, the definition of functioning thing, the definition of permanent phenomenon, one-with-(functioning thing), one-with-pot, conventional truth, uncomposed space, one-with-(permanent phenomenon), one-with-(uncomposed space), the horn of a rabbit, and so on. Thus, the two—phenomena that are 4P with functioning things and phenomena that are 4P with permanent phenomena—compare as 4P.

The procedure for debating this sort of multipart debate is an easy adaptation from what you are already familiar with. As you can see, in order to settle that the two principals above compare as 4P, you would have to debate eight separate little debates in order to establish each part of the larger debate. (Of course, these Christmas tree debates are not always about establishing that two phenomena compare as 4P. Like any debate, the phenomena may compare in any way. Some exercises are provided below.) Beyond these little debates, for which you already understand the procedures, there are only the connecting joints between the little debates that are new. There is no need to play out an entire debate here, but you do need to learn how to round the corner at each turn and how to get started. The "little debates" are not fully shown and breaks in the flow are marked with five horizontal asterisks. Also, this version of the debate is a sterile specimen in which the Defender gives only correct answers. Here is a debate on the comparison given above, supplemented with minimal commentary inside brackets and indented in a prose block in order to help you track what is going on.

C: How do these two compare—phenomena that are 4P with function-ing things and phenomena that are 4P with permanent phenomena?
D: There are four possibilities.
C: It follows that there are not four possibilities. Give an example of something that is both 4P with functioning things and 4P with per-manent phenomena.
D: There is something, The subject, definitions.
C: It follows that the subject, definitions, are 4P with functioning things.
D: I accept it.
C: It follows that the subject, definitions, are not 4P with functioning things. Give an example of something that is both a definition and a functioning thing.
D: There is something. The subject, that which is able to perform a function.

*   *   *   *

C: It follows that whatever is a permanent phenomenon is necessarily not a functioning thing.
D: I accept it.
C: It follows that the subjects, definitions, are 4P with functioning things.
D: I accept it.
   [Imagine here that a Defender has put forth the subject, a hidden phenomenon, as an example of something that is neither a function-

ing thing nor a definition. Then, as the last part of that consideration, the Defender proved that the subject, a hidden phenomenon, is not a functioning thing because of being a permanent phenomenon. Then they checked that pervasion. These lines above then mark the end of the first part of the first foot of the debate, the part establishing that definitions and functioning things are 4P.

Now the debaters proceed to the second part of the first foot, the part establishing that definitions also compare to permanent phenomena as 4P.]

C: It follows that the subjects, definitions, are 4P with permanent phenomena.

D: I accept it.

C: It follows that the subjects, definitions, are not 4P with permanent phenomena. Give an example of something that is both a definition and a permanent phenomenon.

D: There is something. The subject, that which is established by a valid cognizer.

* * * * *

C: It follows that whatever is a definiendum is necessarily not a definition.

D: I accept it.
[These lines are the end of the consideration of something that is neither a definition nor a permanent phenomenon, the last part of the little debate proving that definitions and permanent phenomena compare as 4P. For something that is neither, imagine subjects such as functioning thing, matter, a pot, a consciousness, and so on. This marks the end of the proof that definitions compare as 4P with permanent phenomena.

Now the debaters close out the first set of little debates—something that is both 4P with functioning things and 4P with permanent phenomena:]

C: It follows that the subjects, definitions, are 4P with both functioning things and permanent phenomena.

D: I accept it.
[This marks the end of the first foot of the debate, the part establishing that there is something that is both 4P with functioning things and 4P with permanent phenomena.

Now the debaters proceed to the first part of the second foot, the part proving that there is something that is 4P with functioning things but not 4P with permanent phenomena.]

D: Now, posit something that is 4P with functioning things but not 4P with permanent phenomena.

C: There is something. The subject, different-from-matter.

* * * * *

[The way of debating this and the way of "rounding the corners" to move to the next part of the larger debate can be understood from following the procedures already shown for the first foot of the larger debate.

Thus, imagine that you run through all those parts and now you are at the last part of the little debate proving that there is something that is neither 4P with functioning things nor 4P with permanent phenomena. Imagine that the subject given to prove this is impermanent phenomena, which are MI with functioning things and MX with permanent phenomena. Then imagine that the last bit is proving that impermanent phenomena are not 4P with permanent phenomena:]

C: Why do you say that the subjects, impermanent phenomena, are not 4P with permanent phenomena?

D: Because of being MX with permanent phenomena.

C: It follows that the subjects, the two—impermanent phenomena and permanent phenomena—are MX.

D: I accept it.

C: [Give a reason justifying that] the subjects, the two—impermanent phenomena and permanent phenomena—are MX.

* * * * *

C: It follows that whatever is MX with permanent phenomena is necessarily not 4P with permanent phenomena.

D: I accept it.

[That finishes the last bit of the last little debate, the part proving that impermanent phenomena are not 4P with permanent phenomena, which is itself the final half of proving that impermanent phenomena are not 4P with either functioning things or permanent phenomena. Now, this is how a "Christmas tree debate" is closed out:]

C: It follows that the subjects, impermanent phenomena, are not 4P with permanent phenomena.

D: I accept it.

C: It follows that the subjects, impermanent phenomena, are both not 4P with functioning things and not 4P with permanent phenomena.

D: I accept it.

C: Then it follows that the subjects, the two—phenomena that are 4P with functioning things and phenomena that are 4P with permanent phenomena—are 4P.

D: I accept it.

EXERCISE 26.1

To build up your strength and endurance, debate the following "Christmas tree" comparisons of phenomena with your partner. Notice that, when you go quickly, it is actually easier to remember where you are in the debate. How do these compare?

1. Phenomena that are 4P with functioning things and phenomena that are 4P with permanent phenomena
2. Phenomena that are 3P with functioning things and phenomena that are 4P with permanent phenomena
3. Phenomena that are 4P with functioning things and phenomena that are 3P with permanent phenomena
4. Phenomena that are 3P with functioning things and phenomena that are 3P with permanent phenomena
5. Phenomena that are 4P with one and phenomena that are 4P with different
6. Phenomena that are 4P with definition and phenomena that are 4P with definiendum

EXERCISE 26.2

Make up your own Christmas tree debates and debate them with your partner.

COMPARISONS INVOLVING VARIABLES

Comparisons drawing on variables force you to think about the material in a different way. They are great for helping improve your control of the material and for developing your abilities to think in an abstract way.

An example of a comparison using variables is:

How do these two compare—one is an x and x is one?

For this type of question, the procedure is basically the same as it is for simple comparisons like comparing functioning things and matter. In a simple comparison like that, first you look for things that are functioning things, then you look for things that are matter, and then you look to see if anything is in both groups. Similarly, with the comparisons involving variables, first you look to see what you can put in for the variable x that makes the statement "one is an x" true. For the sentence to be true, this would have to be something that is a quality of the phenomenon one. There are lots of things you can drop in for the x that will work here. For instance, if you substitute "established base" for the x, that makes the sentence "One is an established base," which is certainly true. What about other things? Continuing to ignore the other side of the comparison for now, what else can complete the sentence "one is an x" to make it a true statement? Here are some: permanent phenomenon and all the phenomena MI with permanent phenomena such as conventional truth and so on, definiendum, one, existent and all the phenomena MI with existent, non-(functioning thing), and so on.

Now, what about the other side, the one on the right? What can we put in for the x that makes the statement "x is one" true? Any existent, singular phenomenon works: a chair is one, a table is one, a functioning thing is one, an established base is one, definiendum is one, one is one, and so on.

Now, we need to search to see whether or not there is any subject that can be substituted for the variable x in both parts of the line so that the left side, "one is an x," and the right side, "x is one," are both true statements. If we can find such a subject, a subject that satisfies both the left side and the right side of the line, then we know that the two principals are not mutually exclusive. When you review the lists of things that satisfy the left side and the list of things that satisfy the right side, you quickly see that there is some overlap. For instance, established base, that which is observed by a valid cognizer, permanent phenomenon, one, definiendum, one-with-one, and so on satisfy both sides. Okay! So, this comparison is not MX.

Next, look for something that satisfies the left side of the line, "one is an *x*," but does not satisfy the right side, "*x* is one." At first it seems kind of mystifying, but it is easy. For instance, one is an established base and a permanent phenomenon, but an established base and a permanent phenomenon are not one. There are lots of these you can make up. For instance, an existent and an established base, one and a definiendum, non-(functioning thing) and nondefinition, and so on satisfy the left side but not the right side.

Another, curious possibility that satisfies the left side of this line but not the right is only-a-permanent-phenomenon. One is only-a-permanent-phenomenon, but only-a-permanent-phenomenon is not one. What does this mean? Only-a-permanent-phenomenon is a non-existent, but each and every permanent phenomenon is only-a-permanent-phenomenon. Why is only-a-permanent-phenomenon a non-existent? Because functioning things exist. If only permanent phenomena existed, then there would be no functioning things. Then, why is it said that a permanent phenomenon is only-a-permanent phenomenon? Because it is not sometimes a permanent phenomenon and sometimes not, and because it is not partially a permanent phenomenon and partially not a permanent phenomenon. A permanent phenomenon is only-a-permanent-phenomenon. So, by extension, only-a-product does not exist, only-a-color does not exist, only-one does not exist, and so on; but, for each of these, there are things that have them as a quality. For instance, sound is only-a-product, red is only-a-color, and a pot is only-one. However, only-an-existent exists because non-existents do not exist. Thus, one is only-a-permanent-phenomenon, but only-a-permanent phenomenon is not one because only-a-permanent-phenomenon does not exist; thus, it is not *a phenomenon* that is not diverse, and it is not one. This curious case stresses the difference between the two types of statements used in this system, statements of qualities and statements of pervasion. Please remember the curious case of only-a-permanent-phenomenon as you work your way through the problems involving variables because, at some points, it is the only thing that will work.

For the third foot of this comparison, look for something that satisfies the right side of the line, "*x* is one," but does not satisfy the left side of the line, "one is an *x*." The easy way is just to look for the qualities that one, in and of itself, does not have. For instance, one is not a functioning thing, one is not different, one is not a definition, and so on. Thus, any of these will work here. Functioning thing is one, but one is not a functioning thing. There are limitless things that will work here, such as a chair, a rock, a person, matter, a consciousness, and so on. Different is an interesting subject here. Different is one because of being a phenomenon that is not diverse, but one is not different because of being one.

Finally, for the last part of this comparison, is there anything that does not satisfy either side? Of course. For instance, one is not an impermanent phenomenon and a product, and an impermanent phenomenon and a product are not one. Other possibilities here include a non-existent, the horn of a rabbit, or opposites such as a definition and a definiendum or a permanent phenomenon and a functioning thing.

Thus, the two, one is an *x* and *x* is one, compare as 4P. It seems that 4P is the predominant answer for comparisons involving variables, but it is easy enough to make up ones that require another answer.

Debating comparisons involving variables is just as you might imagine. It is a matter of simply replacing the variable *x* with other terms and just changing the order of those terms as needed between the subject and the predicate to be proven. For instance:

C: How do these two compare—one is an *x* and *x* is one?
D: They are 4P.
C: It follows that they are not 4P. Posit something that works for both.
D: There is something. The subject, an established base.
C: It follows that the subject, one, is an established base.
   [Simply replace the *x* in "one is an *x*" with the subject the Defender has given for the first foot of this debate, "an established base," which is used here as the predicate to be proven.]
D: I accept it.
C: Why do you say that the subject, one, is an established base?
D: Because of being a permanent phenomenon.
C: It follows that whatever is a permanent phenomenon is necessarily an established base.
D: I accept it.
C: Now, it follows that the subject, an established base, is one.
   [Just like above, simply replace the *x* with "established base," but here the sentence is "*x* is one" so "established base" has become the subject and "one" is the predicate.]
D: I accept it.

The debate continues on like that. Just be consistent in the substitutions. Practice the exercises below.

EXERCISE 26.3

Work with your partner to debate the following. How do these compare?

1. One is an x and x is one*
2. Different is an x and x is different
3. One-with-(functioning thing) is an x and x is one-with-existent
4. Form is an x and x is a functioning thing
5. Non-(disintegrating phenomenon) is an x and x is an uncomposed phenomenon
6. Functioning thing is an x and x is an object of knowledge
7. x is a hidden phenomenon and x is a non-(functioning thing)
8. x is an object of knowledge and generally characterized phenomenon is an x
9. x is a nonassociated compositional factor and functioning thing is an x
10. x is a consciousness and consciousness is an x
11. Impermanent phenomenon is an x and x is an impermanent phenomenon
12. Functioning thing is an x and x is a permanent phenomenon
13. x is one-with-x and different-from-x is an x
    [Hint: Functioning thing is one-with-(functioning thing) but different-from-(functioning thing) is not a functioning thing because of being a permanent phenomenon.]
14. Mutually-different-from-x is an x and x is not different-from-x
    [Hint: "Mutually different" means that each of two things are different from each other, as a chair is different-from-(a table) and a table is different-from-(a chair). Thus, the qualification of being *mutually* different works to exclude non-existents because a chair is different-from-(the horn of a rabbit), but the horn of rabbit is not different-from-(a chair). So, a chair and the horn of a rabbit are not mutually different.]
15. x is an x and x is one-with-x
16. Definition is an x and x is a definiendum

---

*As it was with exercise 25.1, some of these comparisons too were drawn from the final exam oral debates of many students over the years in my Buddhist Reasoning and Debate courses. Many were contributed by Chris Runyon.

17. Functioning thing is an x and x is a functioning thing
18. Permanent phenomenon is an x and x is a permanent phenomenon
    [Hint: Of course, anything higher on the chart of the selfless, such as established base and the selfless, works as something that is both. For the possibility of something for which permanent phenomenon is an x but x is not a permanent phenomenon, remember only-a-permanent-phenomenon.]
19. One-with-(functioning thing) is an x and x is one-with-(functioning thing)
20. One-with-x is an x and different-from-x is an x
    [Hint: One-with-(non-existent) is a non-existent because there is no phenomenon that is exactly the same in name and meaning as non-existent. However, different-from-(non-existent) is not a non-existent because every existent is different-from-(non-existent).]
21. Different-from-x is an x and mutually-different-from-x is an x
    [Hint: Different-from-(non-existent) is not a non-existent but mutually-different-from-(non-existent) is a non-existent. For something that is neither, you can use a chair or the horn of a rabbit. In the latter case, with respect to the subject, mutually-different-from-(the horn of a rabbit), it is not the horn of a rabbit because a valid cognizer that realizes it as the horn of a rabbit does not exist.]
22. x is not x and x is one-with-x
23. x is one and x is a permanent phenomenon
24. One is an x and x is a permanent phenomenon
25. Definition is an x and x is a permanent phenomenon
26. Different-from-(functioning thing) is an x and x is different-from-(functioning thing)
27. Nondifferent is an x and non-x is only-an-x
28. Mutually-different-from-(one-with-x) is an x and x is one
29. x is one and different is an x
30. x is mutually-different-from-(one-with-x) and x is one
31. x is one-with-one and different-from-x is an x
32. Phenomena and x is an x
33. x is a definition and one is an x
34. Permanent phenomenon is an x and x is a functioning thing
35. One-with-x is a non-x and one is an x
36. Definition is an x and x is a definition
37. Definition is an x and x is a definiendum

38. Only-a-permanent-phenomenon is an x and x is not only-a-permanent-phenomenon
39. x is non-(one-with-different) and one-with-different is non-x
40. One-with-x is a non-x and x is an x
41. One-with-x is a non-existent and a cup is an x
42. Non-x is an x and x is a definition
43. Non-cow is a non-x and non-x is a non-cow
44. x is able to perform a function and x is one-with-(the definition of functioning thing)
45. Only-an-x is an x and x is a non-(functioning thing)
46. Different is only-an-x and x is only-an-x
47. One-with-x is an x and x is a permanent phenomenon
48. Different-from-x is an x and x is a permanent phenomenon

Conclusion

27. Conclusions and Remarks

B UDDHIST REASONING and debate is of compelling importance for Buddhist practitioners, as you can see in the debaters' passion. The Buddhists have worked hard to develop tools and procedures that are reliable for their efforts to ascertain what exists and what does not exist. It seems that their tools and procedures are simple and elegant, and that is why they are so useful for so many. Also, though their tools and procedures were developed for looking into topics that might lead to a profound, liberating wisdom, those same tools and procedures are also useful for looking into whatever topics are of interest to a person. They provide a useful way for assessing the flood of information that is coming your way, organizing your own thoughts and words, and expressing yourself.

CHECKLIST OF SKILLS YOU SHOULD HAVE AT THE END OF THIS COURSE

Now at the end of *The Course in Buddhist Reasoning and Debate,* you should have developed, or at least begun to develop, a set of reasoning and debate skills. At this point, you should be able to do the following:

1. Assess the extent to which it is purposeful for you to attempt to engage in rational discourse with that person in front of you
2. Assess phenomena in terms of how they compare as 3P, 4P, MX, or MI, or to understand why they do not compare in any of these ways
3. Be mindful of the difference between statements of qualities and statements of pervasion and quietly weigh the value of those statements as you think, speak, hear, or read them
4. Formulate a valid argument in the style of a Buddhist syllogism
5. Convert what others are saying into something you can understand and ask polite questions that will help you do this

6. Stay on the topic in discussions and have better short-term memory
7. Stay in the role of Challenger or Defender to the extent you can in any discussion you are having and gently wrangle others to stay in their role too
8. Consider topics in terms of their definitions, divisions, and illustrations
9. Cast your mind forward to anticipate consequences of statements you think, speak, hear, or read, weighing them in terms of statements of qualities and statements of pervasion and the overall argument
10. Formulate and respectfully fling consequences to others in response to what they are saying
11. Give respectful answers to others' arguments, gently pointing out problems, issues, or uncertainties
12. Assess what a person is saying in terms of how two things compare as 3P, 4P, and so on, and confirm what they are thinking through reasoning together, and address any issues with what they are saying through using the strategies you have learned here
13. Judge when the debate is over and stop*

If you have not yet developed all of these skills, and even the most accomplished person can still improve, there is no reason that you cannot continue your practice. Once you have the basics and have worn in the new connections in your noggin, you can continue this on your own. You will undoubtedly continue it on your own. You will find that you will apply your skills automatically.

ON THE CONTENT

Do not make the mistake of believing that the content offered in this book is typical of the broad content of Buddhist reasoning and debate. The typical things here are the procedures, the strategies, the argument forms, and the basic ontology and consciousness studies. And some of the material here

---

*Remember that when people have run out of answers, they will show that in their body language: they will begin to look around, smile, and maybe giggle. They might also start trying to change the subject. Go ahead and let them change the subject, and show the ability to win gracefully. Also, if you keep talking after your victory, you might find yourself in new entanglements. My brother, who has had a long career in sales and management, sometimes comes forth with folksy wisdom. He said, "When you make the sale, stop talking, or you'll end up buying it back."

is little more than wordplay, especially things like "only-a-permanent-phenomenon." Such things could hardly sustain Buddhist debaters year after year.

It seems to me that the most important lesson in this beginning material, at least besides the procedures and so on, is the difference between statements of qualities and statements of pervasion. Of course, understanding these two types of statements is essential for understanding the argument forms, procedures, and so on. The content of that understanding goes far beyond mere wordplay, for it provides a person with the basis for further analysis of anything of interest. Lati Rinpoche said that, in beginning debate, a student does not learn all the answers but learns how to ask the questions.[1]

Using Your Skills in Reasoning and Debate

Perhaps you have developed some new skills in reasoning and debate in this course or perhaps you have just added a new tool to the skills you already had. In either case, these skills are neither good nor bad on their own. That depends on how you use them. The real measure of value that you will get out of your reasoning and debate skills, whether new or old, is shown by what your motivation is. Here is a story that showed me that.

In the fall of 1978, I had a dream one morning that I often think of still. It was one of those fabulous dreams, one that even at the time—perhaps even during the dream—you know is important. I have come to believe that the dream foretold something of my experience with reasoning and debate in this life. At the time, I was still a graduate student at the University of Virginia. Having finished up all my course work, I was taking my preliminary examinations, which are required before moving on to write the dissertation. I had already been awarded a fellowship to go to India to do my field research work on Buddhist reasoning and debate, but I had to finish the prelims first. It was going to be my first trip to India, indeed my first time out of the country at all. It was a busy and exciting but stressful period with academic preparations and preparations for the trip. Also, I could sense what was ultimately verified, that I was on the edge of great changes in my life. This dream is not like a narrative story but is more like a series of vignettes.

First, I am arriving somewhere. It is hot, and the ground is barren and dusty. It reminds me of backwoods, coastal South Carolina, which I had visited many times as a boy, for there was no grass on the ground, unlike the way I had always known it to be in Virginia. Then I encountered a dark-skinned man, whom I later saw as an East Indian. He and I were immediately hostile, and he grew very brutish in appearance, with a huge ridged brow and a massive jaw. He did not speak but sort of growled and was very aggressive. Then there was a sort of weapon fashioned out of two old British Lee-Enfield .303 rifles as used in the First World War. The rifles were no longer functional; the wood was dry and splintering off, the metal was rusty, and the bolts were missing from both rifles. They were arranged front to back relative to each other, with the muzzle of each at the butt of the other—one pointing one way and the other pointing the opposite way, and they were bound together with rope. That seemed to indicate that aggression would be returned with aggression in equal measure in the opposite direction. The brutish Indian and I used the bonded pair of rifles as a heavy club to fight with each other. At times, we would both hold the rifles and struggle together, and at times one of us would wrestle them away from the other and use them to push the other person in the chest or to hit the other person on the head. This was the tool we had to fight with. Neither of us could win. In the dream, I had the thought that this was senseless. We were just hurting each other and no one could ever win.

Then I moved on. The next thing I remember is sitting alone in a quiet room with a cranberry-colored typewriter. This was the tool I had to write with. It was the machine I would use to compose my dissertation, writing five pages a day, six days a week, for two and a half years. At that time in the dream and later in life during that time of writing, I had fun experiences in classrooms, for the first time on the professor's side of the desk.

Then everything sort of dried up. I remember sitting at a desk in a classroom. There were only a few students, and then there were none. The desks were all really dusty, and so I felt a little sad. During this period in my life, after finishing the dissertation and graduating in 1983, I taught some, though not full-time, and I spent years in dusty India working with Tibetan lamas and scholars.

Then in the next vignette, I was writing again, but now with a more modern keyboard, not a typewriter but a computer, a new and better tool. This was the keyboard I used to write *Debate in Tibetan Buddhism,* my big book on debate. There were now many classes in the dream, still fun, but small groups. This vignette went on for a while.

Then there was an even better keyboard, and there were classes with happy, respectful students, many of them older than college students. Then there were great venues, the kinds where the lights shine in your face and you cannot see the audience, but they were there by the hundreds. By this time in the dream, I was thinking that the purpose of reasoning and debate is to help, not to conquer. The last thing I remember of that dream was laughing with a large audience.

In my reflections on that dream over the years, it seems pretty clear that it has to do with my experiences with debate. It goes to the issues of what debate is for and how debate can help you. I think I first came to debate because I wanted a tool I could use to fight better, but of course I was the brute, and there is no victory in that. Just arguing to fight with somebody is not effective, not purposeful. Then, clearly, the several keyboards—each better than the last—were the new tools, not tools for brutish battle but tools for communication.

The moral of the story is that the tools you have to accomplish your goals and the results that come from the accomplishments are very much the result of the motivation you have. If your purpose in training in reasoning and debate is to gain victories, it will just be brutish competition. If you study to learn, then others will come to listen to the words of a learned person. If you practice to help, the crowds will grow in numbers and be respectful. At least that's the way it seems to me.

Although I have not heard the Dalai Lama speak on this directly, he said something that seems to give support to what I am saying here. In a talk in October 2010, he said about technology that it is not good or bad in and of itself because it depends on how you are using it. He said that in this way, it is like intelligence. If you use it for good purposes, it's a good thing that you are intelligent. But, if you use it for bad purposes, it's too bad that you are bright.[2] Debate and analytical thinking are like that too. If you are just up to bad activities, it would be better if you were dull, unskilled, and had no technology.

Is It Any Different for the Buddhist Debaters?

Is it true that Buddhist debaters too use their wits and skills sometimes for good purposes and sometimes for bad? Of course. When you meet me, you will see that I do not have stars in my eyes. Even within the Buddhist organizations where they practice debate—the monasteries, nunneries, and centers—there are people who use reasoning and debate for bad purposes like just to shame an opponent. But that does not mean the organizations should throw it all away. The guideline is still the same: the value is measured by the motivation of those who practice it. Exactly what a person's motivation is—that is something that is often difficult to discover. Even within yourself, it is often difficult to know.

At the very least, most Buddhist debaters use their skills in the hopes of avoiding a bad rebirth. Perhaps some are trying to use those skills to abandon rebirth entirely. And, perhaps some are trying to use their wits and skills to help not only themselves but everyone to get out of the round of rebirth. That is the hope.

Whatever a person's motivation may be, the process begins with overcoming wrong thoughts, especially your own. Remember the procedure of a physician, who first removes what does not belong in the patient, such as toxins, and then builds up what does belong, such as constitutional balance. In line with this, Geshe Lobsang Tharchin said, "Primarily one uses debate to overcome the abundant misconceptions in one's own and other's thoughts."[3] Beyond that, analytical thinking also helps you to develop what does belong, such as a clear understanding of any topic. Debate for the monks and nuns of Tibet is not mere academics but a way of using direct implications from the obvious in order to generate an inference that is able to understand the ultimate state of phenomena that is not obvious. The debaters are seeking to understand the nature of reality through careful analysis of the state of existence of ordinary phenomena, the bases of reality. This is the essential purpose for religious debate. They are not just arguing over golden pots.

FINAL REMARKS

Since the nature of ultimate reality is "not obvious," the tradition of debate is rooted in the belief that it is possible for us to build up our understanding piece by piece to come to a final understanding of ultimate reality. Standing at the foot of the mountain, it is difficult to see what is on the top of the mountain, so to believe that it is possible to come to know the nature of ultimate reality is at first an article of faith, not knowledge. Within Tibetan Buddhism, one very important avenue of approach to understanding the ultimate state of phenomena is the practice of reasoning and debate. It is a broad avenue for many. Whether or not a student is bright and rational, the study of reasoning and debate will help. In fact, whether or not one is even a Buddhist, the study of reasoning and debate will help.

In my life, as a student in classrooms for twenty-six years and as a professor in classrooms for over thirty years, I have noticed that there are two main ways of learning: learning facts and learning patterns. Especially when people are younger, they spend most of their learning efforts acquiring facts. Often young people struggle with doubts about whether or not these facts are going to help them. But, when you build up more and more facts, you begin to see patterns. Then, even when you meet something you had not known before, you will have a sense of it, simply because you have some awareness of the patterns of things. This may be what is called wisdom. You can see this in every area of human undertaking. You can take a carpenter from Alabama to a wooden structure in Japan, and even though they do things differently there, that carpenter will see the patterns better than those without carpentry experience. Today young people often feel that they need to know only one thing, and that is how to search for things. What I am saying is that you have to build up your own internal "database," which you can search even faster, and only then will you begin to see the patterns in things. If you do not have ready access to an internalized body of facts, it is difficult to progress. This has to be part of what is going on in the process "of using direct implications from the obvious in order to generate an inference that is able to understand the ultimate state of phenomena that is not obvious."

What's more, it has to be easy, or we couldn't do it. I often think that everything is easy. Even brain surgery is easy for a brain surgeon. For most of us, if we were to watch a brain surgeon at work, it would just be a mystery. However, for brain surgeons, it's just another day at work. What they are doing is a series of simple steps that they have built up over the years. They are not in there sweating bullets, trying to figure it out. It's just: they do this, and then they do that, and so on until it's done. When you see a person do something truly amazing like a move on a basketball court, figure skating, or a gymnastics performance, it seems impossibly difficult, and from where I sit, it is. However, they built up their skills bit by bit to get where they are. What we don't see when they get to television are the hundreds, even thousands, of times they missed the shot, fell on the ice, or plopped down flat on the mat. For them, this amazing performance is easy. If it were not, they could not do it. This is part of what Lati Rinpoche meant when he said, "There is no phenomenon that cannot be understood. There is no doctrine that if studied well, cannot be learned, and there is no person who, if he or she studies well, cannot become wise."[4]

HIS HOLINESS THE DALAI LAMA WITH THE AUTHOR,
DHARAMSALA, INDIA, DECEMBER 1984

As the Dalai Lama said about the need for analysis, "An analytical attitude is important at the beginning, middle, and even the end of the spiritual path, since for wisdom to fully mature in Buddhahood you need from the outset to enthusiastically investigate the nature of things and to develop this attitude more and more" (*Becoming Enlightened,* translated and edited by Jeffrey Hopkins [New York: Atria Books, 2009], 27).

Photograph by Sue L. Carrington

Appendix: Table of Definitions

MOST OF THE definitions are arranged according to the outline of the selfless in chapter 9, "Basic Buddhist Ontology 1," and the list of the divisions of functioning things in chapter 10, "Basic Buddhist Ontology 2." So, the order is: the selfless, existents and the phenomena MI with existents, permanent phenomena and the phenomena MI with permanent phenomena, impermanent phenomena and the phenomena MI with impermanent phenomena, and the divisions and examples of functioning things. In addition to these are the definitions associated with the syllogism, the definitions associated with definitions and definienda, and the definitions associated with one and different.

THE SELFLESS	
selfless	that which is without a self
EXISTENTS AND THE PHENOMENA MI WITH EXISTENTS	
existent	that which is observed by a valid cognizer
established base	that which is established by a valid cognizer
object of comprehension	that which is realized by a valid cognizer
object	that which is known by an awareness
object of knowledge	that which is suitable as an object of an awareness

object of comprehension of an omniscient consciousness	an object realized by an omniscient consciousness
hidden phenomenon	an object realized in a hidden manner by a thought consciousness apprehending it
phenomenon	that which holds its own entity
PERMANENT PHENOMENA AND THE PHENOMENA MI WITH PERMANENT PHENOMENA	
permanent phenomenon	a common locus of a phenomenon and the nonmomentary
phenomenon that is a nonthing	a phenomenon that is empty of the ability to perform a function
nonproduced phenomenon	a noncreated phenomenon
uncomposed phenomenon	a nondisintegrating phenomenon
conventional truth	a phenomenon that is ultimately unable to perform a function
generally characterized phenomenon	a phenomenon that is merely imputed by a term or thought consciousness and is not established as a specifically characterized phenomenon
IMPERMANENT PHENOMENA AND THE PHENOMENA MI WITH IMPERMANENT PHENOMENA	
impermanent phenomenon	a momentary phenomenon
functioning thing	that which is able to perform a function
product	a created phenomenon
cause	a producer
effect	an object produced
composed phenomenon	a disintegrating phenomenon

ultimate truth	a phenomenon that is ultimately able to perform a function
specifically characterized phenomenon	a phenomenon that is established by way of its own character without being merely imputed by a term or a thought consciousness
manifest phenomenon	an object explicitly realized by a direct valid cognizer

THE DIVISIONS AND EXAMPLES OF FUNCTIONING THINGS	
matter	that which is atomically established
form	that which is suitable as form
external matter	that which is atomically established and is not included within the continuum of a person
form-source or a visible form	an object apprehended by an eye consciousness
color	that which is suitable as a hue
primary colors	that which is suitable as a primary hue
secondary colors	that which is suitable as a secondary hue
red	that which is suitable as a red hue
shape	that which is suitable to be shown as a shape
sound	an object of hearing
sound-source	an object of hearing of an ear consciousness
odor-source	an object experienced by a nose consciousness
taste-source	an object experienced by a tongue consciousness

tangible object	an object experienced by a body consciousness or an object felt by a body consciousness
earth	that which is hard and obstructive
water	that which is wet and moistening
fire	that which is hot and burning
wind	that which is light and moving
pot	a bulbous, flat-based phenomenon able to perform the function of holding water
internal matter	that which is atomically established and is included within the continuum of a person
eye sense power	a clear internal form that is the uncommon empowering condition for its own effect, an eye consciousness
ear sense power	a clear internal form that is the uncommon empowering condition for its own effect, an ear consciousness
nose sense power	a clear internal form that is the uncommon empowering condition for its own effect, a nose consciousness
tongue sense power	a clear internal form that is the uncommon empowering condition of its own effect, a tongue consciousness
body sense power	a clear internal form that is the uncommon empowering condition of its own effect, a body consciousness
consciousness	that which is clear and knowing

sense consciousness	a knower that is produced in dependence on its own uncommon empowering condition, a physical sense power
eye consciousness	a knower that is produced in dependence on its own uncommon empowering condition, the eye sense power, and an observed-object-condition, a visible form
ear consciousness	a knower that is produced in dependence on its own uncommon empowering condition, the ear sense power, and an observed-object-condition, a sound
nose consciousness	a knower that is produced in dependence on its own uncommon empowering condition, the nose sense power, and an observed-object-condition, an odor
tongue consciousness	a knower that is produced in dependence on its own uncommon empowering condition, the tongue sense power, and an observed-object-condition, a taste
body consciousness	a knower that is produced in dependence on its own uncommon empowering condition, a body sense power, and an observed-object-condition, a tangible object
mental consciousness	a knower that is produced in dependence on its own uncommon empowering condition, a mental sense power
conceptual consciousness	a determinative knower that apprehends a sound-generality and a meaning-generality as suitable to be mixed

meaning-generality of a table [Note: *not* a functioning thing]	that superimposed factor that appears like a table to the thought consciousness apprehending table, although it is not a table
mistaken consciousness	a knower that is mistaken with regard to its appearing object
wrong consciousness	a knower that is mistaken with regard to its object of engagement
uncertain consciousness/doubt	a knower that has qualms with regard to its own object
correctly assuming consciousness	a knower that does not get at an object with respect to which superimpositions have been eliminated, although it adheres one-pointedly to the phenomenon that is its principal object of engagement
inferential cognizer/inferential cognition	a determinative knower that, depending on its basis, a correct sign, is incontrovertible with regard to its object of comprehension, a hidden phenomenon
direct perceiver/direct perception	a nonmistaken knower that is free from conceptuality
valid cognizer	a new incontrovertible knower or a knower that is incontrovertible with regard to its main object
nonassociated compositional factor	a functioning thing that is neither a form nor a consciousness
person	a being who is imputed in dependence upon any of the five aggregates
bear	a being who is imputed in dependence upon any of the five aggregates of a bear

DEFINITIONS ASSOCIATED WITH THE BUDDHIST SYLLOGISM	
reason	that which is stated as a reason
correct sign	that which is the three modes
correct sign in the proof of sound as an impermanent phenomenon by the sign, product	that which is the three modes in the proof of sound as an impermanent phenomenon by the sign, product
something's being the property of the subject in the proof of sound as an impermanent phenomenon	that which is ascertained (by a person for whom it has become the property of the subject in the proof of sound as an impermanent phenomenon) as only existing, in accordance with the mode of statement, with sound
similar class in the proof of sound as an impermanent phenomenon	that which is not empty of impermanence, in accordance with the mode of proof, in the proof of sound as an impermanent phenomenon
something's being the forward pervasion in the proof of sound as an impermanent phenomenon	that which is ascertained (by a person for whom it has become the second mode of the sign in the proof of sound as an impermanent phenomenon) as existing exclusively in the similar class in the proof of sound as an impermanent phenomenon
dissimilar class in the proof of sound as an impermanent phenomenon	that which is empty of impermanence, in accordance with the mode of proof, in the proof of sound as an impermanent phenomenon
something's being the counterpervasion in the proof of sound as an impermanent phenomenon	that which is ascertained (by a person for whom it has become the third mode of the sign in the proof of sound as an impermanent phenomenon) as universally absent in the dissimilar class in the proof of sound as an impermanent phenomenon

DEFINITIONS ASSOCIATED WITH DEFINITIONS AND DEFINIENDA	
definition	that which is a triply qualified substantial existent
definition of a functioning thing	the triply qualified substantial existent of functioning thing
definiendum	that which is a triply qualified imputed existent
definiendum of that which is able to perform a function	the triply qualified imputed existent of that which is able to perform a function
illustration	that which serves as a basis for illustrating the appropriate definiendum by way of [its] definition
illustration of color	that which serves as a basis for illustrating color by way of [being] suitable as a hue
DEFINITIONS ASSOCIATED WITH ONE AND DIFFERENT	
one/singular phenomenon	a phenomenon that is not diverse
one-with-(functioning thing)	a phenomenon that is not diverse from functioning thing
different/different phenomena	phenomena that are diverse
different-from-(functioning thing)	a phenomenon that is diverse from functioning thing

NOTES

PREFACE

1. Daniel E. Perdue, *Debate in Tibetan Buddhism* (Ithaca, N.Y.: Snow Lion Publications, 1992).
2. Ibid., 99.

CHAPTER 1: INTRODUCTION

1. This translation is drawn from *The Way of Lao Tzu (Tao-te ching)*, translated with introductory essays, comments, and notes by Wing-tsit Chan, The Library of Liberal Arts (Indianapolis: The Bobbs-Merrill Company, Inc., 1963), 97.
2. Perdue, *Debate in Tibetan Buddhism*; Lati Rinbochay, *Mind in Tibetan Buddhism*, trans. Elizabeth Napper (Valois, N.Y.: Gabriel/Snow Lion, 1980); Katherine Manchester Rogers, *Tibetan Logic* (Ithaca, N.Y.: Snow Lion Publications, 2009).

CHAPTER 3: REASONING WITHIN THE BUDDHIST CONTEXT

1. *Katha Upanishad* 4.1–2, in *World Scripture: A Comparative Anthology of Sacred Texts*, ed. Andrew Wilson (New York: Paragon House, 1991), 679.
2. In John Barlett, *Bartlett's Familiar Quotations*, 16th ed., ed. Justin Kaplan (Boston: Little, Brown and Company, 1992), 479.
3. Lama Thubten Yeshe, oral commentary in his last verbal teaching, at Kopan Monastery, Nepal, 1983. Lama Yeshe Archive 395, provided by Dr. Nicholas Ribush, Lama Yeshe Wisdom Archive.
4. Chökyi Nyima Rinpoche, oral commentary.
5. Kensur Yeshi Thupten, oral commentary.
6. This is from the *Descent into Laṅkā Sūtra*. See, for instance, D. T. Suzuki, *The Lankavatara Sutra* (London: Routledge, 1932). The translation quoted here is drawn from Geshe Lhundup Sopa and Jeffrey Hopkins, *Cutting Through Appearances: Practice and Theory of Tibetan Buddhism* (Ithaca, N.Y.: Snow Lion Publications, 1989), 149.
7. The dates for Dignāga and Dharmakīrti are from Masaaki Hattori, *Dignāga, On Perception, being the Pratyakṣapariccheda of Dignāga's "Pramāṇasamuccaya" from the Sanskrit Fragments and the Tibetan Versions* (Cambridge, Mass.:

Harvard University Press, 1968), 4 and 14, who in turn takes these dates from E. Frauwallner.

8. The dates for Vasubandhu are taken from Stefan Anacker, "Vasubandhu: Three Aspects" (PhD diss., University of Wisconsin, 1970), 30.

CHAPTER 4: THE COMPARISON OF PHENOMENA

1. Ludwig Wittgenstein, *Philosophical Investigations*, trans. G. E. M. Anscombe, the German text with a revised English translation, 3rd ed. (Malden, Mass.: Blackwell Publishing, 2001), aphorism 43.

2. See, for instance, Perdue, *Debate in Tibetan Buddhism*, 139.

CHAPTER 5: TWO KINDS OF STATEMENTS

1. The system of classification used in this section is drawn from John Stuart Mill, *A System of Logic, Ratiocinative and Inductive* (New York: Harper and Brothers, 1874), especially the section on names and propositions, 32–34.

2. "It Ain't Necessarily So" from the opera *Porgy and Bess* (1935), music by George Gershwin, lyrics by Ira Gershwin.

CHAPTER 6: THE BUDDHIST SYLLOGISM

1. See Hopkins, *Meditation on Emptiness*, 729–33.

2. Mi-nyak Ge-shay Tsul-trim-nam-gyel (Mi nyag dge bshes tshul khrims rnam rgyal), *rTags rigs kyi rnam bzhag chos kun gsal ba'i me long* [The presentation of signs and reasonings, a mirror illuminating all phenomena], in *Rigs lam sgo brgya 'byed pa'i 'phrul gyi lde mig dang po* [The first magic key opening a hundred doors to the path of reasoning] (Mundgod, India: Drepung Loseling Library, 1979), 32–33.

3. Ibid., 36.

4. Ibid.

5. Ibid.

6. Ibid.

7. See Rogers, *Tibetan Logic*, 43 ff.

8. See Mi-nyak Ge-shay Tsul-trim-nam-gyel, *rTags rigs kyi rnam bzhag chos kun gsal ba'i me long*, 36–38.

9. Ibid., 33.

10. Ibid., 38.

11. Ibid., 38–40.

12. Ibid., 33–34.

13. Ibid., 40.

14. Ibid., 40–41.

15. Den-dar-hla-ram-ba (bsTan dar lha ram pa), *Phyogs glang gis mdzad pa'i phyogs chos 'khor lo zhes pa'i bstan bcos gsal bar byed pa'i rin chen sgron me* [Precious lamp illuminating the treatise "Wheel of properties of the subject" formulated

by Dignāga], in *Collected Works of Bstan-dar Lha-ram of A-lag-sha,* vol. 1. (New Delhi: Lama Guru Deva, 1971), 143.5–6.

16. For information on validity and soundness of arguments in Western logic, see, for instance, Benson Mates, *Elementary Logic* (New York: Oxford University Press, 1972), 5ff.

CHAPTER 8: THREE TYPES OF CORRECT SIGNS

1. Kensur Jambel Shenpen, oral commentary.
2. Rogers, *Tibetan Logic,* 155.
3. Dilgo Khyentse Rinpoche, oral commentary.
4. See Rogers, *Tibetan Logic,* 197.
5. Ibid.
6. Ibid., 217.

CHAPTER 9: BASIC BUDDHIST ONTOLOGY 1

1. Lati Rinpoche, oral commentary.
2. Ibid.
3. Hopkins, *Meditation on Emptiness,* 217.
4. Ibid.
5. Ibid., 218.
6. Lati Rinpoche, *Mind in Tibetan Buddhism,* 47.
7. Denma Lochö Rinpoche, oral commentary.
8. Ngak-wang-dra-shi, *sGo mang bsdus grva* [Go-mang collected topics], 396.

CHAPTER 10: BASIC BUDDHIST ONTOLOGY 2

1. Some of the examples in this list are from Gen-dün-drup-ba, *Dam pa'i chos mngon pa'i mdzod kyi rnam par bshad pa thar lam gsal byed,* 29–30 and some are from Hopkins, *Meditation on Emptiness,* 227.
2. The definition is from Pur-bu-jok Jam-ba-gya-tso, *Rigs lam chung ngu* [The introductory path of reasoning] in *Tshad ma'i gzhung don 'byed pa'i bsdus grva'i rnam bzhag rigs lam 'phrul gyi lde mig* [The presentation of collected topics revealing the meaning of the texts on valid cognition, the magical key to the path of reasoning] (Buxa, India: n.p., 1965), 4b.6. *Rigs lam chung ngu* [The introductory path of reasoning] is wholly translated into English in Perdue, *Debate in Tibetan Buddhism.*
3. The division is from Ngak-wang-dra-shi, *sGo mang bsdus grva,* 14.
4. Lati Rinpoche, oral commentary.
5. Kensur Yeshi Thupten, oral commentary.
6. Ibid.
7. Hopkins, *Meditation on Emptiness,* 234.
8. The source for this section on the definitions of an awareness and a consciousness is Losang Gyatso, *Rigs lam che ba blo rigs kyi rnam gshag nye mkho kun btus*

[Compendium of the important points in the presentation of types of awarenesses: An internal division of the greater path of reasoning] (Dharamsala, India: Shes rig par khang, 1974), 4b.1–8a.6.

9. Lati Rinpoche, *Mind in Tibetan Buddhism,* 46.

10. Losang Gyatso, *Rigs lam che ba blo rigs kyi rnam gshag nye mkho kun btus* [Compendium of the important points in the discussion of types of awarenesses], 5b.2–3.

11. The Dalai Lama, "Spiritual Contributions to Social Progress," *Wall Street Journal,* October 29, 1981.

12. Hopkins, *Meditation on Emptiness,* 268.

13. Ibid.

14. Ibid., 268–69.

15. Geshé Rabten, *The Life and Teaching of Geshé Rabten: A Tibetan Lama's Search for Truth,* trans. and ed. B. Alan Wallace (London: George Allen and Unwin, 1980), 18.

16. Vasubandhu, *Abhidharmakośhakārikā* (*Chos mngon pa'i mdzod kyi bshad pa*) [Treasury of knowledge], P5590, vol. 115, 118.3.6.

17. Lati Rinpoche, oral commentary.

18. Ibid.

19. Ibid.

20. Hopkins, *Meditation on Emptiness,* 271.

21. William James, *The Principles of Psychology* (1890; repr., Cambridge, Mass.: Harvard University Press, 1981), 462.

22. The Venerable Mahasi Sayadaw, *The Progress of Insight through the Stages of Purification,* trans. Nyānaponika Thera (Kandy, Sri Lanka: Buddhist Publication Society, 1978), 7.

23. Ibid.

CHAPTER 11: THE PARADIGMS FOR PROVING A COMPARISON OF PHENOMENA

1. Charles Sanders Peirce, *Collected Papers,* vol. 5, *Pragmatism and Pragmaticism* (Cambridge, Mass.: Belknap Press of Harvard, 1935), paragraph 211.

CHAPTER 12: CONSCIOUSNESSES IN RELATION TO WHAT THEY PERCEIVE

1. Charles Sanders Peirce, *Collected Papers,* vol. 7, *Experimental Science, Scientific Method, and Philosophy of Mind* (Cambridge, Mass.: Belknap Press of Harvard, 1935), paragraph 547.

2. Lati Rinbochay, *Mind in Tibetan Buddhism,* 130.

3. Ibid., 50.

4. Ibid., 50–51.

5. Ibid., 130.

6. Ibid., 49.

7. Ibid., 18.
8. Ibid.
9. Ibid.
10. Ibid., 54–74.
11. Ibid., 18.
12. Ibid., 28. For sources of some of the Sanskrit terms given in *Mind in Tibetan Buddhism* and subsequently used in this book, see Lati Rinbochay, *Mind in Tibetan Buddhism*, 163n24.
13. Ibid., 112.
14. Ibid., 30.
15. See Perdue, *Debate in Tibetan Buddhism*, 382–86.
16. Tsong-ka-pa, *Tantra in Tibet*, 192.
17. This definition follows the Ra-dö *Awareness and Knowledge* and is quoted in Lati Rinbochay, *Mind in Tibetan Buddhism*, 106.
18. Lati Rinbochay, *Mind in Tibetan Buddhism*, 108.
19. Ibid., 92.
20. Ibid., 132.
21. Ibid., 91.
22. This definition is from Jam-yang-shay-ba. See Lati Rinbochay, *Mind in Tibetan Buddhism*, 96.
23. This list of three types and the illustrations are adapted from Lati Rinbochay, *Mind in Tibetan Buddhism*, 97.
24. Ibid., 75.
25. Ibid., 91.
26. Ibid., 49.
27. Ibid., 54–55.
28. Ibid., 61–65.
29. Ibid., 64.

CHAPTER 13: VALID COGNITION

1. Lati Rinbochay, *Mind in Tibetan Buddhism*, 118.
2. Dharmakīrti, *Pramāṇavarttikakārikā* (*Tshad ma rnam 'grel gyi tshig le'ur byas pa*) [Commentary on (Dignāga's) "Compilation of valid cognition"], P5709, vol. 130, 88.3.4.
3. This example is adapted from Lati Rinbochay, *Mind in Tibetan Buddhism*, 120.
4. Ibid.
5. Ibid., 117.

CHAPTER 15: CHOOSING YOUR DEBATE PARTNER

1. Thupten Jinpa Langri, oral commentary.
2. Ludwig Wittgenstein, *The Blue and Brown Books* (New York: Harper and Row, 1958), 4.
3. Thomas Jefferson, letter to William Roscoe, December 27, 1820.

4. John Powers, *Introduction to Tibetan Buddhism,* rev. ed. (Ithaca, N.Y.: Snow Lion Publications, 2007), 149.

CHAPTER 16: CHALLENGERS AND DEFENDERS

1. Thupten Jinpa Langri, oral commentary.
2. Georges Dreyfus, "Georges Dreyfus: Cross-cultural Explorer: An Interview with Leah Zahler," *University of Virginia CSAS Newsletter,* Spring 1992, 5, 14.
3. Ibid.
4. Ibid.
5. Kensur Yeshi Thupten, oral commentary.
6. Lati Rinpoche, oral commentary.
7. K. Sierksma, "Rtsod-pa: The Monachal Disputation in Tibet," *Indo-Iranian Journal* 8, no. 2 (1964): 141.
8. Georges Dreyfus, "Georges Dreyfus," 5.
9. Attributed to Josh Billings (1818–85), American humorist.

CHAPTER 17: THE CLAP!

1. Lati Rinpoche, oral commentary.
2. Geshé Rabten, *The Life and Teaching of Geshé Rabten,* 40–41.
3. Denma Lochö Rinpoche, oral commentary.
4. Lati Rinbochay, oral commentary.
5. Ibid.

CHAPTER 18: MAÑJUŚRĪ, THE SPECIAL DEITY OF DEBATE

1. Denma Lochö Rinpoche, oral commentary.
2. Prayer to Mañjuśrī.
3. Lati Rinpoche, *Mind in Tibetan Buddhism,* 44.
4. Denma Lochö Rinpoche, oral commentary.
5. Lati Rinpoche, oral commentary, translated by Joe Wilson, Jr.
6. Tsong-ka-pa, *Tantra in Tibet,* 27.
7. Ibid., 24.
8. Lati Rinpoche, oral commentary.
9. His Holiness the Fourteenth Dalai Lama Tenzin Gyatso, *Kindness, Clarity, and Insight,* trans. and ed. Jeffrey Hopkins, co-ed. Elizabeth Napper (Ithaca, N.Y.: Snow Lion Publications, 1984), 116.
10. Sir Monier Monier-Williams, *A Sanskrit-English Dictionary,* new ed. (Delhi: Motilal Banarsidass, 1976), 87.
11. Kalu Rinpoche, oral commentary.
12. Denma Lochö Rinpoche, oral commentary.

CHAPTER 19: THE THREE PURPOSES OF DEBATE

1. Geshe Lobsang Tharchin, oral commentary, translated by Artemus B. Engle.
2. Lati Rinpoche, oral commentary.

3. Geshé Rabten, *The Life and Teaching of Geshé Rabten*, 14.
4. Geshe Lobsang Tharchin, oral commentary, translated by Artemus B. Engle.
5. Tenzin Gyatso, *The Buddhism of Tibet and The Key to the Middle Way*, trans. Jeffrey Hopkins and Lati Rimpoche, The Wisdom of Tibet 1 (New York: Harper and Row, Publishers, 1975), 56–57.

CHAPTER 20: DEFINITIONS, DIVISIONS, AND ILLUSTRATIONS

1. Lati Rinpoche, oral commentary.
2. Ibid.
3. Pur-bu-jok Jam-ba-gya-tso, *Rigs lam 'bring* [The middling path of reasoning] in *Tshad ma'i gzhung don 'byed pa'i bsdus grva'i rnam bzhag rigs lam 'phrul gyi lde mig*, 9b.2–3.
4. Ibid., 9b.1.
5. Ibid., 10a.1.
6. Denma Lochö Rinpoche, oral commentary.

CHAPTER 21: ONE AND DIFFERENT

1. Denma Lochö Rinpoche, oral commentary.

CHAPTER 22: CONSEQUENCES

1. Denma Lochö Rinpoche, oral commentary.

CHAPTER 23: PROCEDURES IN DEBATE

1. Georges Dreyfus, "Georges Dreyfus," 5.
2. Denma Lochö Rinpoche, oral commentary.
3. Thupten Jinpa Langri, oral commentary.
4. Rogers, *Tibetan Logic*, 202–3.
5. Ibid., 203n.
6. Georges Dreyfus, "Georges Dreyfus," 5.
7. Ibid.
8. From the beginning of debate A.1, which is laid out in Perdue, *Debate in Tibetan Buddhism*, especially 99–131.
9. See Lati Rinbochay, *Mind in Tibetan Buddhism*, 53.

CHAPTER 25: BRINGING IT ALL TOGETHER

1. Lati Rinbochay, *Mind in Tibetan Buddhism*, 50.

CHAPTER 27: CONCLUSIONS AND REMARKS

1. Lati Rinpoche, oral commentary.
2. His Holiness the Dalai Lama, oral commentary, Emory University, October 2010, translated by Thupten Jinpa Langri.
3. Geshe Lobsang Tharchin, oral commentary, translated by Artemus B. Engle.
4. Lati Rinpoche, oral commentary.

Glossary

Sanskrit terms marked with an asterisk are reconstructions from the Tibetan and may not have occurred in Sanskrit literature.

English	Tibetan	Sanskrit
affliction	nyon mongs	kleśha
aggregate	phung po	skandha
animal	dud 'gro	tiryañch
appearance factor	snang ngor	
appearing object	snang yul	*pratibhāsa-viṣhaya
appearing object of a direct perceiver	mngon sum gyi snang yul	
appearing object of a thought consciousness	rtog pa'i snang yul	
apprehended object	bzung yul	grāhya-viṣhaya
ascertainment factor	nges ngor	
ascertainment factor of a direct perceiver	mngon sum gyi nges ngor	
awareness	blo	buddhi
being	yin pa	
being/person	skyes bu	
body consciousness	lus shes	kāya-jñāna

English	Tibetan	Sanskrit
body sense power	lus kyi dbang po	kāya-indriya
boundaries of pervasion	khyab mtha'	
cause	rgyu	hetu/kāraṇa
Challenger	rigs lam pa	
clarification/point of clarification	gsal ba	
clear form	gzugs dvang pa	rūpa-prasāda
coarse impermanence	rags pa'i mi rtag pa	*sthūla-anitya
Collected Topics	bsdus grva	
color	kha dog	varṇa
common being	so so'i skye bo	pṛthak-jana
common locus	gzhi mthun pa	samāna-adhikaraṇa
composed phenomenon	'dus byas	saṃskṛta
compositional factor	'du byed	saṃskāra
consciousness	shes pa	jñāna/vijñāna
consciousness mistaken with regard to its appearing object	'khrul shes	bhrānti-jñāna
consequence/contradictory consequence	thal 'gyur	prasaṅga
contradictory reason	'gal ba'i gtan tshigs	viruddha-hetu
conventional truth	kun rdzob bden ba	saṃvṛti-satya
correct consequence	thal 'gyur yang dag	samyak-prasaṅga
correct sign/correct logical sign	rtags yang dag	*samyak-liṅga
correctly assuming consciousness	yid dpyod	*manaḥ-parīkṣa

English	Tibetan	Sanskrit
counterpervasion	ldog khyab	vyatireka-vyāpti
debating courtyard	chos ra	
Defender	dam bca' ba	
definiendum	mtshon bya	lakṣhya
definition	mtshan nyid	lakṣhana
deity	hla	deva
demigod	lha ma yin	asura
determinative knower	zhen rig	*adhyavasāya-saṃvedana
different/different phenomena/difference	tha dad	nānātva
different-from-pot	bum pa dang tha dad	
direct perceiver/direct perception	mngon sum	pratyakṣha
discrimination	'du shes	samjñā
dispelling objections	rtsod pa spong ba	
dissimilar class	mi mthun phyogs	vipakṣha
division from the point of view of the name	sgras brjod rigs kyi sgo nas dbye ba	
ear consciousness	rna shes	śhrotra-jñāna
ear sense power	rna ba'i dbang po	śhrotra-indriya
effect	'bras bu	phala
element	'byung ba	bhūta
emptiness	stong pa nyid	śhūnyatā
equivocating uncertain consciousness	cha mnyam pa'i the tshom	
established base	gzhi grub	*vastu-siddha

English	Tibetan	Sanskrit
existent/existence	yod pa	sat
external matter	phyi'i bem po	bahirdhā-kanthā
eye consciousness	mig shes	*chakṣhur-jñāna
eye sense power	mig gi dbang po	chakṣhur-indriya
form/visible form	gzugs	rūpa
forward pervasion	rjes khyab	anvaya-vyāpti
four possibilities	mu bzhi	
functioning thing/thing	dngos po	bhāva
ge-shay	dge bshes	kalyāna-mitra
generally characterized phenomenon	spyi mtshan	sāmānya-lakṣhaṇa
hell-being	dmyal ba	nāraka
hidden phenomenon	lkog gyur	parokṣha
horn of a rabbit	ri bong rva	
human	mi	manuṣhya
hungry ghost	yi dvags	preta
ignorance	ma rig pa	avidyā
illustration	mtshan gzhi	
impermanent phenomenon	mi rtag pa	anitya
imputed existent	btags yod	prajñapti-sat
incontrovertible	mi slu ba	avisaṃvādin
inferential cognizer/ inferential cognition	rjes dpag	anumāna
internal matter	nang gi bem po	ādhyātmika-kanthā

English	Tibetan	Sanskrit
knower	rig pa	saṃvedana
lack of being a permanent, unitary, independent self	rtag gcig rang dbang can bdag gis stong pa	
lama	bla ma	guru
limits of pervasion	khyab mtha'	
manifest phenomenon	mngon gyur	abhimukhī
matter	bem po	kanthā
meaning	don	artha
meaning-generality	don spyi	artha-sāmānya
meditating	sgom pa	bhāvana
mental consciousness	yid shes	mano-jñāna
mental direct perceiver	yid kyi mngon sum	mānasa-pratyakṣa
momentary	skad cig ma	kṣhanika
mutually different	phan tshun tha dad	
mutually exclusive/ mutually exclusive phenomena	'gal ba	virodha
mutually inclusive/ mutually inclusive phenomena	don gcig	ekārtha
non-	ma yin pa	
nonassociated compositional factor	ldan min 'du byed	viprayukta-saṃskāra
nonassociated compositional factor that is a person	gang zag yin par gyur pa'i ldan min 'du byed	pudgala-viprayukta-saṃskāra

English	Tibetan	Sanskrit
nonassociated compositional factor that is not a person	gang zag ma yin par gyur pa'i ldan min 'du byed	apudgala-viprayukta-saṃskāra
nonconceptual consciousness	rtog med kyi shes pa	nirvikalpaka-jñāna
nonconceptual mental consciousness	rtog med yid shes	nirvikalpaka-mano-jñāna
non-existent	med pa	asat
nonmistaken	ma 'khrul pa	abhrānta
nonproduct	ma byas pa	akṛta
non-(functioning thing)/nonthing	dngos med	abhāva
nose consciousness	sna shes	ghrāṇa-jñāna
nose sense power	sna'i dbang po	ghrāṇa-indriya
object	yul	viṣhaya
object of comprehension	gzhal bya	prameya
object of comprehension of an omniscient consciousness	rnam mkhyen gyi gzhal bya	sarvākārā-jñāna-prameya
object of engagement	'jug yul	*pravṛtti-viṣhaya
object of hearing	nyan bya	
object of knowledge	shes bya	jñeya
observed by valid cognition	tshad mas dmigs pa	*pramāṇa-ālaṃbīta
observed-object-condition	dmigs rkyen	ālambana-pratyaya
odor	dri	gandha
odor-source	dri'i skye mched	gandha-āyatana

English	Tibetan	Sanskrit
one/singular phenomenon	gcig	ekatva
one-with-pot	bum pa dang gcig	
only-a-permanent-phenomenon	rtag pa kho na	
our own system	rang lugs	
path	lam	mārga
path of reasoning	rigs lam	
permanent phenomenon	rtag pa	nitya
permanent phenomenon that exists for an occasion	res 'ga' ba'i rtag pa	
permanent phenomenon that is stable in time	dus brtan pa'i rtag pa	
person	gang zag	pudgala/puruṣha
pervaded	khyab bya	
pervader	khyab byed	
pervasion	khyab pa	vyāpti
pervasion of being	yin khyab	
pervasion of existence	yod khyab	
phenomenon	chos	dharma
phenomenon that is a non-(functioning thing)/phenomenon that is a nonthing	dngos med kyi chos	abhāva-dharma
pot	bum pa	ghaṭa/kumbha

English	Tibetan	Sanskrit
predicate	bsgrub bya'i chos/gsal ba	
predicate to be negated	dgag bya'i chos	*pratiṣhedhya-dharma
predicate to be proven	bsgrub bya'i chos	sādhya-dharma
presentation of our own system	rang lugs bzhag pa	
produced	bskyed bya	janya
producer	skyed byed	janaka
product/produced phenomenon	byas pa	kṛta
property of the subject	phyogs chos	pakṣha-dharma
proven	bsgrub bya	
reason	gtan tshigs	hetu
refutation of mistaken views	'khrul ba dgag pa	
refutation of others' systems	gzhan lugs dgag pa	
religious conch	chos dung	
same entity	ngo bo gcig pa	eka-rūpatā
self	bdag	ātman
selfless	bdag med	nairātmya
sense consciousness	dbang shes	indriya-jñāna
sense direct perceiver	dbang po'i mngon sum	indriya-pratyakṣha
sense power	dbang po	indriya
shape	dbyibs	saṃsthāna
sign/reason	rtags	liṅga
similar class	mthun phyogs	sapakṣha

English	Tibetan	Sanskrit
sound	sgra	śhabda
specifically character-ized phenomenon	rang mtshan	svalakṣaṇa
subject/logical subject	chos can	dharmin
substantial existent/sub-stantially existent	rdzas yod/rdzas su yod pa	dravya-sat
subtle impermanence	phra ba'i mi rtag pa	*sūkṣhma-anitya
Superior	'phags pa	ārya
syllogism	sbyor ba	prayoga
tangible object	reg bya	spraṣhṭavya
taste	ro	rasa
tenets	grub mtha'	siddhānta
that which is able to perform a function	don byed nus pa	artha-kriyā- śhakti/ artha-kriyā-sāmarthya
that which is to be negated	dgag bya	pratiṣhedhya
that which is to be proven	bsgrub bya	sādhya
thesis	dam bca'	pratijñā
thinking	bsam pa	chintā
thought/thought con-sciousness/conceptual consciousness	rtog pa	kalpanā
three modes	tshul gsum	
three possibilities	mu gsum	
tongue consciousness	lce shes	jihvā-jñāna
tongue sense power	lce'i dbang po	jihvā-indriya

English	Tibetan	Sanskrit
ultimate truth	don dam bden pa	paramārtha-satya
uncertain consciousness/doubt	the tshom	
uncertain consciousness leaning toward believing something that is factual	don 'gyur gyi the tshom	
uncertain consciousness leaning toward believing something that is not factual	don mi 'gyur gyi the tshom	
uncommon empowering condition	thun mong ma yin pa'i bdag rkyen	asādhārana-adhipati-pratyaya
uncomposed phenomenon	'dus ma byas kyi chos	asaṃskṛta-dharma
uncomposed space	'dus ma byas kyi nam mkha'	asaṃskṛta-akaśha
unwanted consequence	mi 'dod pa'i thal 'gyur	
valid cognition/valid cognizer	tshad ma	pramāṇa
wisdom	shes rab	prajñā
wrong consciousness	log shes	viparyaya-jñāna
yogic direct perceiver/yogic direct perception	rnal 'byor mngon sum	yogi-pratyakṣha

Bibliography

Note: The abbreviation P is used for citations in *Tibetan Tripiṭaka*, Tokyo-Kyoto: Tibetan Tripitaka Research Foundation, 1956.

Abe, Masao. *Zen and Comparative Studies*. Edited by Steven Heine. Honolulu: University of Hawai'i Press, 1997.

Anacker, Stefan. "Vasubandhu: Three Aspects." PhD diss., University of Wisconsin, 1970.

Bartlett, John, *Bartlett's Familiar Quotations*. 16th ed. Edited by Justin Kaplan. Boston: Little, Brown and Company, 1992.

Bel-den-chö-jay (dPal ldan chos rje). *Grub mtha' bzhi'i lugs kyi kun rdzob dang don dam pa'i don rnam par bshad pa* [Explanation of the meaning of conventional and ultimate in the four tenet systems]. New Delhi: Lama Guru Deva, 1972.

Buddhaghosa, Bhadantācariya. *The Path of Purification (Visuddhimagga)*. Translated from the Pāli by Bhikkhu Ñyāṇamoli. Berkeley: Shambhala Publications, 1976.

Den-dar-hla-ram-ba (bsTan dar lha ram pa). *Phyogs glang gis mdzad pa'i phyogs chos 'khor lo zhes pa'i bstan bcos gsal bar byed pa'i rin chen sgron me* [Precious lamp illuminating the treatise "Wheel of properties of the subject" formulated by Dignāga]. In *Collected Works of Bstan-dar Lha-ram of A-lag-sha*. Vol. 1. New Delhi: Lama Guru Deva, 1971.

———. *Rang mtshan spyi mtshan gyi rnam bzhag rtsom phrol* [Beginnings of a presentation of generally and specifically characterized phenomena]. In *Collected Works of Bstan-dar Lha-ram of A-lag-sha*. Vol. 1. New Delhi: Lama Guru Deva, 1971.

Dharmakīrti (Chos kyi grags pa). *Hetubindunāmaprakaraṇa (gTan tshigs kyi thigs pa zhes bya ba'i rab tu byed pa)* [Drop of reasons]. P5712, vol. 130.

———. *Nyāyabinduprakaraṇa (Rigs pa'i thigs pa zhes bya ba'i rab tu byed pa)* [Drop of reasoning]. P5711, vol. 130.

———. *Pramāṇavarttikakārikā (Tshad ma rnam 'grel gyi tshig le'ur byas pa)* [Commentary on (Dignāga's) "Compilation of valid cognition"]. P5709, vol. 130.

————. *Pramāṇaviniśhchaya* (*Tshad ma rnam par nges pa*) [Ascertainment of valid cognition]. P5710, vol. 130.

————. *Saṃbandhaparīkṣhāvṛtti* (*'Brel pa brtag pa'i rab tu byed pa*) [Analysis of relations]. P5713, vol. 130.

————. *Saṃtānāntarasiddhināmaprakaraṇa* (*rGyud bzhan grub pa zhes bya ba'i rab tu byed pa*) [Proof of other continuums]. P5716, vol. 130.

————. *Vādanyāyanāmaprakaraṇa* (*rTsod pa'i rigs pa zhes bya ba'i rab tu byed pa*) [Reasoning for debate]. P5715, vol. 130.

Dignāga (Phyogs glang). *Pramāṇasamuchchaya* (*Tshad ma kun las btus pa*) [Compilation of valid cognition]. P5700, vol. 130.

Dreyfus, Georges B. *Recognizing Reality: Dharmakirti's Philosophy and Its Tibetan Interpretations.* SUNY Series in Buddhist Studies. Albany: State University of New York Press, 1997.

————. *The Sound of Two Hands Clapping: The Education of a Tibetan Buddhist Monk.* Berkeley: University of California Press, 2003.

Dze-may Rinpoche (Dze smad rin po che). *Shar rtse bsdus grva* [Shar-dzay collected topics]. Mundgod, India: Drepung Loseling Printing Press, n.d.

Gārgyāyana. *The Science of the Sacred Word.* 2 vols. Adyar, Madras, India: The Theosophist office, 1910–.

Gen-dün-drup-ba (dGe 'dun grub pa). *Dam pa'i chos mngon pa'i mdzod kyi rnam par bshad pa thar lam gsal byed* [Commentary on (Vasubandhu's) "Treasury of knowledge," Illuminating the path to liberation]. Sarnath, India: Pleasure of Elegant Sayings Press, 1973.

Gyatso, Tenzin, the Fourteenth Dalai Lama. *The Buddhism of Tibet and The Key to the Middle Way.* Translated by Jeffrey Hopkins and Lati Rimpoche. The Wisdom of Tibet 1. New York: Harper and Row, 1975.

————. *Kindness, Clarity, and Insight.* Translated and edited by Jeffrey Hopkins. Co-edited by Elizabeth Napper. Ithaca, N.Y.: Snow Lion Publications, 1984.

Hattori, Masaaki. *Dignāga, On Perception, being the Pratyakṣapariccheda of Dignāga's "Pramāṇasamuccaya" from the Sanskrit Fragments and the Tibetan Versions.* Cambridge, Mass.: Harvard University Press, 1968.

Hopkins, Jeffrey. *Emptiness in the Mind-Only School of Buddhism.* Berkeley: University of California Press, 1999.

————. *Maps of the Profound: Jam-yang-shay-ba's "Great Exposition of Buddhist and Non-Buddhist Views on the Nature of Reality."* Ithaca, N.Y.: Snow Lion Publications, 2003.

————. *Meditation on Emptiness.* London: Wisdom Publications, 1983.

Jam-bel-trin-lay-yön-dan-gya-tso ('Jam dpal 'phin las yon tan rgya mtsho). *bLo gsal gling bsdus grva* [Lo-sel-ling collected topics]. Mundgod, India: Drepung Loseling Press, 1978.

Jam-yang-chok-hla-ö-ser ('Jam dbyangs phyogs lha 'ad zer). *Rva stod bsdus grva* [Radö collected topics]. Dharamsala, India: Damchoe Sangpo, Library of Tibetan Works and Archives, 1980.

James, William. *The Principles of Psychology.* Cambridge, Mass.: Harvard University Press, 1981. Originally published 1890.

Khetsun Sangbo Rinbochay. *Tantric Practice in Nying-Ma.* Translated and edited by Jeffrey Hopkins. London: Rider, 1982.

Klein, Anne Carolyn. *Knowing, Naming and Negation: A Sourcebook on Tibetan Sautrāntika.* Translations in Indo-Tibetan Buddhism. Ithaca, N.Y.: Snow Lion Publications, 1991.

———. *Knowledge and Liberation: Tibetan Buddhist Epistemology in Support of Transformative Religious Experience.* Ithaca, N.Y.: Snow Lion Publications, 1986.

Lao Tzu. *The Way of Lao Tzu (Tao-te ching).* Translated with introductory essays, comments, and notes by Wing-tsit Chan. The Library of Liberal Arts. Indianapolis: The Bobbs-Merrill Company, Inc., 1963.

Lati Rinbochay. *Mind in Tibetan Buddhism.* Translated, edited, and introduced by Elizabeth Napper. Valois, N.Y.: Gabriel/Snow Lion, 1980.

Lati Rinbochay and Denma Lochö Rinbochay. *Meditative States in Tibetan Buddhism.* Translated by Leah Zahler and Jeffrey Hopkins. London: Wisdom Publications, 1983.

Losang Gyatso (bLo zang rgya mtsho). *Rigs lam che ba blo rigs kyi rnam bzhag nye mkho kun btus* [Compendium of the important points in the presentation of types of awarenesses, an internal division of the greater path of reasoning]. Dharamsala, India: Shes rig par khang, 1974.

Magee, William. *The Nature of Things: Emptiness and Essence in the Geluk World.* Ithaca, N.Y.: Snow Lion Publications, 1999.

Mates, Benson. *Elementary Logic.* New York: Oxford University Press, 1972.

Mill, John Stuart. *A System of Logic, Ratiocinative and Inductive.* New York: Harper and Brothers, 1874.

Mi-nyak Ge-shay Tsül-trim-nam-gyel (Mi nyag dge bshes tshul khrims rnam rgyal). *rTags rigs kyi rnam bzhag chos kun gsal ba'i me long* [The presentation of signs and reasonings, a mirror illuminating all phenomena]. In *Rigs lam sgo brgya 'byed pa'i 'phrul gyi lde mig dang po* [The first magic key opening a hundred doors to the path of reasoning]. Mundgod, India: Drepung Loseling Library, 1979.

Monier-Williams, Sir Monier. *A Sanskrit-English Dictionary.* New ed. Delhi: Motilal Banarsidass, 1976.

Napper, Elizabeth. *Dependent-Arising and Emptiness.* Boston: Wisdom Publications, 1989.

Nemoto, Hiroshi. "The Role of an Opponent in Buddhist Dialectic: The dGe lugs pa School's Concept of *phyi rgol yang dag.*" Paper presented at the 12th Seminar of the International Association of Tibetan Studies, August 18, 2010.

Newland, Guy. *The Two Truths in the Mādhyamika Philosophy of the Ge-luk-ba Order of Tibetan Buddhism.* Studies in Indo-Tibetan Buddhism. Ithaca, N.Y.: Snow Lion Publications, 1992.

Ngak-wang-bel-den (Ngag dbang dpal ldan). See Bel-den-chö-jay.

Ngak-wang-dra-shi (Ngag dbang bkra shis). *sGo mang bsdus grva* [Go-mang collected topics]. n.p., n.d.

Peirce, Charles Sanders. *Collected Papers.* Vol. 5, *Pragmatism and Pragmaticism.* Cambridge. Mass.: Belknap Press of Harvard, 1935.

———. *Collected Papers.* Vol. 7, *Experimental Science, Scientific Method, and Philosophy of Mind.* Cambridge, Mass.: Belknap Press of Harvard, 1935.

Perdue, Daniel E. *Debate in Tibetan Buddhism.* Translations in Indo-Tibetan Buddhism. Ithaca, N.Y.: Snow Lion Publications, 1992.

Powers, John. *Introduction to Tibetan Buddhism.* Rev. ed. Ithaca, N.Y.: Snow Lion Publications, 2007.

Pur-bu-jok Jam-ba-gya-tso (Phur bu lcog byams pa rgya mtsho). *Tshad ma'i gzhung don 'byed pa'i bsdus grva'i rnam bzhag rigs lam 'phrul gyi lde mig* [The presentation of collected topics revealing the meaning of the texts on valid cognition, the magical key to the path of reasoning]. Buxa, India: n.p., 1965.

Rabten, Geshé. *The Life and Teaching of Geshé Rabten: A Tibetan Lama's Search for Truth.* Translated and edited by B. Alan Wallace. London: George Allen and Unwin, 1980.

Rogers, Katherine Manchester. *Tibetan Logic.* Ithaca, N.Y.: Snow Lion Publications, 2009.

Sayadaw, the Venerable Mahasi. *The Progress of Insight through the Stages of Purification.* Translated from the Pāli by Nyānaponika Thera. Kandy, Sri Lanka: Buddhist Publication Society, 1978.

Sierksma, K. "Rtsod-pa: The Monachal Disputation in Tibet." *Indo-Iranian Journal* 8 (1964): 137–49.

Sopa, Geshe Lhundup, and Jeffrey Hopkins. *Cutting through Appearances: Practice and Theory of Tibetan Buddhism.* Ithaca, N.Y.: Snow Lion Publications, 1989.

Stcherbatsky, F. Th. *Buddhist Logic.* New York: Dover Publications, Inc., 1962.

Tsong-ka-pa. *Tantra in Tibet: The Great Exposition of Secret Mantra.* Translated and edited by Jeffrey Hopkins. London: George Allen and Unwin, 1977.

Vasubandhu (dByig gnyen). *Abhidharmakoshakārikā* (*Chos mngon pa'i mdzod kyi bshad pa*) [Treasury of knowledge]. P5590, vol. 115.

Wilson, Andrew, ed. *World Scripture: A Comparative Anthology of Sacred Texts.* New York: Paragon House, 1991.

Ludwig Wittgenstein. *The Blue and Brown Books.* New York: Harper and Row, 1958.

———. *Philosophical Investigations.* Translated by G. E. M. Anscombe. The German text with a revised English translation. 3rd ed. Malden, Mass.: Blackwell Publishing, 2001.

———. *Remarks on Colour.* Edited by G. E. M. Anscombe. Translated by Linda L. McAlister and Margarete Schüttle. Berkeley: University of California Press, 1978.

INDEX

Toward the spread of virtue and goodness.